The Ventura Publisher Solutions Book

THE BANTAM • ITC SERIES

THE VENTURA PUBLISHER SOLUTIONS BOOK

Recipes for Advanced Results

Covers Version 2 and the Professional Extension

MICHAEL UTVICH

BANTAM BOOKS
NEW YORK • TORONTO • LONDON • SYDNEY • AUCKLAND

THE VENTURA PUBLISHER SOLUTIONS BOOK:
RECIPES FOR ADVANCED RESULTS

A Bantam Book / October 1989

For information address: Bantam Books

ISBN 0-553-34504-4

Published simultaneously in the U.S. and Canada

Bantam Books are published by Bantam Books, a division of Bantam Doubleday Dell Publishing Group, Inc. Its trademark, consisting of the words "Bantam Books" and the portrayal of a rooster, is registered in the U.S. Patent and Trademark Office and in other countries. Marca Registrada, Bantam Books, 666 Fifth Avenue, New York, New York 10103

PRINTED IN THE UNITED STATES OF AMERICA

0 9 8 7 6 5 4 3 2 1

To John and Lola,
with love

Foreword

For graphic professionals entering the brave new world of desktop design and production, International Typeface Corporation (ITC) and Bantam Electronic Publishing have entered into a joint venture to produce a series of definitive desktop reference books.

Most of the books we introduce will show you how to get the most out of a specific technology, but there will also be some that focus on aspects of typeface use, page layout and design. We shall be looking to provide both intermediate and advanced users with clear, professional instructions and advice, and shall package this information so that it is relevant to available technology and to the best standards of practice. It will be clearly and logically presented and copiously illustrated.

The Ventura Publisher Solutions Book is the first of this series. It is a unique, creative tool which provides powerful recipes for getting the most out of Ventura Publisher 2.0 and the Professional Extension.

Included in the following pages are scores of high-utility production techniques, advice on how to best use Ventura tools and third-party add-ons, and valuable cross-references. Key subjects covered include typographic terms, style sheets, page layout and design, designing text, pictures and graphics, working from the screen, coping with publication features, vertical justification, creating automatic document system, tabular work and forms design, tags, graphic templates and much more. Additionally, the book is filled with highly illustrative screen shots and sample documents.

The Ventura Publisher Solutions Book is not for your bookshelf. It is a tool to be kept right next to your computer. It is designed for fast, comprehensive reference to help you not only do the job correctly, but to meet deadlines.

ITC is in the business of producing and promoting high-quality typeface designs. These typefaces are created for designers, graphic artists, people involved in business communications, in fact, everyone who is in the business of communicating information. In addition, ITC seeks to support the many people who use typeface designs by providing them with quality tools that help educate them about type, layout, and design.

This joint venture with Bantam is one more step in ITC's program to help all communicators create highly effective pieces most efficiently. We believe that the intelligent use of technology, allied to necessary traditional skills, and fine tools such as high quality typefaces, will produce effective and efficient high-standard results.

In short, ITC's goal is to help you achieve higher, better standards in less time and for less money.

Mark J. Batty
President and CEO, ITC

Acknowledgments

This book would not have been possible without the help, encouragement, and insight of special people I have worked with over the past several years.

I would like to thank the many people at Xerox Customer Education who worked with me in developing the Xerox Ventura Publisher training classes, including Doreen Aranda, Jane Fairchild, Jan Fradin, Cyndi Holland, and Linda Love. Ann Galdos, Lori Birtley and Carol Clements of Xerox Desktop Software were helpful in assembling material for this book.

Many companies provided software used in the writing and production of this book, including Symsoft Inc., Digital Research, Adobe Systems, Bitstream, Corel Systems, Micrografx and of course Xerox Corporation.

Several people provided technical help and review. John Wilzak of Harvard Systems helped considerably with advice on desktop publishing system hardware that was invaluable. Michael Flanagan of Southern California Printcorp provided advice and technical assistance as well as printing the final Linotronic masters for the book. Bob Mutascio provided invaluable computer system support and advice, especially involving installing and configuring expanded memory.

A special thank you to Cathy Eichlin for her review and editing of the manuscript, and continual support throughout the process.

I would like to thank Michael Roney, my editor at Bantam, for his help, guidance and patience throughout this process. Thanks also to Terry Nasta, Bantam's managing editor, and Nancy Sugihara, who developed the elegant design for the book. I would also like to thank Mark Batty and Skip Wilhelm of ITC for their support throughout the project.

Throughout the writing of this book, my wife Judy and my children, Nicholas and Alexis, have been fully supportive and understanding. Without their help, this truly would have been impossible.

Finally, I would like to express sincere thanks to the four developers at Ventura Software who wrote Ventura Publisher: John Meyer, Don Heiskell, Lee Jay Lorenzen, and John Grant. Their creation has revolutionized the world of publishing, and, in the process, has changed the way we communicate.

Contents

CHAPTER 2

Document Layout and Design 39

CHAPTER 4

Screen-based Layout and Design 163

CHAPTER 5

The Automatic Document 189

CHAPTER 11

Working with Tables 417

Introduction

Recipes for Success

With the release of Version 2.0 and the Professional Extension, Ventura Publisher has gone beyond desktop publishing and has clearly established itself as the most powerful and versatile PC–based publishing system on the market. With a wide range of publishing tools and an open architecture that makes it easy to work with third–party text, databases, spreadsheets, graphics, and fonts, Ventura is the nexus that can integrate all elements in your operation into a single, cohesive professional publishing system.

By harnessing the full power of Ventura you can produce better and more effective documents. For typeset applications, you can set the type yourself, eliminating expensive and time–consuming trips to the conventional typesetter. Ventura makes it easy to enhance the communication power and attractiveness of internal applications with typeset text and professional graphics. With Ventura, your documents communicate better, for less money, in a shorter time.

To get the most out of Ventura Publisher, you need more than just basic information on concepts and features. Rather, you need to understand how to use the available features to create sophisticated design elements on a page. You also have to know how to use the built–in Ventura features that can help to save you time in editing and in the final production of your document. The bottom line is knowing how to meet production deadlines with Ventura...every day.

This is a software cookbook. It contains innovative and practical recipes to help you realize your design goals and meet production deadlines by harnessing the full power of your Ventura publishing system. The focus here is not upon *features*, but on *process*. Each step–by–step recipe demonstrates advanced feature operations to be used in designing and publishing documents. Each recipe contains all the information you need to complete the operation and suggests a number of ways to develop variations of your own.

Learning in Stages

This book is the result of my experience working with Ventura Publisher as a training designer, print production coordinator, and desktop publishing consultant. During this period, I noticed two distinct stages that most people go through when learning Ventura Publisher. In the first stage, one learns the four operating modes, along with how to design simple style sheets and build basic document applications. In the second stage one puts it all together to creatively combine the available tools to design and output more complex document applications. This is where knowledge matures and where you learn to combine features to create sophisticated design effects and reduce editing and processing time.

It takes more than knowing how to use kitchen utensils to be a great chef. And it takes more than simply understanding features to be a successful Ventura publisher.

This book has been designed as a resource to help you build on your existing knowledge of Ventura Publisher features and concepts and get you to the second stage of the learning process. Using fully keystroked techniques, you will learn how to combine features and build on these operations with your own insights and creativity. They are written to help you solve real document design and production problems as they occur. In deadline situations, you don't have time to page through software documentation or narrative descriptions of features. The recipes presented here include specific instructions on how to apply a given operation. Illustrations and sample documents add visual cues to help you understand what the finished effect looks like, as well as to help you when you are "shopping" for ideas and inspiration.

As you work with the techniques, experiment with some of the suggested variations, or add some of your own. You'll enhance your ability to express your creativity as a designer and publisher.

What Your Reference Guide Didn't Tell You

This book is not intended to serve as a replacement for the Reference Guide. The Guide contains complete definitions of Ventura concepts, features, and technical details, but it doesn't always explain the many sophisticated cross–references and connections between features.

The Reference Guide also contains a great deal of valuable information about using Ventura Publisher with third–party products and utilities. However, it doesn't always reveal the specific ways you can use these third–party products in concert with Ventura features.

This book has been designed to support and enhance the technical information presented in the Reference Guide. Recipes in this book have been written specifically to take you beyond the feature definitions and simple utility statements in the documentation.

Book Organization

This book has been set up with *deadline panic* in mind. Maybe the Vice–President of Marketing wants a proposal designed and printed in less than an hour. Or, maybe you've got to create three prototype ad layouts in several hours for a presentation in the afternoon. This is the place to come for ideas, inspiration, and information—fast.

Each chapter contains a group of recipes focused on a specific part of the desktop publishing process. A brief overview of the contents of each chapter follows.

- **Chapter 1: Ventura Concepts, Features and Operations:** Contains a review of basic Ventura information, including an overview of the screen interface; description of basic operations in the four operating modes; and definitions of key Ventura operating concepts.

- **Chapter 2: Document Layout and Design:**Contains layout strategies for different types of documents. Recipes focus on ways to use features of the Frame mode to lay out and design pages, make custom–size pages, and place enhancements in the page design.

- **Chapter 3: Designing Text:** Contains techniques for typesetting text using the features of Ventura's Paragraph mode. Recipes focus on creative ways to design body text, including spacing, multiple–column effects, bullets, and more. Additional recipes illustrate methods to create dynamic headlines and page design elements.

- **Chapter 4: Screen–based Layout and Design:**Shows how to build and edit documents in Ventura directly from the screen. Recipes describe screen–editing techniques which are particularly useful for display applications like advertisements, flyers, and catalogs.

- **Chapter 5: The Automatic Document:**Shows how to set up Ventura documents with automatic features that reduce editing and document processing time. Recipes focus upon powerful automatic features including auto–numbering, headers and footers, and breaks.

- **Chapter 6: Frames and Pictures:**Contains recipes describing creative uses of frame drawing and editing techniques including anchoring, sizing and scaling, cut/copy/paste, captions, and design effects with stacked frames.

- **Chapter 7: Graphic Enhancements:**Contains recipes describing creative uses of Ventura graphics, including master graphics, flowcharts, design effects with stacked graphics, and placing graphic elements into the page design.

- **Chapter 8: Publication Features:**Contains techniques describing creative uses of Ventura publication features. Recipes cover operations in pagination, building publications, indexing, generating tables of contents, and copying finished documents.
- **Chapter 9: Vertical Justification:**Contains complete description of the tools and operations for creating vertical justification systems in Professional Extension documents.
- **Chapter 10: Document Information Networks:** Contains recipes showing creative uses of Professional Extension cross–referencing features.
- **Chapter 11: Working With Tables:**Contains recipes describing creative uses of the Professional Extension Table Editing mode. Techniques include design of simple tables, advanced table editing, designing form masters, and illustrated tables.
- **Chapter 12: Production Power:**Contains information and recipes to help create an efficient Ventura Publisher print production system.

Each chapter begins with an overview that describes the benefits of the featured techniques, a list of applicable Ventura tools, and one or more sample document applications created using the techniques described in that chapter.

Chapter introductions are followed by technique recipes. These recipes are self–contained, step–by–step guides to help you implement the featured technique. Following most recipes is a set of application notes, containing suggestions for enhancing the technique. Other recipes that relate to the current one are cross–referenced with the correct page number. In short, each recipe is written in a form that tells you what the technique is and what it is used for, how to do it, and how to build on it.

Key Words and Conventions Used in the Book

To maintain uniformity throughout the recipes text, a number of key words and conventions are used to describe specific operations and activities:

- **Enable**: Change the operating mode, as in Enable ***Text*** mode.
- **Access**: Open a dialog box, as in Access **FILE•Save Chapter**.
- **Select** Click the left mouse button (the only mouse button Ventura uses) to select a feature inside a dialog box or off a menu, as in Select Turn Column Balance On
- **Features** A group of features on a menu or in a dialog box, as in ...features of the Paragraph menu.
- **Option** An individual selection in a dialog box or feature, as in ...pull up Horz. Alignment and select the Justified option.

In an effort to avoid long, convoluted paragraphs of detail text, the step–throughs are written in a simple shorthand notation to identify menus and dialog boxes. The name of the menu is shown in all caps followed by the name of the dialog box or toggle feature you are to select. So the expression *Access FRAME•Margins & Columns* means Pull down the FRAME menu and select Margins & Columns.

To complete an operation in any Ventura dialog box it is necessary to select OK, or press the Return key. Instructions given in the recipes assume it is understood that you must either select OK to complete the operation, or select Cancel to leave the dialog box.

Your Creative Challenge

This book should be a flexible and inspirational resource for you at any point in your Ventura Publisher education. Use it as a training tool. To get a feel for it, skim through the entire book, reading only the recipe introductions. Mark those you want to practice and experiment with.

Use this book as a regular production resource. Keep it next to your computer. When looking for design or production ideas, open the book at any point and use the illustrations and recipe titles as guides to help you find what you're looking for. Once you've found a technique of interest, check the application notes for additional ideas and cross references to related techniques. The Table of Contents lists all the recipes. A standard index in the back directs you to information about any group of features.

Use this book to increase your desktop publishing skills and creativity. As you "cook" with the recipes and variations featured here, you will discover additional effects and techniques that build naturally upon them. And no matter what the design challenge, you will have access to the tools needed to get the job done.

Happy publishing!

PART I

Using Ventura Publisher 2.0

CHAPTER 1

Ventura Concepts, Features and Operations

Reviewing the Basics

Excellence begins with a solid grasp of the basics. And nowhere is this more true than in desktop publishing. This is not an introductory book on Ventura Publisher, but this first chapter reviews the basic concepts. Those of you already up to speed can skip this material.

Ventura and Traditional Publishing

With an electronic screen and drop down menus, a WYSIWYG page display and mouse–activated features, Ventura Publisher would seem to be worlds away from the old days of traditional typesetting, manual paste–up and art boards. Ventura is actually modeled on traditional publishing methods. Using the power of the computer, Ventura offers electronic solutions to many of the repetitive tasks associated with traditional publishing.

To appreciate this power, think about the amount of time and detailed manual work involved in the traditional publishing process and the number of detailed decisions that go into every publishing project. A layout must be designed—the size of the page, the relative size of columns and gutters. Typesetting text involves a whole new set of choices—the proper typeface, size, and style. Then there's the proper positioning on the page, the amount of space between lines of text and between different text elements. Final layout means deciding about placement of illustrations, captions, plus enhancements and edits to text and visuals. Each of these decisions involves making a number of detailed measurements, and the elements must all be applied consistently throughout the document.

It is easy to understand why traditional typesetting and layout methods take so much time. The work is highly detailed, with the potential for error at every stage of the process. A document passes through the hands of many people, each with specialized skills, making edits and revisions, additions and deletions. The mass of detail that accompanies the design, layout, typesetting, and final publishing of a document is so great that no one person can manage it alone using traditional methods.

With Ventura Publisher, however, one person can publish entire documents from design to completion of final published masters. Ventura has transformed the production process by directly accessing the power of your computer to perform repetitive chores and apply consistent layout and typeset values in a document.

In place of manual operations, Ventura provides you with computerized tools like the *style sheet* and *chapter file* that allow you to record detailed style and layout specs, and apply them consistently throughout a document. At any time, you can refine a page layout or change typesetting elements and see the results applied globally through your document in seconds. The innovative approach Ventura brings to publishing eliminates time–consuming editing, re–typesetting, and paste–up.

Basic Reference

This chapter contains a reference of terms and concepts used throughout the book. The first part contains a complete operations description of the Ventura Publisher Main Screen and all related screen displays. If you are unsure how to operate any of the screen features (i.e.: menus, dialog boxes, Side–Bar, etc.) use this section as a quick guide.

The next section shows how each operating mode is designed to complete specific tasks in the publishing process. There is an overview of key operations in each mode, followed by a list of basic operations.

The two most important operational concepts in Ventura, designing a style sheet and building a chapter file, are covered in detail, with additional information on the six key concepts you should fully understand to complete basic Ventura operations.

Finally, there is a brief discussion of measurement terms, fonts, and other issues which will be referenced during some of the recipes in the book.

Whether you are a beginning or intermediate user, this section can provide you with a direct reference every time you have a question on a basic operation or key concept discussed in the following chapters.

Ventura Publisher Key Concepts

Ventura Publisher lets you design, assemble, and save documents by creating and maintaining a family of computer files that make up that document. In a traditional page layout, individual scraps of paper are pasted to an art board to assemble the page. In the same way, Ventura electronically "pastes" individual text and picture files together to form a complete layout.

The individual files that make up a document always remain freestanding and are not absorbed by Ventura. This lets you continue to make edits to text and picture files in the original word processor or graphics software where they were developed at any time during document development.

The following summary focuses on the six key concepts you must understand to work effectively in Ventura Publisher. You will work with these concepts every day you use Ventura Publisher. This step

VENTURA PUBLISHER KEY CONCEPTS

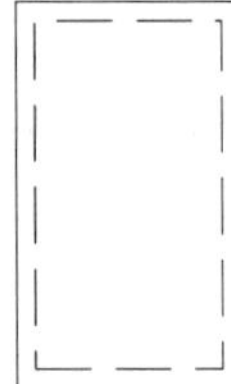

Load Style Sheet

Select the right Width Table

Load text file into Base Page

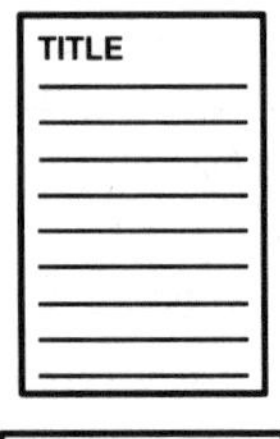

Typeset text with Paragraph Tags

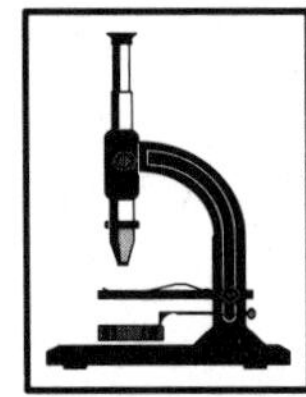

Load pictures into Frames

Save document in Chapter File

through will help you see what each concept means, and how it relates to the others in the process of assembling a document.

Step 1 **Load Style Sheet**

The style sheet is the basis of every document in Ventura Publisher. It contains settings for the page layout, the standard document text attributes (Body Text tag), and a list of paragraph tags which define the typographic attributes for other elements in the document.

Step 2 **Select the right Width Table**

The Character Width Table, or simply Width Table, is the link between the fonts available in your printer and the fonts which are available in the Font/Set Font dialog box to use in designing your document. The style sheet remembers the name of the correct width table. But if you are using more than one printer format, it's a good idea to check to see which width table is installed. If you don't use the correct width table, what you see will not be what you get.

Step 3 **Place text file in Base Page**

The base page is the master frame in every Ventura Publisher document. It automatically expands to the necessary number of pages to display document text file.

Step 4 **Typeset text with Paragraph Tags**

Each style sheet contains a unique list of paragraph tags. Each tag defines typographic values and page positioning for a specific text element in document, such as the Title, Major Heading, Minor Heading, and Bullet. To typeset text, select the text and apply the correct paragraph tag.

Step 5 **Load pictures into Frame**

Frames are controlled areas which "float" on top of the base page. They can contain pictures, Ventura Publisher graphics, or additional text files. Within frames, you can set up layouts and typographic defaults different than those in the base page of the document.

Step 6 **Save document in Chapter File**

Once you have laid out the document, save it in a chapter file. The job of a chapter file is to remember. It remembers the correct names and location of the style sheet and all text and picture files in a document. It also remembers the text and positioning of the headers and footers, and the position of all frames and frame attributes.

The Ventura Publisher Main Screen

Through the Ventura Publisher Main Screen you have access to all the software operating tools. Ventura Publisher's screen and menu design is based in the Graphics Environment Manager (GEM) presentation system developed by Digital Research. If you have any experience working with other GEM applications, such as GEM Draw or GEM Graph, you will already be familiar with many of the screen features and conventions used in Ventura.

The Main Screen is composed of three principal areas. The top of the screen displays the available menus with their Ventura operating features and the name of the active document. The Side–Bar on the left contains the currently selected operating mode and a list of information or special features available with that mode. The Working Area is where the active document is displayed, and where you make edits and revisions.

Current Files and Feature Selection

From two screen–wide bars at the top of the Main Screen you choose the operating features, and monitor the names of currently selected files. Screen elements to note are:

- **Menu line:** Contains the list of each of the menus containing operating features. To display a menu, touch the name of the desired menu with the mouse pointer. To remove a menu display from the screen, click the mouse anywhere outside of the drop-down menu display.

VENTURA PUBLISHER MAIN SCREEN

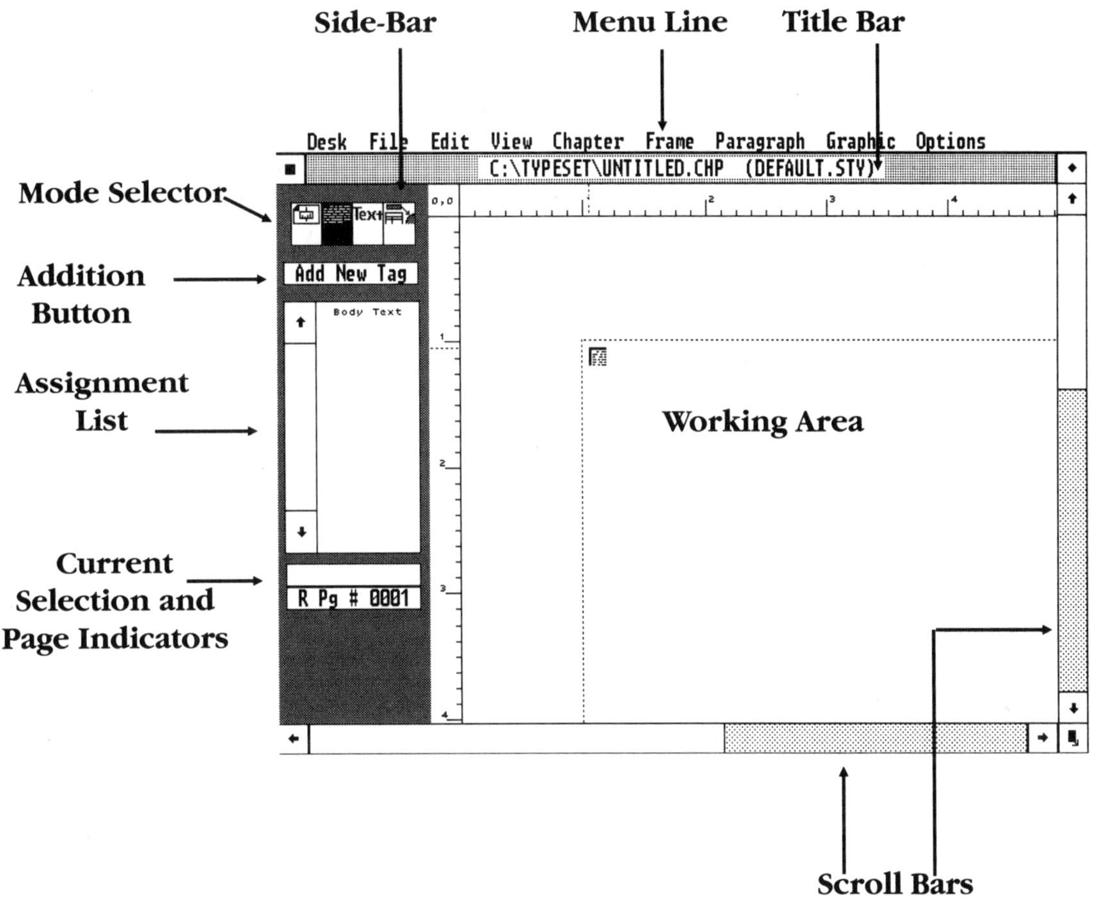

- **Title bar:** Displays the name of the loaded document (chapter file) with its correct path information. The name of the selected style sheet is displayed in parentheses without drive/subdirectory data.

The Side–Bar

The Side–Bar at the left of the screen gives you access to special features unique to each of the operating modes. The four icons of the Mode Selector allow you to select any of the operating modes with the mouse. As you enable a new mode, the Side–Bar changes to display lists of features and options unique to that mode.

The bottom of the Side–Bar indicates the selected element in the Working Area and the currently displayed page. To expand the Working Area to the full width of the screen for a better view of your document page, hide the entire Side–Bar using a selection in the Options menu, or from the keyboard. A number of screen operations can be conducted with the Side–Bar hidden, using keyboard and menu commands. Screen features to note are:

- **Mode selector:** Contains four icons representing each of the four operating modes in Ventura Publisher: Frame, Paragraph, Text, and Graphic. (If you have installed the Professional Extension, a box selector for the Table Editing mode appears as well.) To select the desired mode, click the mouse cursor on the appropriate icon. If the Side–Bar is hidden, use the mode selector on the View menu to change the operating mode.
- **Addition button:** A mode specific feature selection that allows you to perform a key operation in that mode. If the Side–Bar is hidden, access the Addition Button by pressing Control–2 from the keyboard. The features activated by the Addition Button in the four modes are:
  - **Frame mode:** Add New Frame
  - **Paragraph mode:** Add New Tag
  - **Text mode:** Set Font
  - **Graphic mode:** Add New Frame
- **Assignment list:** Displays a list of data or options unique to each of the modes. The Assignment List allows you to load files into a

document, apply paragraph tags to text, and apply text enhancements. To access features shown in the Assignment List, you *must* have an element (i.e.: frame, paragraph, section of text) selected in the Working Area. Then, point to the desired option in the Assignment List and click on it with the mouse. The Assignment List options in the four modes are:

— **Frame mode:** List of text and picture files in the current document. By selecting the file name in the Assignment List, you can load a file into the base page or a selected frame.

— **Paragraph mode:** List of paragraph tags for the currently loaded style sheet. To apply a paragraph tag to text, select paragraph in the Working Area and the name of the paragraph tag in the Assignment List.

— **Text mode:** List of text enhancements and capitalization options. To apply a text enhancement, select a string of text in the Working Area and the enhancement in the Assignment List. To return the text to its original appearance, select Normal at the top of the enhancement list. The Normal Selection *does not work* with capitalization options.

— **Graphic mode:** The Assignment List is replaced by five graphic drawing icons and the selector arrow icon.

- **Current selection indicator:** Shows the name of the currently selected element in the Working Area. This is a valuable reference during editing. It helps you determine instantly whether or not you are working with the correct layout or text element. The elements shown here in the four modes are:

— **Frame mode:** Displays the name of the text or picture file currently loaded in the selected base page or frame.

— **Paragraph mode:** Displays the name of the tag applied to a paragraph selected an the Working Area.

— **Text mode:** When a text cursor has been placed, this displays **Attr. Setting** which marks any text attributes placed in the text, or the name of the Special Edit Item placed at that position. (Special Edit Items include Box Character, Footnote, Index Entry, Fraction, Frame Anchor, or Cross Reference.)

— **Graphic mode:** When a graphic form has been selected in Working Area, this displays the type of graphic selected, such as CIRCLE, LINE, or BOX TEXT.

- **Page number indicator:** Displays the number of the current page as counted from the *beginning of the chapter file.* If you have made special edits to the pagination of a document, *they are not reflected here.* The indicator displays whether the current page is Right (R Pg) or Left (L Pg).

The Working Area

The Working Area is where you design and edit documents. It is, literally, your window onto the page. Depending on your particular needs, you can activate a variety of custom options to the Working Area document display, as noted below:

- **Expand Working Area:** To extend the Working Area to the full width of your screen, hide the Side–Bar using the command available on the Options menu. When the Working Area is expanded, however, you cannot perform all editing functions which require the Assignment List, including loading files into a page, or drawing graphics.

- **View Options:** There are four view options available for the Working Area which allow you to see the entire layout of a page or close in on a focused area. The four view options are:

— **Facing Pages View**: Displays left and right pages of a double-sided document layout. Most standard-size text is not readable in this view, and will appear "greeked," that is, as a pattern of gray lines where the text appears on the page. Each time you press PgDn or PgUp, the next two-page spread is shown.

— **Reduced View:** Displays entire document page so you can see the layout and positioning of text. Like Facing Pages View, most standard-size text appears "greeked" on the screen.

— **Normal View:** Displays a portion of the page, actual size. This view lets you see sections of a page in the exact size and relationship that they will have when printed.

— **Enlarged View:** Displays a smaller portion of a page enlarged to twice its actual size. Make detailed edits from this view. Redraw times for pictures and screens can take significantly longer in this view, so use it sparingly.

- **Zoom–in View:** By using the three keyboard commands for View options, you can "zoom in" to the position of the mouse cursor on the page. To zoom in to a specific point on a page from Reduced View, place the mouse cursor where the upper left corner of the Normal View screen is to appear. Press the keyboard command for Normal View (Control–N), and that section of the page will appear in Normal View. You can also zoom in from Reduced or Normal View to Enlarged View. This operation can save you a great deal of time spent scrolling around pages.

- **Scroll Bars and Arrows:** At the right and bottom edge of the Main Screen are the scroll bars and arrows. These are used to adjust the portion of the page displayed in Normal or Enlarged View. Each scroll bar is composed of white and gray portions. The full length of the horizontal and vertical scroll bars represent the full height and width of the page. The white area represents the approximate portion of the page currently displayed in the Working Area, and its relative position on the page. To scroll the document, place your cursor in the white area, press and hold the mouse and move the white area in the direction you wish to scroll. Scroll arrows move the page in set increments with each click of the mouse.

- **Mouse cursor:** When the mouse cursor is outside the Working Area, it *always* appears as a black selection arrow. When inside the Working Area, the mouse cursor shape changes to indicate the selected mode and feature operation. For example, the mouse cursor changes to represent each of the different graphic drawing shapes. The mouse cursor is another screen guide that helps to orient you as you work with a document.

- **Redraw screen:** If the document image in the Working Area looks messy after a screen operation, you can force Ventura to regenerate the screen and clean out any visual "dirt" by simply pressing the Escape key.

- **Screen rulers:** The optional screen rulers can be turned on in the Options menu and set up in the unit of measure you are most comfortable with. Each of the screen rulers contains a small dotted tracking line that follows the current position of the mouse cursor in the Working Area. This is very helpful when drawing frames or graphics on screen. To reset the zero point of the horizontal or vertical rulers, or both, place the mouse in the box at the intersection of the rulers, press and hold the mouse button and drag the cursor to the position where the zero is to be set.

- **Column Guides:** You can turn on the display of Column Guides in the Options menu. They appear as dotted lines which display the margins and column settings defined in the selected style sheet, and clearly show the relationship of text and picture elements to a page, especially when you are developing a multi–column document.

- **Tabs and Returns:** The display of text marking symbols can be turned off or on using the Show/Hide Tabs & Returns feature on the Options menu. When on, the Working Area displays symbols for the end of each paragraph return, the position of all tab characters and markers for Special Edit Items. When you want to see how the document will look when printed, turn the Tabs & Returns off.

Ventura Menus

Ventura Publisher features are contained in a set of pull–down menus accessible from the Menu line at the top of the screen. Features on the menus change, and their availability varies depending on the enabled operating mode. Features on all menus are operated from the screen using the mouse. In cases where a keyboard command is shown at the right side of the menu, you may elect to access that feature by typing in the appropriate control code.

Menu Design and Operation

Ventura menus are designed for efficiency and ease of operation. The important operating features and design of Ventura menus:

- **Pull Down/Drop Down:** Ventura menus can be set to operate in either Pull–down or Drop–down mode using the Set Preferences dialog box on the Options menu.
  - — **Pull–down** menus operate very much like menus in Microsoft's Windows and other related software. To display a menu, point at the menu name as you press and hold the mouse button. To select a feature, drag the mouse to highlight the desired feature and release the mouse button.
  - — **Drop–down** menus—the Ventura default— appear on screen as soon as you touch the menu name with the mouse cursor. Point at the desired feature so that it appears highlighted, and click the mouse on it to select it.
- **Feature availability:** All features currently available on a menu are shown in black text. Features not available are shown in gray.
- **Dialog indicator:** All features which have a dialog box are indicated by three dots (...) following the feature name.

Ventura Menus

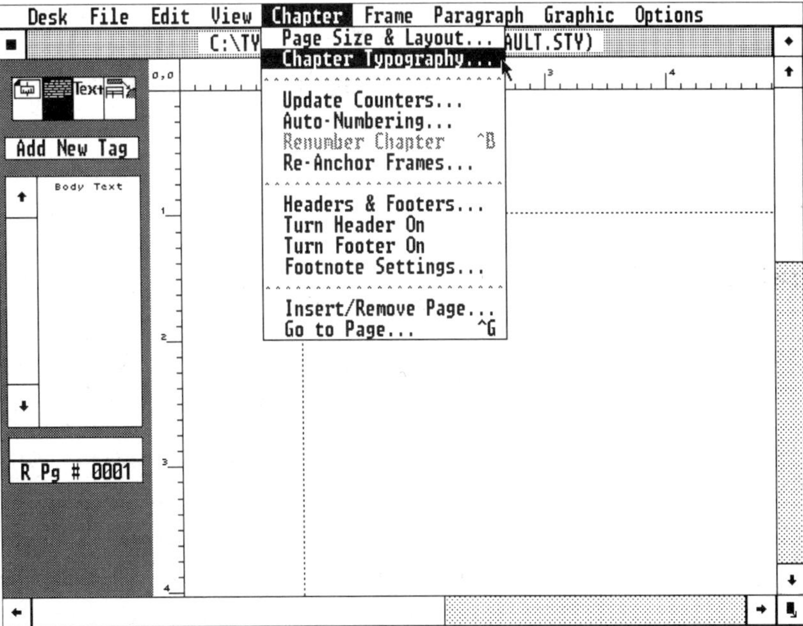

- **Toggle features:** Features which are activated directly from the menu operate like a computer lightswitch. For example, Column Guides are activated by two rotating selections on the Options menu: Turn Column Guides ON and Turn Column Guides OFF. It is important to remember that with toggle features, the name appearing on the menu is the opposite of what is currently enabled in the Working Area. When you have turned Column Guides On in the screen, the Options menu displays the name of the matching toggle feature Turn Column Guides Off.
- **Feature separators:** Some menus contain various groups of related features and selections. To distinguish between these groups, dotted lines appear separating the groups of features on the menu display.
- **Keyboard command equivalents:** All features with keyboard command equivalents display the correct command at the right side of the menu. For these features, you can use either the mouse or the keyboard.
- **Features change with mode:** As you change the mode, some features change entirely to reflect the current mode. For example, in the Edit menu, the Cut/Copy/Paste features change from Cut/Copy/Paste Frames in Frame mode to Cut/Copy/Paste Text in Text mode. It is important to know what mode you should be in to perform a particular editing task.

Description of Features

The Ventura menus contain groups of related features. Understanding the structure of the menus will help you access to the feature you need more quickly. The following is a quick overview of the features contained in each of the Ventura menus, listed in order from the left of the screen.

- **Desk:** The Publisher Info dialog box contains the current installed memory status of the software along with the Version number and other copyright data. Click the mouse on the word *Ventura* in the boxed area containing the expression "Ventura Software, Inc.," and the software diagnostics dialog box which displays detailed data about the apportionment of memory and other technical information will appear.

- **File:** Contains features used for file management and operation, including opening documents, loading text and picture files, saving and printing.
- **Edit:** Contains the Cut/Copy/Paste family of editing features that changes to match the currently enabled mode (these features are not available in Paragraph mode). In addition, Edit has the facilities for removing files from the document and renaming text files *only*, and the list Special Edit Items which are inserted directly to positions in text.
- **View:** Displays the available View options as well as a menu version of the mode selector with the keyboard commands you can use to change modes.
- **Chapter:** Lists special features which are applied globally throughout a document and are recorded in a Chapter (CHP) file, including typography defaults, pagination, headers and footers, and automatic numbering systems.
- **Frame:** Shows a full complement of features for designing and editing the base page and individual frames. These include margin and column settings, frame sizing, picture scaling, plus caption and frame enhancements like rules and shading.
- **Paragraph:** Provides the list of dialog boxes used to design paragraph tags. The paragraph menu is the location from which to design the entire list of paragraph tags in a style sheet.
- **Graphic:** Contains editing features for Ventura Graphics, including line and fill editing, graphic grid, and positioning options.
- **Options:** Presents custom features to configure the Working Area, as well as the set basic printer defaults and install new fonts. The Multi–Chapter selection is a complete editing function for publications, that is, documents made up of more than one chapter file.

Dialog Boxes

Ventura Publisher gives you access to many sophisticated features through a set of screen overlays called *dialog boxes*. From dialog boxes, you select features and enter numeric values and text as part of document design and editing process.

Many of the conventions which apply to menus also apply to dialog boxes. For example, available features are shown in black, unavailable features in gray. For all entries in dialog boxes requiring numeric values or text, the entry line can be cleared by placing a text cursor on the line and pressing the Escape key. Once in a dialog box, screen operations cannot be resumed until you have accepted the dialog box operation by selecting OK, or exiting without making a change using CANCEL. The keyboard equivalent of selecting OK with the mouse is the RETURN key, and the keyboard equivalent of the CANCEL option is Control–X. If you press Control–X when in the Working Area, it will re–display the last dialog box you worked in. The design and operating features of dialog boxes are listed below:

- **Units of measure:** All dialog boxes with features that require entry of measurements or dimensions contain a four–way rotating units of measure selector. To change the units of measure, click the mouse on the units of measure displayed and the next selection will appear, and all measurable entries will be displayed in the new unit of measure. The sequence of appearance is: inches, centimeters, picas & points, fractional points.

- **Selecting features:** For features offering a number of defined selections, there are two types of displays:

  — **Selection boxes:** All feature selections are visible in the dialog box and contained in boxes. Click on the one you want. A good example of this type of dialog box display is the Breaks dialog box on the Paragraph menu.

  — **Pull–up lists:** The feature name appears marked by a vertical up–down arrow graphic. Point at the feature with the mouse cursor and hold the mouse button down, and a list of all available selections "pops up" on the screen. Move to the

Dialog Boxes

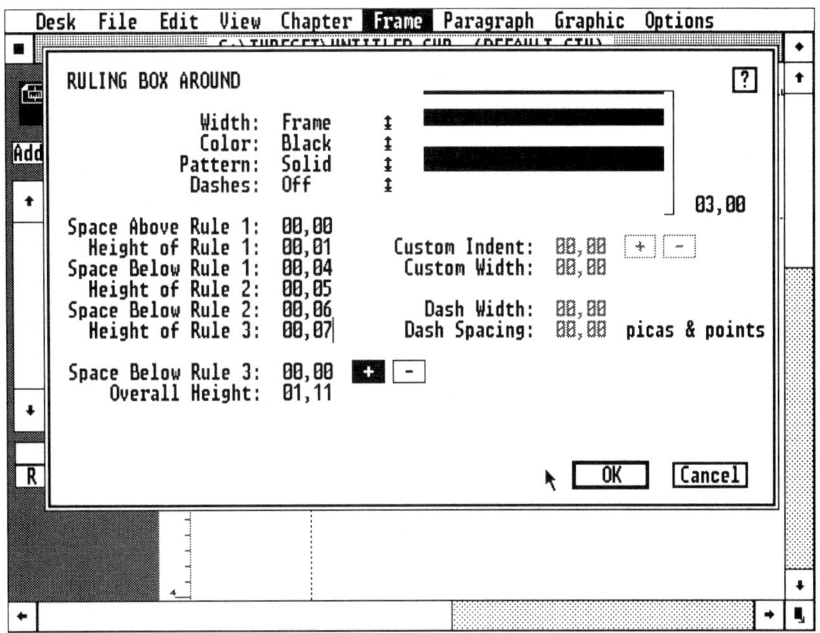

desired selection and release the mouse button. The selection will be displayed in the dialog box. A good example of this type of dialog box display is the Alignment dialog box on the Paragraph menu.

- **Entering data:** Enter numbers and text into Ventura dialog boxes using the lines provided.

  — **Number entry lines:** Enter the number value or measurement required. Be careful about the correct position of zeros in the entry, or you may get the wrong value on the screen.

  — **Text entry lines:** Place a text cursor at the point text is to begin. Do not use the Return key to move between text lines. It closes the dialog box.

- **Screen mimic:** Within some dialog boxes, there is a screen mimic that previews what the selected color, shading, or line appearance will look like on the page. Dialog boxes containing screen mimics include Ruling Lines dialog boxes, Frame Background and Fill Attributes for graphics.

- **Auto–total features:** Some dialog boxes, like the Ruling Lines group and Margins & Columns, have auto– total lines, which automatically total up the settings that you have made.

The Item Selector

The Item Selector is a special type of dialog box for loading files, opening chapters, or saving documents. Essentially, it consists of a file list and filename entry lines, which allow you to select filenames with the mouse pointer, or type the filename directly into the dialog box. But because Ventura accepts many different text and graphic file formats, the Item Selector contains an automatic file filter that displays only the files with the correct extension for the current operation. For example, when you open a chapter, the Item Selector sorts and displays only files with a .CHP extension. Key features of the Item Selector are:

- **Directory line:** Shows the selected drive, subdirectory, and file filter extension. Place text cursor on this line to type in the desired file drive and subdirectory location, or alter the file filter.
- **File list:** Displays the list of files in the current location. Use scroll bars or arrows to move through the list. When loading files into documents, the scroll bar "remembers" your last position so you don't have to continually scroll down a long list of files each time you enter the Item Selector. The file list also displays directories marked with a diamond bullet and drive specifiers marked by a diamond and followed by a colon.
- **Backup Button:** The small black button above the file list is used to back up the location of files displayed until it reaches the list of available drives on your system. At that point, you must select the drive where you wish to display files.
- **Warning beep:** If you have too many files in the selected location for the file list to display, a warning beep will sound. In situations like this, you may have to manually enter the filename on the Selection Line.

The Item Selector

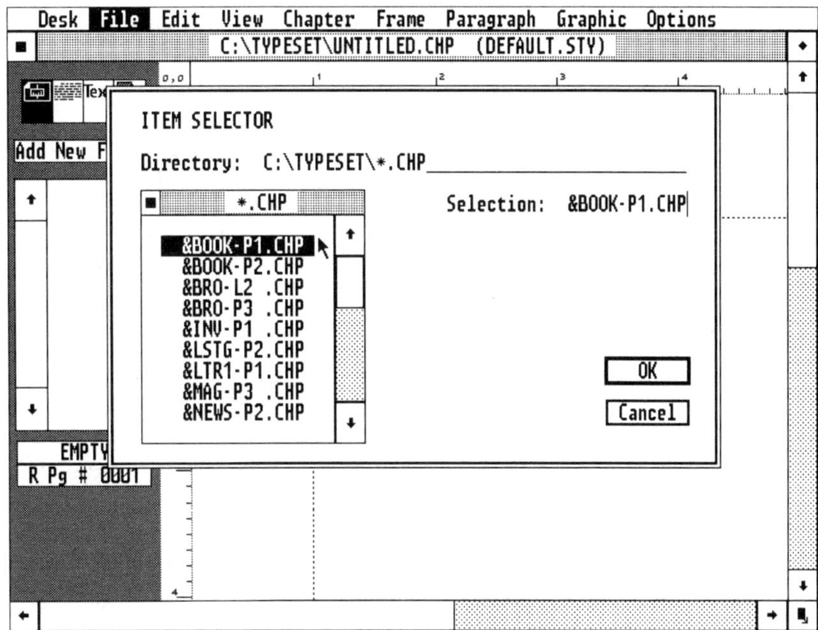

- **Selection line:** The selection line displays the name of the file selected for the current operation. This is where you enter the name of new chapter and style sheets during Save or Save As operations.
- **Overwrite message:** If you are naming a file with a name and extension identical to another file in the current location, an overwrite prompt will be displayed. Overwrite destroys the former file and replaces it with the current one. The new name option allows you to abort the operation and enter a new name for the current file.

The Four Operating Modes

Ventura Publisher is really four programs in one. It is designed around a set of four operating modes, each of which performs a particular aspect of the document preparation process. It is important to understand the modes and how they relate to the process as a whole so you don't get confused by technical labels. It will then be easier to know what mode you should be working in to accomplish a particular operation.

By reading through the mode selector from left to right, the simplicity of Ventura's design is apparent.

- The **Frame** mode has the tools to load files, paste up and layout a document.
- The **Paragraph** mode provides text design and typesetting tools.
- The **Text** mode has tools for text editing, special edit items and additional text enhancements.
- The **Graphic** mode provides visual enhancement tools for pictures, tables, flowcharts, and similar document elements.

The first two modes, Frame and Paragraph, perform powerful design functions that are recorded into the document style sheet. The second two modes, Text and Graphic, primarily perform editing functions, with features to finish and fine–tune a document before final printing.

Each mode transforms the available features of Ventura to conform to its particular function. Some features are available in more than one operating mode, others in only one. To be a successful Ventura user, it is vital to understand the publishing functions specific to each mode. As you build on this knowledge, you will be able to move easily between modes and develop sophisticated document applications for professional results.

Using the Frame Mode for Layout and Paste–up

The Frame mode is where you lay out, assemble, and illustrate documents. It is built around a set of features that allow you to draw, select, and edit space in a page.

The base page in Ventura is the master frame. When you enable the Frame mode and click your mouse in the base page, selection boxes appear around the perimeter of the page. Once the base page

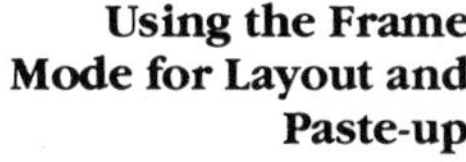

Using the Frame Mode for Layout and Paste-up

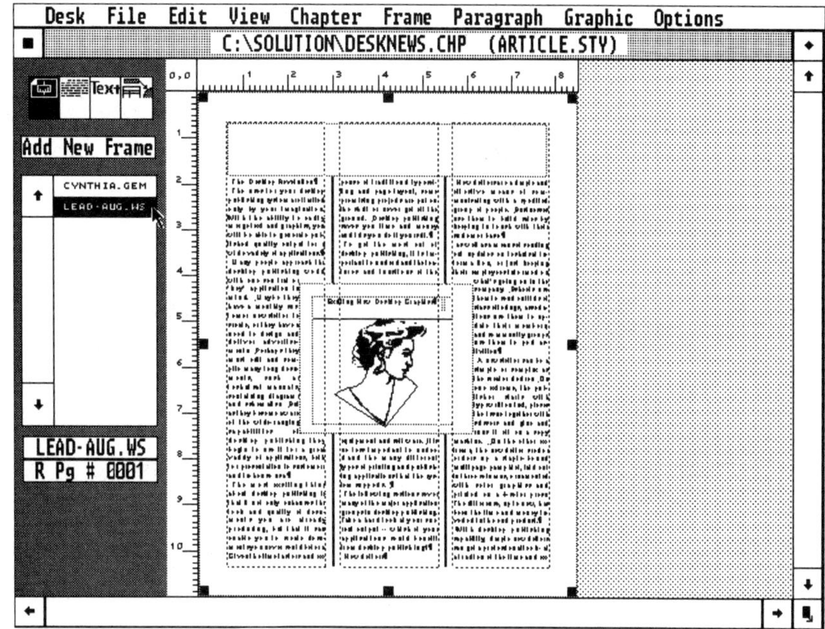

is selected, you can click on the name of a text file in the Frame mode Assignment List, and the text will pour onto the base page. The base page automatically expands to accommodate the entire text file.

You define the default layout specifications of the base page from the Frame mode. They are recorded into the style sheet. These elements include page size, portrait or landscape orientation, and single– or double–sided presentation. The Frame mode is also for setting up the standard margins, columns and gutters for the base page. As you design a document, experiment with different column and margins sizes and page layout characteristics. Text will instantly flow into the new page layout automatically. You can preview a number of different layout options for text in seconds with the touch of the mouse button.

Once you have settled on the layout of the standard page, you can draw controlled areas, or frames on any part of the page. Text automatically flows around the frames, and you can load another text file or illustration. The Frame mode allows you to set up custom values within any frame. This means that special pages with layout characteristics different from those in the base page are possible. At any time, you can resize or move a frame to another page in the document in the click of the mouse. With the Cut/Copy/Paste family of features, you can easily edit your layout and move frames anywhere in your document in seconds.

For documents incorporating a series of text files, use frames to "flow text through" your document pages. All you have to do is draw and position a new frames in the desired location and load the text file into the frame. The text continues in the new frame from the point it ended in the previous one. As additions and deletions to the text are made, the text file automatically repositions between frames so no manual editing or repositioning is necessary.

The Frame mode also contains features that allow you to size, scale, and crop vector and bit–mapped picture files directly on the screen or by entering specific numeric values in a dialog box. You can also add rules, shading and other enhancements to frames or the standard page.

Once your initial layout is developed, you can move on to typeset and edit text. You can return to the Frame mode at any time to fine–tune your layout or edit individual frames and pictures.

Basic Operations in Frame Mode

- **Select base page:** The base page must be selected in the Frame mode before any text can be loaded into it. To select the base page, enable the Frame mode and click the mouse in the Working Area so that the black sizing boxes appear around the perimeter.
- **Load Text/Picture:** To load text or picture files into the Assignment List, access **FILE•Load Text/Picture** and select the desired type of file, and the format of the file. When the Item Selector appears, select filename and select OK. The name of the file will appear in the Frame mode Assignment List.
- **Load text into base page:** From the Frame mode, select the base page and select the name of the text file in the Assignment List. The base page automatically expands and adds enough additional pages to display the entire text file.

- **Draw frame:** To draw a new frame, select Add New Frame in the Frame mode Side–Bar. Place the point of the Frame Drawing cursor at the place where the upper left corner of the frame is to be, press and hold the mouse button and drag the mouse down and to the right. Release the mouse button when the frame is the size you want.
- **Edit frame size:** To edit the size of a frame already drawn, begin by clicking the mouse inside the frame to select it. Place the mouse cursor directly on one of the black sizing boxes surrounding the frame. Press and hold the mouse button. The pointing finger cursor will appear and you drag the mouse to resize the frame.
- **Move frame:** To move the frame to a new position on the page, place the mouse cursor *inside* the frame so that it is *not* touching any of the sizing boxes. Press and hold the mouse button so that the four–way arrow cursor appears. Drag the mouse to move the frame to the desired position on the page.
- **Place file into frame:** To load a file into a frame, click on the frame to select it. Select the name of the desired file in the Assignment List. To replace an existing text or picture file with a new one, simply select the frame containing the old picture, click on the name of the new picture in the Frame mode Assignment List and the new picture will instantly replace the old.

Typesetting in the Paragraph Mode

After the document layout is complete, you can begin typesetting text. In Ventura, typesetting means applying a uniform set of values to an entire paragraph of text, and it accomplishes this through paragraph tags. Each style sheet contains a unique list of paragraph tags which define the unique text elements that make up the document, including document titles, headlines, bullet lists, and others. The Paragraph mode is where you apply paragraph tags to text and design original paragraph tags of your own.

Typesetting in the Paragraph Mode
Page 23

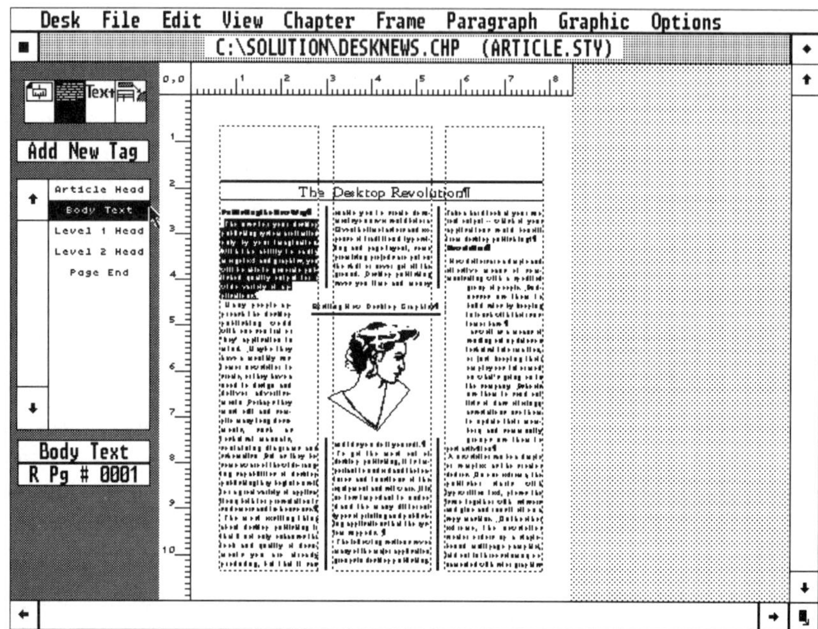

To Ventura, a paragraph is defined as all the text which appears between two paragraph returns. Under that definition, a paragraph can be as short as a single word, or many lines of text. In the Paragraph mode, you can only select complete paragraphs of text at one time. Just point at the desired text and click the mouse.

Every paragraph of text in a Ventura document has a paragraph tag value applied to it. If you haven't applied a custom tag to a paragraph, the default (or automatic) paragraph tag assignment is **Body Text**. Since Body Text is applied automatically, this means that you only have to apply paragraph tags to text elements like headlines, which have different values than the Body Text in the current style sheet.

Body Text and all custom paragraph tags contain an entire set of typographic settings that completely define the look and position of text. The tag for a headline in a newsletter includes the settings for the type face, type size, type style, horizontal alignment, amount of space above and below the text, and more. Once the tag has been designed, all you have to do is click the mouse to apply its values to other paragraphs throughout the document.

Once a paragraph is selected, you can apply to that text any of the custom paragraph tags that appear in the Paragraph mode Assignment List. The Paragraph mode also lets you add new tags to a style sheet, or make edits to existing tags. As you work with a document, you can change values to paragraph tags and the change will be *automatically* reflected in every piece of text with that tag.

The Paragraph mode is a power tool for typesetting and text design. One of the greatest benefits is that it applies *consistent* typographic values to text through paragraph tags.

Basic Operations in the Paragraph Mode

- **Select text:** Click the mouse on the text to be selected. All text in the paragraph will be highlighted in reverse video.
- **Add new tag:** Select a paragraph to carry the new text values. Access Add New Tag in the Paragraph mode Side–Bar. Enter a name for the new tag. For the new tag to begin with the same values as another tag in the style sheet, enter the name of that tag on the Name to Copy From line in the dialog box.
- **Apply tags from Side–Bar:** Click the mouse on the text you wish to tag. Once the text is highlighted, click the mouse on the name of the tag you wish to apply in the Paragraph mode Assignment List.
- **Apply tags with Shift–Select:** To apply the same tag to several paragraphs at once, select the first paragraph of text, press and hold the Shift key as you click on additional paragraphs. Select the name of the desired tag in the Assignment List and all paragraphs will instantly display the tag values.

Text Editing and Enhancement in the Text Mode

The Text mode is primarily for local editing of text. Where the Paragraph mode applies values to *entire paragraphs*, the Text mode lets you make edits within paragraphs. This is valuable when finalizing a document for printing and special edits are required so that the text appears how you want it on the page.

Basic editing features of the Text mode are available when you place a cursor at a position in text. Then you use the keyboard to make additions and deletions just like in a word processor.

Special enhancements like boldface, underlining, or italics to selected sections of a paragraph are applied in the Text mode. Drag the mouse to highlight a single word or an entire sentence and select the enhancement you want from the Text mode Assignment List. To change the type face, or type size for a selected string of text, use the Set Font feature to set custom typeset values for a selected section of text *within* a paragraph.

Cut/Copy/Paste features allow you to move blocks of text around a document without returning to your word processor. In addition, you can place custom non–alphabetic characters and symbols, and enter special editing features like footnotes and index entries while in the Text mode.

Where interactive fine–tuning to copyfit text in a tightly formatted layout is necessary, the Text mode has interactive font sizing and tracking controls that let you adjust text size and spacing incrementally on the screen and see the results immediately.

The Text mode offers a powerful set of document editing options, plus a set of features usable from your word processor that you can use on screen and see the results immediately.

Basic Operations in the Text Mode

- **Place text cursor:** Place mouse cursor at the point where you wish to edit text and click the mouse. The flashing text cursor appears in the text. Control the text cursor using your keyboard.
- **Drag–Select text block:** Place mouse cursor at the beginning of area you wish to select. Press and hold the mouse button as you drag the mouse down to the end of the area you wish to select and release the mouse button. The area will be shown in reverse video.

Text Editing and Enhancement in the Text Mode
Page 25

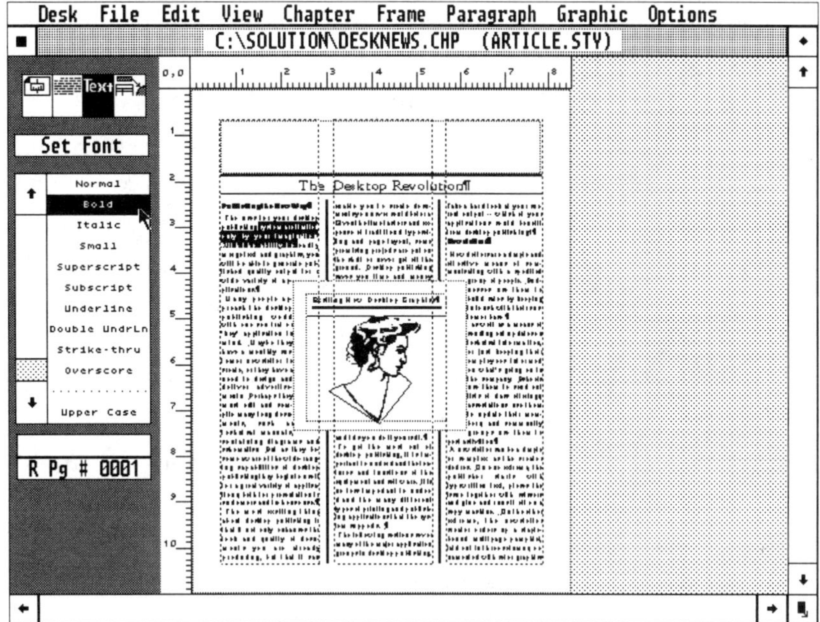

- **Click–Select text block:** Place text cursor at the beginning of the area you wish to select. Press and hold the Shift key as you click the mouse at the end of the area to be selected. The selected area will be shown in reverse video. If you make an error and need to adjust the selected area, hold the Shift key down and drag or click the mouse to the desired endpoint.
- **Apply enhancements from Side–Bar:** Select the text to enhance. Select the desired enhancement in the Text mode Assignment List.

Graphic Drawing and Enhancements in the Graphic Mode

The Graphic mode has the tools for visual editing. Use the simple geometric drawing icons to build art and visual enhancements to documents, or use Ventura graphics to create simple flowcharts and table grids.

One of the most powerful features of the Graphic mode is Box Text. This is a simple graphic form which can contain text and be placed in frames as enhancements to pictures. Ventura graphics can coexist with pictures in the same frame, so you can make last–minute edits and revisions.

In many cases, third–party graphics and illustrations don't have the same high quality fonts offered by Ventura. Using Box Text, you can create title elements using Ventura fonts to present a complete professional look throughout the document.

Ventura graphics operate like a simple line–art drawing program. Select the icon form you wish to create and draw it in the Working Area. Once drawn, move and resize the graphic with sizing boxes just like with frames.

The Graphic mode contains a variety of custom features for drawing and editing forms, including a Cut/Copy/Paste group of features, custom settings for line and shading, and a graphic grid with custom settings. You can alter graphic positioning using Send to Back/Bring to Front options.

From the surface the Graphic mode may appear quite simple, but with practice this mode becomes a powerful editing and design resource for all document applications.

Graphic Drawing and Enhancements in the Graphic Mode
Page 27

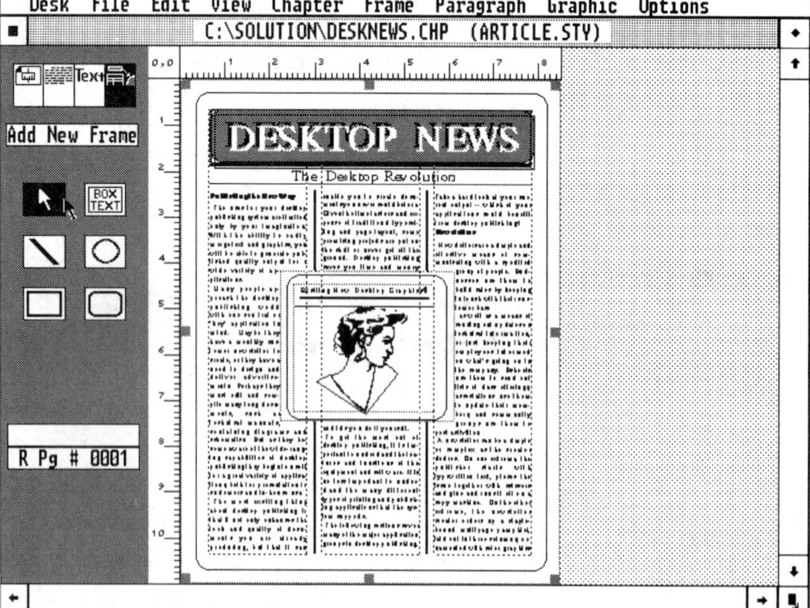

Basic Operations in the Graphics Mode

- **Select frame:** Always draw Ventura graphics with a frame selected. This ties all the individual graphics to a single frame. This in turn makes it much easier to move the graphic on the page and within a document.
- **Draw line:** Select the Line icon and place the cursor where the line is to begin. Press and hold the mouse button as you drag the mouse to the desired endpoint.
- **Draw rectangle forms:** Select the Rectangle, Rounded Rectangle, or Box Text icon. Place the drawing cursor where the upper left corner of the form is to appear. Press and hold the mouse button as you drag the mouse down and to the right. When the graphic is the correct size, release the mouse button.
- **Draw circle:** Select the Circle icon. Imagine the desired circle/ellipse as fitting perfectly into a rectangular box. Place the drawing cursor where the upper left corner of that box would appear. Press and hold the mouse button as you drag the mouse down and to the right. When the circle is the desired size, release the mouse button.
- **Size graphics:** Select the graphic form to be resized and place mouse cursor on one of the sizing boxes surrounding the form. Press and hold the mouse button until the pointing finger cursor appears and drag the mouse to resize the graphic.
- **Move graphics:** Place mouse cursor inside the graphic form you wish to move. Press and hold the left mouse button until the four–way arrow cursor appears. Drag the mouse to move the graphic and release the mouse button when it is in place.
- **Draw multiple graphic forms:** To draw a series of graphic forms with the same icon, press and hold the Shift key as you draw the graphics. You won't have to reselect the drawing icon for each individual graphic.

Designing a New Style Sheet

The style sheet is the mold for a Ventura document which contains all the settings for the standard page layout, plus a list of paragraph tags which have the typographic settings for all text elements in the document. The design of every Ventura document is entered and recorded in a style sheet.

Ventura Publisher comes with a set of standard style sheets which can be found in the \TYPESET subdirectory. To design a custom document, you need to create a new style sheet. There are two principal methods used to design new style sheets. Either design a style sheet completely from scratch, or copy an existing style sheet and make changes to it.

Method 1: Designing a Style Sheet from Scratch

When starting from scratch, begin with the basic style sheet, called DEFAULT.STY, which comes with your software. This style sheet has only a single tag: Body Text. Then use the following process to design your style sheet:

Step 1 **Name the new style sheet**

Access **FILE•Save As New Style** and save the basic style sheet under a new name.

Step 2 **Design page layout**

Access **CHAPTER•Page Size & Layout** to set up the basic page characteristics. Access **FRAME•Margins & Columns** to define desired page margins and columns.

Step 3 **Assign Body Text attributes**

Since Body Text is the standard text and is the basis for many other tags, set all typographic values for Body Text first, using the features of the **PARAGRAPH** menu.

Step 4 **Build list of tags**

Once Body text has been assigned, build a list of paragraph tags from it, using Add New Tag and features of the **PARAGRAPH** menu.

Method 2: Revise Existing Style Sheet

When you want a style sheet that is very close in design and layout to an existing style sheet, use the original style sheet as base for your design, then revise it this way:

Step 1 **Name the new style sheet**

Access **FILE•Save As New Style** and save the original style sheet under a new name.

Step 2 **Revise page layout**

Access **CHAPTER•Page Size & Layout** and make revisions to original page layout settings as necessary. Access **FRAME•Margins & Columns** to change page margins and column settings.

Designing a New Style Sheet
Page 30

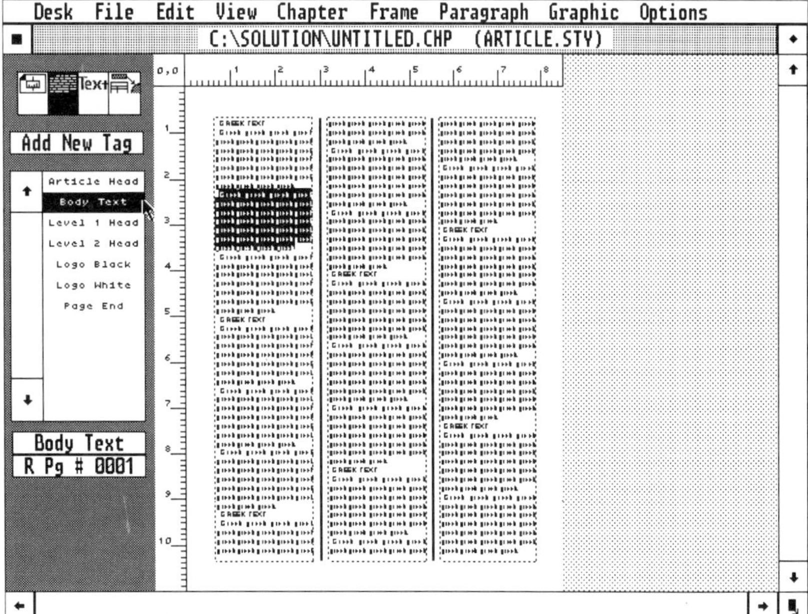

Step 3 **Revise existing tags**

Enable ***Paragraph*** mode. Select text to be edited and use features of the **PARAGRAPH** menu to assign different attributes to any tags currently in the style sheet.

Step 4 **Add new tags**

From the ***Paragraph*** mode, use Add New Tag and features of the **PARAGRAPH** menu to add new tags for text elements not in the original style sheet.

Step 5 **Remove unused tags**

Unused tags are dead weight in your style sheet, consuming memory and slowing screen operations. Access **PARAGRAPH • Update Tag List** and remove all unnecessary tag names.

Optional Method: Designing Style Sheets for Long Documents

For longer documents, you can use a variation on the standard design from scratch approach by entering paragraph tags into a text file *before* designing a style sheet (see *Understanding the Document Skeleton* later in this chapter). Just like designing from scratch, you save the basic style sheet (DEFAULT.STY) under a new name. When you load the tagged text file into the screen, all of the tag names will appear in the Paragraph mode Side–Bar. Since no values have been defined for them, each tag will have the standard attributes of Body Text.

Instead of building a list of tags from Body Text, select text which carries each of the embedded tags and define the values for each tag individually. Once you define the typographic values for a given tag, all occurrences of that tag in the file will instantly display the values you have assigned, allowing you to immediately see the results of your design decisions across a number of pages. This approach makes it easy to see text relationships and adjust page positioning, spacing, and typesize. This design approach can be used for any type of document, but it is especially useful when developing complex long documents which contain multiple levels of headings, bullet lists, and text tables. To design with embedded tags, follow these steps:

Step 1 **Name the new style sheet**

Access **FILE•Save As New Style** and save a basic style sheet (such as DEFAULT.STY) under a new name.

Step 2 **Load the text file**

The embedded tag names will appear in the ***Paragraph*** mode Side–Bar in ALL CAPS. This signifies that Ventura has found the tags but has no values defined for them in the style sheet. The values of Body Text are automatically assigned.

Step 3 **Design page layout**

Access **CHAPTER•Page Size & Layout** and set page layout settings as necessary. Access **FRAME•Margins & Columns** to assign page margins and column settings.

Step 4 **Define individual tag values**

Enable ***Paragraph*** mode. Select a string of text tagged with each of the embedded tags and assign values for that tag. It is a good idea to make a clean progression through the **PARAGRAPH** (Font, Alignment, Spacing, etc.) to reduce confusion and going back and forth.

Step 5 **Check tag relationships**

Page through the chapter to see how the various tags work together. You may need to make some adjustments to horizontal positioning or spacing between elements to achieve the best overall document appearance.

Saving a Chapter File

The Ventura chapter file is the way complete Ventura documents are saved, edited, and printed. The chapter file makes a list of all files included in the document, and records specific information, including the placement of all frames and pictures, the text of header and footer lines, and more.

There are several different methods which can be used to name and save chapter files, depending upon your document and naming preferences. Ventura's default value is to automatically give the chapter file the same name as the text file loaded into the base page. By altering the chapter naming sequence, you can override this approach and give the chapter a name which is not the same as its main text file. The three principal methods which can be used to name chapter files are profiled below.

Method 1: Save a Chapter

Step 1 **Load text file**

Enable ***Frame*** mode and select base page. Access **FILE•Load Text/Picture** to load text file. Note that a chapter name, the same as the text file, appears in the Title Bar.

Step 2 **Save chapter**

To accept the default chapter file name, select **FILE•Save**.

Method 2: Type Document Text in Ventura

Step 1 **Clear screen**

To begin the new document directly in Ventura, select **FILE•New** to clear the screen. Verify that the style sheet name shown in the Title Bar is the one you wish to use.

Step 2 **Enter text**

Enable ***Text*** mode and click mouse in Working Area. A square End of File marker appears. Type document text directly on screen. Note that no chapter file name is assigned, and the name UNTITLED.CHP appears in the Title Bar.

Step 3 **Enter chapter name**

To save the document as a chapter file, access **FILE•Save As** and enter the chapter name in the Item Selector. As the processing overlay appears, note that a text file with the same name as the chapter file is automatically saved, in the word processor format must recent ly selected in the **FILE.•Load/Text Picture** dialog box.

Method 3: Assign Custom Chapter Name

Step 1 **Clear screen**

To create a chapter file which has a different name than the main text file, select **FILE•New** to clear the screen. Verify that the style sheet name shown in the Title Bar is the one you wish to use.

Step 2 **Enter chapter name**

With the Working Area empty, access **FILE•Save As** and enter the chapter file name.

Step 3 **Load text file**

Enable ***Frame*** mode and select base page. Access **FILE•Load Text/Picture** to load text file. Note that the chapter name in the Title Bar is different from the text file name appearing in the Assignment List.

Defining Typographic Terms

Measurement Systems

Ventura Publisher recognizes a number of different measurement systems including the English/American system (inches), the metric system (centimeters), and printer's measure (picas, points, fractional points, and ems).

Standard measurement systems such as inches and centimeters are useful when measuring page size (we automatically think of a letter size page as an 8½ x ll inches), but are useless when measuring type and defining typographic attributes such as spacing and indents.

Printer's measure enables you to define all document measurements in the same system used to measure type. As you move into more sophisticated document applications in Ventura and Professional Extension, it is essential that you understand how to use the integrated system of printer's measure to define all document elements.

Defining Printer's Measure

Techniques in this book use the printer's measure system consisting of **picas & points** and **fractional points** for most operations. Important terms to understand are:

- A **Pica:** A standard unit of printer's measure. Six picas equal one inch.
- A **Point:** A standard unit of printer's measure. Twelve points equal one pica.
- **Fractional points:** Standard units of printer's measure. One hundred fractional points equal one point.
- An **Em:** A variable unit of printer's measure, which is equal to the point size of the current typeface. In 12 point type, the value of one em is 12 points.
- An **En** A variable unit of printer's measure, which is equal to half the point size of the current typeface. In 12 point type, the value of one en is six points.

Fonts

Font Metrics and Width tables

Each set of type has its own unique measurements which uniformly create the characters in that font set. These measurements are called **font metrics**, and they vary between printer formats, even in the same font set. Font metrics for PostScript Helvetica are different from font metrics for HP Laserjet Helvetica.

To create an accurate screen representation of text on the printed page, Ventura Publisher uses character width tables. These contain the font metrics for the fonts available in different formats.

Font Terms and Definitions

When working with fonts on the screen, it is important to understand how they are placed on the page, and how characters in each font set express a consistent design approach through all the characters of the alphabet. The most important font definitions and terms here are:

- **Baseline:** All characters in a line of text sit on the baseline.
- **X–height:** The height of the central element in lowercase characters.
- **Ascenders and Descenders:** Strokes rising above the x–height (ascenders) and dropping below the baseline (descenders)
- **Actual character height:** Fonts are sized by point, but the given point size is not the height of the actual character. The point size for each font includes an amount of built–in space above the character. So for a 12 point font, the actual character height is something less than 12 point. When you select text in Ventura's paragraph mode, the reversed area you see on screen shows an accurate representation of the full cap size. This is the full height of the font, including the built–in space above each character.

Understanding the Document Skeleton

When you are developing your documents in Ventura all paragraph tags and text enhancements are written to, and stored in, a text file. The text becomes the skeleton of the finished document and contains all tags and codes. In Ventura, these codes are translated to the finished design.

By placing the codes for paragraph tags and other special text features directly in a text file, Ventura gives you an easy way to edit and control files. Instead of tagging all files in Ventura, you can enter the tags directly into the text file in the word processor. You can also insert codes for special characters in the text file and enter index entries and other special text features directly into the text file, using your word processor. And when you load the text file into the correct style sheet, the text will appear instantly typeset and the special characters and enhancements will be visible in the document.

The process of inserting tags and other codes directly into text files is called **copymarking** and will be referred to in a number of techniques featured in this book.

C H A P T E R 2

Document Layout and Design

Beginning a New Style Sheet

Every document you design in Ventura Publisher begins with a style sheet. Without a style sheet that meets the needs of your specific document application, you will have to adapt an existing style or design a new one from scratch. And the first task in creating a new style is setting up the standard layout values for the base page.

The base page contains the layout defaults which are written into the style sheet and automatically appear on every page of the document. Once the base page layout has been set, you can override the basic settings by drawing a full page frame to cover one or more pages and set custom values for the individual frame. And at all times, you may refine and adjust the basic page design and see the results reflected immediately on the Ventura screen.

Ventura features offer a number of different ways to approach standard page and document design. Select the appropriate strategy based on the individual design challenge and production require-

Module 3: Publication and File Management

Module 3 overview — **Module Running Time: 1 hour, 54 minutes**

Module agenda

Introduction	2 min
Creating publications	10 min
Creating headers and footers	15 min
Footnotes	20 min
Cutting, copying, and pasting between chapters	5 min
Generating a table of contents	20 min
Generating an index	20 min
Archiving chapters and publications	10 min
Review	10 min
Introduction to the next day's activities	2 min

Instructor summary

Explain key concepts
Direct classroom exercises
Support self-guided activities
Review key points

Checklist

Module inventory

Equipment ❑ Overhead projector

Instructor checklist ❑ OH 4-1

Participant checklist ❑ Participant workbook

Media

Participant Diskette 3

Desktop Publishing Skills 3-1

Instructor Guide: This training document, based upon Xerox publishing standards, illustrates a long document layout in which text position is controlled by spacing offsets built into a system of paragraph tags. Text is typeset in Helvetica.

ments of the individual document. If you are developing a multi–column newsletter, for example, you can build a standard number of columns right into the base page. Your main newsletter text will fit automatically into the defined columns and you can create special sidebars, illustrations, and other features by drawing individual frames directly into the desired pages. For an advertisement or flyer, you may decide to place text and illustrations in frames, and headlines in Box Text graphics, in a large open page layout with no defined columns. This approach lets you move individual elements into position with a click of the mouse. For longer document formats, such as books, technical material, and business reports, you may want to lay out a single text column and control all relative positioning of text using typeset controls on spacing and alignment.

When choosing a document design strategy, consider whether it will enable you to meet the document objectives and be easy to work with in the editing and production phases. Also, keep in mind that Ventura's powerful style sheet features allow you a great deal of room for experimentation. For example: You have loaded a text file into three columns, but you'd like to see what the document would look like with four columns. All you have to do is change the column settings for the page and Ventura redraws it to the new specification, with all text neatly wrapped into place without any manual repositioning or other screen work. This power to experiment is a valuable design tool. Use it! By trying out a number of different effects and layouts at the beginning of the design process, you can select the one that really meets the needs of the document at hand. Continue to make refinements to the page layout at any time in the document development process.

Page Layout Tools

Page Layout tools are contained primarily in the Frame mode, and in features on the Chapter and Frame menus.

- **Frame mode** contains features to select and edit the base page, which is also the *base frame* in Ventura. Most layout operations are performed in this mode.

DESKTOP NEWS

Software Salaries: How Do You Stack Up?

by Joe Smith

How much your software professionals are paid is a function of many variables, and a subject of considerable interest to your organization.

Software salary pay scales

Because of the dynamic growth of the software industry over the last decade, the demand for experienced, qualified programmers has greatly increased, thus leading to a spiraling of salaries.

But what causes managers to pay one programmer more than another? Does the type of organization, its size, or location make a difference? What career path or programming specialty leads to the most remuneration?

To answer these questions, Acme Magazine recently conducted its third annual compensation survey for software professionals. This newsletter article presents the results of this study and explores what the findings may mean to you.

Acme Magazine asked Joe Smith, a compensation consulting specialist for the software industry, to design and conduct the survey. Twenty-four positions, representing four programmer job families plus management, were included.

Data was collected for base pay, bonus and incentive payments, and whether nor not incumbents received stock options or other forms of equity.

Questionnaires were sent to the data processing heads of 2,400 organizations throughout the United States.

Exciting New Desktop Graphics

Compact Disk Read Only Memory (CD-ROM) is a rapidly emerging new technology for the retrieval of vast amounts of information from an optical disk. This new peripheral device allows a totally new level of functionality in the use of microcomputers.

Physically, the CD-ROM device has a laser disk drive (or èplayerò) the same size as a traditional 5 1/4" drive. The removable disk is 4 3/4", and has a capacity of 550M bytes (equivalent to 1500 360K floppy disks).

Theory of Operation

Information stored on a CD-ROM can be loaded into memory (RAM), displayed and printed, as with other media. While that data in RAM may be altered and stored to a conventional magnetic disk, the original information on the CD-ROM is unalterable, always ensuring the original copy is intact, making archiving easy.

The storage capacity, low cost, and read only feature of CD-ROM bring an enormous new capability to microcomputer users Ì that is, information retrieval of very large reference publications. How people receive and use information in the immediate and long term future will be dramatically changed by CD-ROM.

In addition to the huge capacity of raw information storage, specialized software for the search of that information is currently being introduced. This software allows searching the information in areas, methods and speeds not previously feasible.

It now becomes possible to electronically publish reference material more economically than to print the same material in book form. That cost benefit, coupled with search and retrieval software, make an astonishing price/performance ratio.

Newsletter: This desktop publishing newsletter illustrates a display layout in which text position is controlled by column settings in the base page and frames. Text is typeset in ITC Galliard. Artwork was created in GEM Artline.

- **Page Size & Layout** on the Chapter menu contains the default settings for the base page throughout the document, which are applied globally and may not be overridden.
- **Margins & Columns** on the Frame menu is used to set page margins and define the number and size of columns and gutters in the page.
- **Sizing & Scaling** on the Frame menu is used to edit the size of custom document pages and set the position of custom pages in the Working Area.
- **Repeating Frames** on the Frame menu is used to designate frames as repeating frames which can be used to block space in the layout.
- **Ruling Lines** on the Frame menu can be used to add enhancements to the page design.

Ventura Layout Techniques

This chapter presents a group of techniques designed to help you select and implement the best layout and design strategy for any document. These techniques address the different types of design issues for both long documents and short display documents, custom documents with special page configurations and sizes, as well as practical ways to design certain applications in oversize paper sizes. In addition, techniques for enhancements you can build directly into the base page to become part of the overall design are described.

Designing Pages for Long Documents

The keynote of a successful, readable, long document is design consistency over multiple chapters. To accomplish this, design long document pages using Ventura's powerful automatic system processing features to the utmost.

Your design should include readable and clearly defined reference elements on every page such as header and footer lines and automatic section numbering for headings.

Designing Pages for Long Documents
Page 43

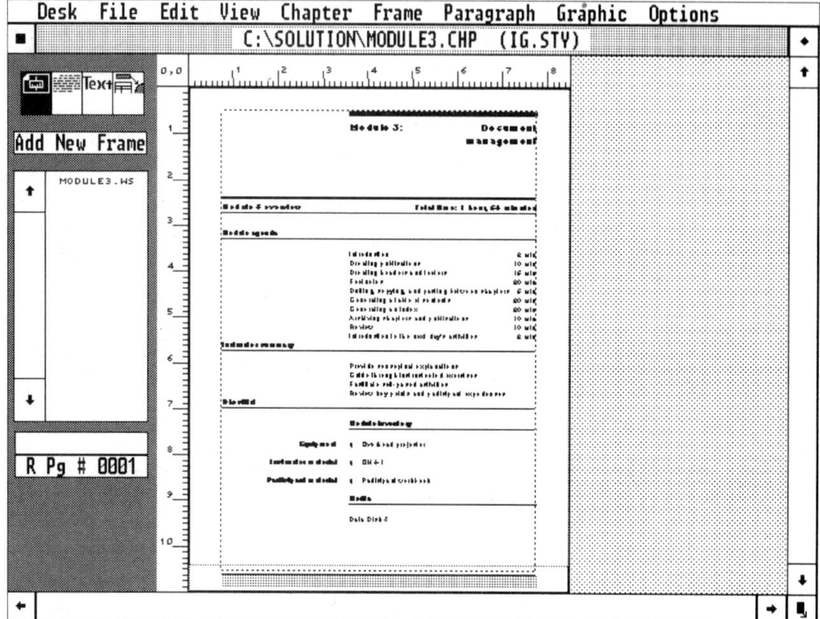

When setting up a long document page, define one or two columns in the base page. Use paragraph tags for all page positioning tasks, including offsetting text in from the page margin, defining multiple column elements and positioning headings, subheadings, and other major document handles.

Recipe: Single Column Long Document Page

Using a single column with text offset by paragraph tags lets you create an open long document layout with effective use of white space to make the page inviting and accessible to the reader.

Step 1 **Outline page**

Draw a sketch of the page including the position of text elements on the page margins and positioning of headlines.

Step 2 **Set up page size and layout**

Access **CHAPTER • Page Size & Layout** and select the correct standard page size, orientation, and single–or double–sided pages.

Step 3 **Set up page margins**

From ***Frame*** mode, access **FRAME•Margins & Columns** and verify that columns are set to 1. Define page margins.

Step 4 **Load text**

Access **FILE•Load Text/Picture** to load text file into page.

Step 5 **Design text**

When developing paragraph tags for your layout, you can offset text from the margin using tag design features. Enable ***Paragraph*** mode, select desired text and access **PARAGRAPH•Spacing**. Use In From Left and In From Right settings to offset your text from the defined page margins. For recipes covering body text and heading design, turn to Chapter 3.

Recipe: Multi–column Long Document Page

Applications requiring a great deal of block text in a long document format, such as a textbook, multi-column catalog, or technical reference material, is often more readable with a double column layout. Double columns narrow the width of the text line and make it easier to read the material.

When setting multiple columns and gutters, Ventura gives you complete freedom to define the size of your columns and gutters. Your selections, however, may not add up to exactly match the width of the current page. When setting up multi-column pages, note the two page measurement lines at the bottom right of the dialog box:

- **Actual Frame Width:** Displays the actual width of the currently selected page
- **Calculated Width:** Represents the sum of all the defined columns, gutters and left/right page margins

If the Calculated Width does not equal the Actual Frame Width, your page layout will be out of balance, or may exceed the actual size of the paper it is to be printed on.

Step 1 **Set up number of columns**

Access **FRAME•Margins & Columns** and select the desired number of columns for the page and define gutters between the columns. The page width is automatically divided into columns of equal width.

Step 2 **Set up different size columns**

To create columns of different sizes, enter the size on the line beneath the Widths heading which corresponds to the number of the column to be changed. (Column 1 is always the column farthest to the left.)

Step 3 **Enter size of gutters**

Each gutter value can be entered individually on the lines provided. Or, enter the desired value in the first gutter entry line and select Make Equal Widths. Check that Actual and Calculated Widths match after this operation.

Step 4 **Copy To facing page**

To place a mirror, reverse copy of the margin and column settings on the facing document page, select Copy To Facing Page. If Copy To Facing Page is *not* selected, the page values will automatically appear on both left and right pages.

Step 5 **Load text**

Access **FILE•Load Text/Picture** to load text file into page.

Step 6 **Design text**

Design body text and other elements to fit within the defined columns with no text offsets. For headlines and title elements to bridge the multiple column layout, **PARAGRAPH•Alignment** and set the Overall Width to Frame–Wide. For recipes covering body text and heading design, turn to Chapter 3.

Application Notes

- **Designing Body Text:** Turn to page 84.
- **Designing text with spacing:** Turn to page 87.

- **Designing headers and footers:** Place long document section names, headlines, and other information automatically in the header or footer line. Turn to page 231.
- **Designing auto–numbering systems:** Use auto– numbering for section numbering, numbered lists and more. Turn to page 192.
- **Production page breaks:** Turn to page 225.

Designing the Display Document Page

Display documents are energetic eye–catching layouts that seek to immediately involve and interest the reader. They include such applications as advertisements, catalogs, brochures, flyers, and newsletters.

In general, display documents involve significantly more complex page design challenges than long documents. The page should be more flexible so you can place visual elements and text exactly where you want them. Some display applications, such as newsletters, are densely set in multiple columns with clear headlines and

Designing the Display Document Page

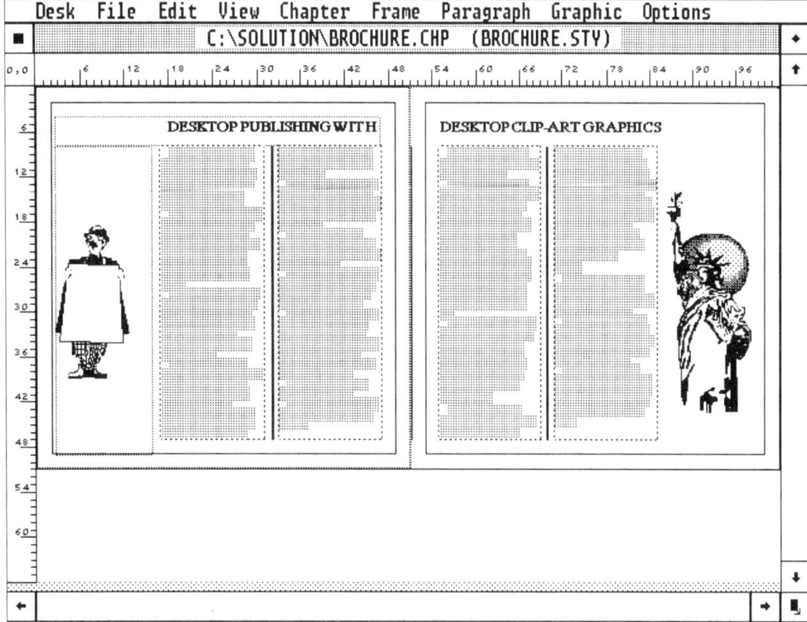

illustrations used to catch the reader's eye. Other display applications are more open, with creative uses of white space, illustrations, text effects and graphics.

When designing a display document page in Ventura, it is best to control the positioning of the main document text using defined margins and columns and not with paragraph tags. Once you have defined the number and position of columns in the main page, text automatically flows where you want it. In addition, the column guides provide a useful guide for drawing frames to position illustrations, text sidebars, and other layout elements. Create tags to define key title and headline elements. Ideally, the display layout should be set up so you can easily edit text from the screen and see the results immediately.

Recipe: Display Document Page

Step 1 **Outline page**

Draw a sketch of the planned page. Identify the core for in which Body Text will appear.

Step 2 **Set up page size layout**

Access **CHAPTER•Page Size & Layout** and select the correct standard page size, orientation, and single–or double–sided pages.

Step 3 **Set up page margins**

From ***Frame*** mode, access **FRAME•Margins & Columns** and verify that columns are set to 1. Use page margins to define the area to contain text.

Step 4 **Set up number of columns**

Access **FRAME•Margins & Columns** and select the desired number of columns for the page and define gutters between the columns. The page is automatically divided into columns and gutters of equal width.

Step 5 **Set up different size columns**

To create columns of different sizes, enter the size on the line beneath the Widths heading which corresponds to the number of the column to be changed. (Column 1 is always the column farthest to the left.)

Step 6 **Enter size of gutters**

Each gutter value can be entered individually on the lines provided. Or, enter the desired value in the first gutter entry line and select Make Equal Widths. Check that Actual and Calculated Widths match after this operation.

Step 7 **Copy To facing page**

To place a mirror, reverse copy of the margin and column settings on the facing document page, select Copy To Facing Page. If Copy To Facing Page is *not* selected, the page values will automatically appear on both left and right pages.

Step 8 **Load main document text**

Access **FILE•Load Text/Picture** to load text file into base page.

Step 9 **Design text**

Design body text and other elements to fit within the defined columns with no text offsets. For headlines and title elements to bridge the multiple column layout, **PARAGRAPH•Alignment** and set the Overall Width to Frame–Wide. For recipes covering body text and heading design, turn to Chapter 3.

Step 10 **Customize layout with frames**

From ***Frame*** mode, draw frames to contain additional text files or picture materials.

Application Notes

- **Designing body text:** Turn to page 84.
- **Designing text with spacing:** Turn to page 87.

- **Letterspacing text:** Create more professional presentation of justified text in multi–column documents using letterspacing. Turn to page 121.
- **Interactive document sketching:** Before designing a final style sheet, you can experiment with different designs using interactive design and editing features. Turn to page 169.
- **Master frames for text:** Turn to page 62.
- **Flow text through frames** Turn to page 64.

Creating Custom–size Pages

In Ventura Publisher, there is a distinction between the size of the *paper* you are printing on and the size of the *page* you are designing. You set the *paper* size in the **CHAPTER•Page Size & Layout** dialog box. Within the dimensions of the defined paper size, you can design a custom *page* of any size and shape by directly sizing the base page like a frame. This allows you to design masters for special applications like business cards, business reply postcards, small brochures, and any other document with non–standard page dimensions.

The base page in Ventura is the base frame, and if you think about it that way, it opens up new creative avenues for design. Not only can you resize the page, but you can also configure it with special rules, and shading values. And to prepare a custom size page for printing, you can print draft copies with crop marks.

Recipe: Custom–size Page

Step 1 **Outline page**

Draw a sketch of the planned page including page size, number and approximate size of columns, page margins, and positioning of text.

Step 2 **Create style sheet**

Access **FILE•Load Diff. Style** and load DEFAULT.STY from the \TYPESET subdirectory. To save this basic style sheet under a new name, acess **FILE•Save As New Style**. Use the Backup Button to

Creating Custom Size Pages

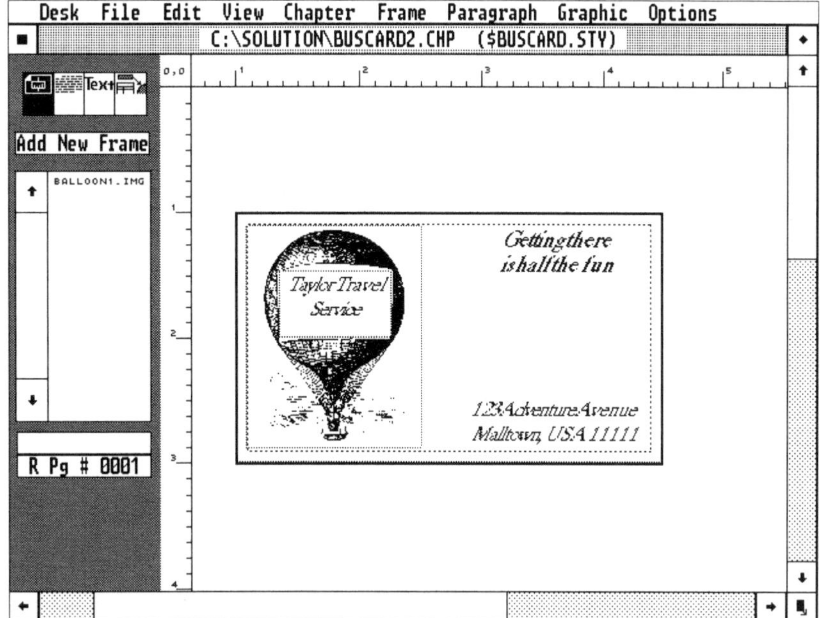

display the target drive and subdirectory where you want the new style sheet to be placed. Enter the name of the new style sheet.

Step 3 **Set up page size and layout**

Access **CHAPTER•Page Size & Layout**, select the desired orientation single–or double–sided pages and a standard size–paper that your printer will accept.

Step 4 **Define custom page size**

Enable ***Frame*** mode, select base page and access **FRAME•Sizing & Scaling**.

▲ **Enter Width:** Enter page width on Frame Width line.

▲ **Enter Height:** Enter page height on Frame Height line.

Step 5 **Position custom page on paper**

The custom–size page can be positioned just like a frame using the Upper Left X and Upper Left Y entries:

▲ **Set horizontal position:** Set distance between left edge of paper and left edge of page on Upper Left X.

▲ **Set vertical position:** Set distance between top of paper and top edge of page on Upper Left Y.

Recipe: Print Custom Pages with Crop Marks

Crop marks are used by printers to denote the edges of a page. When printing a small piece, such as a business card, position the page so that it appears in the middle of the paper, allowing crop marks to display on all sides of the page.

Step 1 **Access printing features**

From any mode, access **FILE•To Print**. Set the desired pages to print and the number of pages.

Step 2 **Enable crop marks**

Turn the Crop Marks feature to On.

Step 3 **Begin Printing**

Crop marks print outside the perimeter of the custom page, not along the page borders. Without sufficient space on the page, crop marks will not appear or only partial marks will appear.

Application Notes

- **Business cards:** Create business card master in any size or shape using custom–size page.
- **Oversize pages** For custom–size pages which are larger than standard letter–size pages, use broadsheet or double paper sizes. Turn to page 54.
- **Custom–size page inserts:** Place an insert of custom size pages inside standard size documents using multi-page frames. Turn to page 59.

Designing Layouts with Unequal Columns

In some applications, you may decide to design a long document or display page using unequal column widths. For example, a special

Designing Layouts with Unequal Columns

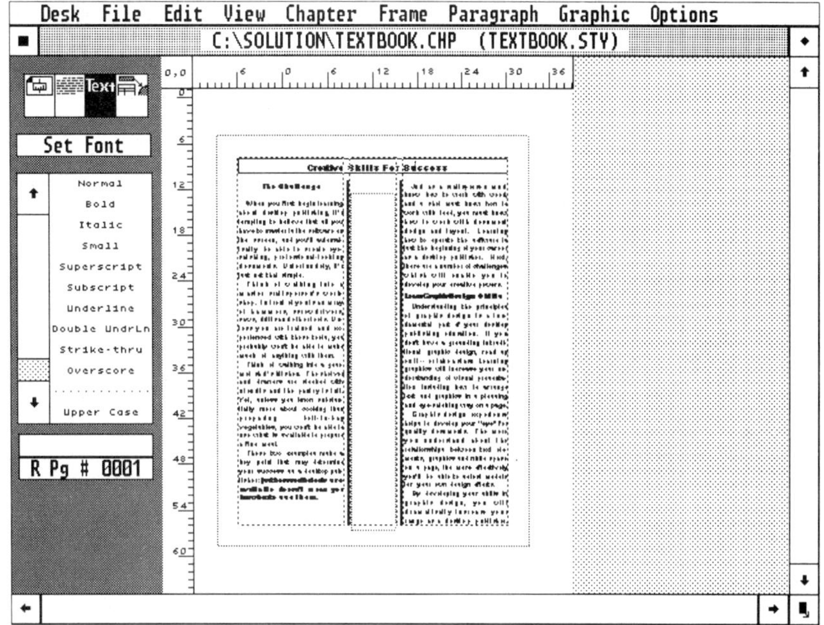

area on a page may be defined for a repeating text block or a special column of reference information. Or, an unequal column be set aside as an area on the page for icons or illustrations.

You can flow text through unequal columns, or you can control the positioning of text by snapping a repeating frame over one or more columns in the layout. Whatever the application need, Ventura has flexibility to design unequal columns on a single page, or over facing pages.

Recipe: Pages with Unequal Columns

Step 1 **Outline page**

Draw a sketch of the planned page including page size, number, and approximate size of columns, page margins, and positioning of text.

Step 2 **Create style sheet**

Access **FILE•Load Diff. Style** and load DEFAULT.STY from the \TYPESET subdirectory. To save this basic style sheet under a new name, access **FILE•Save As New Style**. Use the Backup Button to display the target drive and subdirectory where you want the new style sheet to be placed. Enter the name of the new style sheet.

Step 3 **Set page margins**

Enable ***Frame*** mode and select the base page. Access **FRAME•Margins & Columns** and enter the page margins.

Step 4 **Define columns**

Select the desired number of columns on the page. Individually enter the Widths of each column and the Gutters in the spaces provided.

☞ CAUTION: Verify that values shown for Calculated and Actual Frame Width are the same. Ventura does not automatically force column widths to fit into the defined page when column widths and gutters are entered individually. If Calculated and Actual Widths don't match, your page will not print properly.

Application Notes

- **Block column with repeating frame:** Unequal columns can help in designing a page in which one or more of the columns is covered by repeating frames containing standard text, presentation graphics, or icons. Turn to page 67.
- **Design column breaks:** Special column break tags can make editing columns easier. Turn to page 218.

Designing with Oversize Pages

When designing layouts for larger than standard letter or legal size paper, such as large brochures, tabloid size newspapers, or detailed double page layouts, it is best to use a landscape double page format. By setting up a double page (11" x 17") in the Page Size & Layout dialog box, you can design the double page in any way you like. Graphics and illustrations can easily bridge across the two pages, not possible using standard pages, even in Facing Pages View.

Designing with Oversize Pages

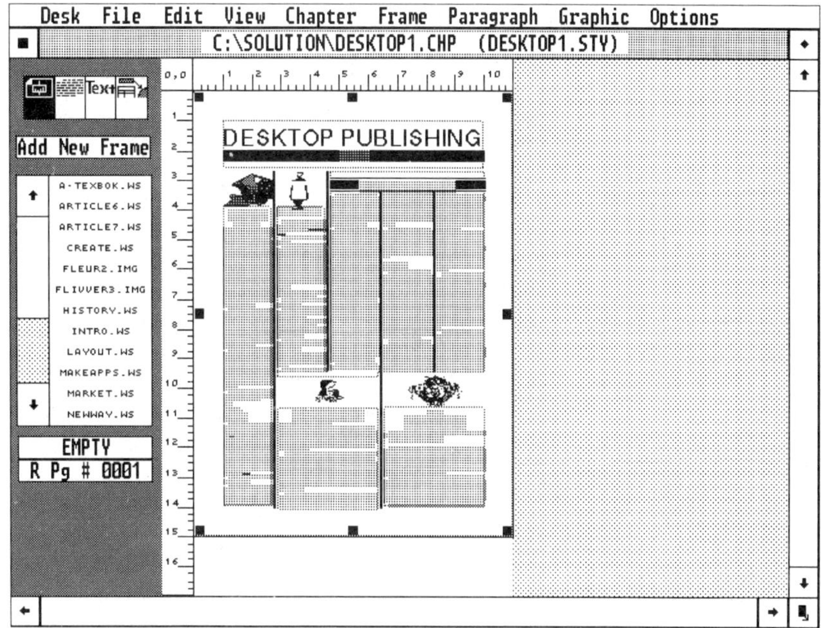

Recipe: Oversize Pages

Step 1 **Outline page**

Draw a sketch of the planned page. Identify core area in which Body Text is to appear.

Step 2 **Create style sheet**

Access **FILE•Load Diff. Style** and load DEFAULT.STY from the \TYPESET subdirectory. To save this basic style sheet under a new name, access **FILE•Save As New Style**. Use the Backup Button to display the target drive and subdirectory where you want the new style sheet to be placed. Enter the name of the new style sheet.

Step 3 **Set up page size and layout**

Access **CHAPTER•Page Size & Layout** and select the correct oversize format, such as Double, or Broadsheet. Set orientation and single–or double–sided pages.

Step 4 **Set up page margins**

From ***Frame*** mode, access **FRAME•Margins & Columns**. Use page margins to define the area to contain text.

Step 5 **Set up number of columns**

Select the desired number of columns for the page. The page width is automatically divided into columns of equal width.

Step 6 **Enter size of gutters**

Enter each gutter value individually on the lines provided or enter the value in the first gutter entry line and select Make Equal Widths.

☞ CAUTION: Check that Actual and Calculated Widths match after this operation. If not, make adjustments to margin, column, or gutter values so that Actual and Calculated Widths match.

Recipe: Printing oversize sheets

Step 1 **Access printing features**

From any mode, Access **FILE•To Print**.

Step 2 **Set print commands**

In Print Information dialog box, identify the desired pages and number of copies.

Step 3 **Turn on crop marks**

Set Crop Marks feature to On. Crop marks defining the edge of the custom page will print if room is available.

Step 4 **Begin print operation**

Select OK in the Print Information dialog box. If you are using a special printer with the capability to print oversize pages, the operation will proceed without further interruption.

Step 5 **Select print option**

If you are using a laser or other printer which can only handle letter and/or legal size paper, shortly after the print operation begins, an overlay dialog box will appear listing the following choices.

▲ **Shrink to fit:** Shrink reduces the entire 11" x 17" page to fit on an 8 ½" x 11" size page.

▲ **Overlap & paste–up:** Overlap is only available for PostScript printers, and will print the entire layout in actual size over four sheets of paper marked with crop marks. The four sheets can then be pasted together to create the finished layout.

Application Notes

- **Tabloid newsletters:** Use portrait broadsheet with multiple columns to develop tabloid format newsletters and newspapers.
- **Large format flyers:** Use portrait or landscape broadsheet to design flyers and posters.
- **Create custom–page sizes:** Create custom pages by resizing base page. Turn to page 50.

Designing Two–page Spreads

When you design a catalog or brochure, you may need to bridge visual elements so that each two–page spread presents a completely integrated effect and doesn't look like two separate pages.

There is no way to bridge visuals without a great deal of trial and error on a single, standard–size page. A double page layout, however, can be designed as a single, unified 11" x 17" page. You can bridge text and visuals across two pages to clearly and easily create a dynamic and unified layout.

Recipe: Two–page Spreads

Step 1 **Outline page**

Draw a sketch of the planned page including page size, number and approximate size of columns, page margins, and positioning of text.

Step 2 **Create style sheet**

Access **FILE•Load Diff. Style** and load DEFAULT.STY from the \TYPESET subdirectory. To save this basic style sheet under a new name, access **FILE•Save As New Style**. Use the Backup Button to display the target drive and subdirectory where you want the new style sheet to be placed. Enter the name of the new style sheet.

Step 3 **Set up page size and layout**

Access **CHAPTER•Page Size & Layout** and select the desired broadsheet page size, orientation, and single– or double–sided pages

Step 4 **Set up page margins**

Enable ***Frame*** mode. Access **FRAME•Margins & Columns** Set page margins to define the area to contain text.

Step 5 **Set columns & gutter**

Select the number of columns for the page. The page width is automatically divided into columns of equal width. To allow for a gutter at the center of the double page spread, set up at least two columns and enter the size of the gutter between them. This helps keep body text from crowding the fold point of the double page spread.

Designing Two-Page Spreads
Page 57

Step 6 **Enter size of gutters**

Enter each gutter value individually on the lines provided, or enter a value in the first gutter entry line and select Make Equal Widths.

☞ CAUTION: Check that Actual and Calculated Widths match after this operation. If not, make adjustments to margin, column, or gutter values so that Actual and Calculated Widths match.

Application Notes

- **Page numbers:** Automatic pagination features do not place correct left and right page numbers on double page spread. Place page number cross–reference in Box Text graphics to place individual numbers on facing pages. Turn to page 93
- **Create custom size layouts** Create custom double page layouts by resizing the base page. Turn to page 50.

Creating Multi–page Frames for Text and Tables

To place a special, multi–page insert containing text or tabular material in a document, you can block off the necessary pages with full page frames and place the text or tables inside them. But an easier way is to create a *multi–page frame* by adding a new base page to contain the insert text.

The base page in Ventura Publisher can be thought of as the *base frame* which defines the basic page characteristics. Whenever you add a new page to a document using **CHAPTER•Insert/Remove Page**, you have added a *second base page* which automatically expands to receive an entire text file.

You may insert a new page at any point in a document using **CHAPTER•Insert/Remove Page**. Each additional base page can be configured with enhancements and attributes different from those in the original base page, including page size, margins and columns settings, frame background, and ruling line enhancements. You cannot, however, override basic settings made in the **CHAPTER•Page**

Creating Multi-Page Frames for Text and Tables
Page 59

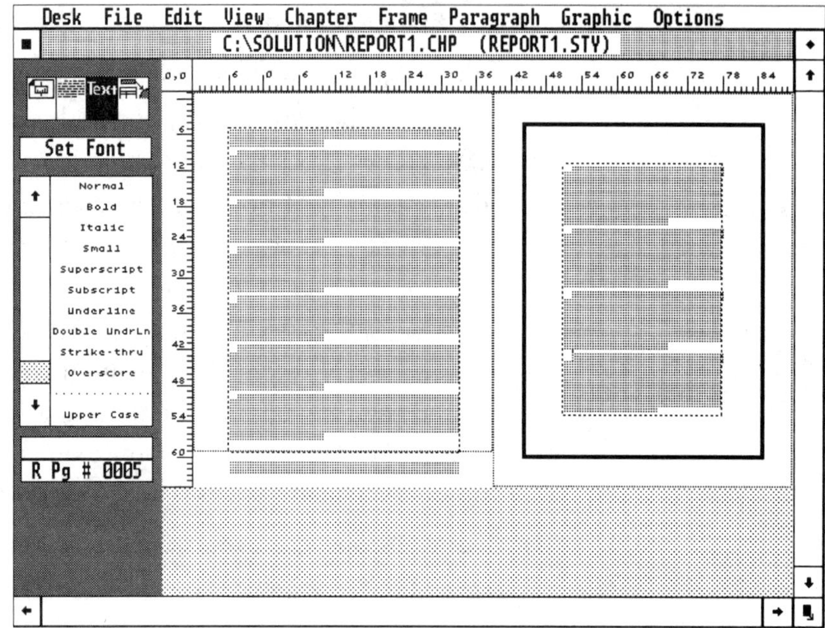

Size & Layout dialog box which define the default paper type, and orientation for *all* pages in the chapter. This technique allows you to easily insert and set off material in documents without a great deal of complex frame editing, or reworking of your text files.

Recipe: Multi–page Frames

Step 1 **Go to position of multi–page frame**

Use keyboard or access **CHAPTER•Go To Page** feature to bring up position where multi–page frame can be added.

Step 2 **Add new page**

From any mode, access **CHAPTER•Insert/Remove Page** and add new page to chapter.

Step 3 **Load text into multi–page frame**

Enable ***Frame*** mode and select the new base page. Load the file containing the text for the insert or tabular material. The new base page automatically adds enough new pages to display the entire text file.

Recipe: Design for Multi–Page Frames

Step 1 **Page size**

From ***Frame*** mode, select the page and access **FRAME•Sizing & Scaling** and change the size of the new base page using the Frame Height and Frame Width lines.

Step 2 **Page position**

For custom–size pages, position the page on the paper using the Upper Left X and Upper Left Y lines.

Step 3 **Page typography**

By setting custom values in the **FRAME•Frame Typography** dialog box, typographic values for the multi–page frame may be different than those set in the **CHAPTER•Chapter Typography** dialog box for the entire chapter.

Step 4 **Margins & columns**

From the ***Frame*** mode, select the page and define margins, columns and gutters for the new base page. Settings in the rest of the chapter will not be affected.

Step 5 **Ruling lines**

From the ***Frame*** mode, select the new base page and define desired ruling lines for the base page. Settings in the rest of the chapter will not be affected.

Step 6 **Vertical rules**

From the ***Frame*** mode, select the page and define inter–column and vertical rules as desired. Settings in the rest of the chapter will not be affected.

Step 7 **Frame background**

From the ***Frame*** mode, select the page and a frame background as desired. Settings in the rest of the chapter will not be affected.

Application Notes

- **Insert special document elements:** Good for special document insert sections including tables, text inserts, groups of illustrations.
- **Place pull–outs:** Create special pull–out insert pages in newsletters, newspapers, and brochures.
- **Text tables with vertical tabs:** Create multi–page text tables using vertical tabs. Turn to page 95.
- **Tables with horizontal tabs:** Use a multi-page frame to display multi–page tables created with horizontal tabs. Turn to page 103.
- **Professional Extension tables:** Turn to Chapter 11.
- **Headers & Footers:** Use header match features to insert name of table into header or footer line. Turn to page 228.
- **Setting pagination:** Use pagination overrides to set up custom page numbering for multi–page frames. Turn to page 338.

Creating Master Frames for Text

Frames provide controlled areas for text. In applications like newsletters and magazines which are made up of multiple text files, use frames to place articles in specific positions in the document. To save time when placing text in frames, you can define all of the characteristics you want for the text materials in a single frame and then copy that frame to any location throughout a document. Creating and copying a master frame can save you a great deal of repetitive frame editing, especially in situations where you are flowing text through multiple frames.

Recipe: Text Master Frame

Step 1 **Set Column Snap**

Select Options•Turn Column Snap On.

Step 2 **Draw frame**

Enable Frame mode and select Add New Frame in the Side–Bar. Draw the frame and edit size and position if necessary.

Step 3 **Set custom typography**

You can set general typographic values for text in a frame which are different from the rest of the chapter. To do this, access **FRAME• Frame Typography** and enter desired settings for Widows & Orphans, Column Balance, Pair Kerning, and Move Down To 1st Baseline.

Step 4 **Set margins and columns**

A custom configuration of margins and columns can be set within the frame to display text. Select the frame and access **FRAME•Margins & Columns**. If you plan to place a ruling box around the frame, enter small margin values to prevent the text from bumping up against the framing line.

Step 5 **Set buffer**

To prevent text outside the frame from bumping up against it, place a space buffer around it. Access **FRAME•Sizing & Scaling** and enter the space buffer for the top and bottom of the frame on the Vertical

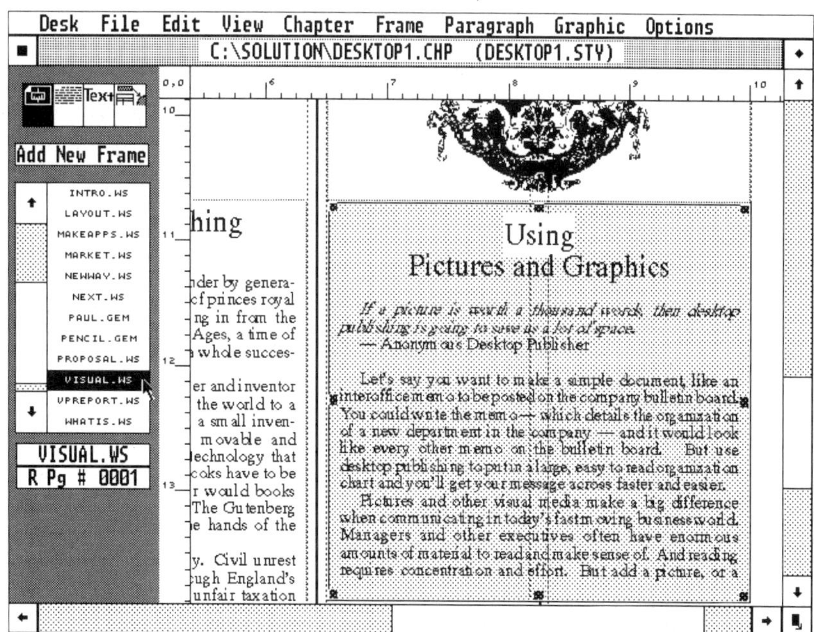

Creating Master Frames for Text

Padding line, and the buffer to the left and right on the Horiz. Padding line.

Step 6 **Set ruling lines**

To enhance the appearance of the frame or set it off from the rest of the page, you can place ruling lines above, below, or around it. Select the frame and access any of the three ruling line dialog boxes on the Frame menu.

Application Notes

- **Setting up Body Text:** Turn to page 84
- **Tracking text through frames:** Use Go to Page features to find the next frame where text file appears. Turn to page 66.

Automatic Text Placement with Master Frames

Magazines and newsletters often feature articles which are broken up and continued at two more more places in the layout. In Ventura, you can accomplish this by flowing a single text file through a set of frames.

Flowing text through frames is a complex operation. The frames must be drawn and positioned throughout the document. Each frame must be configured with the desired margins, buffers, and framing effects. Finally, the text must be loaded into each successive frame.

To save time during document layout, use the master frame technique to position your text. Instead of performing a series of isolated operations, this technique gives you the flexibility to position the text where you want it and see the results instantly on screen. The master frame contains the basic presentation and layout for the text file. When the text file is loaded into the fully configured master frame, you paste copies of the framed text anywhere in the document. As copies are pasted into place, text automatically flows through frames so you can see exactly where text is appearing on the page. You can resize frame copies at any time, and the text will correctly flow into the frame.

Automatic Text Placement with Master Frames

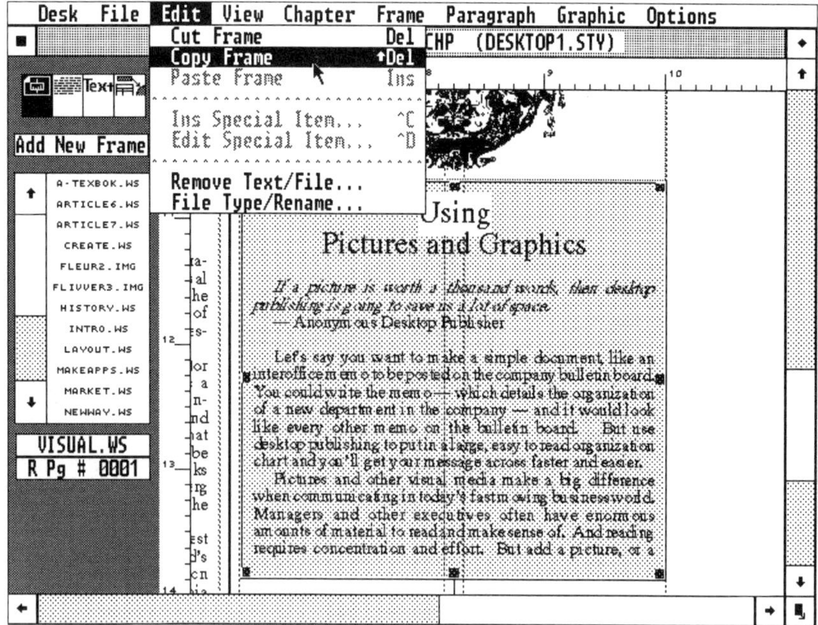

Using this technique can significantly reduce the amount of time you spend laying out and positioning article elements in many document applications. As you make edits to the text, Ventura's flow through features instantly reposition the text through the series of frames. At any time during production, attributes of the individual frames containing the article can be edited as needed.

Recipe: Automatic Text Placement

Step 1 **Place text file in frame**

Enable ***Frame*** mode. Access **FILE•Load Text/Picture** and load the desired text file into the Assignment List. Select frame and select name of text file in the Assignment List.

Step 2 **Copy completed text frame.**

To place a copy of the frame into the copy clipboard, select frame and select **EDIT•Copy Frame**.

Step 3 **Paste copy of text frame**

Use PgUp or PgDn keys to display the page where to continue the file. To place a copy of the frame, select **EDIT•Paste Frame**.

Application Notes

- **Place frame breaks:** When a page break is placed in text which is flowed through a series frames, it acts like a "frame break," and breaks the text to the next frame.
- **Copyfitting:** Using Ventura's interactive font sizing and kerning, fit a given string of text to a frame by increasing/decreasing font size and increasing/decreasing the tracking between individual text characters. Turn to page 185.
- **Designing custom text frames:** Turn to page 62

Tracking Text Files Through Frames

Once a text file has been placed into a series of frames, it is possible to track the file straight through the document without manually going through every page. The Go To Page feature in Ventura works in two ways:

- **Relative to Document:** recognizes the chapter–wide pagination which is showing in the Current Page Indicator
- **Relative to File:** when a framed text file is selected, this will go to the next document page *where that text file appears.*

Using Relative to File tracks files through documents such as newsletters or magazines which contain text files flowing through a variety of different frames.

Tracking text files

Step 1 **Select the frame**

Enable ***Frame*** mode and select the frame and verify that the name of your desired text file is in the Current Selection Box.

Tracking Text Files Through Frames

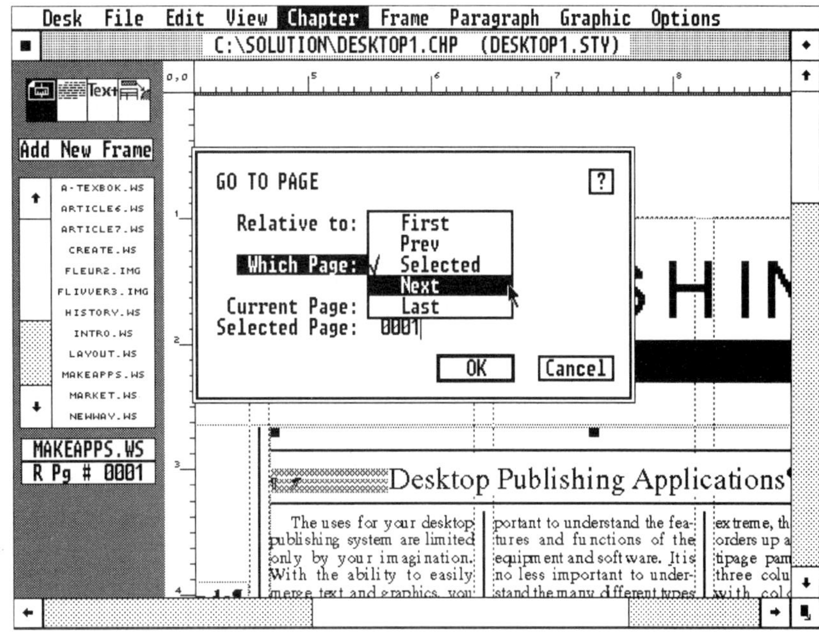

Step 2 **Use relative to file**

Access **CHAPTER•Go To Page**. Select Relative To: File.

Step 3 **Go to desired page**

With Relative to File enabled, the features of the dialog box will take you to pages of the text file in the selected frame. Select Next and it will display the next page where that text file appears.

Application Notes

- **Newsletters:** Follow text files through frames without paging through the entire document.
- **Flow text through frames:** Turn to page 64.

Creating Custom Layouts with Repeating Frames

Many technical documents, training materials, and other business publications require completely different page layouts to appear on facing pages. Applications like this will typically feature document text on the right page with supporting notes and illustrations printed on the left. You can easily design and edit applications like this in Ventura using repeating frames.

Repeating frames are one of the most powerful layout tools available to you in Ventura Publisher. Using this set of features, you can select a frame and force it to repeat on left pages, right pages, or all pages in a document. Ventura allows up to six repeating frames per document. Once repeating frames have been defined, you can hide specific frames on identified pages to create exactly the document layout you wish.

As a layout tool, repeating frames are especially useful in page blocking. For example, if you want left pages to carry a set of illustrations supporting text on the right pages, draw a page size frame on one left page and force it to repeat on all left pages through the document. Instantly, all left pages will be left blank, and all document text will be forced to appear on the right pages. Keep in mind that, although certain editing operations may be performed once a frame has been made a repeating frame, it may not be resized, deleted, or moved until the repeat settings have been turned off.

Recipe: Layout with Repeating Frames

Step 1 **Draw frame**

Draw a frame to use as a repeating frame in document. For the frame to snap to the column guides and cover the entire page, be sure that **OPTIONS•Column Snap** is set to On.

Step 2 **Set frame attributes**

Use features of the Frame menu to set frame attributes before setting up repeating frame.

▲ **FRAME•Margins & Columns:** Set # of columns, gutters, and inside margins of frame as desired in Frame•Margins & Columns.

▲ **FRAME•Sizing & Scaling:** Set Horizontal and Vertical Padding if desired.

▲ **FRAME•Sizing & Scaling:** If frame is to contain a picture, set the size and aspect ratio of the picture in the frame

▲ **FRAME•Ruling Lines & Background:** Set all desired ruling line and background effects using the Vertical Rules, Ruling Line, and Frame Background dialog boxes.

Step 3 **Define repeating frame**

With the frame selected, access **Frame•Repeating Frame**. Select whether the frame is to repeat on Left, Right, or Left & Right pages.

Step 4 **To hide a repeating frame**

To prevent a given repeating frame from appearing on a page, go to the page containing the repeating frame. From the ***Frame*** mode, select the frame and access the **Frame•Repeating Frames** dialog box. Select Hide This Repeating Frame.

Application Notes

- **Place page graphics:** Use repeating frames to place graphics and illustrations into the page layout. Turn to page 330.

Creating Custom Layouts with Repeating Frames

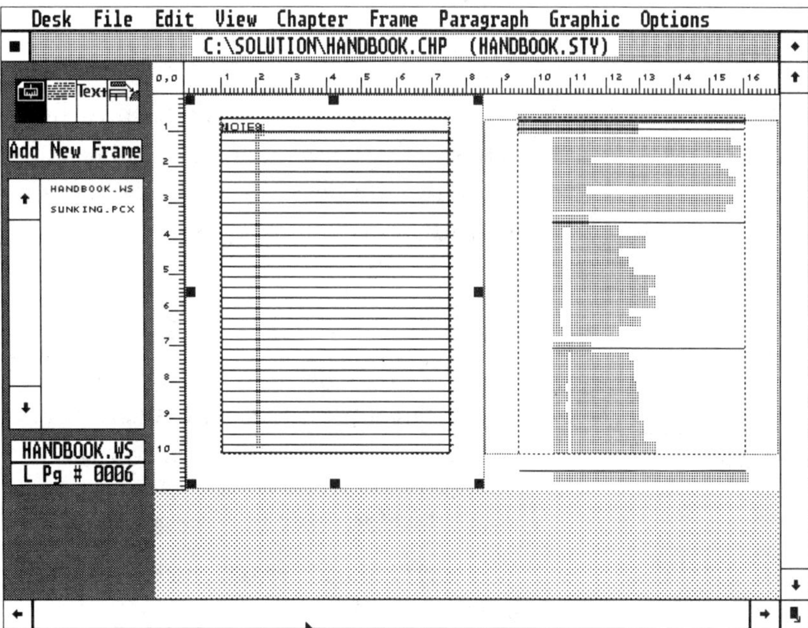

- **Control document space with breaks**: Block pages and columns using breaks features. Turn to page 218.
- **Mailmerge with repeating frames:** Turn to page 297.
- **Designing matching chapters:** Use repeating frames to design complex facing page layouts. Turn to page 347.

Designing Dense Text Documents with Repeating Frames

When working with multi–column dense text documents such as telephone books, databases, and catalogs, you can increase the amount of text placed on a single page by flowing the text file through repeating frames. The repeating frame can trick Ventura into thinking that it is a separate page. The result is that you effectively double the amount of available page memory in the system. This lets you place more text on a single page without having to install extra memory in your system. For this technique to work, some text must always flow into the base page, and then flow into the repeating frame.

This technique is a workaround which should be used only for occasional memory–intensive applications. If you regularly create dense text applications, you should use the Professional Extension with additional memory installed in your system.

Recipe: Dense Text with Repeating Frames

This technique models the process to create a three– column telephone directory listing on a single–sided page. You can vary this process with different column configurations.

Step 1 **Load text file into Assignment List**

Access **FILE•Load Text/Picture**, select Text and the file format. Load text file into the Assignment List.

Designing Dense Text Documents with Repeating Frames

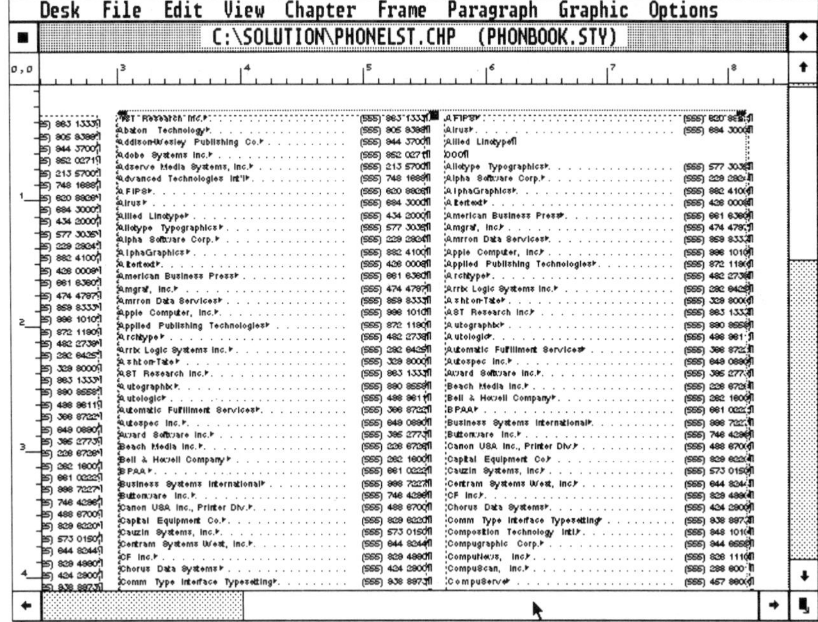

Step 2 **Define page margins and columns**

Enable ***Frame*** mode and select the base page. Access **FRAME•Margins & Columns** and select 3 columns. Define gutters between the columns.

Step 3 **Load text file into base page**

With base page selected, select the text file in the Assignment List.

Step 4 **Draw a frame to cover two columns**

Use Add New Frame to draw a frame covering two columns. Select the frame and access **FRAME•Margins & Columns**. Set the number of columns inside the frame to 2.

Step 5 **Make this frame a repeating frame**

With the frame selected, access **FRAME•Repeating Frame** and set frame to repeat on Right pages only.

Step 6 **Load text into the repeating frame**

With repeating frame selected, select text file name in the Assignment List. Use PgDn and PgUp keys to page through the document to see the text flowing through.

Application Notes

- **Telephone books:** Use this technique to publish multi–column telephone books or sales listings.
- **Professional Extension:** If you regularly produce dense text applications, the Professional Extension can directly access enhanced memory in the system and increase the amount of memory for each page in the document.

Enhancing Pages with Ruling Lines

To enhance the look of a document, Ventura includes a number of ruling lines features which can be assigned to a base page or individual frames. Single or multiple ruling lines can add highlights to the top or bottom of a page, as well as establish framing elements that surround the page outside text margins. Rules are contained in the three ruling line dialog boxes (Ruling Line Above, Ruling Line Below, Ruling Box Around) on the Frame menu.

When placing rules into a base page, they are recorded into the current style sheet and automatically appear on every page in the document. If you don't want ruling lines appearing on every page, it is better to draw page–size frames and assign the ruling line attribute to the frame.

Recipe: Page Enhancements with Ruling Lines

Step 1 **Select base page**

Enable ***Frame*** mode and select base page.

Step 2 **Select ruling lines**

Access any of the ruling line dialog boxes on the **FRAME** menu.

Enhancing Pages with Ruling Lines

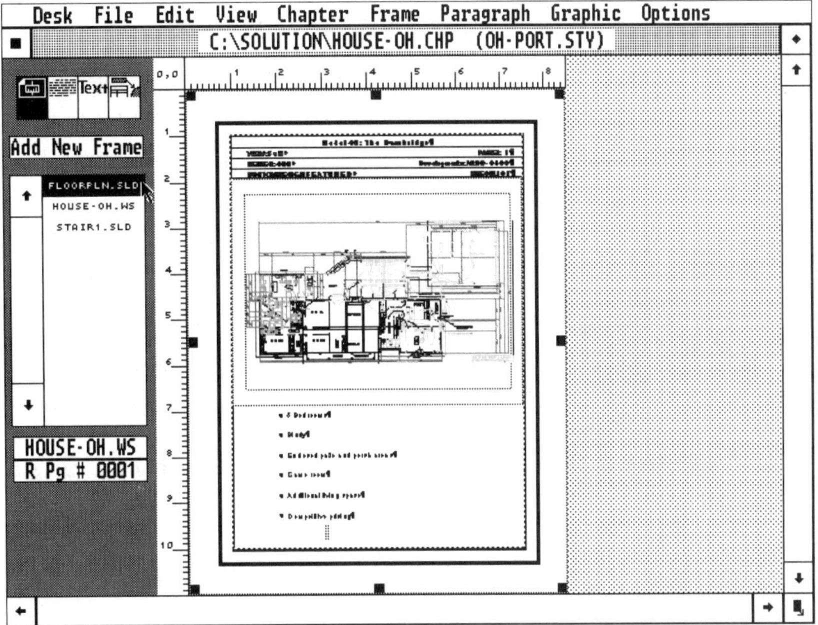

▲ **Ruling Line Above:** Places frame wide rule at top of the page. Move down from the top of the page by entering distance on Space Above Rule line.

▲ **Ruling Line Below:** Places frame wide rule at the bottom of the page. Move up from bottom of page by entering distance on Space Below Rule lines.

▲ **Ruling Box Around:** Places ruling line completely around frame. Move in from page perimeter by entering distance on Space Above Rule line.

Step 3 **Define line characteristics and spacing**

Select color, shading, and dashed patterns if available. Define thickness on Height of Rule lines. Enter space between rules on Space Below Rule lines. The mimic shows what the set of ruling lines will look like.

Step 4 **Define position on the page**

Use Space Above Rule 1 to drop Ruling Lines Above and Ruling Box Around down from the edge of the page, and Space Below Rule 1 to move Ruling Line Below up from the edge of the page.

Application Notes

- **Framing lines:** Use Ruling Box Around.
- **Shaded ruling strips:** Use thick line setting and colored or shaded value for Ruling Line Above or Ruling Line Below.
- **Design elements:** Shaded or solid rules in the page let you create backgrounds and design elements.
- **Experiment with shading, multiple rules, and dashes:** By combining a variety of ruling line effects in the page, you can create a wide variety of backgrounds for your documents in the base page of your document.
- **Master frames for text:** Enhance master text frame with solid or shaded ruling line effcts. Turn to page 62.
- **Master frames for pictures:** Enhance master picture frame with solid or shaded ruling line effects. Turn to page 246.
- **Creating backgrounds with frame rules:** Turn to page 271.

Setting Up Inter–column Rules

Inter–column rules automatically appear between columns of a multi–column style sheet to the height of the currently defined columns. They are hidden when a frame is drawn over them, and may be turned on inside of multi–column frames as well as the base page. By setting the width for inter–column rules at the same value used for page framing lines, or lines around frames in your page, you can enhance page design for multiple column applications.

Setting Up Inter-Column Rules
Page 74

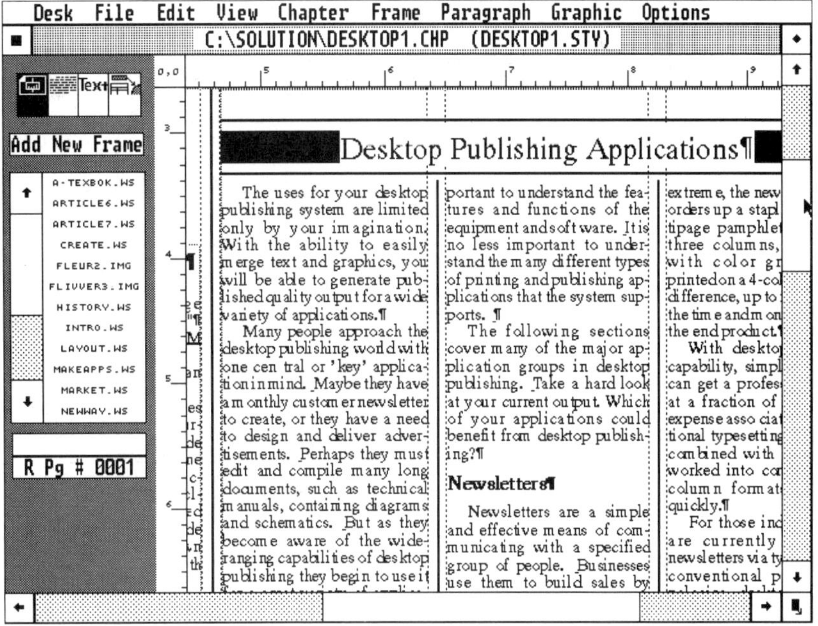

Recipe: Inter–column Rules

Step 1 **Set columns**

Verify that the style sheet has two or more columns defined in the base page.

Step 2 **Turn on Intercol. Rules**

Access **FRAME•Vertical Rules**. Turn Intercol. Rules: On for desired pages. If using a single–sided style sheet, it is only necessary to have the inter–column rules turned on for the correct starting page (left or right) identified in the Page Size & Layout dialog box.

☞ CAUTION: If using a double–sided style sheet, inter–column rules must be turned on for both left and right pages.

Step 3 **Set rule thickness**

Set Intercol. Rules, Width: to the desired thickness.

Application Notes

- **Newsletters:** Use inter–column rules as a design element.
- **Master frames for text:** Place inter–column rules in master text frame. Turn to page 62.

Place Custom Vertical Rules

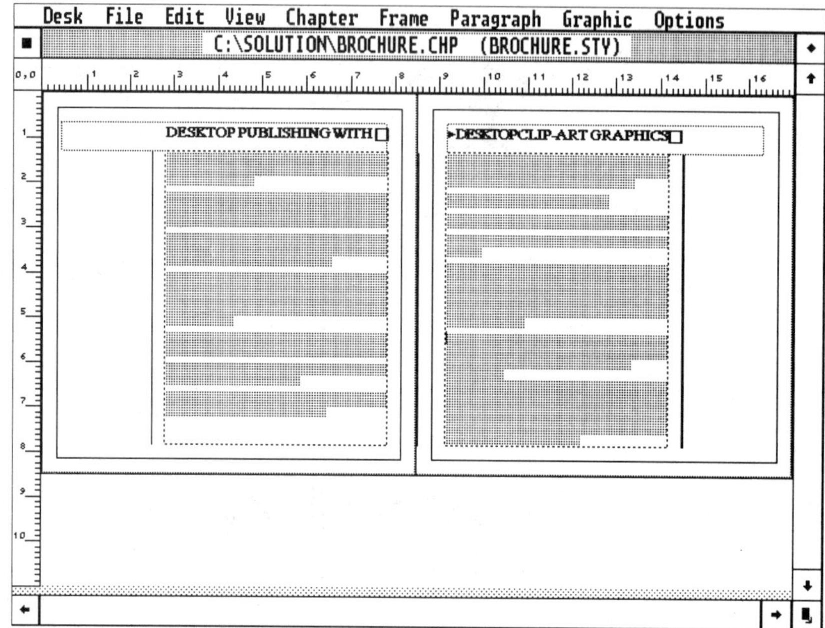

Place Custom Vertical Rules

Two vertical rules can be placed anywhere on the page you desire. Vertical rules allow you to easily create framing effects and design elements with other ruling lines features. They may be used as enhancements to a page, or inside of frames and repeating frames. You can use them as simple framing elements, as complements to inter–column rules, or in conjunction with other page and frame ruling lines.

Recipe: Place Custom Vertical Rules

Step 1 **Set vertical rules**

Enable ***Frame*** mode and select base page. Access **FRAME•Vertical Rules**.

Step 2 **Set rule width**

Enter width for Rule 1 in the Rule 1 Width line.

Step 3 **Set rule position**

Enter position for Rule 1 in the Rule 1 Position line. Vertical rule position is measured from the *left edge of the page*, and *not* the left margin guide.

▲ Entries for Rule 2 may be completely different from those entered for Rule 1

▲ When using Copy to Facing Page with Vertical Rules, it does not mirror the settings across pages, but simply copies the same setting on the right page to the left.

▲ To place mirrored vertical rules on a page, you must measure the correct position for each ruling line from the left edge of the page.

Step 4 **Copy to Facing Page**

In facing page documents, the vertical rule can be copied to exactly the same position, and *not* a mirror position on the facing page using the Copy to Facing Page option.

Application Notes

- **Framing lines:** Use in conjunction with inter–column rules, or Ruling Lines Above and Below.
- **Page side rules:** Place side rules at the edge of page.
- **Table grids:** Inside frames, use in conjunction with underlined text to create simple table grids. Turn to page 103.
- **Master frames for text:** Enhance master text frame with side rules. Turn to page 62.
- **Master frames for pictures:** Enhance master picture frame with side rules. Turn to page 246.

CHAPTER 3

Designing Text

Typesetting with Paragraph Tags

The purpose of every document is to communicate ideas and information. The primary means of communication is almost always the document text, so the design and presentation of that text determines how effectively the document presents its contents to the reader.

Although there are many different types of documents addressing a wide variety of communication needs, there are common text design issues that all documents share. For one thing, all text is structured into a readable and understandable form by text elements such as titles, headlines, subheadings, bullets, lists, footnotes, tables, headers and footers.

Each of these elements requires special presentation on the page to set it off and clarify its purpose and relationship to the whole page. The paragraph tag in Ventura Publisher is one of the most powerful features available to define, place, and edit text elements in documents.

A paragraph tag is a simple code, or copymark, which contains all of the defining typographic and design characteristics for a given

A DYNAMIC SEMINAR THAT WILL
HELP YOU DEVELOP SELF CONFIDENCE
AND BECOME A MORE SUCCESSFUL SALESPERSON

SALES SKILLS

FOR

Success

July 23, 1987
Mariott Hotel
Detroit, Michigan

No matter what you are selling, *Sales Skills for Success* can teach you new ways to consistently close sales. Some of the things you will learn in the two-day program are:

- ❏ Learn how to understand and identify customer interests
- ❏ Develop rapport and communicate with the customer
- ❏ Identify problems and propose effective solutions
- ❏ Overcome obstacles and objections
- ❏ Close the sale and identify new opportunities
- ❏ Build successful, long-term customer relationships

$250 Two Day Seminar

CALL TOLL FREE

1-800-SELL NOW

Direct Mail Brochure: A variety of text presentation effects can be created using features of the Paragraph menu, including matched ruling lines, reverse text, drop caps, and bullet characters. Text is typeset in ITC Avant Garde.

element in a document. It defines the typeface, size, and style; it sets the text alignment on the page; and it contains the exact spacing relationships which separate the text from other elements on the page. In addition, the tag contains other special enhancements, ranging from 16 custom tab settings to automatic controls over line, column, and page breaks. The paragraph tag, a single code, contains all that information.

To manually define all those values for each element in a document would be a time–consuming effort. Additional time would be spent checking and cross checking typographic settings. Paragraph tags also prevent the inevitable errors that would result if each typographic attribute had to be applied individually. They make it easy to apply *consistent typographic values* throughout a document. Within Ventura Publisher, all you have to do is select the text and the correct tag, and the text displays all the correct typographic and design values—immediately.

Once defined, paragraph tags have the seemingly opposed qualities of rigidity and flexibility. As long as the values are unchanged, paragraph tags remain fixed, consistently applying the same attributes to every string of text to which they are applied. This consistency is maintained whether you are working on a two–page brochure or a 500–page technical manual. But, if you wish to change any of the typographic values, the paragraph tag becomes flexible. Enter the changes you want to make *once* and they are *immediately* applied throughout the document. In this way, paragraph tags are using the power of your computer to save you time and effort—consistency when you want it, and flexibility when you need it.

Paragraph tags have another extremely important benefit. They can be applied to a document text from *outside* Ventura Publisher and imported *with* the text. That means you can use Ventura paragraph tags as *copymarks* when writing a document in your word processor. When you bring the text into Ventura using the style sheet designed for the document, all text appears instantly typeset on the screen.

The power of paragraph tags lies in organization and consistency. You define a complex skein of typographic and layout values to text

PROPOSAL TO ACME INSURANCE CORPORATION

Corporate Training

The Corporate Training department has identified an objective to redesign and reformat over 9000 pages of textual and graphic information which constitutes the company's training documentation elements. In addition to redesigning this substantial amount of information, the department will also add new sections to the current training curriculum. The training documentation is currently available in a variety of media, mostly on much copied papers. The documentation is somewhat out of date since the collection of materials dates back ten years. According to the Corporate Director of Training, there is no orderly fashion or design for this information. The corporation has hired a consultant, Ms. Joan Belden who has designed a specific format and process for the training documentation. Ms. Belden will become a member of the Acme Insurance staff to coordinate the processes of rewriting the documentation.

Currently, there is an in-house printing and type-setting shop. Because of delays and priorities, the training department does not have ready access to this facility. Due to the size and nature of this project, a decision has been made to evaluate departmental or work-group desk-top publishing solutions specifically for the training facility. Having an departmental facility for documentation will give the training operation the following benefits:

- Fast turn-around time without having to depend on another corporate department to print documentation.
- Ability to make immediate changes and update training modules.
- Ability to use already installed Personal Computers and Word Processing equipment in association with the new publishing equipment.
- Ability to incorporate the new machinery directly into the day-to-day operations of the department.

The TXN Solution

It is the recommendation of TXN Corporation that Acme Insurance consider the 3544 graphic workstation as the input terminal for the redesign/reformat processes in the training facility. TXN was the first company to offer this unique type of workstation. In 1976, we introduced the 9967 professional computer which had the power of

1

Proposal: For standard, frequently cycled business documents, control text position and define all headings in a set of standard paragraph tags. Text is typeset in Times Roman.

once and can consistently apply those values to any other text *on demand.* Paragraph tags save you hours in late night and early morning editing sessions. Paragraph tags give you confidence that the job is being done, and done correctly.

The Paragraph Toolkit

Defining paragraph tags requires a solid working understanding of the features of Ventura's Paragraph menu. This menu contains the typographic, layout, and special enhancement which you use to make paragraph tags. This menu is a sophisticated workshop for text design. To understand exactly what that means, visualize a work shop, with all of the tools hung on the wall. Each has an individual function: the hammer drives nails, the screwdriver sets screws, the saw makes cuts. To build something in the workshop you must understand not only what the tools and their primary functions are, but you must also understand how to use them together.

The Paragraph menu presents the same challenge. At face value, the features on the menu are a set of simple switches which perform specified functions. But once you understand how to use those switches *in combination*, you can create an astonishing variety of sophisticated document effects.

The most important dialog boxes on the Paragraph menu are the first three. These are the core design dialog boxes:

- **Font:** Defines typeface, size, style, and color.
- **Alignment:** Defines positioning and other key settings for text.
- **Spacing:** Defines the exact amount of space around text.

The values in these dialog boxes determine the major appearance and positioning values for each text element in a style sheet.

The rest of the Paragraph menu contains special enhancements and power features used for customizing tags, including:

- **Breaks:** Defines page, column, and line breaks for each tag.
- **Tab Settings:** Defines up to 16 horizontal tab settings for each tag.
- **Special Effects:** Places bullet or drop cap characters for each tag.

- **Attribute Overrides:** Defines custom values for the text enhancements in the Text mode Assignment List for each tag.
- **Paragraph Typography:** Defines custom typographic values for each tag.
- **Ruling Lines:** Define ruling lines linked to tags.
- **Define Colors:** Supports color separation operations.
- **Update Tag List:** Supports editing of tags in a style sheet.

You can add enhancements to tags using features on one or more of these dialog boxes.

Techniques for Designing Text

This chapter discusses techniques to apply when designing the presentation of the various elements in your document.

Initial techniques focus on the standard paragraph text for your documents, while other techniques show you how to design text presentation with spacing, and how to create special multiple column effects using Spacing and Breaks controls. Recipes detail special effects and tabs features like bullets, drop caps, and other custom text features including tabbed tables and coupons.

The last half of the chapter delves into special text presentations and reverse text effects as elements in eye– catching and sophisticated headlines, subheadings and text for display applications like advertisements, brochures, and catalogs.

All of these techniques illustrate the power of Ventura paragraph tags to record a complex set of typographic values and apply them consistently throughout a document.

Designing Body Text

Typesetting a document begins with Body Text. Body Text is the basic tag in every style sheet. Any text in a document with no tag value assigned to it is *automatically* defined as Body Text.

When designing a new style sheet, it is a good idea to define the values for the Body Text tag before adding any other new tags. As

Designing Body Text

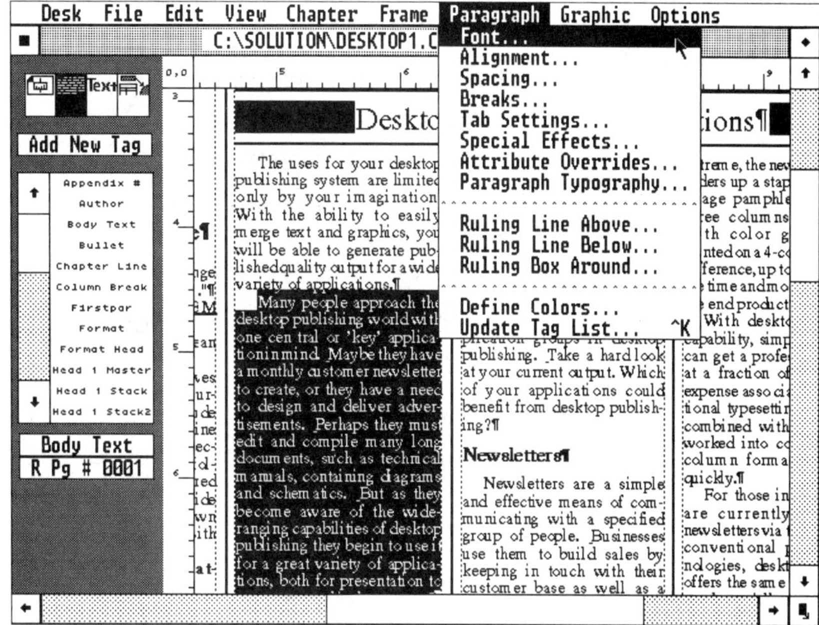

you build a list of paragraph tags, the values for Body Text can form the foundation of each new tag. This allows you to change only those individual values, such as a larger font size, or additional spacing, needed to define the new tag. The following recipe assumes that you are designing a new sheet from scratch.

Recipe: Body Text

Step 1 **Load DEFAULT.STY**

Access **FILE•Load Diff. Style** and use the Backup Button to display the \TYPESET subdirectory. Scroll down to display DEFAULT.STY and select it.

Step 2 **Save as new style**

Access **FILE•Save As New Style**. Use the Backup Button to display the drive and subdirectory where the new style sheet is to be stored. Enter the new style sheet name.

Step 3 **Load text file**

Access **FILE•Load Text/Picture**, select Text, and file format. Display the target drive and subdirectory containing the text file and select the filename. Enable ***Frame*** mode, select the base page in the Working Area and load the text file into the page.

Step 4 **Set chapter typography**

Access **CHAPTER•Chapter Typography**. Set default values for all text in the document.

▲ **Widows & Orphans:** Set how many lines of a paragraph can appear alone at the top or bottom of a page. The higher the setting, the more text tends to pull to following pages leaving large spaces at bottom of the page.

▲ **Column Balance:** Determines whether text in multi–column documents automatically balances equally between all columns or not.

▲ **Move Down to 1st Baseline By:** Sets the position of the first text baseline at the top of the page. Useful for advanced typographic operations such as vertical justification.

▲ **Pair Kerning:** Determines whether is permitted anywhere in the document. If this is turned Off, no kerning values set in any paragraph tag will be expressed. If this is turned on, kerning is enabled in all paragraph tags which are set to kern.

Step 5 **Define Body Text font**

Enable ***Paragraph*** mode and select a paragraph of text. Verify that **Body Text** appears in the Current Selection Box. Access **PARAGRAPH•Font** and select typeface, type size, and type style.

Step 6 **Define Body Text alignment**

With text paragraph still selected, access **PARAGRAPH•Alignment**. Make key alignment selections, including:

▲ **Horz. Alignment:** Most paragraph text is either ragged right, or justified. To set Body Text as ragged right, select **Horz. Alignment: Left**. To set Body Text as justified, select **Horz. Alignment: Justified**.

▲ **Hyphenation:** Enable automatic hyphenation by selecting the **Hyphenation:USENGLSH** option or turn it off. Note that if Body Text justified with no hyphenation enabled, you may have large open spaces between words in your text paragraphs.

▲ **Indent:** If you do not add extra space between Body Text paragraphs, set an indent to mark the beginning of each paragraph. Set **First Line: Indent** and enter the amount of the indent on the **In/Outdent Width** line.

Step 7 **Set Body Text spacing**

With the text paragraph still selected, access **PARAGRAPH•Spacing** and make key selections. (For more detailed information on spacing options, see the next recipe.)

▲ **Interline:** Set interline spacing value.

▲ **Above/Below:** Add space above and below each Body Text paragraph.

▲ **Left Offset:** To offset all lines of a paragraph in from the left margin, enter the size of the offset on the **In From Left** line.

▲ **Right Offset:** To offset all lines of a paragraph in from the right margin, enter the size of the offset on the **In From Right** line.

Application Notes

- **Standard horizontal tabs:** If you are using horizontal tabs in a number of tags, change the values in the Body Text tag. Every tag copied from Body Text then has the same horizontal tab values automatically. Turn to page 101.
- **Design long document pages**: Turn to page 43.
- **Design display documents:** Turn to page 47.

Designing Text with Spacing

One of the most important aspects of document layout is setting up spacing for all text elements, especially Body Text. By understanding the overall spacing of a document, you will be able to make the

Designing Text with Spacing
Page 87

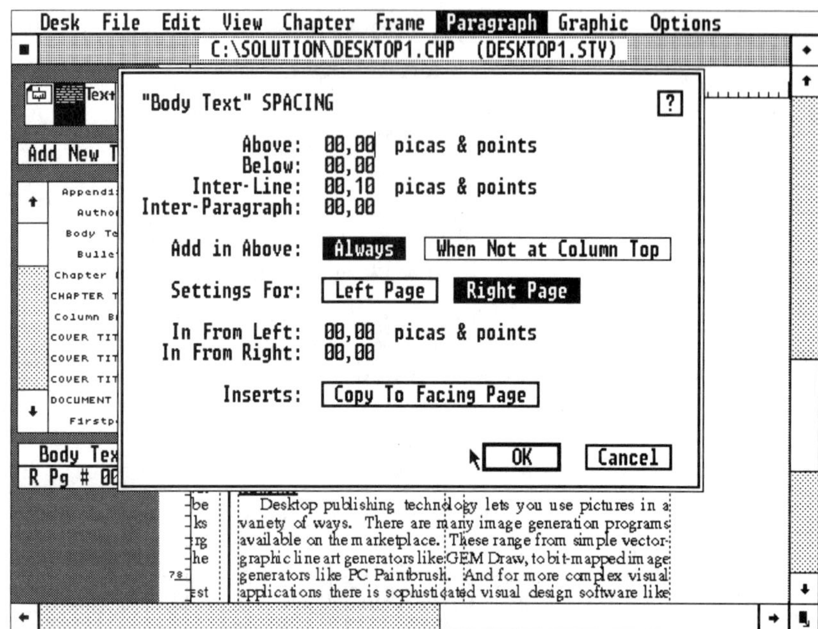

correct spacing settings in the paragraph tags that define your individual text elements.

Before working with spacing it is vital to understand the meaning and function of the key spacing tools in the **PARAGRAPH•Spacing** dialog box.

- **Interline spacing:** This defines the distance from baseline to baseline for text. In a paragraph of text, the interline spacing is the value from the bottom of one line of text to the bottom of the next line. This is the single most important spacing value for every tag in a style sheet.
- **Above and Below spacing:** These settings define buffers of space above and below the text area. Both add space outside of the interline spacing. Use these to control space between different text elements.
- **Inter–paragraph spacing:** This special feature adds a uniform spacing value between tags which share the same interline spacing value. For example, when several tags in style sheet like Body Text, Bullet, List Item, all use the same font, size, and spacing, use

this feature to add identical inter–paragraph spaces between those elements without having to define special above and below spacing values.

Recipe: Text Spacing

Step 1 **Load style sheet**

Access **FILE•Load Diff. Style** and load the style sheet.

Step 2 **Load text file**

Access **FILE•Load Text/Picture** to load text file into base page. Select **FILE•Save** to save as a chapter file.

Step 3 **Set Body Text interline spacing**

Enable ***Paragraph*** mode and select a paragraph of Body Text. Access **PARAGRAPH•Spacing**. The interline spacing value is the sum of the font height plus any additional spacing or leading.

- ▲ **Set solid:** For a 12 point font, set solid with no extra spacing, the Inter–line spacing value is 12 points, or 01,00 picas & points.
- ▲ **Add leading:** For a 12 point font with 2 additional points of extra spacing or leading, the Inter–Line spacing value is 14 points, or 01,02 picas & points

Step 4 **Add Body Text Above/Below spacing**

Entering Above and Below spacing adds the defined values between paragraphs of Body Text, and between Body Text and all other tags. When Above/Below settings meet each other on the page, such as the Below Spacing for a heading tag and the Above spacing for Body Text, the two spacing values do not appear on the page. The larger spacing value of the two tags appears between the paragraphs.

- ▲ **Above spacing:** 01,00 picas & points of Above spacing sets that distance above each paragraph of Body Text.
- ▲ **Always/When Not At Column Top:** For the Above spacing to always be expressed, select Add In Above: Always. Otherwise, the Above spacing value will be automatically suppressed at the top of a page or column.

▲ **Below spacing:** 01,00 picas & points of Above spacing sets that distance below every paragraph of Body Text.

Recipe: Inter–paragraph Spacing

Inter–paragraph spacing automatically adds a specified amount of space between a group of tags sharing the same interline spacing. For this feature to work, all the tags using it *must* have the same interline spacing value and the inter–paragraph value you enter *must* be the same for all tags. To add a uniform 01,00 pica inter–paragraph spacing between all Body Text and Bullet paragraphs each with 01,00 pica interline spacing, the procedure is:

Step 1 **Enter Body Text inter–paragraph value**

In ***Paragraph*** mode, select a paragraph of Body Text. Access **PARAGRAPH•Spacing**. Verify Interline value is 01,00 picas & points. Enter 01,00 picas & points value for Inter–paragraph spacing.

Step 2 **Enter Bullet inter–paragraph value**

In ***Paragraph*** mode, select a bullet paragraph. Access **PARAGRAPH•Spacing**. Verify Interline value is 01,00 picas & points. Enter 01,00 picas & points value for Inter–paragraph spacing.

Application Notes

- **Indent vs. offset:** Use Alignment dialog box to place one line *indent* in text paragraph. Use Spacing dialog box In From Left and In From Right to *offset* entire paragraph from left or right margin.
- **Design long document pages:** Use spacing features to position text elements in long document page. For additional long document design considerations, turn to page 43.

Inserting Special Text Characters

Ventura supports many special characters in addition to those in the standard alphabet and number sequence. These special text charac-

Inserting Special Text Characters

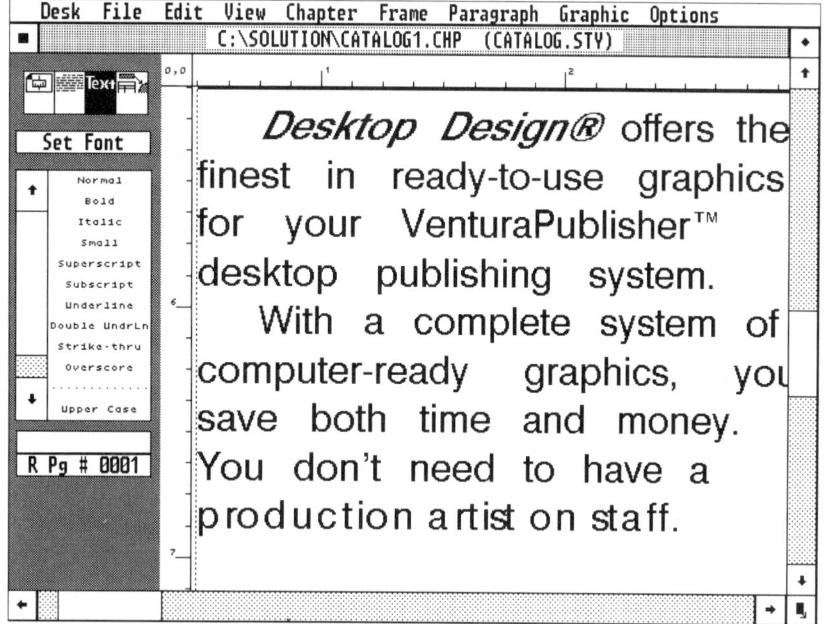

ters include symbols for registered trademarks, bullet characters, and characters used in other languages.

You can insert any of these characters directly into a document using the Alt key and the code number for the character you wish to place. You can even enter special characters from font sets other than the currently selected font, such as Symbol or Zapf Dingbats, by using Set Font to change the character to another set.

Recipe: Special Text Characters

Step 1 **Identify character code**

Check the standard character table (See Appendixes) and identify the code number of the character you wish to enter.

Step 2 **Identify position in text**

Enable ***Text*** mode and place text cursor at the position in text where the character is to appear.

Step 3 **Enter character code**

Press the Alt key and simultaneously enter the numeric code for the character. For example, the character code for an Em–dash is 197. To place an Em–dash, press Alt and type 197.

Recipe: Characters from Special Font Sets

Step 1 **Identify font and character code**

Check the standard character table (see Appendix D) and identify the font name and code number of the character you wish to enter.

Step 2 **Identify position in text**

Enable ***Text*** mode and place text cursor where the character is to appear.

Step 3 **Enter character code**

Press Alt key and simultaneously enter the numeric code for the character. For example, the character code for a Zapf Dingbat drop–shadow box is 111. To place this character, press Alt and type 111.

Step 4 **Set correct font**

Drag the mouse to highlight the individual character in the ***Text*** mode and access Set Font in the Side–Bar. Select the correct font for the symbol you wish to place. For example, if you entered a Zapf Dingbat character code in text, select ITC Zapf Dingbats in the Face selector.

☞ CAUTION: If you do not have the screen font set for Zapf Dingbats installed, the correct character will *not* appear on the screen. However, the correct character will appear when the document is printed.

Place Special Characters with Word Processor

Step 1 **Place cursor**

Open document text file in word processor and scroll to the place where the special character is to appear.

Step 2 **Enter Character Code**

Place the numeric code of the character in delimiter brackets (< >). To place the Em–dash character code directly in your word processor file, you would type: <197>.

Application Notes

- **Interactive document sketching:** Place special text characters directly from the screen. Turn to page 169.
- **Using Ventura as text processor:** Turn to page 167.
- **Pre–formatting text:** Place special characters and text enhancements directly into the word processor file. Turn to page 477.

Using Special Edit Items

Ventura includes a variety of text editing and design features in Special Edit Items.

- **Fractional expressions:** Used to create fractional expressions that are more typographically pleasing than those created using standard text editing.
- **Box characters:** This allow you to place a hollow or solid square box bullet anywhere in text.
- **Page and Chapter cross references:** Allows you to place the current page number, chapter number or both anywhere on the page, and not just in the header or footer line.

The process for placing these items is essentially the same. From a text cursor position, select Special Edit Items and the feature. To delete any Special Edit Item from text, simply delete the small degree symbol appearing in the text.

Recipe: Special Edit Items

Step 1 **Place a box character**

Enable ***Text*** mode and place text cursor in the exact place the item is to appear. Access **EDIT•Ins Special Item** and select Box Char.

Using Special Edit Items
Page 93

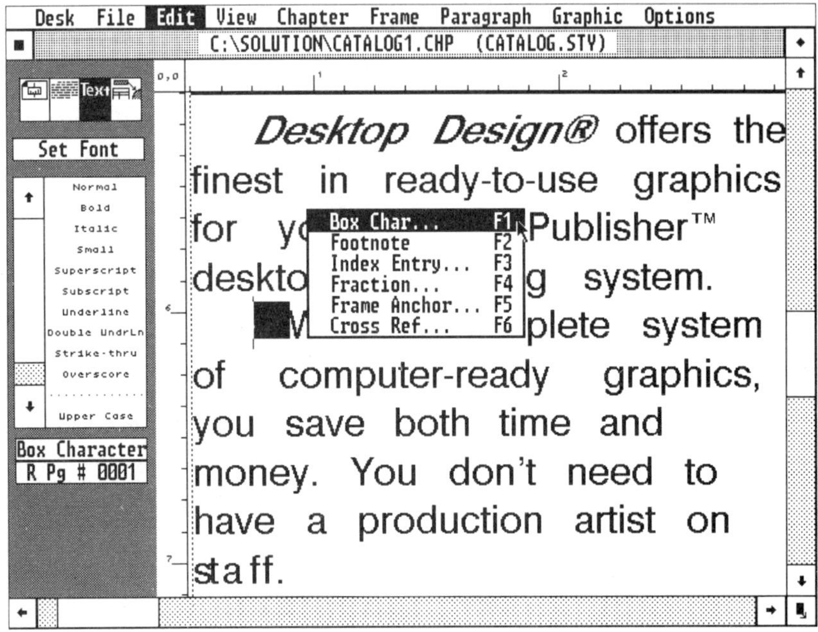

Select either Hollow or Filled. The box will be inserted at the cursor position, marked with a small degree symbol.

Step 2 **Place a fractional expression**

Enable ***Text*** mode and place text cursor in the exact place the item is to appear. Access **EDIT•Ins Special Item** and select Fraction. Type the fraction on the fraction editing line. Allow Ventura a moment to convert the fraction, then press Control–D to insert the fraction into your text.

Step 3 **Place a page or chapter number cross–reference**

Enable ***Text*** mode and place text cursor in the exact place the item is to appear. Access **EDIT•Ins Special Item** and select Cross Ref. Select Page # or Chapter #. The number of the current page will appear at the text position. To place a reference containing both page and chapter numbers, enter an individual reference for each one.

Application Notes

- **Interactive document sketching:** Place special edit items directly from the screen. Turn to page 169.
- **Using Ventura as text processor:** Turn to page 167.
- **Pre–formatting text:** Place special edit items and text enhancements directly into the word processor file. Turn to page 477.
- **Page number thumbtabs:** Place page and chapter cross references into Box Text graphics linked to repeating frames at the edge of the page for special thumbtab pagination effect. For more on using graphics with repeating frames, Turn to page 328
- **Setting up pagination systems:** Turn to page 338

Designing with Vertical Tabs

Vertical tabs are a standard Ventura Publisher operation in which two or more tags are set up to align to the same vertical position on the page. The effect is created by editing spacing offsets and break settings in a series of paragraph tags. Vertical tabs can be used to create multi–column text tables in which column size and placement is completely controlled through the paragraph tag, not through margin and column settings in the base page. In addition, the vertical tabs process can be used to position other text elements, including hanging indents, side heads and Ventura–generated auto–numbers.

To create vertical tabs, make an individual paragraph tag for each column, or horizontal position of text. Use In From Left and In From Right text offsets in the **PARAGRAPH•Spacing** dialog box to define column size and position on the page. To allow all columns to align to the same vertical point on the page, the line breaks between them must be removed. To do this, you set the column which is farthest to the left to have the line break *before* the text. All columns in the middle have *no* line break at all, and the final column has a line break *after* the text. With no line breaks between any of the tags, the text is free to float up to the same vertical position.

Designing with Vertical Tabs
Page 95

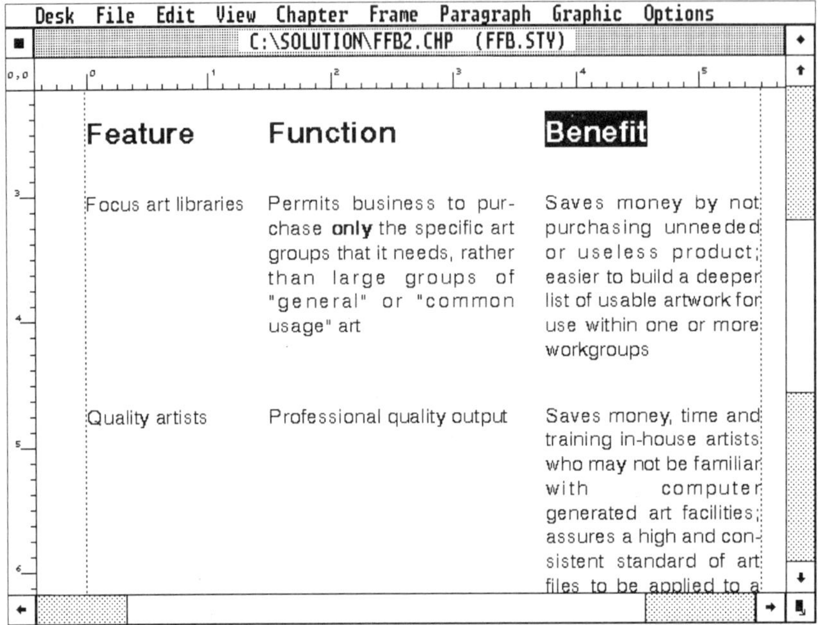

Recipe: Three–Column Vertical Tabs

Step 1 **Sketch layout**

Determine relative positioning of vertical tab elements on the page, and the size and position of columns.

Step 2 **Create Column 1 tag**

Enable ***Paragraph*** mode and use Add New Tag to create the tag for the text in Column 1 of the vertical tab design.

Step 3 **Set Column 1 attributes**

Access **PARAGRAPH•Font** and select typeface, size, and style for the column text.

Step 4 **Create Column 1 with spacing offset**

Access **PARAGRAPH•Spacing** and enter the distance between the right edge of Column 1 and the right margin on In From Right .

Step 5 **Copy Columns 2 & 3**

With Column 1 tag selected, use Add New Tag on the Side–Bar to create tags for Column 2 and Column 3.

Step 6 **Create Column 2 with spacing offset**

Select the Column 2 tag. Access **PARAGRAPH•Spacing** and define the left edge of Column 2 by entering the distance between it and the left margin on the In From Left line. Define the right edge of Column 2 by entering the distance between it and the right margin on the In From Right line.

Step 7 **Create Column 3 with spacing offset**

Select the Column 3 tag. Access **PARAGRAPH•Spacing** and define the left edge of Column 3 by entering the distance between it and the left margin on the In From Left line. Define the right edge of Column 3 by entering the distance between it and the right margin on the In From Right line.

Step 8 **Set column line breaks**

To allow the three column tags to align to the same vertical position on the page, remove the line breaks between them.

▲ Select Column 1 tag and access **PARAGRAPH•Breaks**. Verify Line Break: Before.

▲ Select Column 2 tag and Access **PARAGRAPH•Breaks**. Set Line Break: No.

▲ Select Column 3 tag and access **PARAGRAPH•Breaks**. Set Line Break: After.

Step 9 **Set keep with next breaks**

Use the Keep With Next feature in **PARAGRAPH•Breaks** to force the three columns to stay on the same page.

▲ Select Column 1 tag and access **PARAGRAPH•Breaks**. Set Keep with Next to Yes.

▲ Select Column 2 tag and access **PARAGRAPH•Breaks**. Set Keep with Next to Yes.

▲ Select Column 3 tag and access **PARAGRAPH•Breaks**. Verify that Keep with Next is set to No.

Recipe: Complex Vertical Tabs

The vertical tabs technique is built upon the concept of removing line breaks between a series of tags so that they can all appear at the same vertical position on the page. For more than 3 columns, follow these steps to assign breaks settings.

Step 1 **Set line break for first column**

Select tag for first column and access **PARAGRAPH•Breaks**. Set Line Break: Before.

Step 2 **Set line break for last column**

Select tag for last column and access **PARAGRAPH•Breaks**. Set Line Break: After

Step 3 **Set line breaks for middle columns**

Select tags for all columns in the middle. For each one, access **PARAGRAPH•Breaks** and set Line Break: No.

Step 4 **Set keep with next breaks**

Select tags for all columns except the final column, access **PARAGRAPH•Breaks**

Application Notes

- **Text tables:** Set up vertical tabs to display text tables, such as Feature/Function/Benefit charts
- **Multi–page text tables** Use multi–page frames to create special page layout for long text table. Turn to page 59.
- **Hanging Indents:** Position hanging indent tag using **PARAGRAPH•Spacing** In From Right to set the position for the right edge of text. Use **PARAGRAPH•Alignment** to change Horz. Alignment to Right.
- **Create table grid:** Add ruling lines and vertical rules and to a grid for text tables. Use the same technique as for horizontal tab tables. Turn to page 103.

Creating Fitted Text

For some applications, *interlinked* tags which fit together like pieces of a puzzle help coordinate the design of a document. This effect is useful in creating custom lead–in lines to paragraphs with oversize characters or special fonts. This effect can also be used to create a set of special tags with boldface or italic enhancements to Body Text values that automatically fit into a Body Text paragraph. By manipulating alignment and break values, fitted tags automatically indent to the length of the previous line, and begin on that line.

As with vertical tabs, there are no line breaks between fitted tags. Using the Relative Indent feature of the **PARAGRAPH•Alignment** dialog box, the first line of the fitted tag indents the length of the last line of the preceding paragraph. With the line break removed, the text would normally overprint the preceding paragraph. But using the Next Y Position feature in the **PARAGRAPH•Breaks** dialog box, the text automatically begins following the last line of the preceding paragraph.

Creating Fitted Text

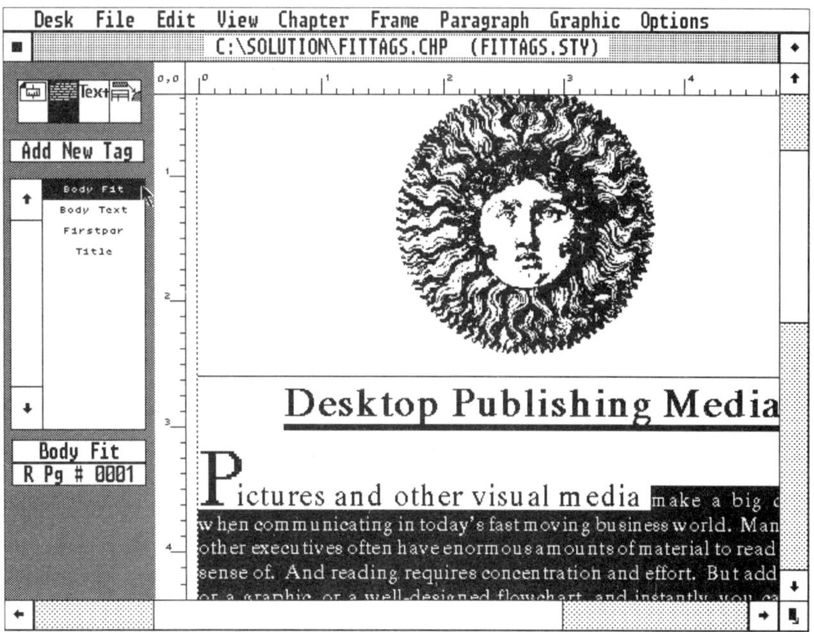

Recipe: Fitted Tags

Step 1 **Create lead tag**

Enable ***Paragraph*** mode and select the text. Use Add New Tag in the Side–Bar to create the lead tag. Use features of the Paragraph menu to set font, alignment, and spacing. Access **PARAGRAPH•Breaks** and set Line Break to Before.

Step 2 **Create fitted tag**

With the lead tag selected, use Add New Tag in the Side–Bar to create the fitted tag. Access **PARAGRAPH•Font** to set font values for text.

Step 3 **Set fitted tag relative indent**

Access **PARAGRAPH•Alignment**. Turn Relative Indent to On. This indents the first line of the fitted tag by the exact length of the last line of the lead tag. Verify that First Line is set to Indent and enter an In/Outdent value of 01,00 picas & points to set a small buffer between the two tags.

Step 4 **Set fitted tag breaks**

Access **PARAGRAPH•Breaks**. Set Line Break to After. Set Next Y Position to Beside Last Line of Previous Paragraph. This forces the fitted tag to begin right beside the last line of text tagged with the lead tag.

Application Notes

- **Paragraph lead:** For lead sentence of Firstpar that includes drop cap and all cap lead line or lines, you can create a special tag for the lead text and use this technique to fit it naturally into body copy.
- **Drop words:** To create entire lead word in oversize text or custom font, create a drop word tag and a fitted Firstpar tag for the fitted Body Text tag.
- **Use drop cap effects:** Use standup drop cap in the lead line. Turn to page 114.

Designing with Horizontal Tabs

The Tab Settings dialog box on the Paragraph menu lets you set horizontal tabs for each tag in a style sheet. The most obvious use for these tabs is the same as in your word processor—tables and columnar data. But Ventura tab stops can do more than just tables. They offer many levels of design flexibility for other types of applications. Not only can you define 16 tab stops for each paragraph tag, but you can define leaders to appear between selected stops and not others. You can use any character as a leader, and control how it is spaced between tab stops. The tab auto–leader automatically extends selected leader character to the right margin without placing tabs individually.

All tab stops are measured from the left margin guide. The easiest way to set tabs is to set the zero point of screen rulers to align with the left margin guide. Then you can instantly pinpoint the correct measure on the screen.

Designing with Horizontal Tabs

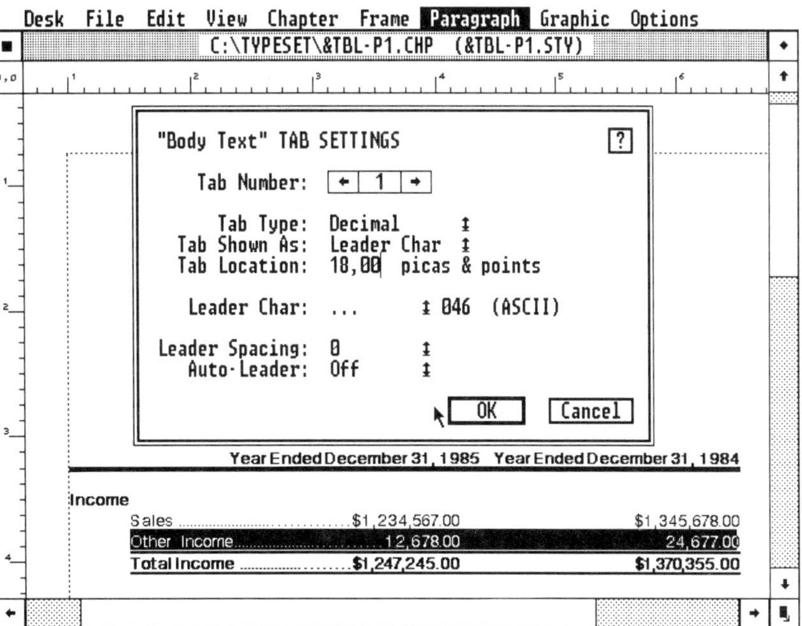

Recipe: Horizontal Tabs

Step 1 **Reset screen rulers**

The location of each tab is defined by its distance from the left margin guide. By resetting the zero point of the screen rulers at the left margin guide, you can use the tracking lines to easily measure the correct location for all tab stops. Place mouse cursor at the intersection of screen rulers; press and hold the mouse button as you drag the cross–arrow cursor to align the zero point with the left margin guide.

Step 2 **Select text**

Enable ***Paragraph*** mode and select text to be tabbed. Access **PARAGRAPH•Tab Settings**

Step 3 **Set values for tab 1**

To set the values for the first tab stop, enter the type, location, and leader format, if desired:

▲ **Select Tab Number:** Use the scrolling indicator to display tab 1.

▲ **Set Tab Type:** Decide how the text is to align at the tab location. Select left and the left edge of text aligns at the tab stop. Right tabs align the right edge of text at the tab stop and so forth.

▲ **Set leader:** To use a leader character, set Tab Shown As to Leader Char. Set the leader on the Leader Char. line and the spacing between leader characters on the Leader Spacing line.

▲ **Set Tab Location:** Set Tab Location identifies the position of the tab stop. Remember that the position of *each tab stop* must be measured from the left margin guide. Measure the distance and enter it on the line.

Step 4 **Set auto–leader**

If a leader character has been specified, that leader character can be placed automatically from the end of your text line to the right margin if auto–leader is turned on.

Step 5 **Repeat the process for additional tabs**

Repeat the above process for each additional tab stop. To turn leaders on and off between tab stops, use different leaders between different tab stops to create a variety of effects.

Step 6 **Place tab characters in text**

For tab stops to work, you must place tab stops in text. You can place them from the ***Text*** mode directly into a page. Ventura also reads tab stops placed in your text by some word processors.

Application Notes

- **Display financial data:** Use tabs to display columns of numbers and data.
- **Position page enhancements:** Use tabs to position a string of special text characters or characters from Zapf Dingbats to create page dividers or design elements.
- **Invoices:** Make your own invoices and position all financial information using tabs.

Creating Table Grids with Tabs

When tabs are used in conjunction with ruling lines and graphics, you can create simple table grids easily without having to draw a complex box text grid. This technique is no substitute for the powerful Table Editing mode in the Professional Extension, but it can be used to design many table applications simply and quickly.

For best results, place table text into a frame. By placing a ruling line under the tag used to tab financial data, you can add a ruling line around the frame and draw vertical graphic rules into the frame to complete the effect.

Recipe: Table Grid with Horizontal Tabs

Step 1 **Sketch table**

Sketch the planned table. Identify the number of columns in the table and how data is to be spaced on the line. Write down the size of the table columns for later reference.

Step 2 **Draw frame**

Enable ***Frame*** mode and use Add New Frame to draw a frame to hold the table.

Step 3 **Load table text**

Access **FILE•Load Text/Picture** select Text and the file format. Select the file containing the table text and load it into the frame.

Step 4 **Define table tag**

Enable ***Paragraph*** mode, and select a line of the table text. Use Add New Tag to create a new tag for the table text.

Step 5 **Set font values**

Access **PARAGRAPH•Font** and set the font for the table. When

Create Table Grids with Tabs
Page 103

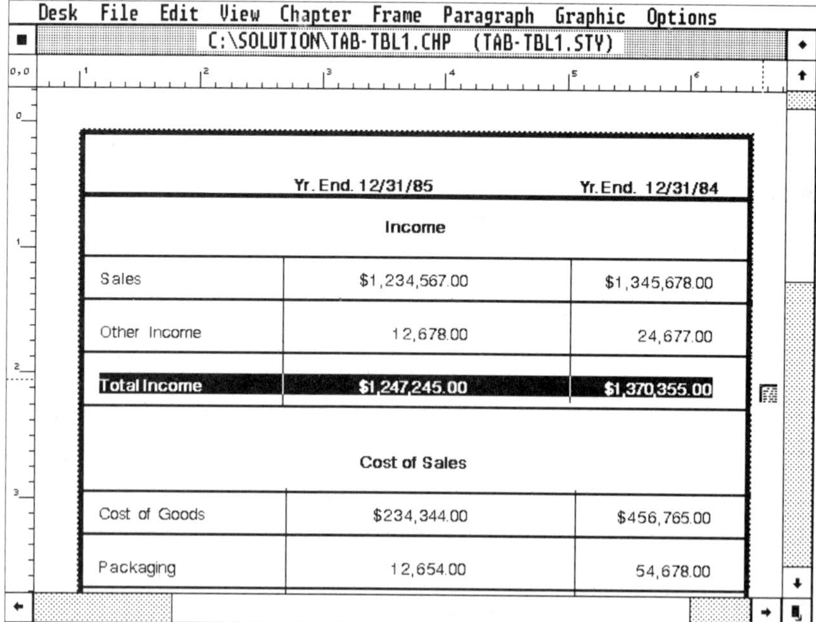

entering columns of numbers, avoid using fonts which are proportionally spaced, because characters may not align correctly. Use monospaced fonts, such as Courier, which use the same space width for each character.

Step 6 **Set table tab stops**

Access **PARAGRAPH•Tab Settings**. For financial data, select decimal tab type for all positions and enter the position of each tab stop. Avoid using leaders because you will be placing a ruling line under the entire line of data.

Step 7 **Place ruling line below data**

Access **PARAGRAPH•Ruling Line Below** and define a frame–wide, solid black horizontal line to extend across the frame. Enter the line thickness on the Height of Rule 1 line and write it down for reference. To add space between the line and the data, enter the distance in the Space Above Rule 1 line.

Step 8 **Place vertical rules**

Enable ***Graphic*** mode and select table frame. Select line cursor and position it at the top of the frame in the position where the vertical table rule is to appear.

▲ Press and hold the Alt key as you drag the mouse down to draw a perfect vertical line.

▲ Access **GRAPHIC•Line Attributes**. Select Thickness: Custom and enter the exact thickness used for the horizontal rule.

▲ Select **EDIT•Copy Graphic** and Select **EDIT•Paste Graphic** to make a copy of the vertical rule and drag it into place in the table. Repeat this process until all vertical rules are in place between columns.

Step 9 **Place framing line around tables**

Enable ***Frame*** mode and select table frame. Access **PARAGRAPH•Ruling Box Around**. Define a frame–wide, solid black ruling line which is the same thickness as the horizontal and vertical rules. Enter the thickness on Height of Rule 1.

Application Notes

- **Create table template:** Once you have created the table grid, it is easy to enter new data into the same format. As long as you are using the same style sheet, just use the table text tag to display new data.
- **Copy table across chapters:** The frame containing the table may be copied into another chapter. If you copy the table grid frame with the vertical rules into a chapter using a different style sheet, you will have to re–enter design values for the table text tag in that style sheet. Turn to page 249.
- **Create table headings and custom presentations:** To create special paragraph tags to display the table headings, copy the table text tag and change font a ruling line values for the headline. You can also make special versions of table text in boldface or italic to place emphasis on certain rows of data.
- **Place data emphasis with Set Font:** Use Set Font in the ***Text*** mode to place emphasis on individual data elements in the style sheet.
- **Multi–page tables:** Use multi–page frame to create special page layout and presentation for multi–page tables. Turn to page 59.
- **Professional Extension table features:** This simple technique is not intended to develop long, highly complex or frequently edited tables. If you regularly produce such applications, use the Professional Extension. Turn to Chapter 11.

Publishing Spreadsheets with Tabs

Data entered into spreadsheet software such as Lotus 1–2–3 can be published in Ventura. Begin by exporting spreadsheet data to an ASCII file. To position the spreadsheet text using Ventura's standard features, all columns in the spreadsheet must have tab characters inserted between them. There are several third–party software

Publishing Spreadsheets with Tabs

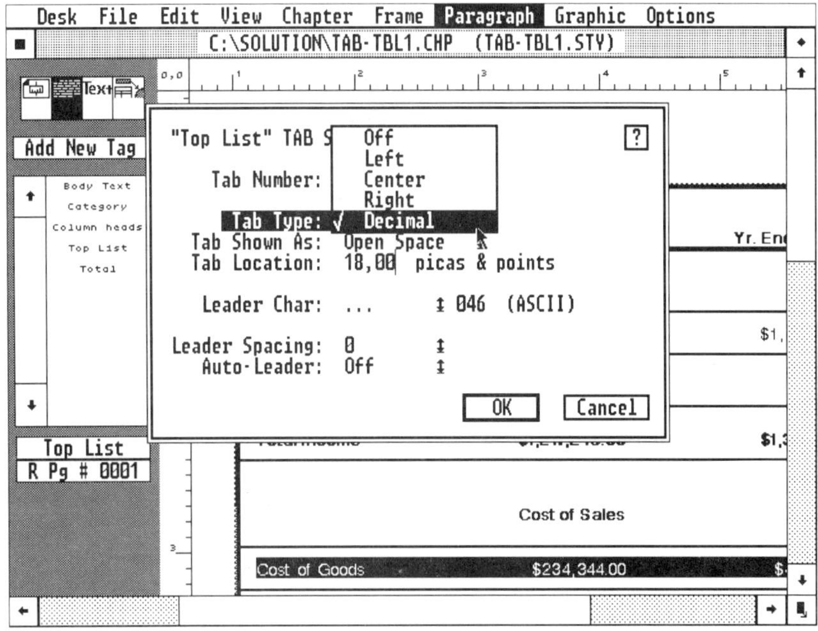

utilities capable of performing this function, including Corel Tabin and VP Tabs.

Tab conversion is necessary only if you are publishing tables in Ventura Publisher 2.0 standard product. The Professional Extension directly accepts ASCII spreadsheet files without tab insertions.

Recipe: Published Spreadsheets

Step 1 **Export spreadsheet data**

In spreadsheet software, export the file to ASCII format. To load as an ASCII file, give the file the .TXT extension.

Step 2 **Insert tab characters**

Place tab characters between columns in the text file using a tabbing utility such as VP Tabs or Corel Tabin.

Step 3 **Load spreadsheet file**

Enable ***Frame*** mode and use Add New Frame to draw a frame to contain the spreadsheet. If you are publishing the spreadsheet by itself, load it to the base page.

Step 4 **Set spreadsheet font**

Enable ***Paragraph*** mode and select a row of spreadsheet text. Access **PARAGRAPH•Font** and select the font for the spreadsheet.

Step 5 **Set spreadsheet tabs**

Access **PARAGRAPH•Tab Settings** and set the location and type of all tabs to position the spreadsheet text.

Application Notes

- **Copy table across chapters:** The frame containing the table may be copied into another chapter. If you copy the table grid frame with the vertical rules into a chapter using a different style sheet, you will have to re–enter design values for the table text tag in that style sheet. Turn to page 249.
- **Place data emphasis with Set Font:** Use Set Font in the ***Text*** mode to place emphasis on individual data elements in the style sheet.
- **Multi–page tables:** Use multi–page frame to create special page layout and presentation for multi–page tables. Turn to page 59.
- **Professional Extension table features:** Professional Extension tables features accepts Lotus 1–2–3 files in the .PRN format. Turn to page 430.

Using Tabs to Create a Coupon

A coupon is any application involving fill–in–the– blank information, such as Name, Address, and so forth. To make a simple coupon, use tab auto–leaders to create the line elements and use define horizontal tabs to place the Name, Address, and Telephone detail text beneath the line.

Recipe: Coupon Design

Step 1 **Sketch out coupon**

Sketch out the design for the coupon.

Using Tabs To Create a Coupon

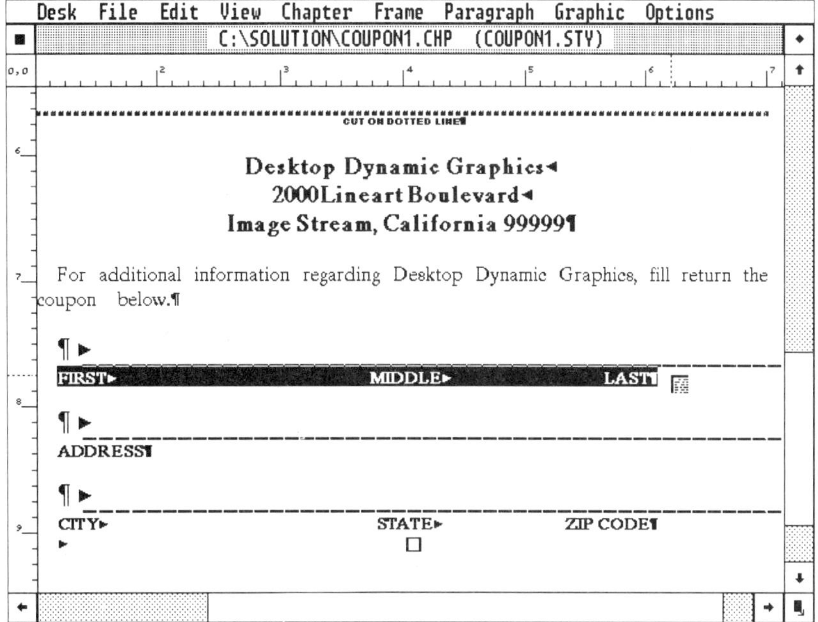

Step 2 **Draw a frame and load text**

If you are placing a form or fill–in–the–blank design into a newsletter, brochure, or advertisement, it is best to design this element in its own frame. Enable ***Frame*** mode and draw a frame for the coupon. Load a prepared text file into the frame, or enable ***Text*** mode and click the mouse inside the frame and start typing.

Step 3 **Create entry lines with auto leader**

Place the blank lines to be filled in with the tab auto–leader.

▲ Enable ***Paragraph*** mode, select a free paragraph return and use Add New Tag to create the tag for the coupon line.

▲ Access **PARAGRAPH•Tab Settings**. Turn Tab Type to any setting but Off. Set Tab Shown As to Leader, select the Leader Character and turn Auto–Leader On. You don't have to specify a location for the tab.

▲ If you get an error message that the Text alignment is set to justified, the auto–leader will work anyway.

Step 4 **Set coupon line spacing**

To maintain space between entry lines in the coupon, assign Above spacing values to the coupon line. Access **PARAGRAPH•Spacing**. Enter the distance you want to place between lines in the coupon on the Above spacing line, and select Add In Above: Always.

Step 5 **Set coupon labels**

Enable ***Text*** mode. Enter the text to appear beneath the lines in the coupon. Place a tab character before the text and between each element to appear under the line. Type a coupon label line for each line in the coupon.

Step 6 **Design coupon label tag**

Enable ***Paragraph*** mode and select one of the coupon label lines. Use Add New Tag to create a new tag for the coupon label text. Apply the tag to the other coupon label lines.

Step 7 **Reset screen rulers**

Place cursor at the intersection of the screen rulers and drag the cross–arrow cursor to set the zero point at the left page margin or the left edge of the frame containing coupon. Use the screen tracking rulers to specify the position where text is to appear.

☞ CAUTION: When setting position for text from the screen, remember the tab type used. Text centered at the tab stop will be at a different position from text entered left of the tab stop.

Step 8 **Enter coupon label tab settings**

With a coupon label line selected, access **PARAGRAPH•Tab Settings**. Specify the location and type for each tab setting. To place text in different places on different lines, you have two choices:

▲ Enter all tab stops into a single master coupon line tag.

▲ Create separate coupon label tags with specific settings for text in each label line.

Application Notes

- **Design reply forms:** To design business reply cards or forms to accompany brochures.
- **Design questionnaire or survey material:** Use coupon design process to create questionnaires, surveys and forms.
- **Design effects with ruling lines:** Ruling lines can also be used to create coupon lines, by placing a ruling line above the Coupon Text tag.

Designing Bullet Lists

Ventura lets you define a variety of standard and custom bullet characters to display bulleted lists. The most common format is the round, filled dot which precedes each separate entry in the bullet list. There are many more applications for bullets in documents, especially if you think of the bullet character as a mini–graphic which precedes a line of text in your document.

There are special font sets available made up of nothing but bullet characters. The most well–known of these is ITC Zapf Dingbats, and it features minigraphics, including pointing fingers, stars, check marks, and other lively images. These graphics can become custom bullet tags which give a specific visual character to many kinds of lists. In addition to displaying lists in text, bullet characters can be enlarged to add special emphasis to overhead transparencies, advertisements, flyers, and posters.

Standard Bullets

Step 1 **Create bullet tag**

Enable ***Paragraph*** mode and select a paragraph of text you wish to accent with a bullet. Select Add New Tag in the Side–Bar and enter the name for the new tag.

Step 2 **Assign bullet character**

With text selected, access **PARAGRAPH•Special Effects** and select Bullet. Select any of the standard bullet characters available in the Show Bullet As selector.

Step 3 **Set distance between bullet and text**

Enter the distance between the bullet character and the first character of the text line on the Indent After Bullet line.

Step 4 **Indent bullet from margin**

To set the distance the bulleted line is indented from the text margin, access **PARAGRAPH•Spacing** and enter the indent value on the In From Left line. If a text offset amount is already entered on this line, increase the value by the amount you wish to indent the bullet.

Recipe: Custom Bullets

Designing Bullet Lists
Page 111

To create a custom bullet element, use the Set Font Properties feature of the **PARAGRAPH•Special Effects** dialog box. This allows you to select a custom font and size *for the bullet character only.* This font

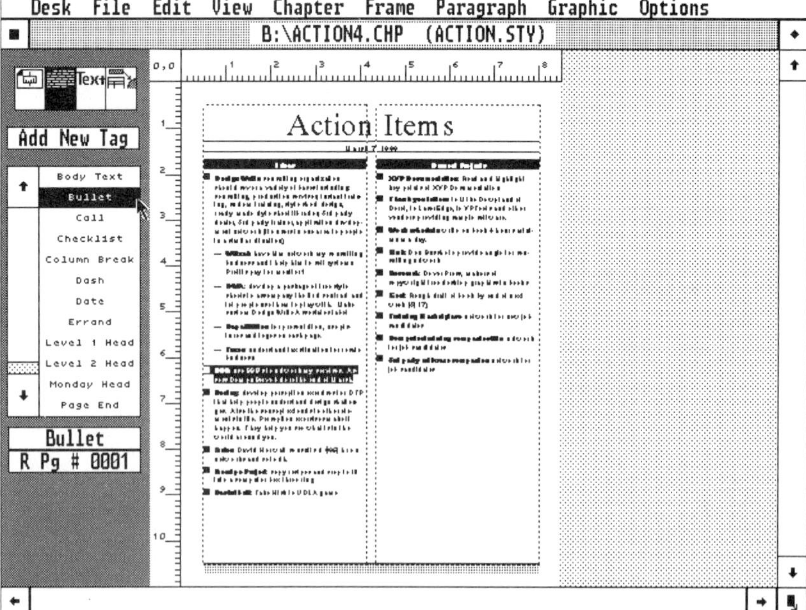

can be different from that used for the text. The following recipe assumes you are creating a custom font using a drop–shadow box character from ITC Zapf Dingbats.

Step 1 **Create custom bullet tag**

Enable ***Paragraph*** mode and select a paragraph of text you wish to accent with a bullet. Select Add New Tag in the Side–Bar and enter the name for the new tag.

Step 2 **Access Set Font Properties**

With text selected, access **PARAGRAPH•Special Effects** and select Bullet. Select Set Font Properties to bring up a version of the Font dialog box.

Step 3 **Select custom font**

Select the typeface containing the custom font character, ITC Zapf Dingbats. For the character to be of a larger or smaller size than the bullet text, select the size. Select OK to return to the Special Effects screen.

Step 4 **Enter custom font code**

To enter bullet character, consult the code list for the custom font set. (For Zapf Dingbats character codes, see the Appendixes.) To enter the code for the drop shadow box dingbat, select Show Bullet As: Other and enter the correct code **111** on the Bullet Char entry line.

☞ CAUTION: If you do not have screen fonts for the custom bullet font set installed, you will not see a correct display of the bullet on the screen. However, the bullet will print out on paper.

Application Notes

- **Experiment with sizing:** Some bullet characters work best at a size slightly larger than that of the reference text. Experiment with different sizing of bullets.

- **Experiment with vertical shift:** The Set Font Properties option includes a built–in shift control which lets you move the bullet character up or down from the baseline.
- **Rest bullet on ruling line:** By shifting the bullet character up and down, you can make it touch a ruling line above or below text for interesting design effects.

Designing with Drop Caps

Drop caps are large initial characters which begin a paragraph. They can be nested into the paragraph or placed standing up from the baseline. A drop cap does not have to be the same font or style as the rest of the paragraph.

To create a drop cap, create with a special tag for the first paragraph, such as Firstpar. In the Special Effects dialog box, specify the drop cap, and use the Set Font Properties option to select the typeface, size, and style desired.

Recipe: Drop Caps

Step 1 **Create Firstpar tag**

Enable ***Paragraph*** mode and select text. Use Add New Tag to create the Firstpar tag.

Step 2 **Define drop cap**

Access **PARAGRAPH • Special Effects** and select Drop Cap. Select Set Font Properties and a Font selector appears. Select the desired typeface, size, style, and color for the drop cap. Select OK to return to the Special Effects dialog box.

Step 3 **Set drop cap position**

There are two ways to present the drop cap. Either nest it into the text paragraph, or standing up from the top line of the paragraph. Space for the drop cap is controlled by the Space for Big First option on the Special Effects dialog box.

▲ **Nested:** To place the drop cap into the text paragraph, compare the relative point size of the drop cap and the body text. If the body text is 12 points and the drop cap character is 24 points, accept the Space For Big First Normal setting of two lines. If the drop cap is 36 points, set a custom Space For Big First of 3 lines.

▲ **Standup:** To force a drop cap of any size to snap to the baseline of the first line in the paragraph, set a custom Space for Big First of one line.

Step 4 **Shift drop cap position**

The drop cap character automatically snaps to the nearest body text baseline. If Space for Big First is set to two, the drop cap sits on the baseline of the second line of text. To shift the drop cap up or down from the baseline, access Set Font Properties and enter the shift desired on the line provided.

Application Notes

- **Create drop words:** To place a word or phrase in large type at the lead of a paragraph, use fitted text technique. Turn to page 99.

Designing with Drop Caps

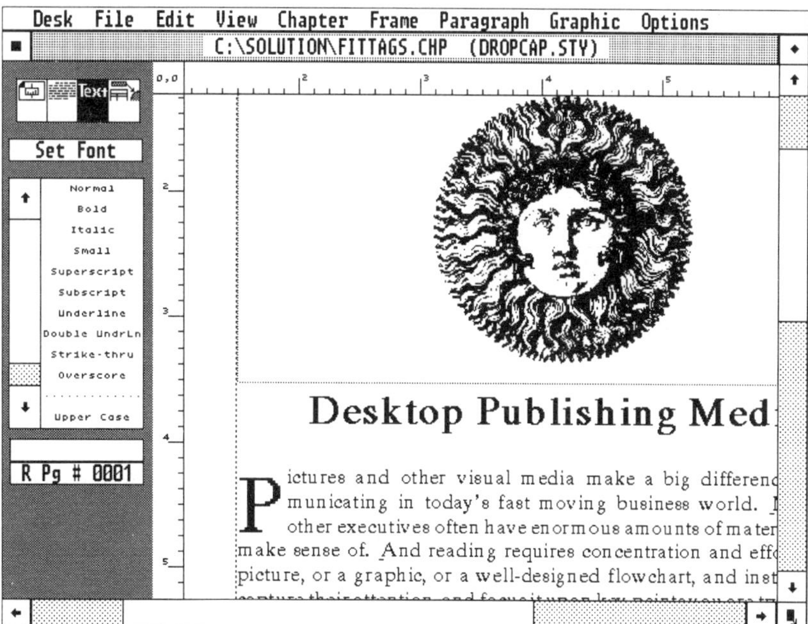

- **Scanned characters:** To use characters scanned from special font sets, such as ornate medieval characters and other display fonts, scan the character and load it as a picture file. Use automatic frame anchoring to place it in the paragraph. Turn to page 295.
- **Reverse text drop caps:** To place a reverse text drop cap, use fitted text technique and create a separate tag for the drop cap. Place drop cap tag in reverse text. Turn to page 127.
- **Rotated drop caps:** To place a rotated drop cap, place the character in an auto–anchor frame, and create a special tag, defining the character size and degree of rotation. Turn to page 291.

Designing with Dashed Lines

Dashed lines may be placed around frames or in text tags. They can be used to create highly graphic effects by themselves or in combination with other tags in a stacked tag application.

Ventura lets you control the width of the individual dash as well as the spacing between dashes. By varying these values in combination with line thickness, color and shading, you can create long or tall clusters of dashes. Use dashes for emphasis and as a creative tool in designing a document.

Recipe: Dashed Lines

Step 1 **Select ruling line format**

Enable ***Paragraph*** mode and select text. Access the ruling line dialog box on the PARAGRAPH menu.

Step 2 **Define line attributes**

Define the width, color and line shading for the ruling line.

Step 3 **Enter line height**

Enter the thickness of the line on the Height of Rule 1 dialog box.

Designing with Dashed Lines

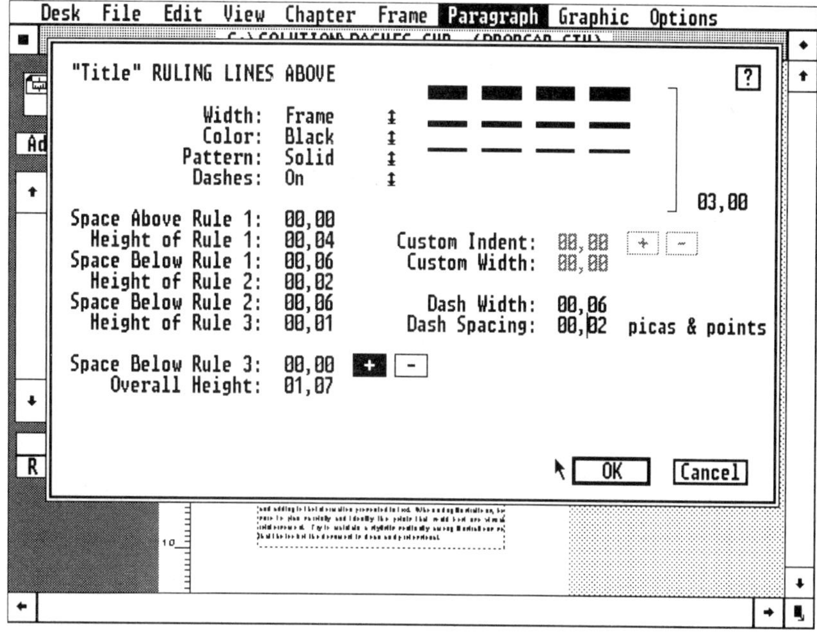

Step 4 **Set dash values**

To set dashes for ruling lines, complete three steps:

▲ **Set Dashes On:** Dash features are not available unless turned on.

▲ **Set Dash Width:** Enter the width of the individual dashes.

▲ **Set Dash Spacing:** Enter the amount of space between individual dashes. Experiment with a variety of dash spacing, dash width and line height and see the result in the dialog box screen mimic.

Application Notes

- **Use with multiple rules:** Set up multiple ruling lines and dashes for a multi–level pattern of dashes and line thicknesses.
- **Experiment with color and shading:** Change color and shading of dashed lines for a variety of interesting background effects.
- **Use with stacked tags:** Use dashed lines in combination with solid backgrounds and other ruling lines in stacked tag applications. Turn to page 130.
- **Use as framing elements:** Set up dashes to add emphasis or focus to framed text.

- **Create checkerboard effect:** Stack two dashed lines, same height, different shading. Indent the stack tag the width of one dash. The result is a checkerboard background pattern. Or, accomplish this effect by drawing a solid black line and then stacking a solid white dashed line on top.

Designing with Rotated Text

Rotated text elements allow you to position text in ways which can be used for ornamental purposes. Ventura Publisher supports three positions of rotated text:

- 90° text line is vertical; text reads bottom to top.
- 180° text line is inverted; text begins at right margin.
- 270° text line is vertical; text reads top to bottom.

Text rotation applies to all text in a given tag. The maximum allowable height of vertically rotated text (at 90 and 270) is controlled by the Maximum Rotated Height setting at the bottom of the Alignment dialog box.

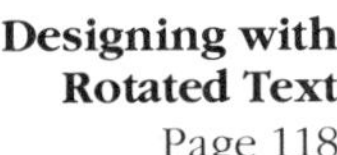

Designing with Rotated Text
Page 118

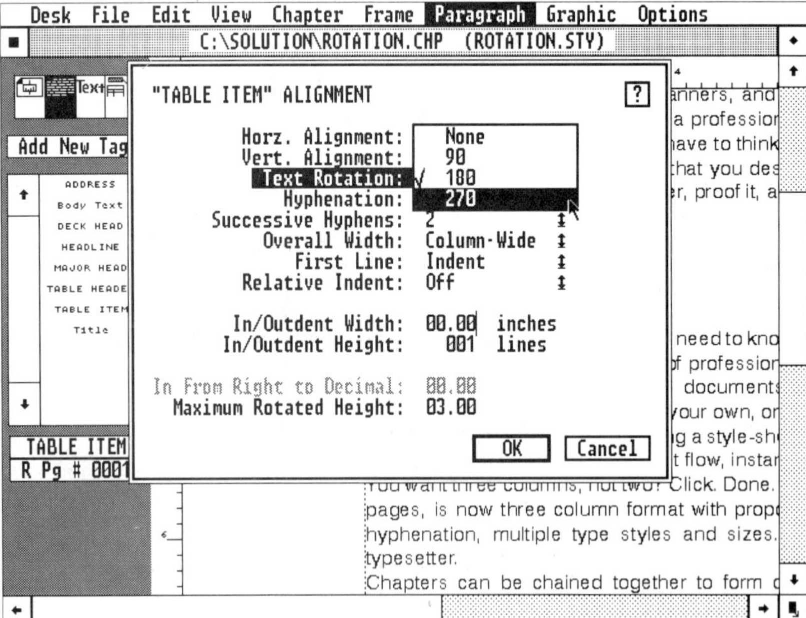

Because rotated text is a special text presentation, it is better to contain rotated text elements in frames or box text to avoid conflicts with other text elements on the page. When selecting rotated text in the Paragraph mode, you must place the cursor in the original location of the text *before* it was rotated.

Recipe: Rotated Text

Step 1 **Draw framing element**

Place rotated elements in a frame or a box text graphic to avoid conflict with normally aligned text.

Step 2 **Create special tag**

Enable ***Paragraph*** mode. Select text and use Add New Tag to create special tag for rotated text. Access **PARAGRAPH• Alignment** and specify degree of rotation.

Application Notes

- **Use in headings and logos:** Rotate document titles or headings to the side of the page or frame.
- **Upside down elements:** Invert text at the bottom of page or frame, or as a design element.
- **Rotated reverse text strip:** Combine rotation with reverse text or shaded effects for headlines and display text effects.
- **Use with automatic frame anchoring:** Place rotated characters or words into text using automatic anchoring. Turn to page 291.
- **Landscape tables in portrait documents:** Place landscape Box Text or Professional Extension tables into portrait documents. Turn to page 324.

Create a Multi–element Headline

Tab settings allow you to position two or more separate text elements in a single line of text. This is useful when creating column headings for tables and similar layouts, but you can also use this technique to

Creating a Multi-element Headline

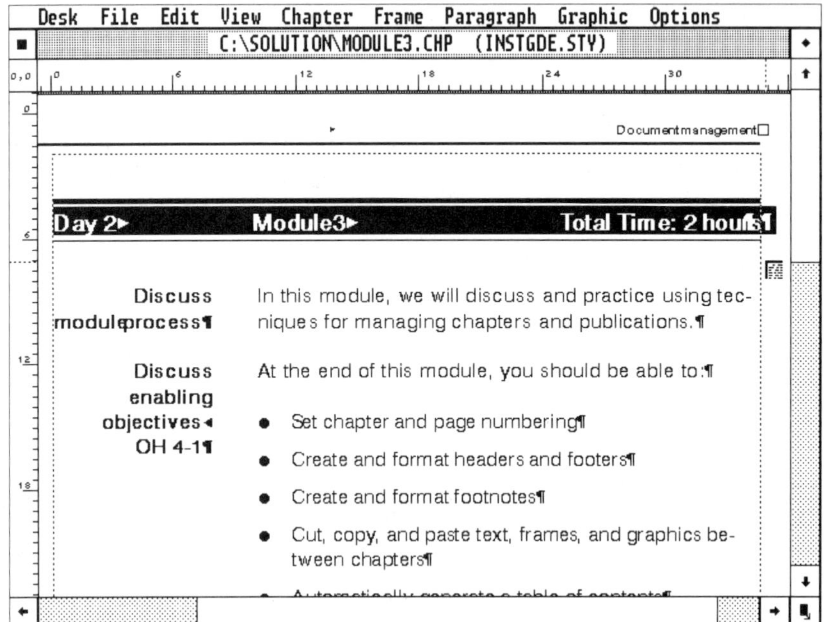

combine two or more separate tags into one. In an application where the title element must be shown near the current date, place both on the same line, and position the date with tabs. Similarly, for technical training materials, you can place the module title and its current running elements in the same line using a single tag rather than creating multiple lines. One of the best examples of the utility of this technique is a left aligned text heading which shows a date on the same line.

Recipe: Multi–element Headlines

Step 1 **Enter headline text**

Enable ***Text*** mode. Enter headline text, press the tab key and the text to be right aligned.

Step 2 **Create tag**

Enable ***Paragraph*** mode and select text. Use Add New Tag to create new tag for the headline. Access **PARAGRAPH•Font** and define the headline font. Access **PARAGRAPH•Alignment** and set Horz. Alignment to Left.

Step 3 **Measure position of right margin**

Reset the zero point of the screen ruler to align with the left margin. Use screen rulers to measure the exact position of the right margin.

Step 4 **Set position of right element**

Access **PARAGRAPH • Tab Settings**. Set Tab 1 to Tab Type: Right. Enter the distance to the right margin in the Location line. The second text element now aligns perfectly with the right margin.

Application Notes

- **Section headings:** Section headings can include time or date information tabbed to right align with the right column guide.
- **Table headlines:** Multi–column presentations can have a single tag displaying the table heading. This is useful in vertical tab applications and eliminates the need for multiple tags

Fine–Tuning Typography with Letterspacing

Letterspacing is a typographic feature that allows you to automatically increase spacing between letters to present a more even flow of text. This feature is especially useful in multi–column applications using justified body text, such as newsletters or magazines. When text is justified, each line is forced to align to both left and right column edges. In this process, large spaces appear between words as text is pulled into alignment. The text looks choppy and unprofessional.

The way to correct this problem is to increase the letterspacing limit, defined in the **PARAGRAPH • Paragraph Typography** dialog box. As the letterspacing limit is increased, Ventura adds more space between letters on an individual line of text. This distributes the large open spaces between the words throughout the line and eliminates the holes in the text. Letterspacing is not entered as a set value, like picas & points. It is set in *ems* which is a relative measure of type size. One em is equal to the current typesize—one em in 12 point type is

12 points. As you increase the limit for letterspacing, Ventura adds space up to the limit you have defined in fractions of an em.

Letterspacing by itself is not enough to completely solve the problem of large spaces in justified text. In some cases, the holes are caused by large, unhyphenated words that wrap to the next available line of text, leaving the line before them stretched, with large open spaces between words. Lines such as this are called loose lines. A loose line is one in which the spacing between words is greater than the maximum word spacing value defined in the Paragraph Typography dialog box. Ventura automatically displays loose lines when the **OPTIONS•Show Loose Lines** is enabled. To break the loose line, simply place a cursor in the unhyphenated word and type Control–Hyphen (–) to insert a discretionary hyphen.

Recipe: Letterspacing and Loose Lines

Step 1 **Select text**

Enable ***Paragraph*** mode and select a paragraph of Body Text or the text to be letterspaced.

Fine-Tuning Typography with Letterspacing
Page 121

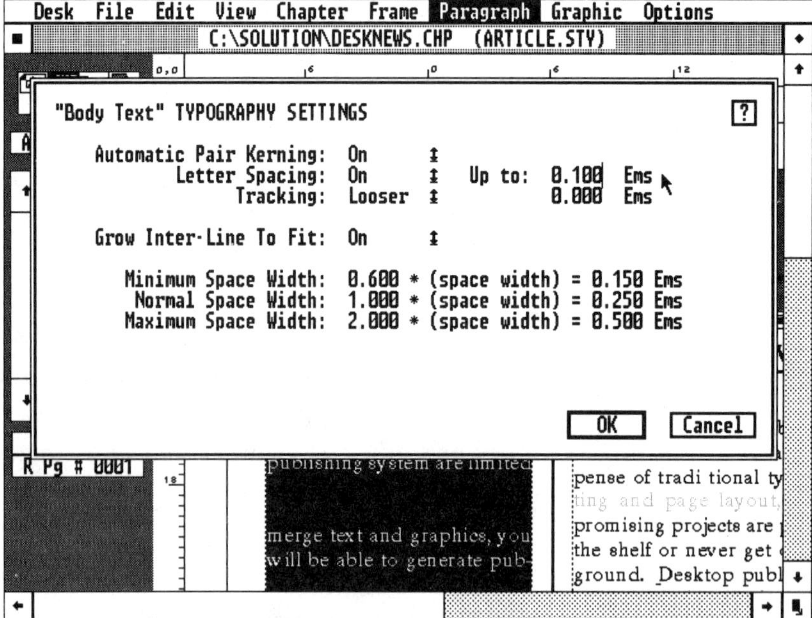

Step 2 **Set letterspacing value**

Access **PARAGRAPH•Paragraph Typography**. Set Letter Spacing to On. Increase the letterspacing value by a small increment. For example, if letterspacing is set at 0.100 em, increase it to 0.300 em. Select OK and check the results on screen. Experiment with different letterspacing values to see the effect they have on the text.

Step 3 **Check document text**

Page through the document on the screen and check the text for even flow. Note if any large open spaces remain.

Step 4 **Show loose lines**

Select **OPTIONS•Show Loose Lines**. All loose lines are shown in reverse video on screen. For some color monitors, they are displayed in red text.

Step 5 **Place discretionary hyphen**

Enable ***Text*** mode. Start at the beginning of the file. As you place discretionary hyphens in text, the text will re–wrap in the columns and possibly generate new loose lines. Go to each loose line and look at the line immediately beneath it. Place text cursor at a logical break in the unhyphenated word and press Control–Hyphen to insert a discretionary hyphen.

Application Notes

- **Designing Body Text:** Turn to page 84.
- **Designing display documents:** Multi–column display documents, like newsletters, often need to letterspace text. For more display document design considerations, turn to page 47.

Creating Illustrated Text

One method for enhancing the appearance of document pages, or design elements within pages is to create illustrated text. Illustrated text appears inside a special ornamental frame or is printed inside an open area of an illustration. This technique makes for high–impact illustrations in advertisements, newsletters, and eye–catching graphic enhancements for books and technical materials.

Many border designs for text can be found in clip–art packages, such as Publisher's Picture Pak or PC Quik–Art. In addition, there are clip art sets available in art resource books which you can use with a picture scanner. Finally, you can design and create your own illustrated text frames using Ventura graphics, or a third–party package such as Corel Draw, Adobe Illustrator, Micrografx Designer, or GEM Artline.

Recipe: Illustrated Text

Step 1 **Place background illustration**

Enable ***Frame*** mode and use Add New Frame in Side–Bar to create a frame. Access **FILE•Load Text/Picture** to load the picture file. Load the picture into the frame. Access **FRAME•Sizing & Scaling** to size, scale and crop the artwork as desired.

Creating Illustrated Text
Page 123

Step 2 **Create box text graphic**

The simplest way to place text inside the border or over the picture is to load it into a box text graphic. Enable ***Graphic*** mode, select the frame containing the illustration and draw a box text graphic over the open area in the border or picture.

Step 3 **Set graphic attributes**

To remove all line and fill attributes so that the box text graphic is truly invisible, access **GRAPHIC•Line Attributes** and set Thickness: None. Access **GRAPHIC•Fill Attributes** and set Pattern: Hollow. The color selected doesn't matter.

Step 4 **Enter text**

To type text directly into the graphic, enable ***Text*** mode and place the text cursor on the End of File Marker in the box text graphic. If you have prepared a text file, you can load it to the position of the text cursor in the Box Text graphic. Make sure the cursor is in position, then access **FILE•Load Text/Picture**, select Text, the desired word processor format and Location: Text Cursor. Then select the file containing the text to be displayed in the frame.

Step 5 **Set text attributes**

To control the presentation of the text in the ornamental frame, it is best to create a custom paragraph tag to display it. Enable ***Paragraph*** mode, select the text and use Add New Tag in the Side–Bar to create a new tag name. Define all special text presentation values in the tag.

Recipe: Illustrated Text with Stacked Frames

To incorporate an illustrated text effect which requires greater control over the placement and display of the text, you should use a stacked frame instead of a box text graphic. This allows you to set text in multiple columns and more easily control margin values. This approach is best used when you are developing full– page illustrated text effects with larger and more complex text files.

Step 1 **Place background illustration**

Enable ***Frame*** mode and use Add New Frame in Side–Bar to create a frame. Access **FILE•Load Text/Picture** to load the picture file with the ornamental frame. Load the picture file into the frame. Access **FRAME•Sizing & Scaling** to size, scale and crop the frame as desired.

Step 2 **Draw stacked frame**

Enable ***Frame*** mode and use Add New Frame to draw stacked frame directly where text is to appear.

Step 3 **Load text into frame**

With the stacked frame selected, access **FILE•Load Text/Picture**, select Text and the desired word processor format. Select the desired text file.

Step 4 **Position text in frame**

To display text in multiple columns, access **FRAME•Margins & Columns** and set the desired column settings to display the text.

Step 5 **Set text attributes**

To control the presentation of the text in the ornamental frame, it is best to create a custom paragraph tag to display it. Enable ***Paragraph*** mode, select the text and use Add New Tag in the Side–Bar to create a new tag name. Define all special text presentation values in the tag.

Application Notes

- **Illustrated headlines:** Link picture and text to form illustrated headlines for article headings, departments and table of contents.
- **Graphic headers and footers:** Text printed over a graphic background or illustration can be placed in a repeating frame at the top or bottom of the page and displayed on all.
- **Drop shadow text:** Create drop–shadow text with Ventura graphics. Turn to page 311.

Designing with Reverse Text

Reverse text is a special text presentation in which white letters appear against a black (or shaded) background. In Ventura, this effect is created by placing a ruling line above text which has a height equal to or greater than the type size for the text, and dropping this line down *behind* the text.

The reverse text process may be used to create a wide variety of text presentation effects for headlines and special feature elements of body text. Combining the basic process with variations in text and background color and shading can yield a virtually infinite number of text design options.

Recipe: Reverse Text

Step 1 **Select typeface**

Set the desired typeface, size, and style using the Font dialog box on the Paragraph menu. Display text in Black for the initial phase of the operation.

Designing with Reverse Text
Page 127

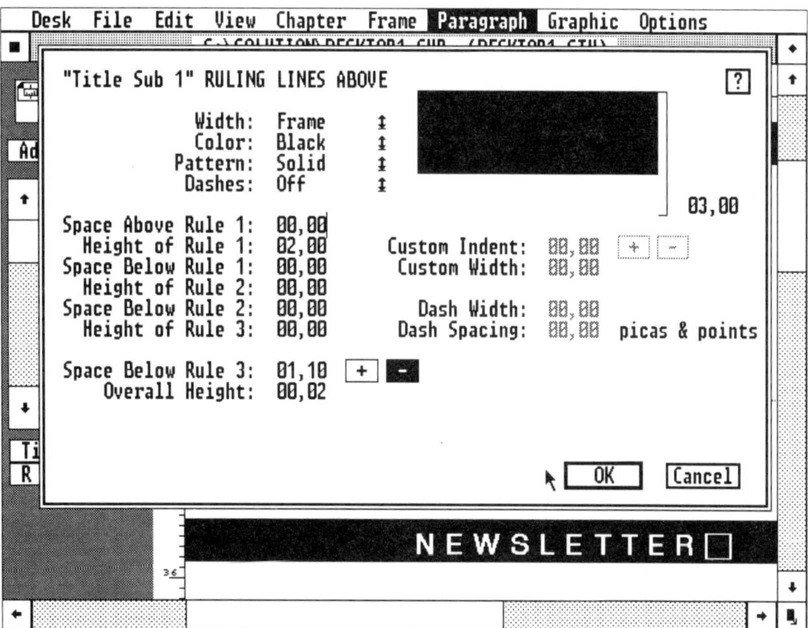

Step 2 **Set background line attributes**

To create the ruling line which will act as the black background, access the Ruling Line Above dialog box on the Paragraph menu and set the color and shading pattern of the background.

Step 3 **Compute background line height**

Determine the height of the background line by adding the size of the typeface with the above and below spacing values (for example: 24 point type with 4 point buffers above and below result in a 32 point high background line).

Step 4 **Position background line**

The standard formula to determine the drop–down distance is to add the type size to the height of the line and divide by two. (For example, 24 point typesize plus 32 point line height equals 56 points. Half of 56 points is 28 points. Enter 28 points on Space Below Rule 3 line.)

▲ **Set rule height:** Enter the height of the background line in the Height of Rule 1 line.

▲ **Set rule drop:** Place the amount the ruling line is to be dropped down on the Space Below Rule 3 line. To drop the line down, select the Minus option.

Step 5 **Reverse text color**

To display text in white (or one of the available text color options), change the font color using the Font dialog box

Application Notes

- **Headings and subheads:** Place headings and subheadings in reverse text for emphasis.
- **Experiment with color and shading:** Create different effects by varying shading and color.
- **Use with stacked tags:** Turn to page 130.

Placing Ruling Lines Behind Text

Ruling lines can be placed not only above, below, and around text, but also behind text to create special effects for headlines and other document elements. The process used to place ruling lines behind text is exactly the same as that used to create reverse text, except that you enter multiple ruling lines and the spaces between them.

Recipe: Ruling Lines Behind Text

Step 1 **Set typeface**

From ***Paragraph*** mode, access **PARAGRAPH•Font** and set the typeface, size, and style. Display text in Black for the initial phase of the operation.

Step 2 **Create background line pattern**

Access **PARAGRAPH•Ruling Line Above** and select color and shading pattern for the background lines.

Placing Ruling Lines Behind Text

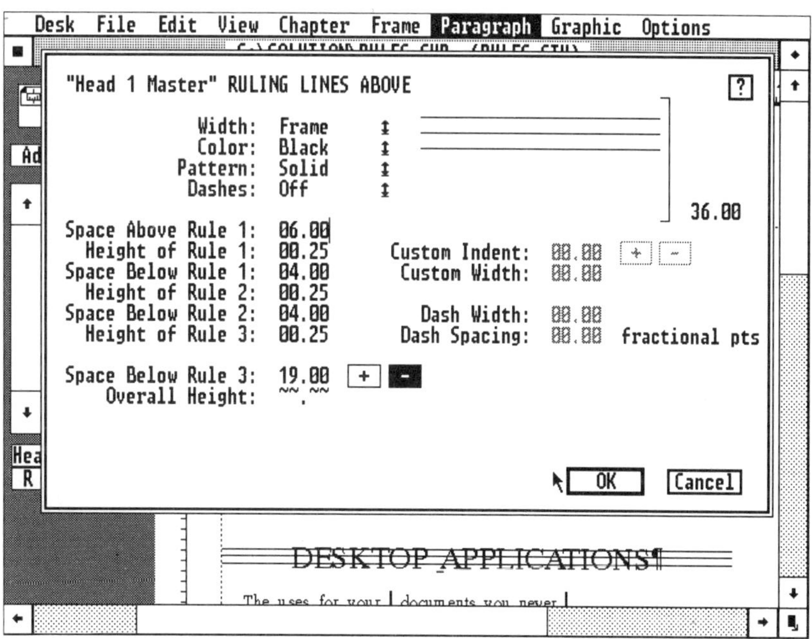

Step 3 **Set height of ruling lines**

To create the ruling lines, enter line thickness on the three Height of Rule lines. To place space between the lines, enter the amount of space in the Space Below Rule lines.

Step 4 **Measure and set line pattern height**

Determine the height of the background line by adding the size of the typeface with the additional amounts to add extra background above and below the text.

Step 5 **Position the ruling line**

Place the amount the ruling line is to be dropped down on the Space Below Rule 3 line. To drop the line down, select the Minus option.

▲ **Standard drop–down formula:** The standard formula to determine the drop–down distance is to add the type size to the height of the line and divide by two.

Step 6 **Set text color**

To display text in white (or one of the available text color options), change the font color using the **PARAGRAPH•Font** dialog box.

Application Notes

- **Document headings:** Use ruling lines behind text for emphasis.
- **Dashed variations:** Experiment with dashed forms of multiple lines.
- **Shaded variations:** Place black or colored text against background of shaded rules. Experiment with different combinations of line thickness and spacing using shaded patterns.

Designing with Stacked Tags

Ventura does not permit a Ruling Line Above or Below to be assigned to the same tag as a Ruling Box Around. To get around this limitation, you can stack a set of tags directly on top of one another to create elaborate text effects such as shaded reverse text surrounded by a ruling line. Stacked tags are very similar in concept to vertical tabs and fitted text that create a set of one or more tags and remove the line breaks between them.

Stacked tags are created in two operations. First, the master tag is created which defines the typographic values and positioning for the text. Next, a copy of the master tag is made and additional ruling lines enhancements are assigned to it. Then, the line break between the two tags is removed and the master tag text now appears with the additional ruling line enhancements in the stacked tag. The two tags appear as a single design element on the page. Finally, to force all tags in the stack to appear on the same page or in the same column, all tags in the stack *except the last one* should be set up with **PARAGRAPH•Breaks**: Keep With Next set to Yes.

Stacked tags is an easy technique to master which can be used to create an astonishing variety of headline and special text presentation effects. Depending upon the particular application, stacked tags may be added immediately *before* or *after* the master tag text to create sophisticated presentation effects for text. Using the full com-

Designing with Stacked Tags
Page 130

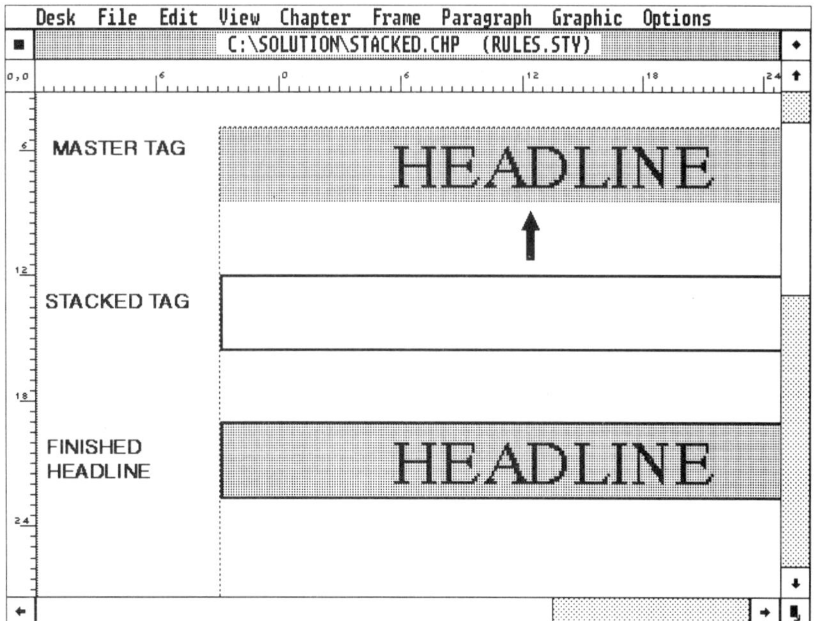

plement of width, color, shading, and dashed design options in the Ruling Lines dialog boxes, this technique can be used to create graphic text designs which are stored in a set of paragraph tags.

Recipe: Stacked Tags

Step 1 **Create master tag**

Assign values to the base tag using features of the paragraph menu (for example: MASTER TAG).

Step 2 **Pull free paragraph return**

Enable ***Text*** mode, place the cursor at the end of the line tagged with the Master tag text and pull down a free paragraph return.

Step 3 **Create first stacked tag**

Enable ***Paragraph*** mode, select the return and create the first stacked tag. Give it a name which clearly links it to the name for the master tag (for example MASTER TAG A).

Step 4 **Edit stack tag**

Select the tag. Access the appropriate **PARAGRAPH•Ruling Line** dialog boxes and delete any unnecessary ruling line attributes copied from the master tag and set desired ruling line values in stacked tag.

Step 5 **Remove line break from stacked tag**

To make stacked tag rise up and "stack" on top of base tag, select the tag and access **PARAGRAPH•Breaks** and change its Line Break to No.

Step 6 **Create second stack tag**

For an effect requiring additional stack tags, create Master Tag B and repeat the process.

Recipe: Editing Stacked Tags

Multiple stacked tags can create a variety of text presentation effects. When editing stacked tags, it may need to unstack them to edit the master or one or more of the stacked tags.

Step 1 **Replace line break in stacked tag**

In ***Paragraph*** mode, select stacked tag and change Line Break to Before.

Step 2 **Place line break in text**

In ***Text*** mode, force the stacked tags apart by placing cursor at the end of the Master tag text and pressing Return.

Application Notes

- **Stacking tags with vertical tabs:** When using stacked tags with any vertical tabs operation, such as auto–numbering or side headings, carefully check the sequence of line breaks in all of the related tags. For vertical tabs and stacked tag effects to work, it is vital that line breaks between all elements be removed.
- **Heading effects:** Place framed heading text on shaded background.
- **Use different line formats:** Integrate more than one line format or shading variation into a single heading.
- **Editing stacked tags in the word processor:** Placing tag names for stacked tags in word processor saves time over placing them manually in Ventura.
- **Use Keep with Next:** Force all elements in a stacked tag group to appear on the same page or in the same column by turning Keep With Next to Yes for all tags in the stack.

Stacking Multiple Rules Behind Text

Using stacked tags, you can place a pattern of hairline rules or a pattern of lines of different thicknesses and shadings behind headline or special text. Begin by placing a pattern of ruling lines behind the master tag text, and add a stacked tag with additional ruling lines. This approach permits text to be placed over a grid of six or more hairline rules.

This effect can be expanded by changing the line thickness, shading, color, or position in the stacked tag. Place a pattern of hairline rules in the headline tag, and a pattern of light, shaded background lines in the stacked tag. The two tags together make up an interesting design element which can easily be consistently reproduced throughout the document using the pair of stacked tags.

Multiple Rules Behind Text

Step 1 **Create master tag**

Enable ***Paragraph*** mode and select text. Use Add New Tag to assign name for master tag. Use features of the **PARAGRAPH** menu to set font, alignment and spacing for tag.

Step 2 **Set master tag ruling lines**

Access **PARAGRAPH•Ruling Line Above**. Set line width, color and pattern. Enter thickness of lines on Height of Rule entry lines and define space between lines on Space Below Rule lines. Use the preview at the top of the dialog box as a guide.

Stacking Multiple Rules Behind Text
133

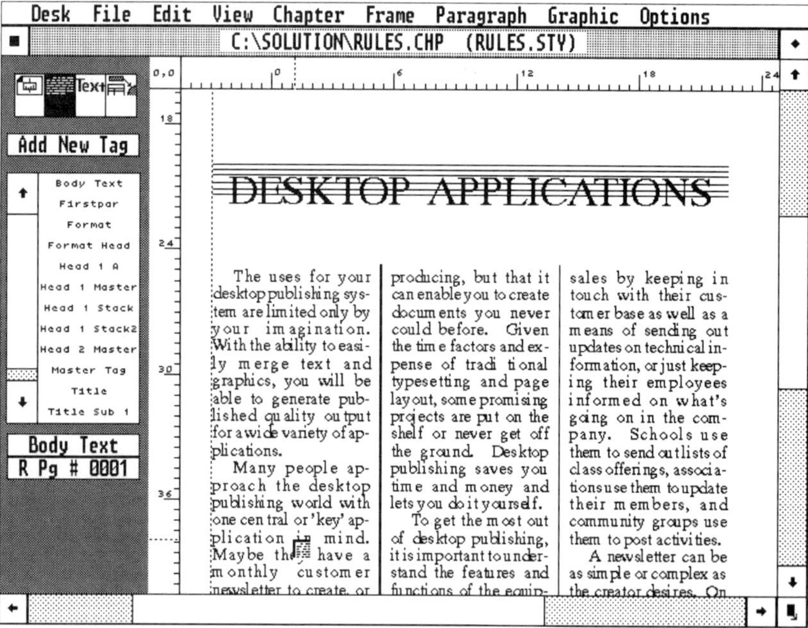

Step 3 **Place ruling lines behind master tag**

Enter distance to drop the ruling lines down for Space Below Rule 3, and select Minus. If you enter values in the Space Above Rule 1 line, the ruling line cluster will drop further down. Experiment on screen to establish position.

Step 4 **Create stacked tag**

Enable ***Text*** mode, place cursor on the paragraph return at the end of the master tag text and press Return to bring down a free paragraph return. Enable ***Paragraph*** mode, select the free return and apply name of stacked tag (i.e.: MASTER TAG A).

Step 5 **Adjust ruling line position**

Access **PARAGRAPH•Ruling Line Above**. Increase the drop down distance for Space Below Rule 3. Move the stacked group of lines far enough down to clear the first group of lines and you can create a pattern of six lines behind text.

Step 6 **Set keep with next**

To force the master tag and its stacked tag to always appear together, select master tag and **PARAGRAPH•Breaks**. Set Keep With Next to Yes. To force the complete stacked tag effect to appear on the same page or in the same column with the next paragraph of text, select the stacked tag and repeat the process.

Step 7 **Remove line break from stacked tag**

To make stacked tag rise up and "stack" on top of base tag, select the tag and access **PARAGRAPH•Breaks** and change its Line Break to No.

Application Notes

- **Different ruling line effects:** Vary the thickness and position of the ruling lines in the stacked tag to create a thick/thin pattern of lines.

- **Multiple shading patterns:** Change the shading pattern of the ruling lines in the stacked tag to create a different texture. Alternate between solid and shaded.
- **Overprint ruling lines:** Use different color and/or shading in the stacked tag. Use this effect to overprint thin solid lines over thicker shaded background lines.

Overprinting Text with White Ruling Lines

If a stacked tag is placed after the master tag, the stacked tag prints on top of the master tag. It literally *overprints* the text of the master tag. If the overprinting pattern of ruling lines is white, the white lines appear to slice through text, or white shading effects adding texture to text. You cannot create this effect by placing ruling lines behind the master tag. You can only create the white grid overprint using the stacked tag method.

Recipe: White Lines Over Text

Step 1 **Create master tag**

Enable ***Paragraph*** mode and select text. Use Add New Tag to assign name for master tag. Use features of the **PARAGRAPH** menu to set font, alignment, and spacing for tag.

Step 2 **Create stacked tag**

Enable ***Text*** mode, place cursor on the paragraph return at the end of the master tag text and press Return to bring down a free paragraph return. Enable ***Paragraph*** mode, select the free return and use Add New Tag to add name of stacked tag (i.e.: MASTER TAG A).

Step 3 **Create line pattern**

Access **PARAGRAPH•Ruling Line Above**. Enter any width value except Text. Enter line thickness on Height of Rule lines and distance between lines on Space Below Rule lines. You have two options for line shading:

Overprinting Text with White Ruling Lines

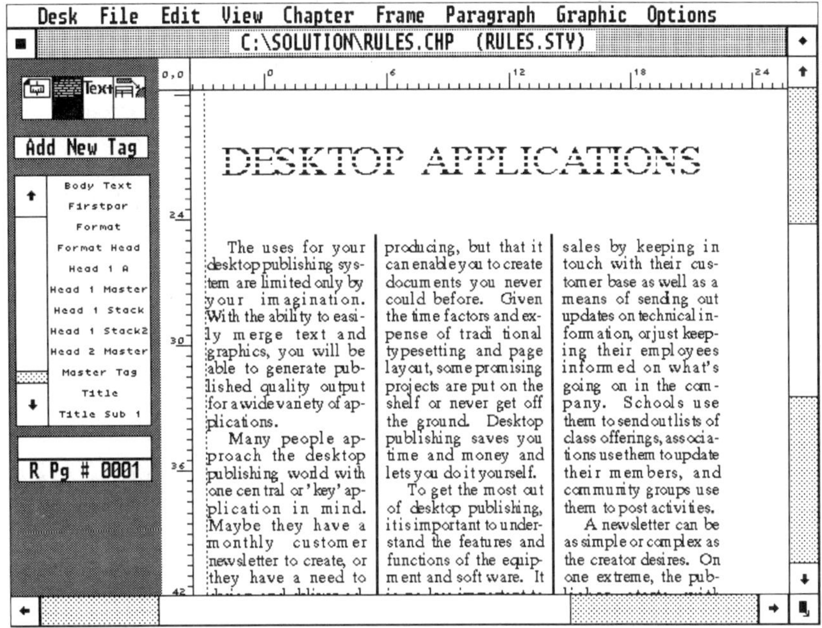

▲ **Solid lines:** Solid white lines will cut a clean strip through the text.

▲ **Shaded lines:** Shaded lines will print out a muted gray effect.

Step 4 **Position line pattern**

Enter drop down value on the Space Below Rule 3 line and select Minus.

☞ CAUTION: Run a print test with any shaded overprint effects. They may not print depending on the individual capabilities of your printer.

Step 5 **Set keep with next**

To force the master tag and its stacked tag to always appear together, select master tag and **PARAGRAPH•Breaks**. Set Keep With Next to Yes.

Step 6 **Remove line break from stacked tag**

To make stacked tag rise up and "stack" on top of base tag, select the tag and access **PARAGRAPH•Breaks** and change its Line Break to No.

Application Notes

- **Print test effects:** Always print test overprint effects to make sure your printer is capable of producing them.
- **Overprint shaded backgrounds:** Place white lines over shaded text and backgrounds.
- **Vary line thickness:** Experiment with thicker overprint lines with different fonts.
- **Vary shading and color:** Try placing white text against a shaded or solid background and overprinting a pattern of hairline rules.

Create Boxed and Shaded Headlines

For a dramatic headline effect, place text on a shaded background and frame it with ruling lines above and below. Or vary this technique by placing ruling box completely around the shaded block. This professional–looking graphic effect can only be accomplished using stacked tags.

Recipe: Shaded Headline with Rules

Step 1 **Create master tag**

Enable ***Paragraph*** mode and select text. Use Add New Tag to assign name for master tag. Use features of the **PARAGRAPH** menu to set font, alignment and spacing for tag.

Step 2 **Place master tag shaded reverse text background**

Access **PARAGRAPH•Ruling Line Above**. Select width, color and background shading pattern. Set the height of background shading strip on Height of Rule 1 line. Enter amount to drop shaded line down for Space Below Rule 3 and select Minus.

Step 3 **Create stacked tag**

Enable ***Text*** mode, place cursor on the paragraph return at the end of the master tag text and press Return to bring down a free paragraph return. Enable ***Paragraph*** mode, select the free return and use Add New Tag to add name of stacked tag (i.e.: MASTER TAG A).

Step 4 **Clear shaded background**

Access **PARAGRAPH • Ruling Line Above** and select Width: None.

Step 5 **Assign top and bottom ruling lines**

With stacked tag selected, access **PARAGRAPH • Ruling Line Above**, set color and solid pattern and set thickness of ruling line above on Height of Rule 1 line. Access **PARAGRAPH • Ruling Line Below** and repeat the process. Above and below rules may be of different thicknesses.

Step 6 **Set keep with next**

To force the master tag and its stacked tag to always appear together, select master tag and access **PARAGRAPH • Breaks**. Set Keep With Next to Yes.

Step 7 **Position stacked tag**

Access **PARAGRAPH • Breaks** and select Line Break: No.

Creating Boxed and Shaded Headlines

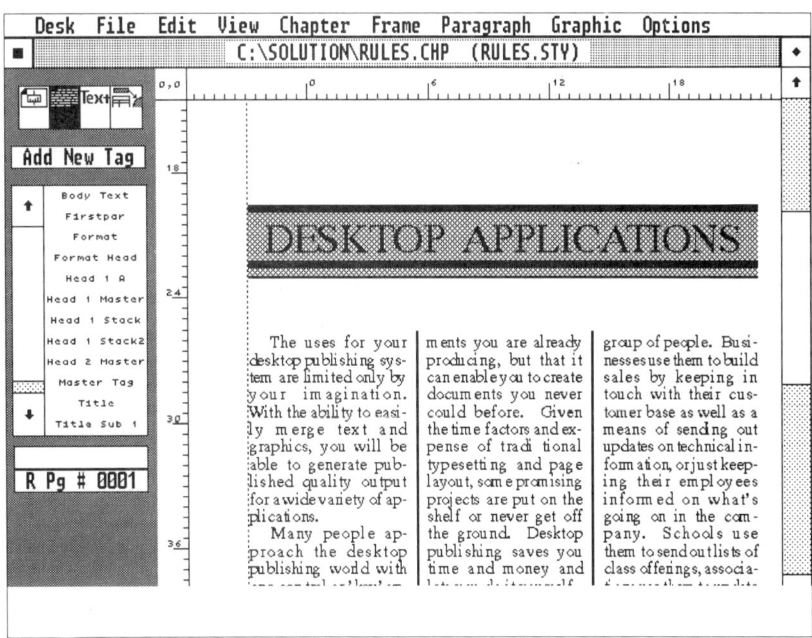

Recipe: Shaded Headline with Framing Box

Step 1 **Define master tag**

Enable ***Paragraph*** mode and select text. Use Add New Tag to assign name for master tag. Use features of the **PARAGRAPH** menu to set font, alignment, and spacing for tag.

Step 2 **Place master tag shaded reverse text background**

Access **PARAGRAPH•Ruling Line Above**. Select width, color and background shading pattern. Set the height of background shading strip on Height of Rule 1 line. Enter amount to drop shaded line down on Space Below Rule 3 line and select Minus.

Step 3 **Define stacked tag**

Enable ***Text*** mode, place cursor on the paragraph return at the end of the master tag text and press Return to bring down a free paragraph return. Enable ***Paragraph*** mode, select the free return and use Add New Tag to add name of stacked tag (i.e.: MASTER TAG A).

Step 4 **Assign ruling box around**

Access **PARAGRAPH•Ruling Box Around**. Define width, color and solid shading. Define thickness of ruling box which will frame the shaded area on Height of Rule 1.

Step 5 **Control master text position**

When using a ruling box around, right and left aligned text can bump up against the ruling box. To control for this, use special offsets in the **PARAGRAPH•Spacing** dialog box:

- ▲ **Left–aligned text:** From ***Paragraph*** mode, select the master tag and access **PARAGRAPH•Spacing**. Enter a small offset value, like one pica, on the In From Left Line. Select the stacked tag and delete this offset.
- ▲ **Right–aligned text:** From ***Paragraph*** mode, select the master tag and access **PARAGRAPH•Spacing**. Enter a small offset value, like one pica, on the In From Right Line. Select the stacked tag and delete this offset.

Step 6 **Set keep with next**

To force the master tag and its stacked tag to always appear together, select master tag and access **PARAGRAPH•Breaks**. Set Keep With Next to Yes.

Step 7 **Position stacked tag**

Access **PARAGRAPH•Breaks** and select Line Break: No.

Application Notes

- **Spacing between line and shaded block:** To add vertical space between ruling lines or ruling box and shaded block, access **PARAGRAPH•Ruling Line Above**. Enter the space buffer on Space Below Rule 1 for Ruling Lines Above and Ruling Box Around. Enter space buffer on Space Above Rule 1 for Ruling Line Below.
- **Vary positioning:** Move shaded block or ruling line to change the relative position.
- **Multiple shadings:** Place text against multiple background textures by stacking lines with different shading values.

Setting Custom–size Shaded Backgrounds

Using custom ruling line widths, you can set shaded backgrounds to any width. You can control the height of the shaded area using the Height of Rule 1 line, and set up of custom–size shaded backgrounds for your text. You can also frame a custom–shaded area using ruling lines or a ruling box.

To create a custom–shaded line, define the Custom Width of the line, and the Custom Indent, used to indent the custom ruling line from the left margin. For example, to create a shaded background centered in a single column page that is 39 picas wide and indented two picas from both right and left margins, deduct the total amount of indented space from width of the column. 39 pica column minus four picas total indent equals 35 picas. So, the Custom Width is *35 picas.* To position the custom line, enter the left indent only. So your Custom Indent is *two picas.*

Step 1 **Measure current column**

Using screen rulers, determine the width of the column that will contain the custom shaded background. Another way to check this value is to enable ***Frame*** mode, select the page and access **FRAME•Margins & Columns** and check the width of the current column.

Step 2 **Determine custom width**

Decide how wide the custom ruling line is to be. Deduct this amount from the width of the current column to arrive at the total indent.

Step 3 **Determine custom indent**

Divide the total indent in half and you have the custom indent.

Step 4 **Set up custom shaded background**

Enable ***Paragraph*** mode. Select master tag text and access **PARAGRAPH•Ruling Line Above**. Select Width: Custom, and define color and shading patterns. Enter the thickness of shaded line on Height of Rule 1 line.

Step 5 **Enter custom line values**

Enter Custom Width on the Custom Width line. Enter Custom Indent on the Custom Indent line.

▲ **Custom Indent/Outdent:** By selecting the Minus option for Custom Indent, the line will be *outdented* from the current margin by the defined amount.

Recipe: Add Ruling Box Around

Once the custom–shaded line is defined, you can add a ruling box around which is buffered by the same distance on all sides. Using the figures from the example above, you could place the ruling box a uniform one pica around on all sides of the shaded box by entering the vertical buffer amount in the Space Below Rule 1 line.

Setting Custom Size Shaded Backgrounds

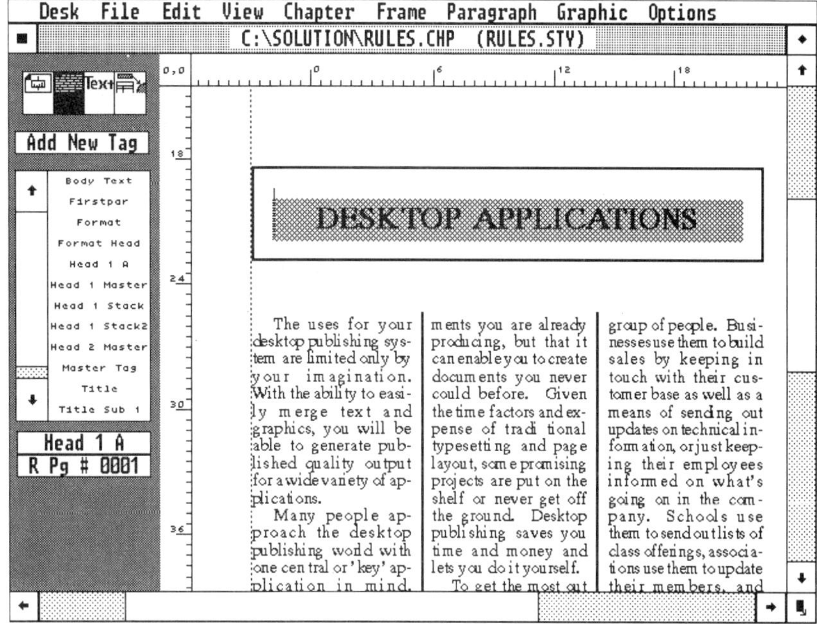

Step 1 **Create stacked tag**

Create a stacked tag (i.e. MASTER TAG A), based upon the attributes of the MASTER TAG. Access **PARAGRAPH•Ruling Line Above** and set Width to None.

Step 2 **Set up ruling box around**

With stacked tag selected, access **PARAGRAPH•Ruling Box Around** and enter the width. Use *Frame* wide for a line between left and right page margins, and *Column* wide for a line the width of the current column. Set the color and solid pattern.

Step 3 **Set box line values**

Enter the thickness of the ruling box line on the Height of Rule 1 line.

Step 4 **Set space buffer**

To set a vertical space between the ruling line and the shaded pattern, enter the same amount entered for the master tag Custom Indent on the Space Below Rule 1 line.

Step 5 **Set keep with next**

To force the master tag and its stacked tag to always appear together, select master tag and access **PARAGRAPH•Breaks**. Set Keep With Next to Yes.

Step 6 **Remove line break from stacked tag**

To make stacked tag rise up and "stack" on top of base tag, select the tag and access **PARAGRAPH•Breaks** and change its Line Break to No.

Application Notes

- **Asymmetrical positioning:** By altering the Custom Indent, you can place a custom shaded background anywhere on a page. This allows you to change its position in relation to its reference text. Experiment with different Custom Indent settings and see how many design effects you can create.
- **Matching rules above and below:** To create a stacked effect in which ruling lines above and below appear at the top and bottom of the custom–shaded line, create a stacked tag and enter the same custom width and indent values for both ruling line above and below.

Change Bars and Side Rules

The **PARAGRAPH•Ruling Box Around** feature can be used to place ruling line to the *side* of a paragraph as a marker for certain paragraphs or as an element in your overall page design.

While the **FRAME•Vertical Rules** dialog box places a vertical line which is automatically the height of the current column, side rules in the paragraph tag automatically adjust to the height of the current paragraph.

Create this effect by placing a ruling box around the text and setting the Custom Width of the box to zero. With the width set to zero, all that's left of the box is the vertical line. Use the Custom Indent feature to place that vertical line beside text.

Recipe: Creating Change Bars and Side Rules

Step 1 **Create tag**

Enable ***Paragraph*** mode and select text. To apply the side rule to all body text in a document, build it into the Body Text tag. Generally it is better to create a special tag (i.e. BODY RULE or CHANGE BAR) for this special attribute.

Step 2 **Define text attributes**

Use features of **PARAGRAPH** menu to set font, alignment, and spacing for tag.

Step 3 **Measure custom outdent**

Using screen rulers, measure how far to the left of text you wish to place the side rule, for example, one pica. Write this value down as Custom Outdent before accessing the dialog box.

Step 4 **Set side rule display attributes**

Access **PARAGRAPH • Ruling Box Around**. Select Width: Custom. Set color and shading.

Step 5 **Set side rule thickness**

Enter the thickness of side rule on Height of Rule 1 line.

Step 6 **Set custom rule and position**

Make sure that Custom Width is set to zero. Enter the value for Custom Outdent on the Custom Indent line and select Minus (–). The Minus selection causes the side rule to *outdent* by the amount entered on the Custom Indent line.

Step 7 **Set tag breaks**

Access **PARAGRAPH • Breaks** select Allow Within: No. This prevents any paragraph with this tag from breaking between two pages or columns. If the side rule tag breaks over two pages (or columns), the side rule will not appear after the break.

Change Bars and Side Rules
Page 144

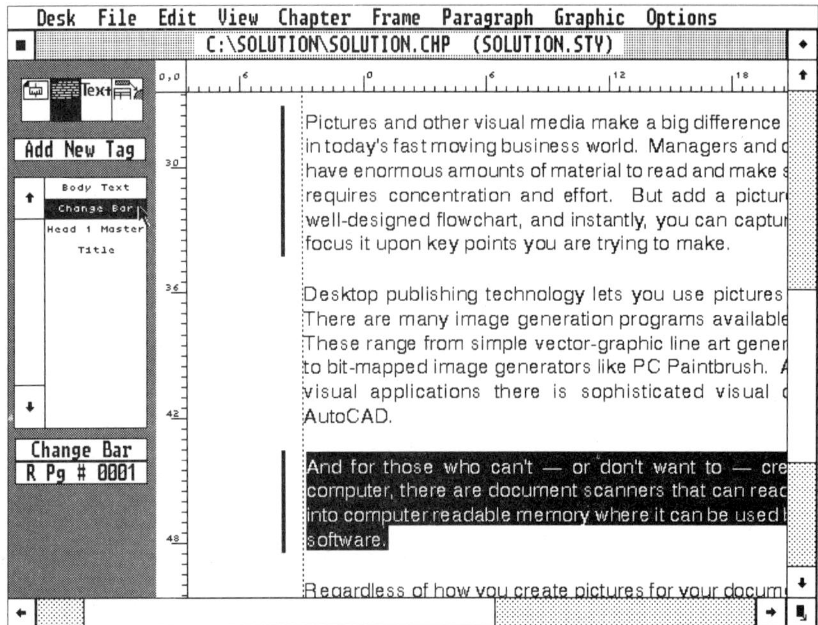

Application Notes

- **Use shading:** Vary color and shading for different levels of emphasis or design effects.
- **Vary line thicknesses:** Make thicker lines in combination with color and shading effects to create different presentation effects.
- **Use dashed lines:** Set the ruling box line as dashed for a dashed side rule.
- **Multiple side rules:** To create different levels of emphasis, define a series of tags with different side rules. Base all tags on a common standard, such as Body Text, and simply vary the side rule presentation for each.
- **Apply with function keys:** When using side rules for editing purposes, such as a change bar, apply the tag easily in the text mode by assigning it to a function key. Enable ***Text*** mode and press Control–K. Enter the names of side rules onto available function keys. *Write down key assignments* for use during editing.
- **Place change in word processor:** When editing in word processor, create a key macro for side rule or change bar tag and place the change bar tag directly into the text file during the editing process.

When you open the chapter in Ventura, change bars will be in place in the document.

Creating Wrap Box Headings

Applying the principle of stacking tags, you can combine a side rule in the master tag with a stacked tag containing a ruling line above to create half–box wrap around line. In longer technical documents, this effect can help visually reinforce the beginning of a section or sequence of data and information.

The procedure creates a master tag and assigns an automatic side–rule to the text. Instead of outdenting the rule to the left, the rule is indented to align with the right page or column margin. Then a stacked tag is created with a ruling line above. When stacked, the two lines merge to create an integrated wrap box effect.

Recipe: Wrap Box Heading

Step 1 **Create the master tag**

Enable ***Paragraph*** mode and select text. Use Add New Tag to assign name for master tag. Use features of the **PARAGRAPH** menu to set font, alignment and spacing for tag.

Step 2 **Measure custom indent**

Using the screen rulers, measure the distance from the left edge of the text block to the right page or column margin. Write this measurement down as Custom Indent.

Step 3 **Assign side rule to master tag**

Access **PARAGRAPH•Ruling Box Around**. Select Width: Custom. Enter line color and shading. Enter side rule thickness on Height of Rule 1 line. Write down all thickness and shading settings for reference when designing the matching ruling line above.

Creating Wrap Box Headings
Page 147

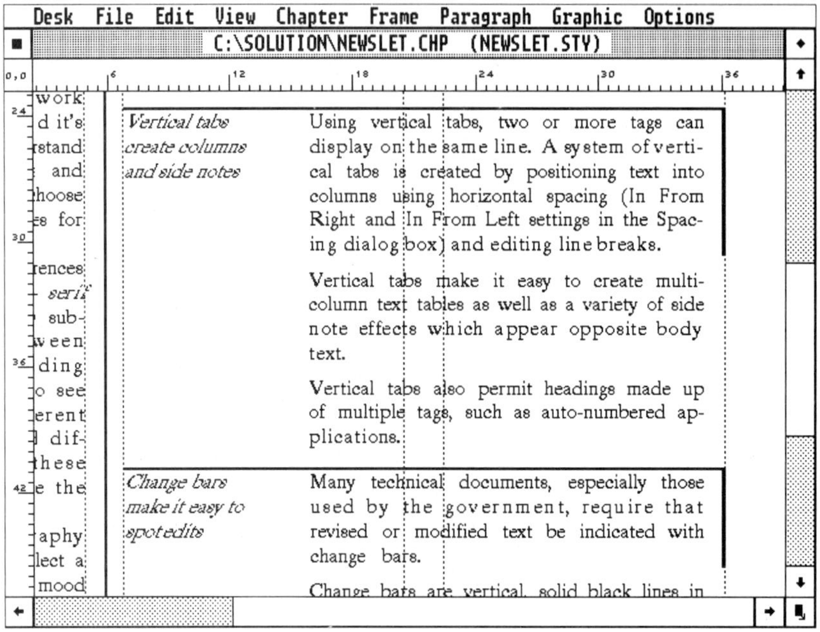

Step 4 **Set side rule width and position**

Set Custom Width to zero. Enter the Custom Indent value measured earlier on the Custom Indent line and verify that Plus is selected. The side rule should appear aligned at the right margin.

Step 5 **Set right text buffer**

To prevent text from touching the side rule, place a small space buffer between the side rule and the text by entering a small value (such as one pica) on the Space Below Rule 1 line.

Step 6 **Create stacked tag**

Enable ***Text*** mode, place cursor at the *beginning* of the end of the master tag text paragraph and press Return to bring up a free paragraph return. Enable ***Paragraph*** mode, select the free return and use Add New Tag to create stacked tag (i.e.: MASTER TAG A).

Step 7 **Assign ruling line above width**

With stacked tag selected access **PARAGRAPH•Ruling Line Above**. Select the desired line width. Use *Frame* for a line extending between left and right margins, *Column* for a line extending the width of the current column, or *Margin* for a line extending from a spacing offset to a margin. (For example, from In From Left position to Right margin).

Step 8 **Match ruling line values**

Match color, pattern, and dashed settings to those entered for the side rule. Enter the same line thickness as that entered for the side rule to create a uniform effect.

Step 9 **Set line breaks**

▲ Select stacked tag text and access **PARAGRAPH•Breaks**. Select Line Break: Before.

▲ Select master tag text and access **PARAGRAPH•Breaks**. Select Line Break: After.

Recipe: Custom Wrap Box Headings

To place more space between the text and the ruling line above and maintain contact between the two ruling lines, add an equal amount of space below both the side rule and the ruling line above.

Step 1 **Move up ruling line above**

Enable ***Paragraph*** mode, select the stacked tag. Access **PARAGRAPH•Ruling Line Above** and enter the amount you wish to raise the line on the Space Below Rule 1 line.

Step 2 **Move up side rule**

From ***Paragraph*** mode, select the master tag. Access **PARAGRAPH• Ruling Box Around** and enter the same amount on the Space Below Rule 1 line.

Application Notes

- **Lead tags:** Wrap box headings are a visually interesting way to begin a section, especially in long technical manuals, instructional materials, or reference documents.

- **Design elements:** Create wrap box headings for elements in a brochure catalog and save the time and effort required to draw and position Ventura graphics. As you edit the document, the effect moves with the text.

Creating Reverse Box Match Heading

For an especially dramatic heading that coordinates with a series of side headings or auto–numbering elements, create a match heading that displays the auto–number in reverse text and matches it to the reference text contained in a ruling line around. The overall effect is a uniform heading with both reverse and normal text elements. A match heading gives a unified and professional look to technical documents and book designs.

The following process assumes you have created an auto–numbered heading. It shows how to set up the two tags to match to a unified text element.

Recipe: Create Boxed Heading

This operation places a ruling line around the heading text with a slight buffer to the left to prevent the ruling line from touching, or crowding heading text.

Step 1 **Design heading tag**

Enable ***Paragraph*** mode. Use Paragraph menu features to set up heading font and spacing. Access **PARAGRAPH•Alignment** and select Horz. Alignment: Left.

Step 2 **Measure heading text line**

Measure width of text block from left to right using screen rulers.

Step 3 **Set heading ruling box around**

With heading tag selected, access **PARAGRAPH•Ruling Box Around**. Set Pattern to Solid and the color and enter the thickness on Height of Rule 1.

Creating Reverse Text Box Match Heading

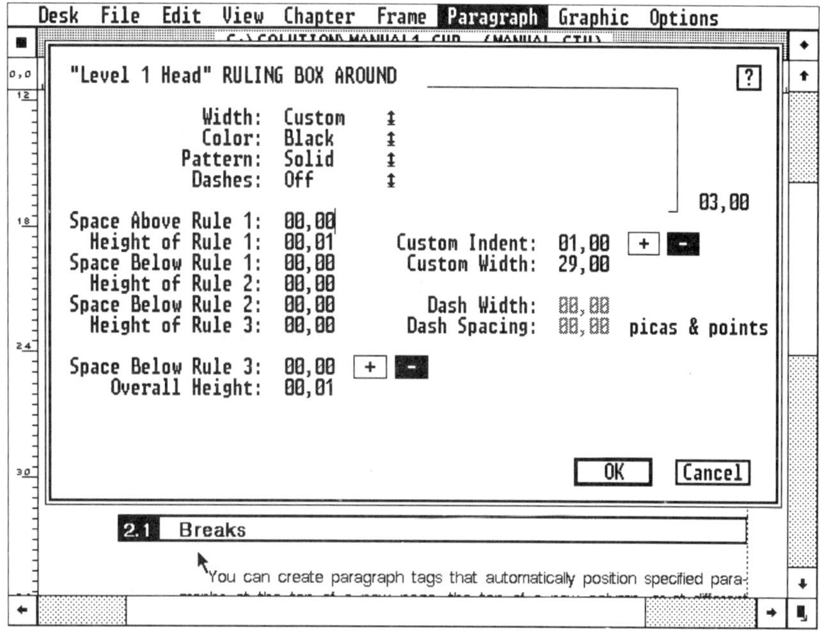

- ▲ Select Width: Custom.
- ▲ Enter the width of the text block on the Custom Width line and display the measure in picas & points.
- ▲ Add 1 pica (01,00) to the Custom Width and enter the result on the Custom Width line. Write down the Custom Width for later use.
- ▲ Enter 1 pica (01,00) on the Custom Indent line and select Minus. This outdents the ruling line by one pica.
- ▲ Compute the height of the heading plus ruling lines by adding height of the interline spacing for the heading to the Overall Height of the Ruling Box around shown in the dialog box. For example, a heading set with a 14 point interline spacing and a 1 point Overall Height has a total height of 15 points. Record the total height for later reference.

Recipe: Reverse Text Auto–Number

This operation places the side heading or auto–number tag in a reverse text block which is equal to the Overall Height of the heading text with ruling lines.

Step 1 **Position tag**

Enable ***Paragraph*** mode and select the generated auto–number tag. Access **PARAGRAPH•Spacing**. Enter the Custom Width for the heading line, and enter it on the In From Right line. This places the auto–number just to the left of the ruling line box.

Step 2 **Set auto–number reverse text**

Access **PARAGRAPH•Ruling Line Above**. Select Width: Text, Pattern: Solid and the color. Enter the value recorded for the total height of the heading into the Height of Rule 1 line. Enter the *same* value into the Space Below Rule 3 line and select Minus.

Step 3 **Set auto–number font**

Access **PARAGRAPH•Font** and set Color: White.

Step 4 **Print test result**

Depending on the accuracy of your screen display, it may be necessary to test print this effect to verify that lines are correctly displayed.

Application Notes

- **Set up auto-numbering:** Turn to page 192.
- **Expand reverse text block:** To add more reverse text area at the beginning and end of the side head, place the text cursor in text and press the Spacebar. To add more reverse text around the auto–number, use the Spacebar to enter a space at the beginning and end of the bracketed auto–number entry in the **CHAPTER•Auto–Numbering** dialog box.
- **Use with side headings:** The match heading effect can be used with a hanging indent or similar vertical tab application. Turn to page 95.
- **Vary shading & color:** Switch the process to create a reverse text headline with a boxed auto number. Experiment with shading values in both elements.

Paired Ruling Line Effects

Using the stacked tag principle, you can generate paired ruling lines made up of different widths and thicknesses for headline effects in which a thick ruling line over the text is paired with a slender frame or column wide ruling line.

By varying the widths, thicknesses, shading patterns and dashed attributes, this technique makes an infinite number of effects possible for text headlines and other elements in documents.

Recipe: Paired Ruling Line

Step 1 **Create master tag**

Enable ***Paragraph*** mode and select text. Use Add New Tag to assign name for master tag. Use features of the **PARAGRAPH** menu to set font, alignment and spacing for tag.

Step 2 **Assign text wide ruling line above to master tag**

Access **PARAGRAPH•Ruling Line Above** and select Width: Text. Set color, pattern and enter line thickness on Height of Rule 1 line.

Step 3 **Create stacked tag**

Enable ***Text*** mode, place cursor on the paragraph return at the end of the master tag text and press Return to bring down a free paragraph return. Enable ***Paragraph*** mode, select the free return and use Add New Tag to add name of stacked tag (i.e.: MASTER TAG A).

Step 4 **Change stacked tag ruling line**

Access **PARAGRAPH•Ruling Line Above** and change Width to the value. Use *Frame* for a line extending from left to right margins or use *Column* for a line extending the width of the current column.

Step 5 **Position stacked tag**

Access **PARAGRAPH•Breaks** select Line Break: No.

Step 6 **Adjust stacked tag line position**

With the stacked tag in position, you may wish to raise or lower its ruling line relative to the ruling line on the master tag. Access **PARAGRAPH • Ruling Line Above**. To raise line, enter amount to raise line on Space Below Rule 1. To lower line, enter amount on Space Below Rule 3 and select Minus.

Application Notes

- **Shading patterns:** Experiment with shading of one or both ruling lines for different design effects
- **Dashed patterns:** Experiment with setting up single or multiple line dashes for different design effects.
- **Multiple rules:** Enter multiple ruling lines in the master tag, the stacked tag, or both to create a variety of enhancements to text.
- **Overprint rules:** Experiment with overprinting rules. Using this variation, you can stack a colored rule over black, or a frame wide pattern of red lines over a thick black line. You could also overprint

Paired Ruling Line Effects
Page 153

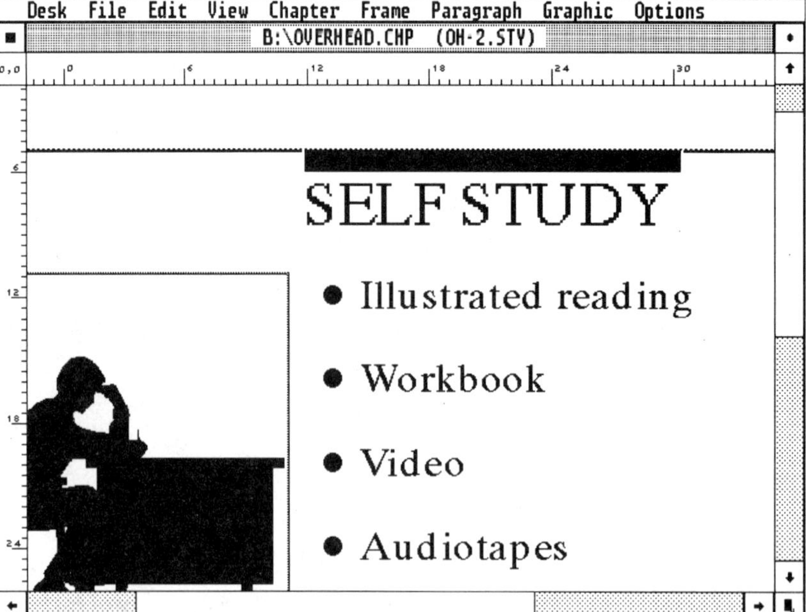

a single or multiple white dashed line over a thicker black line to create an ornamental effect.

- **Triple stacks:** By creating a triple stack of tags, you can create a cluster of ruling lines with differing widths and characteristics.
- **Place stacked tags in word processor:** By entering tag values using a macro or a simple insert file in your word processor, the combined ruling line effects are visible in document as soon as you open Ventura.

Create Paired Ruling Lines Below

Paired ruling lines can be drawn beneath your text without using a stacked tag thanks to the peculiarities of the Ruling Lines Above and Below dialog boxes. Ruling lines Above can be dropped to print below your text using the same principle as reverse text. And you can define a ruling line below the same text with entirely different characteristics to create a matched set.

This effect can be used to place a number of paired ruling line effects, including thick text–wide ruling line below text paired with a thinner frame, column or margin wide ruling line below text.

Recipe: Paired Ruling Lines Below

Step 1 **Create the tag**

Enable ***Paragraph*** mode and select text. Use Add New Tag to assign name for the tag. Use features of the **PARAGRAPH** menu to set font, alignment and spacing for tag.

Step 2 **Assign text wide ruling line below**

Access **PARAGRAPH•Ruling Line Below** and select Width: Text. Define color, shading and dashed patterns. Enter line thickness on Height of Rule 1 line.

Step 3 **Assign frame wide ruling line above**

Access **PARAGRAPH•Ruling Line Above** and select Width: Frame. Define color, shading and dashed patterns. Enter line thickness on Height of Rule 1 line.

Step 4 **Measure ruling line drop**

Access **PARAGRAPH•Spacing** and note the value for interline spacing (Above and Below entries don't matter). Use this value as a guide in determining the drop value to place the Ruling Line Above *below* its text.

▲ If the drop value is the same as the interline spacing for the text, the ruling line will appear at, or on, the text baseline.

▲ If you want to put the ruling line above completely beneath the text, make the drop down value greater than the interline spacing. For example, for 12 point text with 14 point interline spacing, a drop down value of 18 points will place the line cleanly beneath the text.

Step 5 **Enter and position ruling line above**

Reagan **PARAGRAPH•Ruling Line Above**. To drop the line beneath its text, you must enter the drop value in two places in the dialog box:

▲ Enter the drop value on the Space Above Rule 1 line. Note that the line shown in the screen mimic drops down.

▲ Enter the drop value on Space Below Rule 3 line and select Minus.

Application Notes

- **Relative positioning:** Experiment with relative positioning of the two lines. Adding space above a ruling line below pushes it down. If values are entered for Space Above Rule 1, the ruling line above will drop farther down as the drop value on Space Above Rule 3 line is increased.

- **Underlined shaded block effect:** The ruling line above can be a shaded block which matches with the solid ruling line beneath.

- **Shaded patterns:** Experiment with shading of one or both ruling lines for different design effects.
- **Dashed patterns:** Experiment with setting up single or multiple line dashes for different design effects.
- **Multiple rules:** Enter multiple ruling lines in the master tag, the stacked tag, or both, to create a variety of enhancements to text.
- **Overprint rules:** Experiment with overprinting rules. Using this variation, you can stack a colored rule over black, or a frame wide pattern of red lines over a thick black line. You can also overprint a single or multiple white dashed line over a thicker black line to create an ornamental effect.
- **Triple stacks:** Create a triple stack of tags to form a cluster of different ruling lines with differing widths and characteristics.
- **Enter tags in word processor:** Use macros to insert tag clusters into document text. The multiple tag effect is visible when the Ventura document is opened.

Create Paired Ruling Lines Below
Page 155

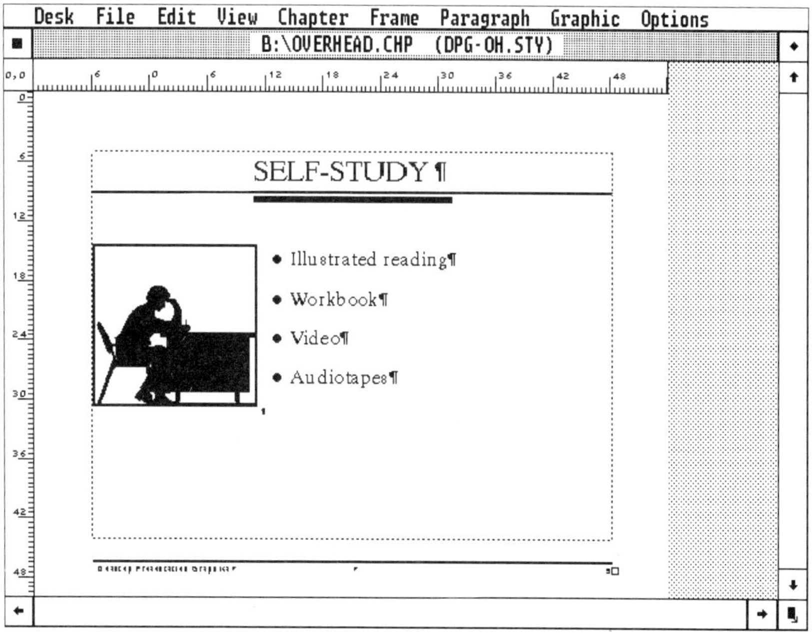

Placing Ruling Lines Beside Text

Stacked tags following a master text tag *overprint* text and stacked tags appearing before master text *underwater* text. You can use this principle to place ruling lines *beside* text.

In this technique, a solid white, text–wide ruling line is placed behind your text in the master tag. Then, a frame or column wide ruling line tag is defined to stack *before* the master tag. The result is that a white ruling line overprints the black line, leaving text framed by a ruling line to the right and left of it. This is useful for newsletter headings or other text effects in display documents.

Recipe: Ruling Lines Beside Text

Step 1 **Create the master tag**

Enable ***Paragraph*** mode and select text. Use Add New Tag to assign name for master tag. Use features of the **PARAGRAPH** menu to set font, alignment and spacing for tag.

Step 2 **Create master tag white ruling line**

Access **PARAGRAPH•Ruling Line Above** and select Width: Text. Select Color: White and Pattern: Solid. Enter a ruling line thick enough to provide a complete background for the whole font. For example, for 18 point type, enter a 24 point rule.

Step 3 **Position master tag white ruling line**

Using the reverse text drop formula (divide the sum of the font size and ruling line height by 2), enter the result on Space Below Rule 3 and select Minus.

Step 4 **Pull down free paragraph return**

Enable ***Text*** mode and place cursor at the *beginning* of master tag text so free return is *above* text.

☞ CAUTION: If you place the stacked tag after the master tag this technique will not work.

Placing Ruling Lines Beside Text
Page 158

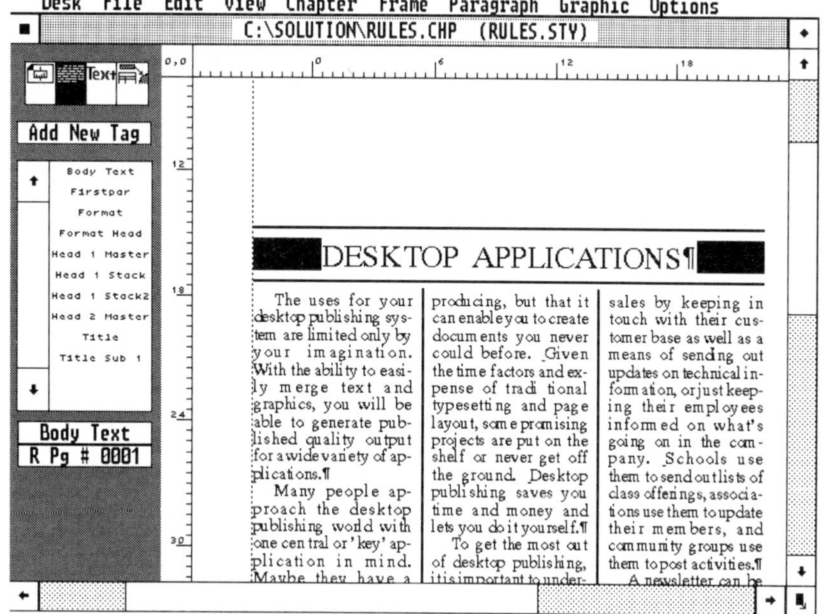

Step 5 **Create stacked tag**

Enable ***Paragraph*** mode, select the free return and use Add New Tag to add name of stacked tag (i.e.: MASTER TAG –1).

Step 6 **Set stacked ruling line attributes**

Access **PARAGRAPH • Ruling Line Above**. Select width (i.e.: Frame or Column) for the ruling line to appear beside text. Select color (any but white) and shading. Determining the line correct width right may require some experimentation. Begin by entering the line thickness as equal to the point size in the master tag (i.e.: for 18 point type, enter an 18 point line thickness).

Step 7 **Position ruling line**

Enter the value from Height of Rule 1 on the Space Below Rule 3 line and select Minus. This positions the background line behind the text when the tags are stacked.

Step 8 **Check stacked tag break**

Select stacked tag. Access **PARAGRAPH•Breaks**. Because the master tag will *follow* this tag, the breaks must be set to Before.

Step 9 **Remove master tag line break**

Select master tag and access **PARAGRAPH•Breaks**. Select Line Break: After to stack the tag on top of the background ruling line.

Application Notes

- **Variable alignment:** Change horizontal alignment of master tag to any value.
- **Add text buffers:** To add space between the ruling line and the text string, use the text mode to insert an em (Ctrl–Shift–M) or en (Ctrl–Shift–N) space at the beginning and end of the text line. This expands the text line and its solid white background. To save time, enter em and en spaces using text attribute codes directly in your word processor.
- **Inset text in background rule:** Decrease the height of the white background and expanding the height of background rule to inset a white box containing text into a black or colored background line.
- **Shading variations:** Set up the background rule as a pattern of multiple solid or shaded lines for a variety of presentation effects.
- **Triple stacks:** Create more elaborate effects by stacking two tags to build the background rule. Using this technique, one tag with a pattern of shaded rules, stacked behind another tag with solid rules is possible. The master tag with its solid white background box creates a white space to show the text.

Designing Multiple–use Paragraph Tags

Each Ventura style sheet can contain up to 128 paragraph tags. But when designing style sheets, avoid creating long lists of tags. Creating an individual tag for every special design situation in your document

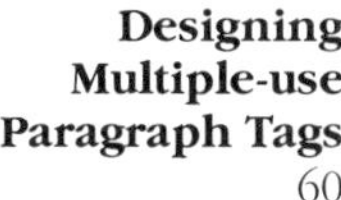

Designing Multiple-use Paragraph Tags
60

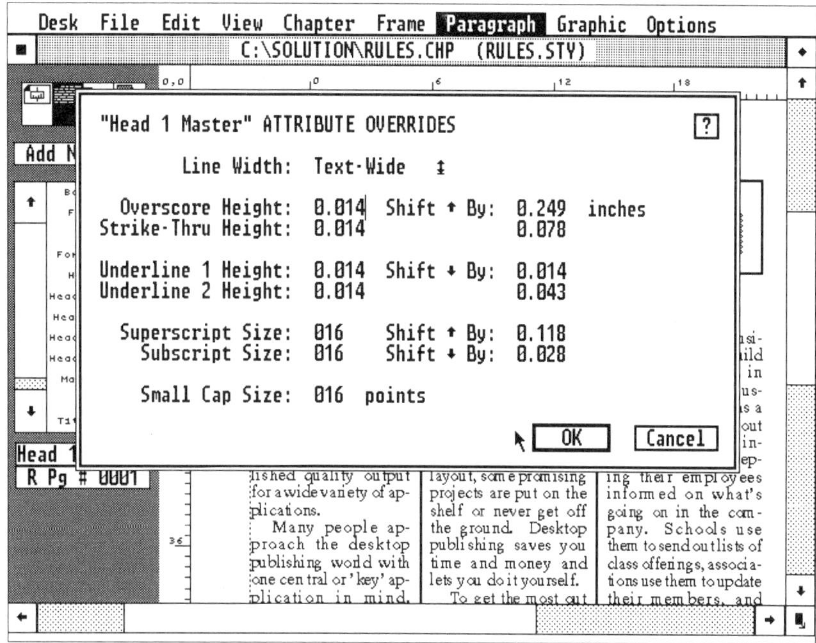

makes style sheets needlessly unwieldy and difficult for others to understand. In addition, too many tags in your style sheet makes you more vulnerable to triggering system errors and memory problems.

There is a group of features in Ventura that help you get more mileage out of each paragraph tag in your style sheet. These features let you build in additional values and variables which may eliminate the need for lots of additional tags.

- **Custom Attribute Overrides:** Allow custom values to be set for the text attribute Side–Bar for *each paragraph tag in the style sheet.* Use this dialog box to assign build special text enhancement features into a tag which can be accessed in the text mode. For more information, turn to page 177.

- **Custom Horizontal Tab settings:** Allows sixteen custom horizontal tab stops to be defined for *each paragraph tag in the style sheet.* Use this feature to place multiple text elements in a single headline. Tab stops can also be designed to place tagged text at several positions on the page, so that multiple tags are not necessary. For more information, turn to page 101.

- **Soft paragraph return** This text attribute forces a line break in text without breaking to a new paragraph. This makes it easy to position title text without making a set of different paragraph tags.
- **Typeset selected text with Set Font:** To assign custom values to selected elements of text, use Set Font in the ***Text*** mode to assign the values and avoid creating a lot of tags to cover one–time problems or special cases. For more information, turn to page 169.
- **Interactive copyfitting:** To adjust font size and tracking of tagged text, use interactive font sizing and tracking to edit text size and tracking values. This also can help avoid creating tags to cover one–time problems and special cases. For more information, turn to page 185.
- **Setting frame wide alignment:** For headline elements which are used both in the page and inside of frames, access **PARAGRAPH• Alignment** and set overall width to frame–wide. This feature forces the headline to expand to the width of the current frame, or across the page, even if columns have been defined in the page. This makes it possible to get more use out of one heading.

CHAPTER 4

Screen-based Layout and Design

Interactive Document Design

When you bring a document into the Ventura screen, you are looking at a flexible sheet of paper. Your layout has text and graphics in place. Yet, with a touch of the mouse, you can transform that page by moving pictures and graphics, or by changing the look and position of text. The page has been made flexible by electronic paste–up, typesetting, text editing, and graphic design. To understand the power and the magic in this, remember that an edit you make with a stroke of the mouse may once have taken hours of paste–up and manual type resetting.

Many early page layout software programs were designed as electronic emulations of the traditional publishing process. The screen was conceived as an electronic facsimile of the designer's art board. Typeset text and illustrations could then be assembled and pasted up to build documents. A major reason for Ventura Publisher's success is that it went beyond this early approach. It includes system

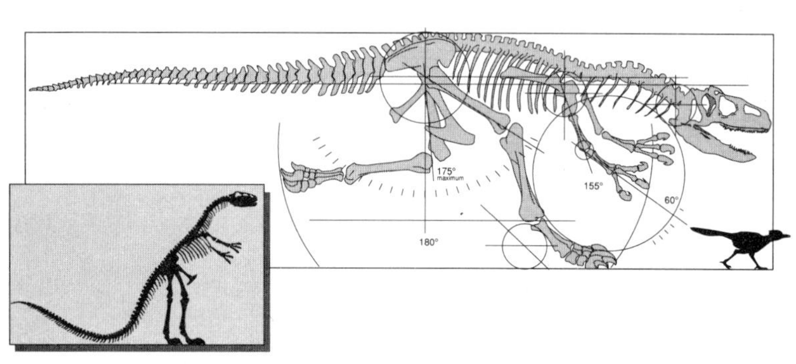

TWILIGHT *of the*
DINOSAURS

Millions of years ago, the dinosaurs suddenly vanished.
The reason for their mysterious disappearance
has puzzled scientists for decades.
New research has revealed a number of surprising possibilities
and opened new questions about the disappearance
of these gigantic prehistoric creatures.
Experience the *Twilight of the Dinosaurs*.

CENTRAL EXHIBITION HALL

February 12 to May 18

Flyer: This layout illustrates how screen-based editing techniques allow you to create special text effects, including individual character editing, placement of special text characters and special text positioning. Text is typeset in Palatino. Artwork was created in Adobe Illustrator/Windows Version.

design features such as paragraph tags which draw upon the processing power in your computer to perform repetitive tasks. To fully access the power of these features, detailed document design decisions are entered in Ventura dialog boxes. By moving back and forth between the document surface and the dialog box, you build a document design by defining set values for fonts, alignment, spacing, and other variables.

For some design challenges, however, dialog boxes can be confusing and cumbersome. Before you can enter a set value, you have to know what that value is. In some cases, the best way to determine a design value is by experimenting and designing your layout directly on the screen. For display applications, such as advertising layouts, brochures, illustrated catalogs, and newsletters, designing on the screen is often the best way to build and complete your design. It is generally not as important for long documents which maintain a set format over many pages.

The principal difference in designing from the screen is how you place and typeset text. Ventura's Paragraph mode contains an array of tools which let you define automatic typeset codes, or paragraph tags. Ventura's Text mode provides features that let you edit, position and typeset selected pieces of text, including individual characters. Using the interactive design features available in Text mode, you can do many things which are impossible in the Paragraph mode by itself. Where the Paragraph mode defines uniform values for entire paragraphs, the Text mode cursor lets you get inside a paragraph. Once inside, you can change the character of individual words, set custom fonts, force line breaks where you want them and interactively experiment with font sizing, kerning and tracking. Special features in the Text mode allow you to move text above and below the baseline, something which cannot be accomplished using the Paragraph mode.

Every document you create in Ventura will involve some direct screen editing. The Text mode is designed to provide the necessary tools to perform simple edits, Cut/Copy/Paste sections of text, and add enhancements to selected words or phrases. But if you wish, you can develop some simple style sheets which will let you use the

Text mode as a complete interactive document design system. You will be able to edit and position your text almost entirely from the screen level using only the mouse and keyboard.

Ventura's interactive design and editing features allow you to work with your document as you would on a conventional page layout program like Aldus Pagemaker. You can enjoy the freedom of experimentation and the power to shape your design directly on screen. Once your design has been completed, you have the option to convert your screen settings into a custom style sheet to make your finished design easy to use regularly in print production. How you use interactive editing features will depend largely on the type of applications you are developing and your preferred working style.

Interactive Design Tools

Features used in interactive design are contained primarily in the Text mode, which is the primary focus of all interactive design operations.

- **Text mode** contains features for text editing, special edit items, text characters and text enhancements.
- **Frame mode** contains features to layout the page and position pictures and text.
- **Attribute Overrides** on the Paragraph mode permits custom settings for enhancements shown in the Text mode Assignment List *for each paragraph tag in a style sheet.* This can be used to set up custom style sheets for interactive design.
- **Set Font** in the Text mode Side–Bar sets custom typeface, size and style values to a string of selected text. It also permits custom kerning and text shift above and below the baseline.
- **Function keys** apply paragraph tags to text selected in the Text mode which significantly speeds up interactive operations.
- **Special Edit Items** in the Edit menu insert special characters and text features at the cursor location, including hollow or filled box characters and fractions.
- **Cut/Copy/Paste** in the Edit menu move or remove selected elements of text.

- **Keyboard commands** shown at the right of all drop–down menus permit some features to be activated while typing on the keyboard without the mouse.

Style Sheets for Hands–on Design

This chapter contains a variety of techniques to help you turn Ventura's ***Text*** mode into a powerful interactive screen editing system. The most important concept linking all of these techniques is the generic, or open, style sheet. In regular Ventura documents, you create a series of custom paragraph tags which define a series of unique, uniform text elements. For interactive editing, you create open tags to position your text and set default font values which you can then edit as needed.

Even if you don't want to design extensively from the screen, the techniques in this section can help you get more use and value out of features available for text editing. Using features such as custom Attribute Overrides in your regular Ventura style sheets can make editing easier and increase your design options.

If you work in a production department, a thorough understanding of how to use the Text mode can get you out of the office a lot faster. This mode is one of the most important tools in the document production process. As you finalize documents, you invariably have to make last–minute edits to text and correct paragraph tagging problems. Setting up the Text mode for power production is your solution to those late nights spent over the printer.

Using Ventura as a Text Processor

In situations where a word processor is unavailable, you can configure Ventura to work efficiently as a text processor by using the keyboard editing shortcuts and assigning often–used tags to function keys so you can apply tags directly from the ***Text*** mode.

When typing your text on the screen, remove the Side–Bar display so you can display more of your page width in the Working Area. This can significantly reduce the amount of back and forth scrolling you must do and increase your working efficiency. Bring back the Side–Bar when you need to apply text enhancements.

Keep a reference sheet with all of the keyboard commands handy (Turn to Appendix B). Using keyboard shortcuts reduces the number of times you stop typing to select features with the mouse and can greatly increase your working speed in text editing.

Recipe: Using Ventura as a Text Processor

Step 1 **Open chapter**

Access **FILE•Open Chapter** and select the chapter file you wish to edit.

Step 2 **Assign function keys**

Enable ***Text*** mode and press Control–K. Assign the 10 most commonly used tags in your style sheet to the function keys and write the assignments down for reference.

Step 3 **Remove Side–Bar for typing**

Select **OPTIONS•Hide Side–Bar**. By removing the Side–Bar, you can

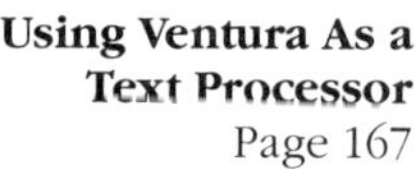

Using Ventura As a Text Processor
Page 167

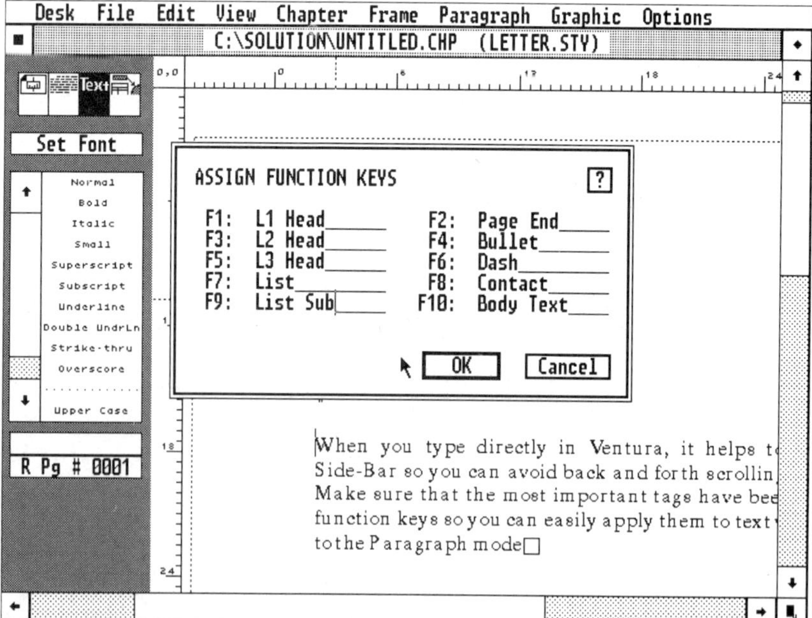

usually display the entire width of your page so you don't have to interrupt typing with side–to–side scrolling.

Step 4 **Hide All Pictures**

To prevent long delays as your screen redraws pictures, select **OPTIONS•Hide All Pictures**.

Step 5 **Using keyboard commands**

Note the keyboard equivalent commands appearing on the right edge of all the pull–down menus. Use keyboard commands to perform a variety of key document editing functions, including:

▲ Changing modes
▲ Cut/Copy/Paste text
▲ Place Special Edit Items
▲ Change document view
▲ Save the chapter

Application Notes

- **Deadline editing:** When a word processor is unavailable, take time to use these techniques, especially function keys and keyboard commands to speed up text editing in Ventura.
- **Production editing:** When preparing documents for production, use this approach to set up your screen to make quick edits. Use Reduced View and Go To Page features to quickly bring up desired page for tag corrections and text editing.
- **Insert special text characters:** Turn to page 90.
- **Insert special edit items:** Turn to page 93.

Interactive Document Sketching

Designing complex style sheets can be very time– consuming and exacting work, often involving a great deal of back and forth between the document on the screen and various dialog boxes. Interactive document sketching is a way to experiment directly on the screen with different fonts, text spacing, and positioning. When you have settled on the design, you can record the decisions you have made into a custom Ventura style sheet.

A sketching style sheet consists of a handful of body text tags, each defining a different alignment or special text presentation option. Once these tags have been created, you assign them to the function keys so that all tagging and direct editing to text can be done without leaving the ***Text*** mode.

Recipe: Sketching Style Sheet

Step 1 **Create new style sheet**

Access **FILE•Load Diff. Style** and load a basic style sheet or DEFAULT.STY from the \TYPESET subdirectory. Access **FILE•Save As New Style** to save it under a new name.

Step 2 **Load or type in text**

Access **FILE•Load Text/Picture**, select Text and the desired file format. Select the text file for your document. To type text directly on the screen, enable ***Text*** mode, click the mouse on the screen to set a text cursor and begin typing.

Step 3 **Define page defaults**

Access **CHAPTER•Page Size & Layout**. Set the options to define the default values for the document page.

Step 4 **Define custom page size**

If you wish to create a page which is not the same as one of the standard paper sizes, enable ***Frame*** mode and select the base page. Access **FRAME•Sizing & Scaling**. Enter the dimensions of the custom size page in Frame Width and Frame Height. Center the custom page on the paper using Upper Left X and Upper Left Y.

Step 5 **Define Margins & Columns**

Access **FRAME•Margins & Columns**. Enter the desired margins and columns for the page.

Step 6 **Set Body Text font and interline spacing**

Enable ***Paragraph*** mode and select a paragraph of Body Text. Access **PARAGRAPH•Font** and select the desired font, size, and style. Access **PARAGRAPH•Spacing** and set the desired inter–line spacing. This setting is important for two reasons:

▲ It is the spacing for standard document text.

▲ When Line Snap is On, all frames snap vertically in increments of Body Text interline spacing.

Step 7 **Define basic tags**

To easily position text anywhere you wish during the design process, use Add New Tag to create three tags based on Body Text with different alignment values:

▲ **Body Left:** Access **PARAGRAPH•Alignment** and set Horz. Alignment to Left.

▲ **Body Center:** Access **PARAGRAPH•Alignment** and set Horz. Alignment to Center.

▲ **Body Right:** Access **PARAGRAPH•Alignment** and set Horz. Alignment to Right.

Interactive Document Sketching
Page 169

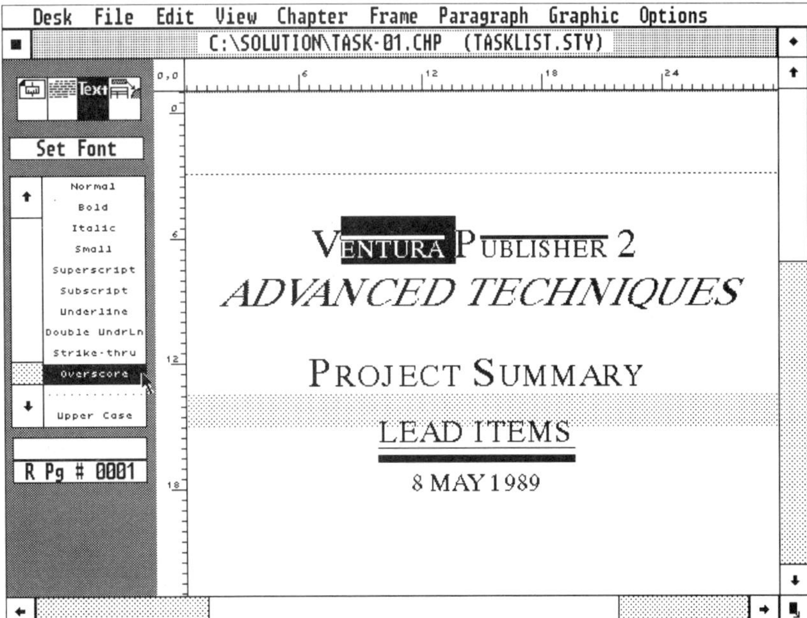

Step 8 **Define custom tags**

If you wish, use Add New Tag to create several additional tags which position text for special applications.

▲ **Body Table:** Access **PARAGRAPH•Tab Settings** and define a set of standard tab stops for tabular material.

▲ **Bullet:** Set a bullet tag to display listed items.

▲ **Point size tags:** To insert defined space values into your text at any point, create several tags whose interline spacing is set to specific point sizes. For example, 2 point, 6 point, and so forth.

▲ **Break tags:** To conveniently break text over pages or columns, create Page Break or Column Break tags.

Step 9 **Assign tags to function keys**

To quickly apply the tags during text editing, assign them to function keys. Select **FILE•Save** to save the chapter file. Access **PARAGRAPH• Update Tag List** and select Assign Func. Keys. Enter each tag name on a line in the dialog box and write down all function key assignments for reference.

Recipe: Using the Sketching Style Sheet

Once your sketching style sheet has been completed, you can use it to create a document layout in the Text and ***Frame*** modes. Use the function keys to tag your text with one of the generic tags. To assign custom font values to selected strings of text, use features in the ***Text*** mode Assignment List and Set Font. Block space in the page using frames. In addition, with Line–Snap set to On, you can draw one–line–high frames to add spacing between text elements.

Step 1 **Layout page with frames**

Select **OPTIONS•Turn Line Snap On**. Enable ***Frame*** mode. Use Add New Frame to draw frames to block out space on the document page.

Step 2 **Load or type in text**

Access **FILE•Load Text/Picture**, select Text and the desired file format. Select the text file for your document. To type text directly on the screen, enable ***Text*** mode, click the mouse on the screen to set a text cursor and begin typing.

Step 3 **Position text with generic tags**

To tag text, select any part of a text paragraph and press the function key for the tag you wish to apply.

Step 4 **Change text attributes with Set Font**

To change the typeface, size, or style of text, select the text in ***Text*** mode and access Set Font in the Side–Bar. Select the desired typeface, size, style and color for the text.

Step 5 **Shift text from baseline**

You can adjust the vertical position of a single letter or a string of selected text. Select the desired text, access Set Font in the Side–Bar. Use the Shift feature provided to move the text up or down from the baseline.

Application Notes

- **Insert special text characters:** Turn to page 90.
- **Insert special edit items:** Turn to page 93.
- **Interactive copyfitting:** Fit text to a defined area by increasing or decreasing font size and space between letters. Turn to page 185.

Creating a Designer's Style Sheet

Another approach to designing documents on the screen is to create a sketching style sheet with Body Text interline spacing at a very small value, such as one point. By developing a set of left–center–right tags based on this value, you can place text virtually anywhere on the page. Each time you press the Return key, you position the text down by the value defined for the interline spacing. In addition, when Line Snap is On, frames snap vertically in increments of the Body Text interline spacing value.

This technique gives you greater control over positioning text on a page. However, it should be used *only* when designing a complex layout that requires this degree of flexibility. It is easier and less time consuming to create a sketching style sheet using a larger body text interline spacing value, as described previously.

Because the Body Text interline spacing value is set so small, all text must be typed directly into the Ventura screen and spaced as it is being typed. If you load a prepared text file into this style sheet, Body Text paragraphs will cluster and overprint each other due to the small interline spacing value.

If you wish to use the complete design on a regular basis, translate the layout and text values into a permanent Ventura style sheet using custom paragraph tags. This will make the design easy to use and reproduce in a production environment.

Recipe: Designer's Style Sheet

Step 1 **Create new style sheet**

Access **FILE•Load Diff. Style** and load a basic style sheet or DEFAULT.STY from the \TYPESET subdirectory. Access **FILE•Save As New Style** to save it under a new name.

Step 2 **Type text in base page**

Enable ***Text*** mode and click the mouse in the Working Area. Type a string of text to use in setting up the style sheet.

Step 3 **Define page defaults**

Access **CHAPTER•Page Size & Layout**. Set the options to define the default values for the document page.

Step 4 **Define custom page size**

If you wish to create a page which is not the same as one of the standard paper sizes, enable ***Frame*** mode and select the base page. Access **FRAME•Sizing & Scaling**. Enter the dimensions of the custom–size page in Frame Width and Frame Height. Center the custom page on the paper using Upper Left X and Upper Left Y.

Creating a Designer's Style Sheet
Page 173

Step 5 **Define Margins & Columns**

Access **FRAME•Margins & Columns**. Enter the desired margins and columns for the page.

Step 6 **Set body text interline spacing**

Set Body Text interline spacing at a very small value—for example, one point. This lets you get to any place on the screen by hitting the Return key multiple times. Make sure that this value is the *same* for all designer text tags to avoid problems in positioning text.

☞ CAUTION: If you load a text file into this style sheet, the small value for interline spacing will cause lines of text to overprint on the screen. With this style sheet, you should type all text directly on the screen and position it as you type.

Step 7 **Define basic tags**

To position text anywhere during the design process, use Add New Tag to create three tags based on Body Text with different alignment values. All of these tags should be created *after* you have set the interline spacing value for Body Text:

▲ **Body Left:** Access **PARAGRAPH•Alignment** and set Horz. Alignment to Left

▲ **Body Center:** Access **PARAGRAPH•Alignment** and set Horz. Alignment to Center

▲ **Body Right:** Access **PARAGRAPH•Alignment** and set Horz. Alignment to Right

Step 8 **Define custom tags**

You can also use Add New Tag to create several additional tags which position text for special applications.

▲ **Body Table:** Access **PARAGRAPH•Tab Settings** and define a set of standard tab stops for tabular material.

▲ **Bullet:** Set a bullet tag to display listed items.

▲ **Point size tags:** To insert defined space values into your text at any point, create several tags whose interline spacing is set to specific point sizes. For example, 2 point, 6 point, and so forth.

▲ **Break tags:** To conveniently break text over pages or columns, create Page Break or Column Break tags.

Step 9 **Assign tags to function keys**

To quickly apply tags during text editing, assign them to function keys. Select **FILE•Save** the chapter file. Access **PARAGRAPH•Update Tag List** and select Assign Func. Keys. Enter each tag name on a line in the dialog box and write down all function key assignments.

Using the Designer's Style Sheet

The designer's style sheet gives you the power to place text and design your document almost entirely from the working screen. With tag values set and assigned to function keys, you won't need to access the ***Paragraph*** mode unless it is to make changes to one of your generic tags.

This style sheet is best used for direct entry of text onto the screen. Because the Body Text interline spacing value is significantly less than the actual font height, loading a text file onto the screen can produce a blur of stacked text. Press the appropriate function keys to tag your text as you type it into the page and use the Return key to space text elements on the page.

Step 1 **Layout page with frames**

Select **OPTIONS•Turn Line Snap On**. Enable ***Frame*** mode. Use Add New Frame to draw frames that block out space on the document page.

Step 2 **Type in text**

Enable ***Text*** mode, click the mouse on the screen to set a text cursor and enter text at the cursor. You may wish to enter headline elements in frames, or Box Text graphics to make them easier to move around the page.

Step 3 **Position text with generic tags**

To tag text, select any part of a text paragraph and press the function key for the tag you wish to apply.

Step 4 **Change text attributes with Set Font**

To change the typeface, size, or style of text, select the text in ***Text*** mode and access Set Font in the Side–Bar. Select the desired font for the text.

Application Notes

- **Insert special text characters:** Turn to page 90.
- **Insert special edit items:** Turn to page 93.
- **Interactive copyfitting:** Fit text to a defined area by increasing or decreasing font size and space between letters. Turn to page 185.

Creating Designer Text Tags

One of the benefits of interactive design is speed. You see results quickly. Making changes to a long string of tags takes time to plan and execute. To give yourself even greater efficiency in on–screen

Creating Designer Text Tags
Page 177

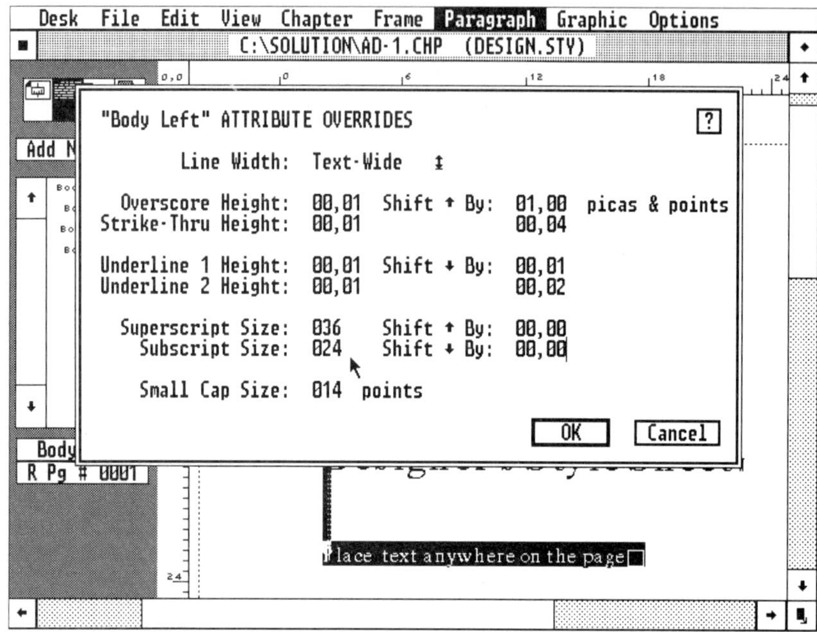

design, use Ventura's Attribute Overrides to build a system of designer text tags.

Attribute Overrides allow you to set custom values for the attributes displayed in the ***Text*** mode Side–Bar *for each paragraph tag in your style sheet.* You can use this capability to add additional features to the generic tags in your sketching style sheet, including:

- Assign up to four separate font sizes in a single tag.
- Assign up to two separate underline sizes in a single tag.
- Set underscores and overscores to automatically extend to the width of the current column.
- Define custom font size and baseline shift values for each tag.

By customizing the generic tags and keeping a key reference of special attributes defined in each one, you can design even more quickly from the screen and define text values *as* you type and see results immediately. In addition, you can assign up to 16 tab stops for each of the basic tags, permitting you to build a variety of different values into the tags for interactive design.

Recipe: Designer Text Tags

Step 1 **Identify design requirements**

Determine what specific design needs you want the style sheet to meet. List the font sizes and underlines you will be using most frequently with each of the generic tags.

Step 2 **Create master reference sheet**

To keep track of the custom elements assigned to each designer style sheet tag, create a reference sheet. Write down the name of each generic tag and leave space to record specific values encoded in it.

Step 3 **Set generic tag Attribute Overrides**

Enable ***Paragraph*** mode and select text for one of the generic tags in your style sheet. Access **PARAGRAPH•Attribute Overrides**.

Step 4 **Set multiple font sizes**

In addition to the default font size specified in the tag, you can assign up to three additional font sizes using Attribute Overrides features:

▲ **Small Cap Size:** Small caps can be any size you wish. Set the desired size in the space provided. To apply this font size in the ***Text*** mode, select Small in the Assignment List.

▲ **Superscript Size:** If you don't need superscript for this tag, zero out the Shift Up value, and enter another font size. To apply this font size in the ***Text*** mode, select Superscript in the Assignment List.

▲ **Subscript Size:** If you don't need subscript for this tag, zero out the shift down value, and enter another font size. To apply this font size in the ***Text*** mode, select Subscript in the Assignment List.

Step 5 **Set multiple underline sizes**

The ***Text*** mode lets you place a line over text (Overscore), through text (Strike–Thru), under text (Underline), and a double line under text (Double UnderLn). By altering the settings for these lines you can assign two custom underline sizes for each tag:

▲ **Underline 1 Height:** Enter the desired custom value for the ruling line and the desired shift down from text. Make this the thinner of the two rules. To apply this underline in the ***Text*** mode, select Underline in the Assignment List.

▲ **Underline 2 Height:** If you don't need the double underline effect, you can zero out, or match the Shift Down value for the first underline, and enter a thicker ruling line value. When you select Double UnderLn in the ***Text*** mode, this thicker line will overprint Underline 1.

Step 6 **Setting line width**

Depending on the key uses of the tag, you can define all rules to appear as the Text–Wide or Margin–Wide, which makes them automatically extend to the column margins.

Step 7 **Assign tab settings**

Access **PARAGRAPH•Tab Settings**. To build additional positioning values into each tag, you may assign up to 16 custom tab stops for each generic tag.

Application Notes

- **Multi–purpose tags:** Attribute overrides are one way to get multiple uses from a single paragraph tag. For other techniques, turn to page 160.
- **Brochures:** This technique is excellent for fast sketching out a brochure or other display layout. Assigning the enhanced tags to the function keys lets you see effects instantly on screen.
- **Save multiple drafts:** As you develop designs, save versions you like under different chapter file names. Ventura will automatically save a version of the text file which is loaded in the base page with the same name as the chapter. Print different chapter versions to view results.

Designing a Document with Frames

Text spacing is one of the most complex processes in document design. When determining spacing for multiple paragraph tags in a style sheet, it can be very time consuming going back and forth between the screen and a dialog box to get it just right.

When designing interactively, it is often helpful to use frames instead of ***Paragraph*** mode spacing controls. Then you can adjust spacing between text elements right on screen. There are two ways to use frames to draw space:

- **Snap to Interline:** When Line Snap is On, frames vertically snap in increments of Body Text interline spacing. So, if interline spacing is 1 pica, the smallest frame you can draw is 1 pica high but you can drag to resize it in increments of 1 pica each. However large or small the frame, it must be an exact multiple of Body Text interline spacing.
- **Freeform:** When Line Snap is Off, frames may be drawn to any height desired. Once the frame has been drawn, determine its exact height using the *Frame Height* line of the Sizing & Scaling dialog box.

Once you have completed the design, you can use the spacing frames as guides to build the spacing values into paragraph tags and transform the design into a permanent style sheet for use by yourself and others in the production department. Just select a spacing frame and access the **FRAME•Sizing & Scaling** dialog box. The Frame Height line will show you the exact space you have defined.

Recipe: Document Design with Frames

Step 1 **Set body text interline spacing**

Enable ***Paragraph*** mode and select a paragraph of Body Text. Access **PARAGRAPH•Spacing** and enter value for Interline spacing.

Step 2 **Set column grid**

Enable ***Frame*** mode. Access **FRAME•Margins & Columns** and set up desired number of columns in the page to serve as a column grid.

▲ Select **OPTIONS•Turn Column Snap On**. This forces a frame drawn close to a column guide to automatically "snap" to the column guide.

Designing a Document Using Frames
Page 180

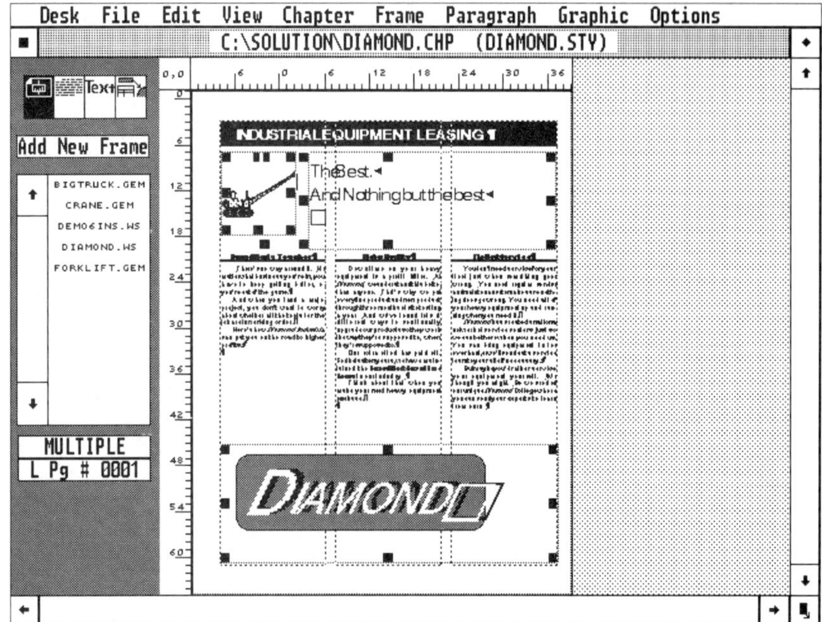

▲ Use this technique even if you don't want body text to pour into the columns. To let body text flow over the defined columns, enable ***Paragraph*** mode and access **PARAGRAPH•Alignment**. Set Overall Width to Frame–Wide.

Step 3 **Create headline frames**

Enable ***Frame*** mode and draw a frame to block an area for a headline. Enter headline text into frame or place it using a Box Text graphic.

Step 4 **Create illustration frames**

Draw frames to place illustrations in the layout. Use the column guides to snap them into the correct position.

Step 5 **Create text spacing frames**

Instead of building a system of paragraph tags with complex spacing values, draw one–line high frames between text paragraphs. This is an easy way to space text elements on–screen.

Application Notes

- **Use frames to determine spacing:** Designing interactively with frames allows you to see and accurately measure the amount of space between text elements on the page. For documents that are regularly produced, these spacing values should be encoded into paragraph tags in a finished style sheet.
- **Spacing with paragraph tags:** Turn to page 87.
- **Measure space with frames:** To measure space between different text elements, draw a frame and access **FRAME•Sizing & Scaling** to turn off Text Flow Around. Resize the frame over the area to be measured. To check the exact measurement, select the frame and access **FRAME•Sizing & Scaling**. The frame height line shows vertical distance and frame width shows horizontal measure.

Using Graphics to Position Text

In interactive design, determine the advantage of all layout tools before using them. For example, frames force text in the base page to flow around them, creating controlled areas on the page to display pictures, blocks of text, and block the layout. Graphics, on the other hand, do *not* displace text, so they do not help to block the layout. Ventura graphics, however, offer a wider selection of shapes and customizing attributes than frames do, and can easily contain short segments of text which makes them ideal for headlines, flowcharts, tables, and custom–design elements.

Graphics have the additional advantage that they can be linked to a frame, and can coexist with a picture file which is displayed in the frame. When you place text in a Box Text graphic and attach it to a frame, you can move the text anywhere you wish inside or outside of the frame. When the frame is copied or moved to another position, the Box Text graphic automatically travels with it.

In interactive design, graphics offer several advantages. After blocking out the page space with frames, Box Text graphics let you place headline and title elements anywhere in the frame with a stroke of your mouse. For elaborate headline or design elements, create a special frame and use graphic drawing forms with Box Text to draw

Using Graphics to Position Text
Page 183

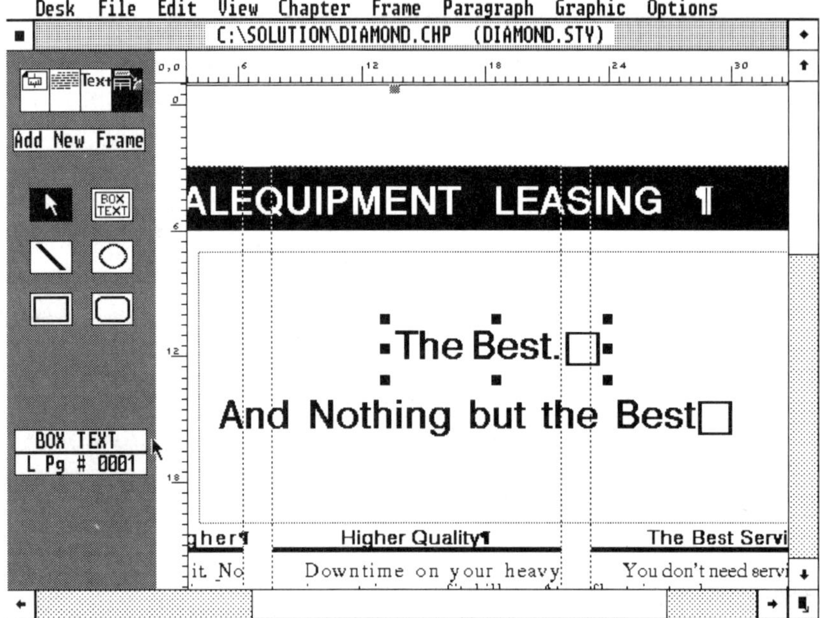

your design. The entire graphic cluster attaches to the frame and moves with it, on the page, to any place in the current chapter and between different documents.

Recipe: Graphics to Position Text

Step 1 **Draw blocking frame**

Enable ***Frame*** mode and use Add New Frame in the Side–Bar to draw the blocking frame.

Step 2 **Place text in box text graphic**

Enable ***Graphic*** mode and select the blocking frame. Select Box Text icon and draw the graphic in the blocking frame. Enter the desired text from the keyboard or load a file to the Text Cursor position.

Step 3 **Set Box Text attributes**

Set the desired attributes of the Box Text graphic using **GRAPHIC•Line Attributes** and **GRAPHIC•Fill Attributes**. If you want the graphic to be an invisible base for text, set the Line Attributes to None and the Fill Attributes to Hollow.

Step 4 **Position box text graphic**

Within the blocking frame, use the mouse to position the Box Text graphic. This avoids disrupting the rest of the layout while experimenting with placement of certain elements in the document.

Application Notes

- **Framing line:** Add framing lines around Box Text title graphics.
- **Background shading:** Set headline shading in the blocking frame or in the title graphic itself.
- **Drop shadow text:** Stack multiple graphics to create drop shadow text for headlines. Turn to page 311.
- **Soft text frame:** Use rounded rectangle graphic under box text graphic which has no framing line to create a soft, rounded box frame.
- **Stacking graphics:** Create a variety of design effects with stacked graphic forms. Turn to page 310.

Interactive Copyfitting

When designing documents interactively, you will often need to fit a particular string of text into a defined area in your layout. Ventura's two key features to help you copyfit your documents interactively are interactive kerning and interactive font sizing.

- **Interactive kerning:** allows you to adjust space between individual characters or track entire lines of text with tighter or looser character spacing.
- **Interactive font sizing:** This feature allows you to increase or decrease the font size of selected text in one point increments and see the results on screen. This feature works best when a printer format, such as PostScript, which supports incremental fonts, has been selected.

Recipe: Individual Character Kerning

Step 1 **Select character**

Enable ***Text*** mode. For a better view, select **VIEW•Enlarged View** and use the mouse to select the individual character to be kerned.

Step 2 **Kern character**

Individual character kerning adds or removes space to the right of the selected character.

▲ To decrease space between the selected character and text to its right, press and hold the Shift key while repeatedly pressing the Left Arrow key on your keyboard.

▲ To increase space between the selected character and text to its right, press and hold the Shift key while repeatedly pressing the Right Arrow key on your keyboard.

Recipe: Headline and Text Tracking

Step 1 **Select text**

Enable ***Text*** mode and select entire string of text to be tracked.

Interactive Copyfitting
Page 185

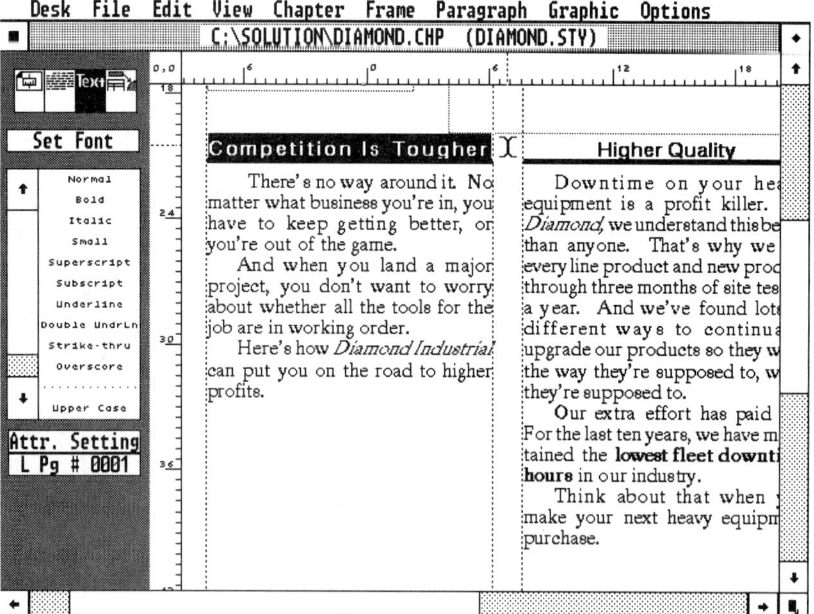

Step 2 **Track text tighter or looser**

Interactive tracking adds uniform spacing between all characters in the selected text string.

▲ To decrease character spacing and tighten the appearance of the text, press and hold the Shift key while repeatedly pressing the Left Arrow key on your keyboard.

▲ To increase character spacing and loosen the appearance of the text, press and hold the Shift key while repeatedly pressing the Right Arrow key on your keyboard.

Step 3 **Setting tracking value in the tag**

When tracking selected text interactively, the exact tracking value is recorded in the Set Font dialog box. By entering the tracking value from Set Font into the **PARAGRAPH•Paragraph Typography** box for the paragraph tag, you can uniformly apply the same tracking to all text using the tag. This is useful when creating special headlines and other text elements.

Recipe: Interactive Font Size Editing

Step 1 **Select text**

Enable ***Text*** mode and select the individual character or string of text you wish to resize.

Step 2 **Resize text**

Interactive font sizing increases and decreases the font size in one point increments, providing you have installed a printer format, such as PostScript, which supports fonts in one point increments.

▲ To increase the font size of selected text, press and hold the Shift key while repeatedly pressing the Up Arrow key.

▲ To decrease the font size of selected text, press and hold the Shift key while repeatedly pressing the Down Arrow key.

Application Notes

- **Preview tracking:** The exact numeric value for the amount that selected text has been kerned is displayed in the Set Font dialog box. By interactively tracking text on screen, you can then enter the numeric value into a paragraph tag and track all text to that same value. To do this, enter the kern value displayed in Set Font into the Tracking line in the **PARAGRAPH•Paragraph Typography** dialog box.

- **Preview font size:** The exact font size for interactively copyfit text is displayed in the Set Font dialog box. By interactively sizing text on screen, you can then enter the correct point size into a paragraph tag using the **PARAGRAPH•Font** dialog box.

CHAPTER 5

The Automatic Document

Letting Your Computer Do the Work

Think for a moment about all of the steps necessary to publish a book: Planning, outlining, writing, editing, revising, illustrating, and proofreading are just a few. To produce a quality book and on deadline takes many skilled individuals and a great deal of time and effort. Wouldn't it be great if your computer could do a lot of the work...automatically?

With Ventura Publisher, it is possible to do just that. Ventura is designed to perform *batch processing*. In layman's language, that means Ventura uses the computer's power to perform repetitive editing and processing tasks, leaving you free to work on more important things.

Paragraph tags are the most visible example of Ventura's batch processing power. Tags enable you to set typeset values for specific text elements in every style sheet. When you want to change the font for a headline, you change the font in the tag for that headline *once*...and every other occurrence of that headline is changed *automatically*. Even on a 500–page book!

5.0 VENTURA USER INTERFACE

5.1 WYSIWYG

Ventura Publisher is designed to provide What You See (on the screen) Is What You Get printed (WYSIWYG). This means that the computer display should match as closely as possible, at all times, what you will see on the final printed page. Of course, the difference between the technology used to display a page on a CRT screen, and the technologies used to print a page on a laser printer or typesetter, do create some unavoidable differences. In particular, because the computer CRT screen cannot produce anywhere near the same resolution of a printer or typesetter, and because what is displayed is shown in a different aspect ratio (height to width ratio), the space between words and between lines may appear to be bigger or smaller than the printed page under certain circumstances. Several thin ruling lines, with little space between, may show on the screen as one thick line.

Keyboard Keys

Various keys on the keyboard perform special functions:
- The keyboard Cursor keys control the Text Cursor.
- The Home key goes to the first page of the document.
- The End key goes to the last page of the document.
- The Pg Up key goes to the previous page.
- The Pg Dn key goes to the next page.

5.2 ITEM SELECTOR

Description and Application

The display shown in Figure 10-2 is called an Item Selector. The Item Selector is used for saving and retrieving files.

The Item Selector allows you to save and retrieve files by pointing to the file name, or by typing the file name.

The Item Selector also provides a simple way to move between various DOS subdirectories (sometimes called folders) where text, Line Art, Image, chapter, and publication files may be stored.

Finally, the Item Selector automatically "filters" the files displayed so that you need only search for files which match specified criteria. For instance, only chapter files (which are stored with a file extension CHP) are displayed when loading or saving chapters. The method for filtering the files to be displayed follows standard DOS conventions, including wildcard characters (e.g. * and ?).

Ventura Publisher Features & Operations 5-1

Technical Reference Manual: For long documents containing technical material or reference information, auto-numbering and other automatic features can be used to make it easier to locate specific information anywhere in the document. Text is typeset in ITC Bookman.

And paragraph tags are just one of the automatic features in Ventura Publisher. This section presents a series of techniques you can use to set up automatic features throughout documents—long *and* short—that will save you time and effort in editing, revising, and publishing even the most complicated documents.

Using Tags as an Organizing System

As mentioned before, paragraph tags are used to typeset text. Each style sheet contains a list of custom tags which contain the correct values for all document elements.

In addition to typesetting text, the list of tags in the style sheet acts as key codes in the automatic document organizing system. For example, when you want to place sequential numbers on all major headings throughout your document, you use the name of the tag for the major heading to identify the text to be numbered.

A number of Ventura features have the capability to search and access information directly from a document using the tag names in a style sheet, including auto–numbering, headers & footers and table of contents. So when using automatic features, it is important to develop a simple, consistent system of paragraph tags for the major elements in a document.

Tools for Automatic Documents

Tools for automatic editing and organizing are found primarily on the Chapter and Paragraph menus. These tools let you develop document–wide systems in the style sheet and the chapter file that reduce the amount of production organization and special handling, especially for long document applications.

- **Auto–Numbering** sets up custom document–wide automatic numbering systems based upon paragraph tags in the style sheet. Auto–numbering features can be configured to automatically number sections and subsections, lists, and outlines.

- **Headers & Footers** sets up header and footer lines which automatically appear on each page of the document. Custom features allow automatic insertion of the current heading or other information directly into the header and footer line.

- **Breaks** permit sophisticated control of text positioning between pages and columns, as well as building linkages that force two more tags to appear on the same page or in the same column with each other.
- **Paragraph menu** contains typographic design features which are used to create custom presentation of Ventura–generated elements like auto–numbers and header and footer lines.

Automatic Document Organization

This chapter contains recipes describing the use of Ventura features for automatic document organizing and editing. Initial techniques cover applications with auto–numbering features, including outlines and auto–numbered section and sub–section headings. Recipes cover special applications with auto–numbering including automatically numbered lists and special methods to customize auto–numbering capability.

Additional recipes cover automatic text positioning and editing with breaks which can significantly reduce editing time on long document applications. Header and footers are covered, including a variety of enhancements they include for automatic insertion of text.

By designing documents to get the most out of Ventura's automatic document features, a publishing system can more easily meet its deadlines.

Designing Auto–numbering Systems

Ventura gives you the power to automatically number the text associated with one or more tags in a style sheet. The value of this is obvious for technical documents and legal applications which contain numbered sections and subsections. But there is much more to Ventura's auto–numbering capability than that.

To begin with, you can automatically "number" text with both number *and* letter sequences. You can control the start point of the

Designing Auto-numbering Systems

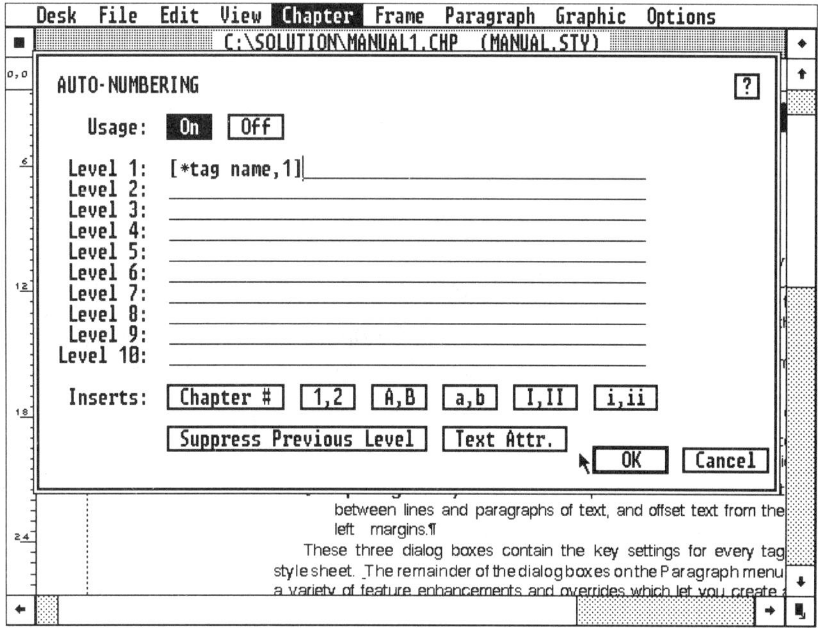

numeric sequence and automatically force the numbering to begin at any point in the document. You may develop a complete multi–level document numbering system to number many different elements in your document.

It is important to plan auto–numbering requirements before setting them up in the dialog box. The many different techniques and effects you can create with auto–numbering are detailed in the sections that follow, but the basic effects can be broken down into these four areas:

- **Outlines:** Use upper and lowercase alphabet and Roman numerals, to automatically number multiple level outlines.
- **Section numbering:** Set up automatic numbering of sections in a document. Then, when edits are made to the text, all sections automatically renumber to reflect the new order.
- **Multi–level section numbering:** Automatically number a series of levels in a document. Assign a different numbering system for each level, or develop an incremental multi–sectional system in which each level reflects the numbers of the sections above it.

- **Automatically restarting lists:** You can number lists and steps in your documents and automatically restart the numbering to 1 or any other number at specific points in text.

Auto–numbering uses paragraph tags to find the text to be numbered. To set up auto–numbering, you must specify a *tag name* to be auto numbered. Ventura then searches straight through the chapter and numbers each occurrence of the tag.

This planning process for setting up auto–numbering makes short work of designing a system for your application.

Recipe: Style sheet for Auto–numbering

Auto–numbering is a generated feature of Ventura Publisher. Each auto–number is a separate generated paragraph which is placed opposite its reference text by manipulating the line breaks of the auto–number and its reference text. Setting the generated auto–number tag with a Line Break: Before and the reference text with a Line Break: After allow the two of them to appear opposite one another on the same line.

When designing a style sheet which includes auto–number features, you should begin by setting the line break for Body Text to After. All headlines and other standard document elements based upon Body Text will also have a line break After. Using this approach, you can simply set the generated auto–number tags with Before line breaks and they can vertically align without the need to create special matching tags with complicated configurations of line breaks.

If you are designing the document using a text file containing embedded tag names, change the Body Text line break in the new style sheet *before* loading the text file. By doing this, all embedded tags in the style sheet will automatically be given the same After line break as Body Text, saving you a great deal of tag editing time.

Step 1 **Create new style sheet**

Load DEFAULT.STY from the \TYPESET subdirectory or another basic style sheet. Access **FILE•Save As New Style** to save the style sheet under a new name.

Step 2 **Set Body Text line breaks**

Enable ***Text*** mode and click the mouse on the Working Area. Type a few words on screen. Enable ***Paragraph*** mode and select the text. Access **PARAGRAPH • Breaks** and set Line Break to After.

Step 3 **Load text file**

Enable ***Frame*** mode. Access **FILE • Load Text/Picture** to load text file into document.

Step 4 **Design paragraph tags**

Design the special headings in the style sheet using the appropriate method.

▲ **Build from Body Text:** If you have placed no tag names into the text file, build all new tags from Body Text so they all carry a Line Break: After.

▲ **Set embedded tag values:** If you have placed tag names into the text file, select text for each tag and define values individually for each tag.

Recipe: Single Level Auto–numbering System

Step 1 **Identify text to number**

Decide which text elements you want to number. Make sure that all text for a given element carries the same tag name.

Step 2 **Select number format**

Access **CHAPTER • Auto–Numbering** and turn Usage to On. Place the cursor on Level 1. Select the numbering format for Level 1 by pointing at one of the alpha–numeric formats at the bottom of the screen. A bracketed entry will appear at Level 1.

Step 3 **Enter tag name**

Use keyboard arrow keys to move cursor inside the bracketed entry. Delete only the words *tag name*, leaving all other characters and brackets untouched. Type the name of the tag to be numbered inside the brackets. For example, to auto–number the tag name MAJOR

HEADING with Arabic numerals, the bracketed entry will appear: **[*MAJOR HEADING,1]**.

Step 4 **Specify punctuation**

Imagine that the bracketed expression is the auto–number itself. If the auto–number is to be followed by punctuation such as a period or dash, type it immediately after the final bracket, or leave extra space as desired.

Recipe: Auto–number Tag Position

Ventura generates auto–numbers internally and places them on the screen as *generated text* which carry *generated paragraph tags.* You may not make text edits to the numbers you see on the screen. All changes to the number sequence must be made through settings in the Auto–Numbering dialog box.

You can control the typographic attributes and position of the auto–number text by directly editing its generated tag. All auto–number tags begin with Z_SEC. For example, the tag for the Level 1 auto–number is Z_SEC1.

When auto–numbers are first printed into your document, they appear as separate paragraphs on a different line from the reference text. To place auto–numbers on the same line as reference text, you must change the break settings to remove the line break between the auto–number and the reference text.

Step 1 **Set auto–number font**

Enable ***Paragraph*** mode and select the auto–number tag. Verify that the correct Z_SEC tag appears in the Current Selection Box. The auto–number will appear in the same font as Body Text. To change it, access **PARAGRAPH•Font** and select the desired typeface, size, and style.

Step 2 **Set auto–number line break**

With the auto–number tag selected, access **PARAGRAPH•Breaks**. Set Line Break to Before.

Step 3 **Set text alignment and offset**

There are two ways to align the auto–number opposite its reference text. Using alignment features sets a standard distance between the auto-number and its reference text. As the auto-number gets longer, the reference text indents more to accommodate it. Using spacing features locks the auto-number to a set position on the page. As it gets longer, it expands to the left of that position.

▲ **Offset with Alignment:** Select the tag for reference text. Verify that the correct tag appears in the Current Selection Box. Access **PARAGRAPH•Alignment**. To automatically offset the reference text the width of the auto number, set Relative Indent to On. To add additional space between the auto number and the text, set First Line to Indent, and set In/Outdent Width to 01,00 picas & points. To ensure that all lines of the paragraph line up correctly, change In/Outdent Height to 100 lines.

▲ **Hanging indent with Spacing:** Select the tag for the auto–number, beginning with Z_SEC. Place cursor where you wish the right edge of all auto–numbers to appear and measure the distance to the right margin guide. Access **PARAGRAPH•Spacing** and enter the measurement on the In From Right line. The auto–number characters will all line up at the same point on the page opposite their reference text.

Step 4 **Remove line break**

With text tag selected, access **PARAGRAPH•Breaks**. Change Line Break to After. This removes the line break between the number and the text and allows the two tags to appear on the same line in your document.

Recipe: Custom Number Sequences

For some applications, you will want to begin the auto–numbering sequence with a number other than one. To do so, place the beginning number inside the auto–number bracketed entry in the **CHAPTER•Auto–Numbering** dialog box.

Step 1 **Select beginning number**

Decide on the number to begin auto–numbering sequence. Access **CHAPTER•Auto–Numbering** and place cursor on the auto-number level line to be edited.

Step 2 **Enter start number**

Use keyboard arrow keys to move inside the bracketed entry. Place the cursor on the final bracket. Type a comma (,) and the new starting number. You can enter any pure number even if it has more than one digit. For example, to begin the numbering sequence for the tag MAJOR HEADING with the number 5, the bracketed expression would be: **[*MAJOR HEADING,1,5]**

▲ To start numbering with zero, enter 0.

▲ To start numbering with 1,000, enter 1000.

▲ To start numbering with 587, enter 587.

☞ CAUTION: Use only complete numbers. Do not enter any numbers containing letter characters, such as A100.

Step 3 **Enter start for roman or alphabet numbering**

To start alphabet sequence at a number other than A or a, enter the sequence number of the desired alphabet character into the brackets. For example, to begin the numbering sequence for the tag MAJOR HEADING with the letter C, the bracketed expression would be: **[*MAJOR HEADING,A,3]**. Use the same technique to set custom number starts for Roman numerals.

▲ To start numbering with F, enter 6.

▲ To start numbering with Z, enter 26.

▲ To start numbering with IX, enter 9.

Application Notes

- **Automatic chapter number:** Integrate chapter number with any level of auto–numbering by placing the Chapter # symbol in the appropriate place on the desired level. Set chapter number start and format in **CHAPTER•Update Counters**

- **Match heading:** Combine the auto–number with heading to form a unified design element. Turn to page 150.

Create Multi–level Auto–numbering Systems

Auto–numbering enables you to simultaneously number multiple levels within your document. You can use this capability to create a continuous section numbering system, an automatic alphanumeric outline, or a combination of both.

When you design multi–level auto–numbering, you assign numbers to a series of different tags in the style sheet. And, you may specify a completely different number or alphabet format for each level in the system.

When designing auto–numbering, keep in mind that the auto–numbering default is to "carry down" numbers from level to level. In a system in which all levels are numbered with Arabic numerals, each level down includes the numbers of all the levels that have gone before it.

Create Multi-level Auto-numbering Systems

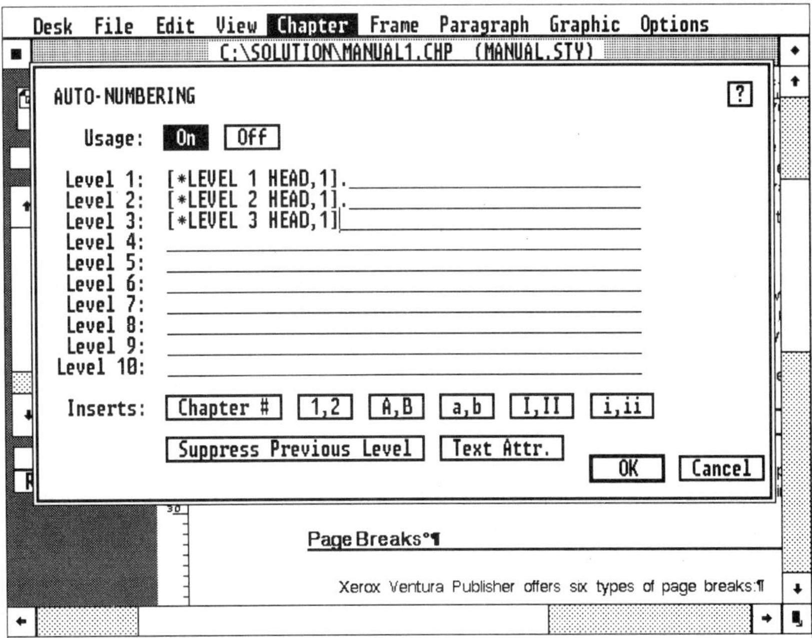

- Level 1 is **1**
- Level 2 is **1.1**
- Level 3 is **1.1.1**
- Level 4 is **1.1.1.1**

You can override the default using the Suppress Previous Level selection at the bottom of the Auto–Numbering dialog box. When the Suppress Previous Level symbol is placed at the beginning of a level entry line, it prevents the auto–number from the previous level(s) from carrying down, allowing the number on this level to stand alone. Using Suppress Previous Level, you can design many custom auto numbering systems including standard outline formats that look like this:

- Level 1 is **I.** (Upper case Roman Numerals)
- Level 2 is **A.** (Upper case alphabet)
- Level 3 is **1.** (Arabic numerals)
- Level 4 is **a.** (Lower case alphabet)

Design multi–level auto–numbering systems with Body Text and all standard document elements with line breaks set to After. This allows each level of generated auto–number elements to be tagged with a line break Before and vertically align to the correct position opposite its reference text.

The techniques shown here describe various ways that you can configure your multi–level auto–numbering system to meet the particular requirements of your application.

Recipe: Multi–level Auto–numbering

Step 1 **Identify text to number**

Decide which text elements are to be numbered. Make sure that all text for a given element carries the same tag name. To number more than one tag, decide the order of the tags to be numbered.

Step 2 **Select number format**

Access **CHAPTER•Auto–Numbering** and turn Usage to On. Place the cursor on Level 1. Select the numbering format for Level 1 by selecting one of the alphanumeric formats at the bottom of the screen. A bracketed entry will appear on the Level 1 line.

Step 3 **Enter tag name**

Use keyboard arrow keys to move cursor inside the bracketed entry. Delete only the words *tag name*, leaving all other characters and brackets untouched. Type the name of the tag to be numbered inside the brackets.

Step 4 **Specify punctuation**

Imagine that the bracketed expression is the auto–number itself. If the auto–number is to be followed by punctuation such as a period or dash, type it immediately after the final bracket, or leave extra space as desired.

Step 5 **Enter additional levels**

Place text cursor on the next available level in the **CHAPTER•Auto–Numbering** dialog box. Enter the tags to be auto–numbered.

▲ **To suppress previous level:** To prevent the number from the previous level from carrying down to the present level, place the cursor at the beginning of the current level line and select Suppress Previous Level. A bracketed minus sign [–] appears.

Application Notes

- **Match heading:** Combine auto–number with heading to create a uniform design element. Turn to page 150.
- **Designing long documents:** Turn to page 43.

Creating Auto–numbers with Built–in Text

To create more sophisticated auto–numbering effects, you can enter text directly on any level line in the **CHAPTER•Auto–Numbering** dialog box and the text will print out *as part of the auto–number itself.* This makes step numbering throughout a document possible. Enter the word *Step* on the auto–numbering line and it will appear in the document as part of the auto–number.

Text can be placed before or after the auto–number bracketed entry. To understand how the expression will look on the page, imagine that the bracketed entry is the auto–number character. Type text, set punctuation, and leave space accordingly.

Recipe: Auto–numbers with Built–in Text

Step 1 **Identify text to number**

Decide which text elements are to be numbered. Make sure that all text for a given element carries the same tag name. To number more than one tag, decide the order of tags to be numbered.

Creating Auto-numbers with Built-in Text

```
Desk  File  Edit  View  Chapter  Frame  Paragraph  Graphic  Options
E:\BANTAM\05-VPSB.CHP  (VP-BOOK.STY)

AUTO-NUMBERING                                          [?]

   Usage:  [On]  [Off]

   Level 1:  [-][*L1 HEAD][*L2 HEAD][*L3 HEAD]
   Level 2:  Step [*STEP,1]
   Level 3:
   Level 4:
   Level 5:
   Level 6:
   Level 7:
   Level 8:
   Level 9:
  Level 10:

   Inserts:  [Chapter #] [1,2] [A,B] [a,b] [I,II] [i,ii]
             [Suppress Previous Level] [Text Attr.]
                                              [OK] [Cancel]
```

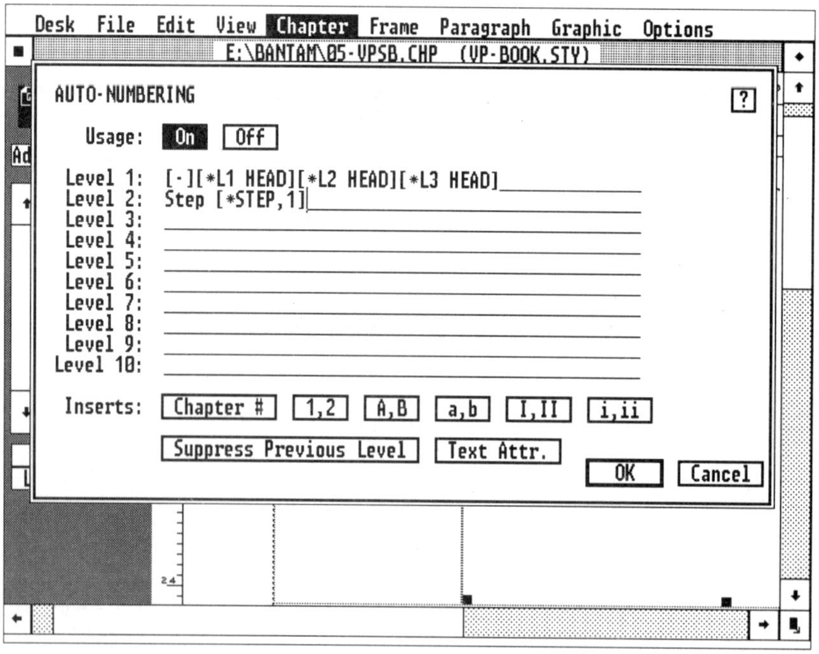

Step 2 **Select number format**

Access **CHAPTER•Auto–Numbering** and turn Usage to On. Place the cursor on Level 1. Select the numbering format for Level 1 by selecting one of the alphanumeric formats at the bottom of the screen. A bracketed entry will appear on the Level 1 line.

Step 3 **Enter tag name**

Use keyboard arrow keys to move cursor inside the bracketed entry. Delete only the words *tag name*, leaving all other characters and brackets untouched. Type the name of the tag to be numbered inside the brackets.

Step 4 **Enter text**

Use keyboard arrows to position cursor where text will appear on the Level line. Enter the text either before or after the bracketed expression. Use the Spacebar to leave a space between the bracketed expression and the text.

Step 5 **Specify punctuation**

Imagine that the bracketed expression is the auto–number itself. If the auto–number is to be followed by punctuation such as a period or dash, type it immediately after the final bracket, or leave extra space accordingly.

Application Notes

- **Automatic text placement:** Auto–numbering can place a set string of text for every occurrence of a named tag *without the auto–number*. Enter the name of the tag in the brackets on the auto–number line, and delete the number format inside the brackets. Type text on the same auto–number level line.
- **Use custom text attributes:** Assign text enhancements or custom font values to the auto–number text or the number itself. The procedure is the same as those used for custom edits to headers and footers. Turn to page 239.

- **Cross referencing:** Place auto–number cross–references into text using Professional Extension cross–referencing features. Turn to page 408.

Numbering Lists Automatically

Auto–numbering features can be configured to number lists and automatically restart numbering at 1 (or any defined alphanumeric value) at any place in the document. This application is very useful if you are editing a long document containing a series of numbered lists. As you edit the elements in the list, Ventura will *automatically* renumber all of the lists without any editing or reentry on your part. This feature was used to number all of the steps in this book.

To create an automatically restarting list, you must set auto–numbering values for two tags:

- **Restart tag:** This tag, usually a heading, or subheading, that is set to restart the auto–numbering.
- **List tag:** This tag displays the listed item.

Numbering Lists Automatically

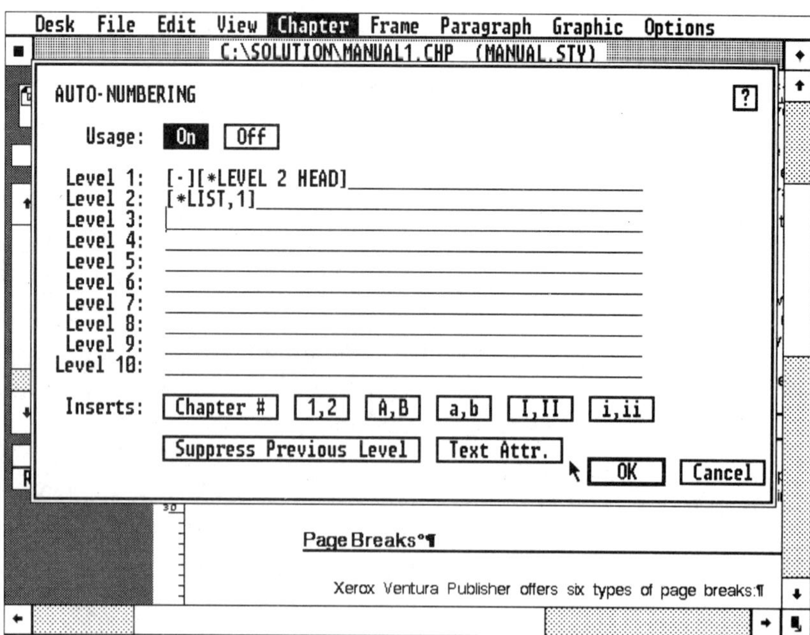

To set up a simple auto–numbering system for restarting lists, place the restart tag on Level 1 or the next available level in the **CHAPTER•Auto–Numbering** dialog box. Then delete the number format character inside the brackets to suppress the numbering and a Suppress Previous Level before it. Now set the list tag to auto–number on the next level.

When Ventura searches through your file and finds the restart tag, it doesn't number it because you have disabled the numbering, and the Suppress Previous Level resets all numbering up to this point back to the original point for tags on levels below. The result is that the List tag restarts numbering.

By using a subheading as the restart tag, set up a system where Ventura goes through a file sequentially numbering all List tags it finds after a certain subheading. When it finds that subheading again, it restarts numbering the List tags after that from 1, or the beginning number you have specified. If you have more than one list in subsections of the document, use Body Text as the restart tag. Every paragraph of body text in your document will then automatically restart a list sequence to 1.

Recipe: Automatically Numbering Lists

Step 1 **Identify list and restart tags**

Decide which text element in your document is to be numbered and which will be the restart tag. Make sure that all the text for a given element carries the same tag name.

Step 2 **Set–up restart tag**

Access **CHAPTER•Auto–Numbering** and turn Usage to On. Place cursor on Level 1, or next available Level. Select Suppress Previous Level. Now, select number format **1,2** from the bottom of the screen. Using keyboard arrows, move cursor inside the bracketed entry. Delete the text *tag name, 1* from inside the bracketed entry. Type in the name of the restart tag. *Enter no text or punctuation on this line.*

Step 3 **Select List number format**

Place the cursor on Level 2, or next available Level. Select the numbering format for Level 1 by pointing at one of the alphanumeric formats at the bottom of the screen. A bracketed entry will appear at Level 1.

Step 4 **Enter List tag name**

Use keyboard arrow keys to move cursor inside the bracketed entry. Delete only the words *tag name*, leaving all other characters and brackets untouched. Type the name of the tag to be numbered.

Step 5 **Specify List punctuation**

Imagine that the bracketed expression is the auto–number itself. For the auto–number to be followed by punctuation such as a period or dash, type it immediately after the final bracket, or leave extra space accordingly.

Step 6 **Position number and text**

To place the auto–number and its reference text on the same line, set line breaks so that the auto–number tag has a Line Break value of Before and the reference text has a Line Break value of After.

Recipe: Multiple Level Restart System

In some documents, you may have lists appearing under a major heading and a variety of subheadings and therefore cannot set up a single restart tag. In these cases, set up multiple restart tags on the same Level. This allows you to set list numbering to automatically restart after two or three different tags. This technique was used in this book to force lists of steps to restart to one after both topic headings and recipe headings.

Step 1 **Identify list and restart tags**

Decide which text element is to be numbered and which will be the restart tags. Make sure that all the text for a given element carries the same tag name.

Step 2 **Setup restart tag**

Access **CHAPTER•Auto–Numbering** and turn Usage to On.

▲ **First restart tag:** Place cursor on Level 1, or next available level. Select Suppress Previous Level. Now, select number format **1,2** from the bottom of the screen. Using keyboard arrows, move cursor inside the bracketed entry. Delete the text *tag name, 1* from inside the bracketed entry. Type in the name of the restart tag.

▲ **Additional restart tags:** *Leave cursor on the same level as the first restart tag.* Verify that cursor is placed immediately after the last bracket in the bracketed entry. Select number format **1,2** at the bottom of the screen and delete the text *tag name, 1* from inside the brackets. Type the name of the second restart tag inside the brackets. To place a third restart tag name, repeat this process, staying on the same level as the first restart tag.

Step 3 **Enter the List tag**

Place the cursor on Level 2, or next available level. Set up the List tag as described previously.

Recipe: Set up a Free Restart

For some applications, it may be helpful to define a tag to restart list numbering at any place you like. This can be accomplished by creating a free restart tag which you can insert into the text at any point.

A free restart tag works very much like a page break. It is a simple body text tag which you apply to a free paragraph return. By giving the free restart tag no line break, no line height, and outdenting it slightly from your document margin, it doesn't affect the display of your document text. Then it is set up in the **CHAPTER•Auto–Numbering** dialog box as the restart tag for lists.

To use the restart tag, pull down a free paragraph return and apply it to the return, and Renumber the chapter. When selected, it has no effect on the rest of your text except to restart the auto-numbered lists.

Step 1 **Define free restart tag**

Enable ***Text*** mode and place your cursor on the end of a paragraph. Pull down a free paragraph return. Enable ***Paragraph*** mode and select the free return. Use Add New Tag in the Side–Bar to name the free restart tag.

Step 2 **Position free restart**

To outdent the free restart, access **PARAGRAPH•Alignment**. Change First Line to Outdent and set In/Outdent value to 01,00 picas & points. This places the free paragraph return slightly outside left margin or in the gutter to the left of column.

▲ If the free restart does not move outside the left margin, it may contain a spacing offset. To remove this offset, access **PARAGRAPH•Spacing** and zero out the In From Left line.

Step 3 **Remove extra spacing**

To remove extra spacing that could affect your document text from the free restart, Access **PARAGRAPH•Spacing** and zero out the Above, Below, and Inter–paragraph entries.

Step 4 **Adjust free restart line breaks**

Access **PARAGRAPH•Breaks** and change Line Break to No. This permits the document text to flow naturally as if the free restart tag were not there.

☞ CAUTION: If the free restart tag appears at the top of a page preceding a heading or other tag with a line break Before, Above space for that tag will be added in. To eliminate this problem, set Body Text and all standard document headings with line break After.

Step 5 **Set free restart auto–numbering**

Access **CHAPTER•Auto–Numbering**. Place cursor on Level 1, or next available level. Select Suppress Previous Level. Now, select number format **1,2** from the bottom of the screen. Using keyboard arrows, move cursor inside the bracketed entry. Delete the text *tag name,1* from inside the bracketed entry. Type in the name of the free restart tag.

Step 6 **Set List auto–numbering**

Place the cursor on Level 2, or next available level. Set up the List as described before.

Application Notes

- **Auto–numbering style sheet:** Design auto–numbering style sheet with all line breaks set to After to save time and special tags. Turn to page 192
- **Step lists:** Number all steps or similar items in a document. Step numbers in this book were placed and sequenced using automatic restarting lists.
- **Numbered bullets:** For ease of reference, use automatically restarting lists instead of bullets to display key data.
- **Cross referencing:** Place auto–number cross–references into text using Professional Extension cross–referencing features. Turn to page 408.

Designing Production Auto-numbering Systems

Auto–numbering systems can be used even for documents that do not include auto–numbered elements. A document production auto–numbering system can be created which numbers headings, subheadings, and any other document element. These auto–numbers can be used as the basis of marker names used for cross–referencing and other production purposes.

By outdenting the auto–number from the left margin and removing all line breaks, the auto–number won't affect the text layout in the page. Yet the auto–numbers can be used for a variety of final production purposes. When placing markers for Professional Extension cross–referencing systems, enter names based on the auto–

numbers. When printing drafts of the document, the auto–numbers printed on the side of the page make it easy to edit and find specific sections of information. To hide the auto–numbers on screen or the printed page, simply change the font color for the auto–number tags to white.

Recipe: Production Auto–numbers

Step 1 **Set up auto–numbering system**

Access **CHAPTER•Auto–Numbering** and set up auto–numbering system for all headings and other document elements.

Step 2 **Set outdent from margin**

Enable ***Paragraph*** mode and select the auto–number generated tag. Access **PARAGRAPH•Alignment**. Set First Line to Outdent and enter a small value for In/Outdent Width, about 01,00 picas & points.

▲ If the paragraph return does not appear outside the left margin guide, it may have a spacing offset built in. To correct this, access **PARAGRAPH•Spacing** and zero out In From Left.

Designing Production Auto-numbering Systems

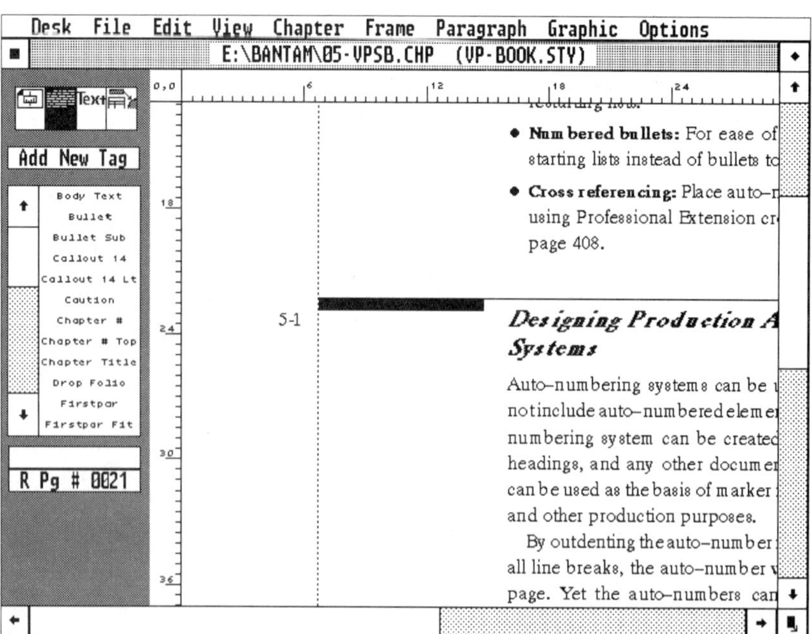

Step 3 **Remove extra spacing**

To remove extra spacing which could affect the position of the production auto–number, access **PARAGRAPH • Spacing** and zero out Above, Below, and Inter–Paragraph spacing values.

Step 4 **Remove line break**

Set Line Break to No. This makes the tag invisible to other tags and lets them align normally beside it.

☞ CAUTION: If production auto number tags appears at the top of a page preceding a heading or other tag with a line break Before, Above space for that tag will be added in. To eliminate this problem, set Body Text and all standard document headings with line break After.

Step 5 **Outdent additional tags**

Repeat the process described above for each additional level of auto–numbering.

Step 6 **Hide production auto–number**

To hide the production auto–number on screen or for draft printing, enable ***Paragraph*** mode and select auto–number tag. Access **PARA-GRAPH • Font** and set color to White.

Application Notes

- **Cross–reference markers:** Use sequential auto–numbers to set marker names for Professional Extension cross–referencing. Number a system of headings, subheadings and other elements in long documents.
- **Frame anchor names:** For each illustrated heading or subheading, use the same auto–number to enter the frame anchor name.
- **Print production auto–number list:** Use table of contents feature to sort a reference list of all headings with the correct production auto–number. Turn to page 370.

Editing Automatically with Breaks

Longform and technical publications often have complex designs which make use of bullets, auto–numbered headings, lists, and illustrated elements. One of the most time–consuming tasks in publishing such documents is repeatedly printing out and reviewing text to make sure all elements appear on the correct pages.

Ventura Publisher gives you the power to control a great many text/design relationships *automatically* through the use of breaks.

On a typewriter, you have one type of break: a carriage return at the end of each line. Ventura breaks are simply custom carriage returns which can be placed before and after lines. In addition, you can use Ventura breaks to control the relationship of text elements between pages and columns. And finally, Ventura lets you define break relationships between tags which force certain tags to appear with other tags and to prevent breaks within a text paragraph.

Some of the automatic features that you can build into a style sheets with breaks are:

- **Headings & Subheads:** Use breaks to force them to appear on the same page or in the same column as their reference text.
- **Section headings:** Use breaks to automatically position them at the top of a page or column. Page breaks provide the option of forcing the text to appear either at the top of the next left page or right page.
- **Section endings:** Use breaks to automatically move the next text element to the following page or column.
- **Fitted paragraph element tags:** Use breaks to create a series of tags with different attributes that fit into a single paragraph.
- **Page blocking:** Use breaks to automatically block specified pages in a document without drawing frames.
- **Solid paragraphs:** Use breaks to prevent paragraphs from breaking over pages or columns.
- **Link lists and sections:** Use breaks to force elements in a list to appear on the same page.

Editing Automatically with Breaks

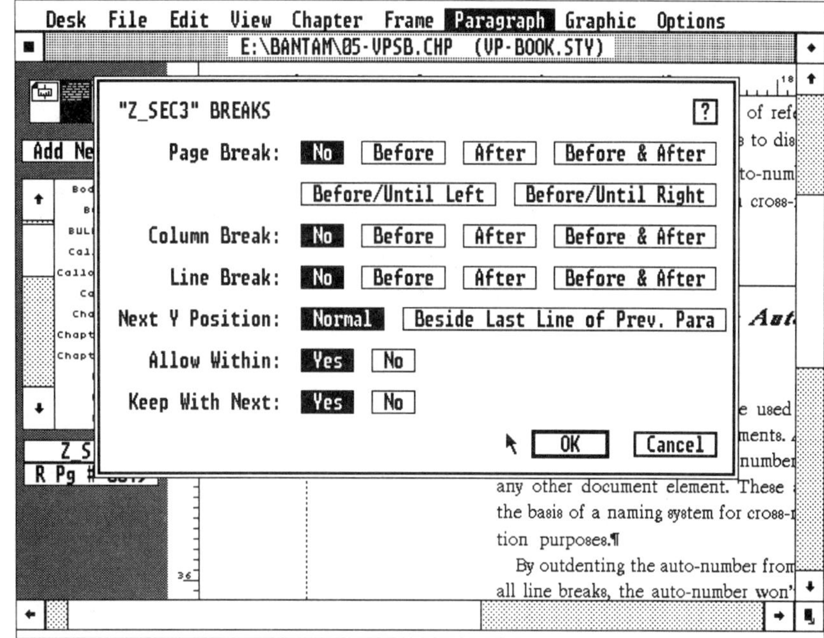

Recipe: Designing with Breaks

Step 1 **Select text**

Enable ***Paragraph*** mode and select the text carrying the tag to be edited.

Step 2 **Set line break**

Access **PARAGRAPH • Breaks**. Check the line break setting for the tag. There are basically two ways that tags can be set up to relate to other text in the document.

▲ **Standard document elements:** To prevent text from different tags from overprinting on screen, there must be a line break between each paragraph. For example, if Body Text is set with a Line Break: After, then line breaks for tags for most other document elements including headings, bullets, and lists should be set with Line Break: After as well.

▲ **Special text effects:** Many special text presentation effects including stacked tags, vertical tabs, auto–numbering, and production page breaks are created by removing line breaks between two or more tags. Check line breaks to make sure that tags for these special text effects have line breaks set correctly.

Step 3 **Set page or column break**

If a tag is to carry an automatic page or column break, set the value.

- ▲ **Break Before:** These push the tagged text to the top of the next page or column.
- ▲ **Break After:** These push text *following* the tag to the top of the next page or column.
- ▲ **Breaks Before & After:** These place the tagged text as the *only* text on the page or in the column.

Step 4 **Set automatic controls**

To automatically control relationships between tags, there are two special features.

- ▲ **Keep With Next:** Forces tagged text to appear on the same page or in the same column with the tagged text immediately following. Use for headings and multiple–tag effects like stacked tags and vertical tabs.
- ▲ **Allow Within:** Prevents paragraph breaks over pages or columns.

Application Notes

- **Vertical tabs:** Turn to page 95
- **Stacked tags:** Turn to page 130
- **Fitted tags:** Turn to page 99
- **Auto–numbering systems:** Turn to page 192

Using Keep With Next for Headings and Subheads

Keep With Next is a valuable automatic feature which forces a tag to appear on the same page as the one that follows it. This lets you keep headings on the same page as the first paragraph of text beneath them, and helps you prevent orphan headings stuck at the bottom of a page.

Using Keep With Next for Headings and Subheadings

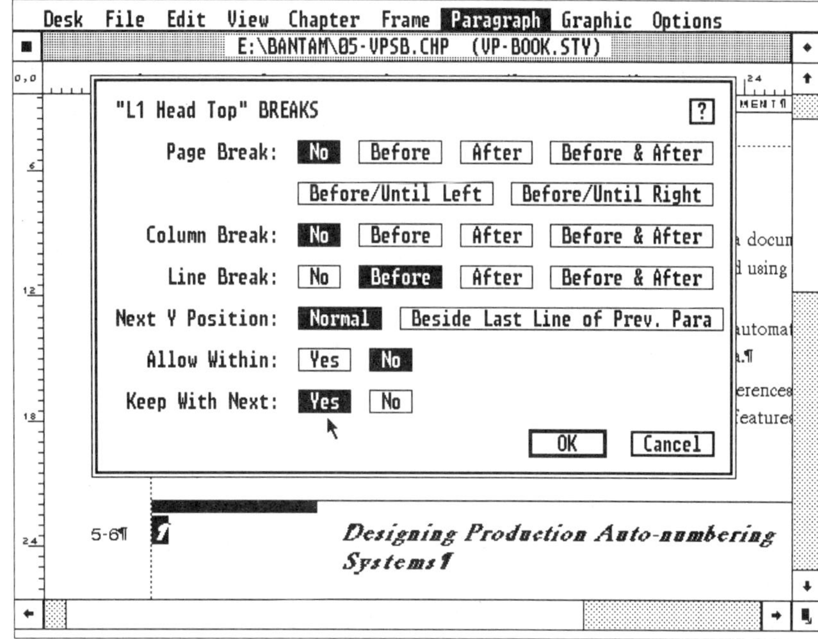

This feature also keeps clustered elements, such as multiple columns created with vertical tabs together so that they don't split up over pages. Time–saving is the greatest benefit to designing with this feature. You are spared from reprinting and making additional edit passes to place text on the correct page.

One warning, if Keep With Next is turned on for tags which display large sequential paragraphs of text, like the Body Text tag, there is a good chance a whole series of paragraphs will "chain" together and disappear from your screen. Keep With Next is best applied to small heading tags, column headings, and auto–number tags to prevent splitting these elements in different pages or columns.

Recipe: Link Two Tags Together

Step 1 **Create core heading tag**

Enable ***Paragraph*** mode and select the text. Use Add New Tag in the Side–Bar to create the heading tag. Use Paragraph menu features to set the desired font, alignment, and spacing.

Step 2 **Set Keep With Next**

Access **PARAGRAPH•Breaks** and set Keep With Next to Yes. This forces the heading to appear on the same page or column as the paragraph of text which immediately follows it.

Step 3 **Build additional headings**

When designing additional headings, select this heading tag before using Add New Tag, or enter the name of this tag on the Tag Name to Copy From line in the Add New Tag dialog box.

Application Notes

- **Auto–numbers:** Prevent generated auto–number from appearing on separate pages or columns from its reference text using Keep With Next. Turn to page 192.
- **Vertical tabs:** Force rows of multi–column tables to appear together without breaking over pages. Turn to page 95.
- **Stacked tags:** Use Keep With Next to force all stacked tag elements to appear in the same page or column. Turn to page 130.
- **Prevent stranded headings:** Use Keep With Next to prevent stranded headings at the bottom of a page or column.

Position Headings Automatically

The positioning of page elements can be controlled using a simple page break tag applied to a paragraph return. But in longer documents, additional passes may be necessary to break pages and position the text correctly.

If your document design places certain section headings at the top of a page, or other elements at the end of a page, automatically build these values into a tag. Then text is forced automatically to where you want it, whether at the top of the next page, the next left page, or the next right page.

Recipe: Automatically Position Headings

Step 1 **Create design spec**

Identify which section headings in your document are to begin at the top of the pages. Specify if they are to begin at the top of left or right pages only.

Step 2 **Design section heading tag**

Enable ***Paragraph*** mode and select text for the heading. Use Add New Tag in the Side–Bar to create the heading tag. Use features of the Paragraph menu to assign the desired font, alignment, and spacing.

Step 3 **Apply page break**

There are four ways to automatically position your section heading at the top of the page.

- ▲ **Page Break Before** places the heading automatically at the top of the next left or right page.
- ▲ **Page Break After** moves text following the tag to the top of the following page. Assign this value to another tag preceding the section heading, such as a freestanding Page Break tag.

Position Headings Automatically

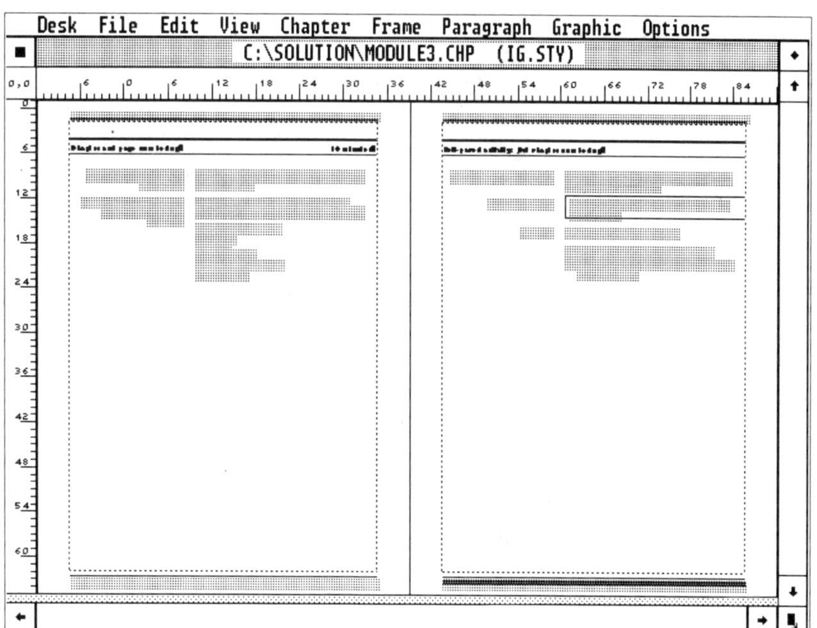

▲ **Page Break Before/Until Left** forces the section heading to the top of the next left page. If necessary, the text will jump past a right page to position on the next left page.

▲ **Page Break Before/Until Right** forces the section heading to jump to the top of the next right page.

Application Notes

- **First page position:** If a tag carrying a Page Break Before value is used as a title tag and appears at the top of page 1 in document, it will *not* break to the next page.
- **Long documents:** Design system of automatically positioning headings for long documents. For other long document design considerations, turn to page 43.

Page and Column Blocking

In some documents, you may need to block entire pages for illustrations or insertion of framed text material. One way to accomplish this

Page and Column Blocking

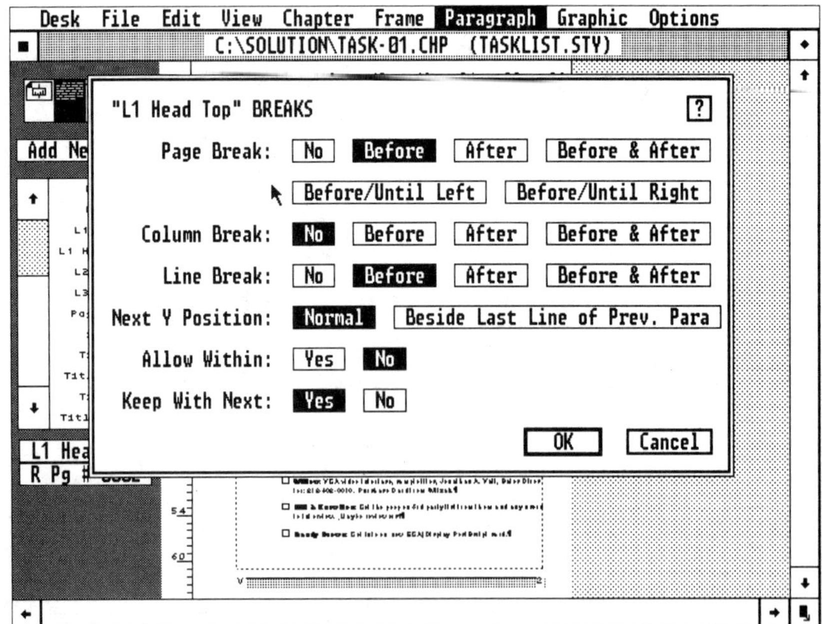

is to use left– or right–page repeating frames to force text to flow around them.

To block specific pages in a document, create a special tag with Before & After page or column break settings. This automatically clears a page and or column text flows to the following page.

In addition to saving printing and editing time, this approach also saves the time required to manually draw and edit frames. You have the ability to control page breaks and layout with a few simple operations in your word processor. The time saved with this technique can be especially significant when you are working on a long document with many open pages for frames or tables.

Recipe: Page and Column Blocking

Step 1 **Create blocking tag**

Enable ***Paragraph*** mode and select the text. Use Add New Tag in the Side–Bar to create the blocking tag.

Step 2 **Assign Break Before & After**

Access **PARAGRAPH•Breaks** and select the desired blocking effect:

▲ To block an entire page, select Page Break: Before & After.

▲ To block an entire column, select Column Break: Before & After.

Step 3 **Apply to free paragraph return**

Enable ***Text*** mode and pull down a free paragraph return. Enable ***Paragraph*** mode and apply the blocking tag. The page or column following the return is empty.

Step 4 **Enter in word processor**

To create blocked pages or columns in a document to hold pictures or other material, apply the blocking tag to a free paragraph return as you write text files in the word processor.

Recipe: Automatic Blocking Headings

You can create headings which automatically block page or column space in your document. In cases where pictures or text will be inserted into your document at a later time, this technique allows you to create a heading which both describes the inserted material and blocks space in the document for it.

Break Before & After settings for the page or column allow you to clear the entire page or column beneath the heading line. For pages, you can automatically place the heading directly onto Left or Right pages, providing you follow it with a simple Page Break After to complete the page blocking.

Step 1 **Create heading tag**

Enable ***Paragraph*** mode and select the text. Use Add New Tag in the Side–Bar to create the heading tag.

Access **PARAGRAPH•Breaks** and select the desired blocking effect.

- ▲ To place the heading at the top of a blank page select Page Break: Before & After.
- ▲ To block an entire column, select Column Break: Before & After.
- ▲ To place the heading at the top of the next left page, select Page Break Before/Until Left. Follow the heading with an additional Page Break tag, set to Page Break After.
- ▲ To place the heading at the top of the next right page, select Page Break Before/Until Right. Follow the heading with an additional Page Break tag, set to Page Break After.

Step 2 **Enter in word processor**

To save time, enter these heading and page break assignments directly in your word processor text file using macro keys. The empty pages will be in position when you open the document in Ventura.

Recipe: Continue Pages

Applications such as training materials often require blank page insertions with short text messages, like "Continue to the following page" or "Stop at this page." You can easily insert and position such a message by means of a Break Before & After tag.

Step 1 **Create message tag**

Enable ***Paragraph*** mode and select the text. Use Add New Tag in the Side–Bar to create the new tag.

Step 2 **Set message position**

Use features of the Paragraph menu to set the desired font, alignment, spacing, and ruling line values.

Step 3 **Assign Page Break Before & After**

Access **PARAGRAPH•Breaks** and select Page Break Before & After.

Step 4 **Enter in word processor**

To place these pages, enter the message text into your word processor and apply the message tag. You may be able to encode the message with its paragraph tag using a macro key.

Application Notes

- **Anchor frames to blocking tag:** Use frame anchoring to link pictures and graphics to page blocking tag or heading. Turn to page 251.
- **Blocking with repeating frames** Turn to page 67.

Creating Unbreakable Paragraphs

Unless designed otherwise, all text in Ventura Publisher can break across pages or columns. This means that paragraphs beginning near the bottom of a page or column will automatically flow to the top of the next page or column.

To suppress this flow–through process and force an entire paragraph to appear on the same page, or within the same column, turn off the Allow Within command in the Breaks dialog box. This command is useful to prevent document headings from breaking over pages or columns. You can also use it to force any body text or bullet list paragraph from breaking over columns and pages. Avoid using this feature with tags that carry very long paragraphs of text.

Creating Unbreakable Paragraphs
Page 221

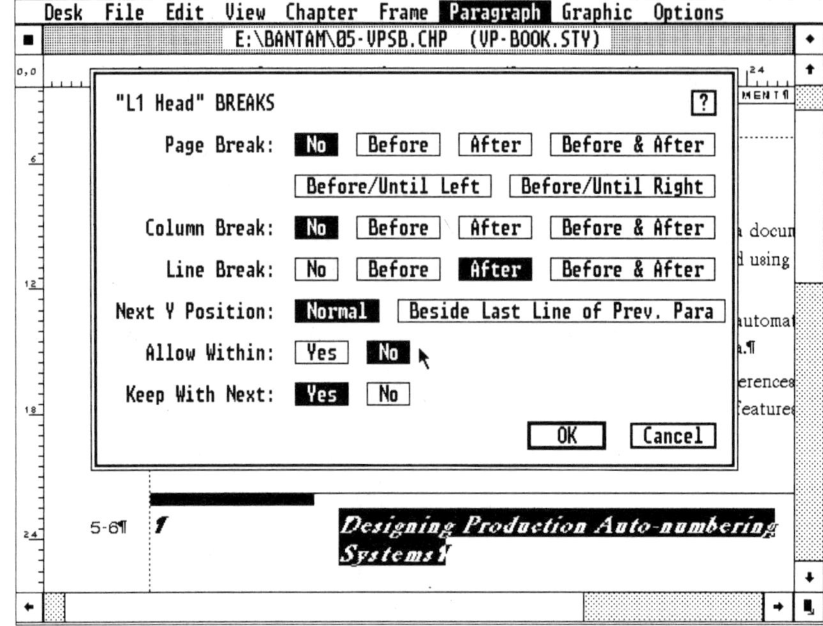

By forcing a long paragraph to the following page, Ventura can leave a large empty area on the preceding page.

The real value of this feature is that it lets you force certain elements to stay in the same page or column. When used in long document applications, this can save you hours of editing and reprinting time.

Recipe: Solid Paragraphs

Step 1 **Select desired tag**

To set up any tag in a style sheet with solid paragraphs, enable ***Paragraph*** mode and select the desired tag.

Step 2 **Set Allow Within**

Access **PARAGRAPH•Breaks** and set Allow Within to No. The text will not break over columns or pages.

Step 3 **Check pages**

Page through the document and observe the effect of the allow within settings. Large empty spaces may appear at the bottom of pages as complete paragraphs pull to the following page. You can diminish this effect by enabling the ***Text*** mode and breaking long paragraphs into two or more shorter paragraphs.

Application Notes

- **Headings:** In multi–column documents, prevent headings from splitting across columns.
- **Body text:** Prevent body text paragraphs from splitting across pages or columns.
- **Bullet lists:** Prevent awkward breaks of bullet lists or other copy across columns or pages.

Linked Lists and Sections

Lists are usually most effective when all elements in the list appear in the same column or page. And for short lists, it is a simple operation to accomplish.

To force all elements in a short list to appear in the same page or column, develop a pair of matched tags. For the principal tag covering all elements in the list, turn Keep With Next On, to force each item to appear on the same page as the item that follows it.

For the last item in the list, make a copy of the main list and turn Keep With Next Off. This List End tag will prevent the list from chaining itself to the next paragraph of text, and possibly disrupting your document.

Recipe: Linked Lists

Step 1 **Create list tag**

Enable ***Paragraph*** mode and select the text. Use Add New Tag in the Side–Bar to create the list tag.

Step 2 **Set list Keep With Next**

Access **PARAGRAPH•Breaks** and set Keep With Next to Yes. This forces each list tag to appear on the same tag as the tag that follows it, and keeps all list elements together.

Linked Lists and Sections
Page 223

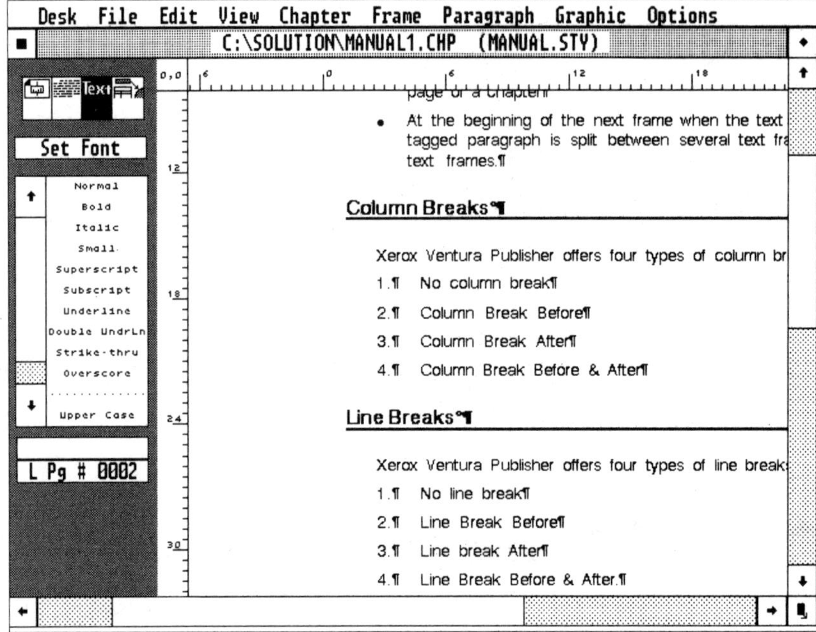

Step 3 **Create list final tag**

With the list tag selected, use Add New Tag in the Side–Bar to create the list final tag.

Step 4 **Set list final Keep With Next**

Access **PARAGRAPH•Breaks** and set Keep With Next to No. This enables the connected list to relate normally to other elements in the document.

Application Notes

- **Short list material:** Use this technique to prevent short lists from spreading over two pages or columns.
- **Stacked heading tags:** Use this technique for heading effects created with stacked tags. Link two or more stacked tags together to prevent them from splitting over pages. Turn to page 130.

Designing Production Page Breaks

For documents with different left and right page layouts, you can easily position text on left and right pages by creating a system of production page breaks which are positioned at the upper left corner of your document page.

If page length in your document is uneven, placing page breaks at the bottom of the page can lead to a a lot of vertical scrolling as you search for the page breaks.

Production page breaks help streamline final production. All custom page break tags appear at the upper left corner of the page, just outside the document margin. During final editing passes, you can assign all your custom page breaks to function keys and page through your document checking your breaks. The only time you will have to scroll through the page is when you wish to add a new page break near the bottom of the page.

Production page breaks are outdented from the left margin guide and have no line height or line breaks. When set up this way, the tag can control the position of text in your document, yet be entirely "invisible" to the rest of your document text.

Tagged text will rise to the top of the next page, and yet the break handle will always be easy to find and select because it is slightly outside the text margin.

When breaking the page to the left or right, Ventura requires that the break take place before the tagged text. Accordingly, you create three tags:

- **Page Before:** Breaks text to the top of the next page, left or right.
- **Page Left:** Breaks text to the top of the next left page.
- **Page Right:** Breaks text to the top of the next right page.

Production page breaks make it easy for you to break text to the next page, the left page, or the next page at the stroke of a mouse.

Recipe: Production Page Breaks

Step 1 **Pull down free paragraph return**

Enable ***Text*** mode and place text on a paragraph return symbol. Press the Return key to pull down a free paragraph return.

Step 2 **Create Page Break Before tag**

Enable ***Paragraph*** mode and select the free return. Use Add New Tag in the Side–Bar to create the page before handle tag.

Step 3 **Set outdent from margin**

Access **PARAGRAPH•Alignment**. Set First Line to Outdent and enter a small value for In/Outdent Width, about 01,00 picas & points.

▲ If the paragraph return does not appear outside the left margin guide, it may have a spacing offset built in. To correct this, access **PARAGRAPH•Spacing** and zero out any In From Left spacing value.

Step 4 **Place page break**

Access **PARAGRAPH•Breaks** and select Page Break: Before.

Designing Production Page Breaks
Page 225

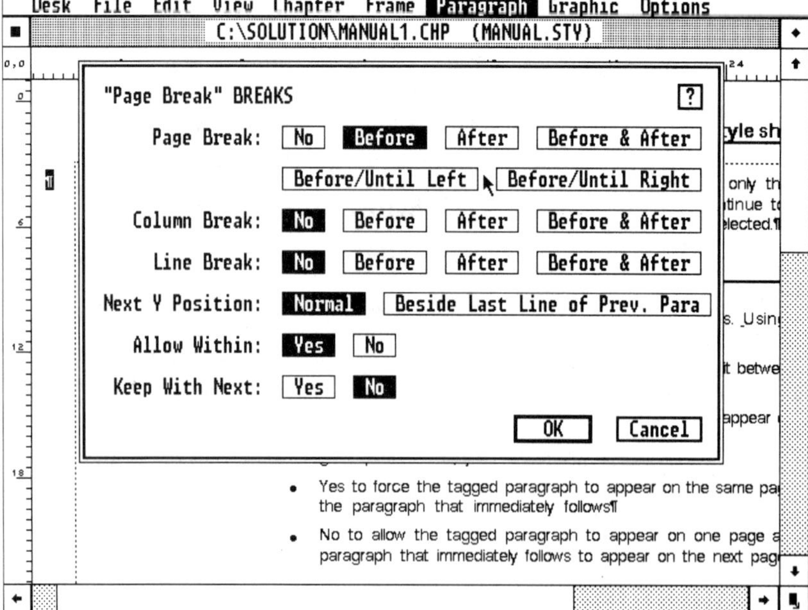

Step 5 **Remove extra spacing**

Access **PARAGRAPH•Spacing** and zero out Above, Below, and Inter–Paragraph spacing values.

Step 6 **Remove line break**

Set Line Break to No. This makes the tag invisible to other tags and lets them align normally beside it.

☞ CAUTION: If the production page break tag appears at the top of a page preceding a heading or other tag with a line break Before, Above space for that tag will be added in. To eliminate this problem, set Body Text and all standard document headings with line break After.

Step 7 **Copy tag to page left**

With the tag selected, use Add New Tag to create Page Left. Access **PARAGRAPH•Breaks** and set Page Break Before/Until Left.

Step 8 **Copy tag to page right**

With either of the break tags selected, use Add New Tag to create Page Right. Access **PARAGRAPH•Breaks** and set Page Break Before/Until Right.

Recipe: Edit with Production Page Breaks

Step 1 **Assign tags to function keys**

Enable ***Text*** mode and press Control–K. Assign break tags to available function keys.

Step 2 **Place page breaks on–screen**

To position text in your document using production page breaks, enable ***Text*** mode and pull down a free paragraph return and apply the tag with function keys.

Application Notes

- **Long documents:** Design system of production page breaks for long documents. For other long document design considerations, turn to page 43.
- **Headings:** Use production page breaks to control position of headings during onscreen Ventura text editing.
- **Outdented column break:** Create column breaks outdented to fit into the gutter between columns in your document.
- **Block pages with repeating frames:** Turn to page 67.

Creating Custom Headers and Footers

Headers print running text at the top of pages and Footers print repeating text at the bottom of pages. For long document applications, these are extremely powerful automatic elements. They not only display running text, but can automatically display the text from your current document headings. Used in concert with the typesetting capabilities of the Paragraph mode, and custom text attributes, an infinite number of design effects are possible.

Creating Custom Headers and Footers

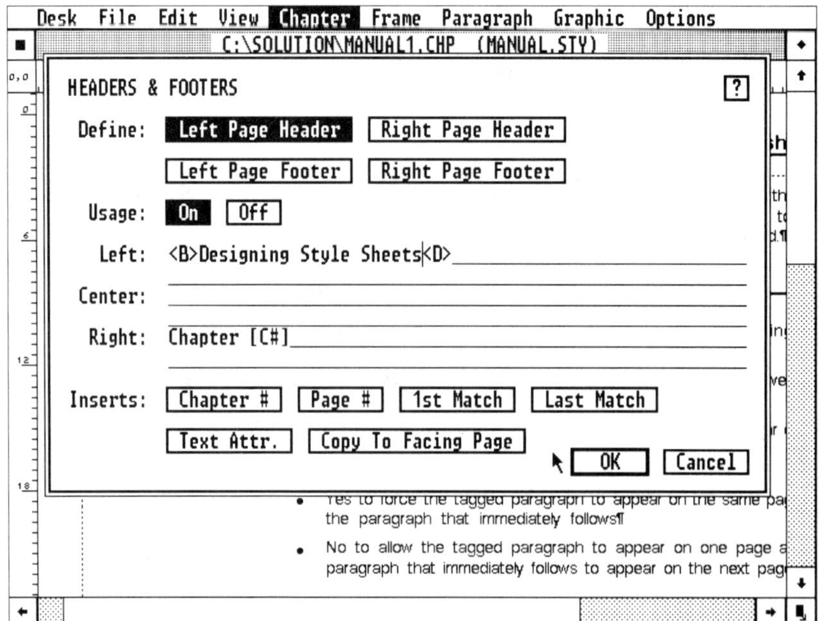

Recipe: Custom Headers and Footers

Step 1 **Select header and positioning**

Access **CHAPTER•Headers & Footers**. To create the right header, make the appropriate selection and turn usage on.

Step 2 **Enter text**

Enter text on the Left, Center, and Right lines as needed.

Step 3 **Enter page and chapter numbers**

To place page and chapter numbers in the header and footer line, place cursor where the number is to appear and select Page # or Chapter # at the bottom of the screen.

Recipe: Header and Footer Placement

To control placement of headers and footers, you must manually turn them off and on using the toggles on the Chapter menu. If a Header or Footer is turned off on the current page and you reaccess the Headers & Footers dialog box to make edits, the Headers and Footers *on the current page only* will be turned on again.

When defined, headers and footers automatically appear on the current page displayed in the Working Area, and all pages *following* it. Any pages before the current page do not display the header or footer. To place headers and footers throughout an entire chapter automatically, display the first page of the chapter at the time you design them.

Step 1 **Turn header off**

Display the page where you wish to suppress headers and select **CHAPTER•Turn Header Off**. Reselect the same toggle feature to turn the header back on.

Step 2 **Turn footer off**

Display the page where you wish to suppress footers and select **CHAPTER•Turn Footer Off**. Reselect the same toggle feature to turn the footer back on.

Recipe: Mirror Headers and Footers

Mirror headers and footers present text in opposite positions on facing pages. If text is right aligned on the right page, it will be left aligned on the left page. Mirror headers and footers are useful for positioning text and data on facing pages to the edge of the page.

Step 1 **Set up page layout**

Mirrored headers and footers are possible only in facing page layouts. Access **CHAPTER•Page Size & Layout** and set Sides to Double.

Step 2 **Select right page header and positioning**

Access **CHAPTER•Headers & Footers**. Select Right Page Header. Enter the desired text for Right Page Header.

Step 3 **Copy to facing page**

To mirror text to the facing page, select Copy To Facing Page. Mirror positioning places Right aligned elements on the Right page and Left aligned elements on the Left page. Select Left Page header to check mirror positioning.

Step 4 **Repeat for footers**

Repeat the above process when creating mirroring footers.

Recipe: Non–mirror Headers and Footers

Step 1 **Select right page header and positioning**

Access **CHAPTER•Headers & Footers**. Enter text for Right Page Header.

Step 2 **Enter left page header text**

Select Left Page Header and enter header text in the desired text.

Step 3 **Repeat for footers**

Repeat the process when creating non–mirror footers.

Application Notes

- **Illustrated headers and footers:** Turn to page 123.
- **Graphic headers and footers:** Use repeating frames and graphics to create custom graphic headers and footers on facing pages. Turn to page 328.
- **Setting up pagination systems:** Turn to page 338.

Creating Automatic Header and Footer References

In addition to displaying information about document elements, and page and chapter numbers, header and footer lines can create automatic page indexing and reference systems by performing a simple field sort using paragraph tags as a handle.

1st and Last Match allows you to insert the name of a designated tag (usually a heading or subheading) into a position on the header and footer line. In that position, Ventura pulls the text associated with most recent occurrence of that tag into the header and/or footer line.

- **1st Match** pulls in the text from the first occurrence of the tag on the current page.
- **Last Match** pulls in the text from the last occurrence of the tag on the current page.

You can use multiple matches in header and footer lines to place automatic references to the current section and other information directly in your header and footer lines.

Recipe: Automatic Heading References

One of the simplest applications for 1st Match is to place the name of the current document section heading in the page header. As the document header text changes, the changes are automatically reflected in the header line.

The following technique describes the steps necessary to place the name of the current document section heading in the header line. Instructions are the same when used in a footer line.

Step 1 **Select tags for match:**

Identify the title, heading, or subheading tags to be displayed in the header or footer line.

☞ CAUTION: Be sure that the text associated with the selected tag will not be so long that it cannot be displayed in the Header or Footer line. The typesize currently set in the header or footer tag determines how much text appears.

Step 2 **Place 1st match in header line**

Access **CHAPTER•Headers & Footers**. Turn header on and place cursor where the text element is to be inserted. Select 1st Match at the bottom of the screen.

Step 3 **Enter match tag name**

Use keyboard arrows to move inside the brackets and delete only the words *tag name* from inside the brackets. Enter the name of the tag name to match inside the brackets.

Recipe: Telephone Book References

1st and Last Match lets you automatically enter the first and last occurrence of a particular element on a page into the header or footer line, like the first and last names listed in the header line of a telephone directory. First to last references are especially helpful to readers searching for specific information in long technical or reference documents.

Step 1 **Place 1st match in header line**

Access **CHAPTER•Headers & Footers**. Turn header on and place cursor where the text element is to be inserted. Select 1st Match at the bottom of the screen.

Step 2 **Enter match tag name**

Use keyboard arrows to move inside the brackets and delete only the words *tag name* from inside the brackets. Enter the name of the tag name to match inside the brackets.

Creating Automatic Header and Footer References
Page 234

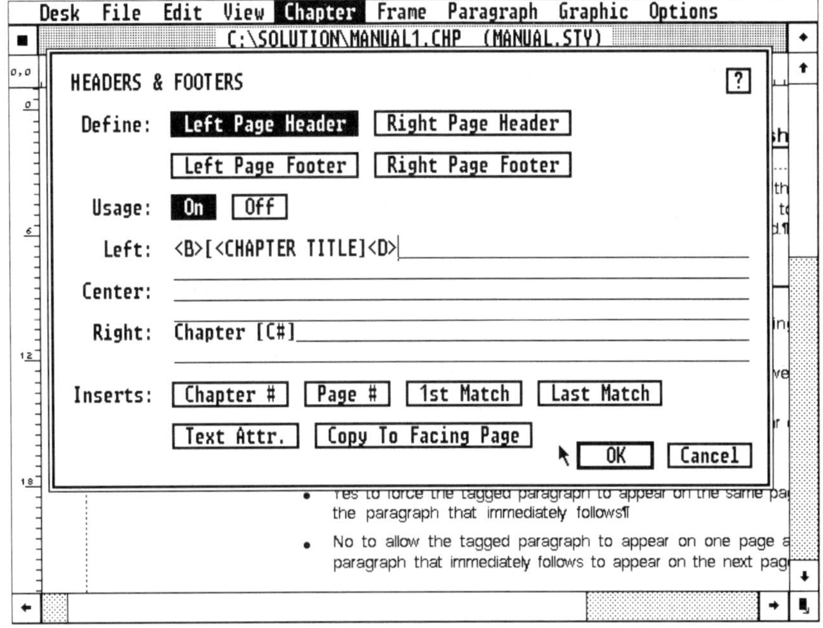

Step 3 **Place Last Match in header line**

Place cursor where the last match is to be inserted. Select Last Match at the bottom of the screen.

Step 4 **Enter match tag name**

Use keyboard arrows to move inside the brackets and delete only the words *tag name* from inside the brackets. Enter the name of the tag name to match inside the brackets.

Step 5 **Enter punctuation**

To place special punctuation between the 1st and Last Match text, insert it outside of the bracketed expressions in the Header & Footer dialog box.

Application Notes

- **Long documents:** Use 1st/Last Match to create customized headers and footers for long documents. For other long document design considerations, turn to page 43.

- **Custom header text** Apply text enhancements and custom font and style settings to selected text in the header or footer line. Turn to page 239.

Creating Automatic Document Updates

1st and Last Match may be used as many times as desired in the same header or footer line as long as there is room to display all the automatically placed text. This allows you to place updatable document information in your header line, including the date, issue number, and other elements without making any additional edits or entries in the Headers & Footers dialog box.

One of the most obvious applications for this technique is the document date. If you create a special Date tag in the style sheet, that tag can be automatically displayed in the header or footer line. When you make revisions to the document, change the revision date in the text file, and print the document in Ventura. The new date will automatically show up in the header and footer line without even opening the Headers & Footers dialog box.

Use this technique for regularly cycled documents, or document drafts going through a series of revision cycles by different individuals. Any information that has its own paragraph tag can be automatically placed into the header line, including the current date, document issue, name of current document reviewer, chapter title, section headings, or other information. This technique is also useful for standard boilerplate documents, such as letter proposals. By making a few simple edits to the text file, the name of the customer, the current date, and the proposal subject display automatically in the proposal header or footer line.

Creating Automatic Document Updates

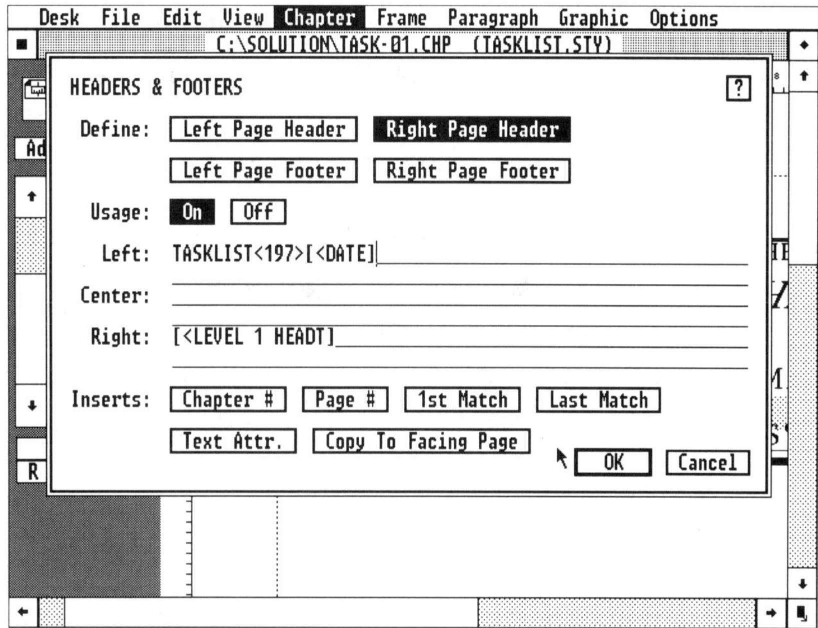

Recipe: Automatic Document Updates

Step 1 **Select document information updates**

Decide which text elements you would like to automatically display in the header or footer line and write down the tag name for each. These might include elements such as:

▲ Current chapter title

▲ Major headings

▲ Date

▲ Issue

▲ Name of editor/reviewer

Step 2 **Create special tags**

Enable ***Paragraph*** mode and use Add New Tag to special tags for document updates.

Step 3 **Enter document information**

Enter the updated document information in the word processor text file (or in Ventura) and assign correct tag.

Step 4 **Place document information tags in header**

Access **CHAPTER•Headers & Footers**. Place cursor where you want to place date in your header line. Select 1st Match, delete the words *tag name* and enter the date tag inside the brackets.

Step 5 **Revise document information data**

At any time, change the document information in the word processor text file or in Ventura. The revised date will automatically read into your header or footer line. No changes to the **CHAPTER•Headers & Footers** dialog box are necessary.

Recipe: Auto–Number Match in Header Line

Use multiple–match selections to place auto–numbered elements in the header or footer line. For example, in a legal or technical document using automatic section numbered headings, you can create an on–page index in the header or footer by displaying the first occurrence of the heading with its section number and the final occurrence of the heading with its section number.

Step 1 **Identify headings for match**

Identify the auto–numbered heading or subheading to be placed in the header or footer line. Write down the name of the tag and the tag name of its related auto–number.

Step 2 **1st match heading auto–number**

Place cursor where the auto–number for the heading is to appear and select 1st Match. Delete the words *tag name* from inside the brackets and enter the name of the generated auto–number tag.

Step 3 **1st match heading text**

Access **CHAPTER•Headers & Footers**. Select which line to define and turn Usage to On. Place cursor where heading text is to appear and select 1st Match. Delete the words *tag name* from inside the brackets and enter the name of the heading tag.

Step 4 **Place punctuation**

To place punctuation between the heading text and its auto–number, enter that punctuation between the bracketed expressions.

☞ CAUTION: If your auto–number text already has built–in punctuation, placing punctuation in the header line will result in double punctuation.

Step 5 **Repeat process for Last Match**

To have a 1st–Last Match of the heading, repeat the process using Last Match for the heading tag and the auto–number tag.

Step 6 **Select mirror or non–mirror presentation**

To place mirror version of header line on the facing page, select Copy to Facing Page. For the same presentation on the facing page, select the facing page header or footer and enter the information again.

Application Notes

- **Frequent–cycle business documents:** Set up a standard chapter file with all headers and footers defined with automatic elements in place. Load updated text into the *same* chapter file and print. Headers will automatically show the new data for titles and dates.
- **Track document drafts:** Use automatic updating concept to automatically place draft and date information in header or footer line.
- **Custom header text:** Apply text enhancements and custom font and style settings to sections of text in the header or footer line. Turn to page 239.

Setting Header and Footer Typography

Typographic values for header and footer lines are controlled by two generated tags, Z_HEADER and Z_FOOTER. You can set the general typography for the header line by editing these tags. But because headers and footers are special text elements contained in generated frames, you cannot edit their tags as completely as some others. For

Setting Header and Footer Typography
Page 239

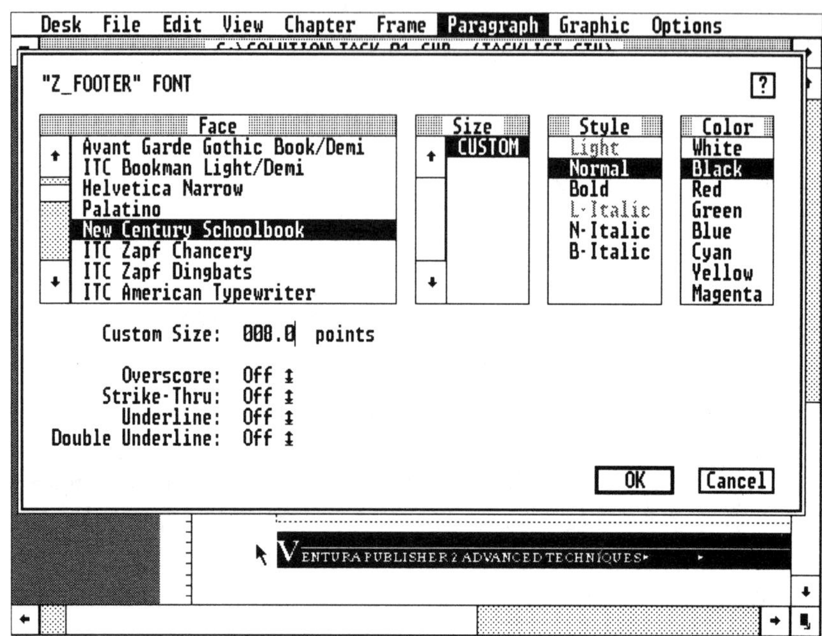

the most part, when editing these tags, you will make changes to the font. You can alter the position of the header or footer by adjusting the spacing above and below the line. The settings you make for the generated header and footer tags are applied uniformly to all text in the line.

Recipe: Header and Footer Typography

Step 1 **Set typographic values**

Enable ***Paragraph*** mode and select header tag. Note that Z_HEADER appears in the Current Selection Box.

Step 2 **Set custom values for selected text**

Use the features of the Paragraph menu to set the desired Font and Spacing for the header tag.

Step 3 **Repeat process for footer line**

Use the same process to edit the tag for the footer line. Note that the name of the generated footer tag is Z_FOOTER.

Application Notes

- **Add ruling lines and enhancements:** Use Ruling Line features on the **PARAGRAPH** menu to enhance header and footer text.
- **Illustrated headers and footers:** Turn to page 123.
- **Graphic headers and footers:** Use repeating frames and graphics to create custom graphic headers and footers on facing pages. Turn to page 328.

Using Text Attributes with Headers & Footers

Header and footer tags allow you to set global typographic values which are applied uniformly to the entire header or footer line. For a more stylish effect, you can make alterations to specific sections of the header or footer text. Because headers and footers are *generated text* elements, processed inside of Ventura and not written to your text file, you cannot edit them directly from the ***Text*** mode. To add enhancements and custom text edits, you must place text attribute entries in the **CHAPTER•Headers & Footers** dialog box. The Text Attr. selection in the dialog box places text attribute brackets at the cursor position on the header or footer line. Use the keyboard to enter the desired text attribute codes inside them.

When using text attributes, remember that each one has an *initial code* placed where the effect begins, and a *Return to Normal* code placed where the text effect is to end. The codes are designed so that a number of different enhancements can be assigned and controlled independently of each other. Simple text enhancements, like boldface, use letter codes. The code <B> begins a boldface string and the standard Return to Normal code <D> ends it. Changes to typeface, size, and color use unique number codes to begin and end the effect. For example, to increase the font size of one word in the header line to 36 points, enter the point size increase code containing the desired size <P036> and return the effect to normal using the point size Return to Normal command <P255>.

Using Text Attributes with Headers and Footers

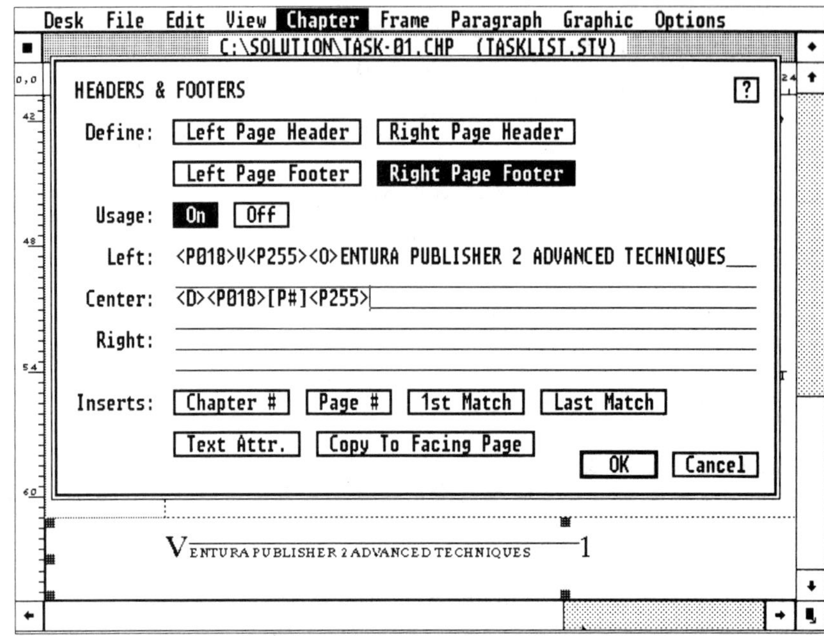

Recipe: Header Text Typeface

Step 1 **Place text attribute codes**

Access **CHAPTER•Headers & Footers**. Enter header text.

Step 2 **Enter desired Font Code**

Using keyboard arrows, place cursor at beginning of text to be customized and select Text Attr. at the bottom of the screen. Move inside the delimiter brackets at the beginning of the text and delete the letter **D**. Enter the code of the desired font in the format <Fnnn>. (A list of font codes can be found in the Ventura documentation.)

Step 3 **Enter Return to Normal**

Place text cursor at the end of bracketed entry. Select Text Attr. and delete the letter **D** from inside the brackets. Enter the Return to Normal font code: <F255>.

Recipe: Header Text Point Size

Step 1 **Enter point size code**

Place text cursor where the point size change is to begin. Select Text Attr. and delete the letter **D** from inside the brackets. Enter the point size code in the format: <Pnnn>. The code *nnn* refers to the point size expressed in three digits. For example, 36 points, is **036**.

Step 2 **Enter return to normal**

Place text cursor at the end of bracketed entry. Select Text Attr. and delete the letter **D** from inside the brackets. Enter the Return to Normal point code: <P255>

Recipe: Header Text Color

Step 1 **Place color codes**

Place text cursor where the color change is to begin. Select Text Attr. and delete the letter **D** from inside the brackets. Enter the Color code in the format: <Cnnn>. (For list of color codes, turn to Appendixes.)

Step 2 **Enter return to normal**

Place text cursor at the end of bracketed entry. Select Text Attr. and delete the letter **D** from inside the brackets. Enter the Return to Normal color code: <C255>.

Application Notes

- **Oversize characters:** Create oversized characters for special applications design effects.
- **Set custom text:** Use different styles of the same font in the header text.
- **Place special characters:** Use text attributes to place special symbol characters, such as Zapf Dingbats, into header and footer lines.
- **Auto–numbering:** For auto–numbering systems which include text on the auto–number line, use the same procedures to place enhancements. Turn to page 202.
- **Table of Contents:** Use these procedures to place enhancements to table of contents text. Turn to page 366.

CHAPTER 6

Frames and Pictures

Visual Dimensions

Pick up a pair of scissors and cut out a small square of paper. Now place the scrap of paper on top of a full piece of paper. You have just demonstrated how a Ventura frame sits on a document page. It is a controlled area or space in your document that floats on top of the base page.

Frames are the key to the layout process in Ventura Publisher. The base page in every document is a frame, which can be edited and customized in a variety of different ways. Within the page, individual frames represent controlled areas which can be individually configured to hold pictures, graphics, or text.

Electronics give the Ventura frame much more flexibility than your little piece of paper. Touch a frame with the mouse and you can resize and move it. Make a few simple changes to the background settings and it becomes hollow or opaque. Place a picture inside a frame and you can stretch, distort, and size it as if it were printed on elastic.

Within each frame, you can create a unique environment. Assign custom margins and columns inside it. Place ruling lines above,

Increase the Quality of Your Communications

CLIP-ART LIBRARIES

Architectural Symbols

A complete library of standard architectural symbols for use in mapping floor plans and decorative design plans. Individual drawings represent elements in architectural layouts for highly realistic and professional representative drawings. Furnishing graphics include tables, chairs, bedroom furnishings, couches, shelving, grand piano and lamps. Fixture drawings include kitchen cabinetry and major appliances, bathroom fixtures, furnace, water heater, furnace, staircases, fireplace and more.

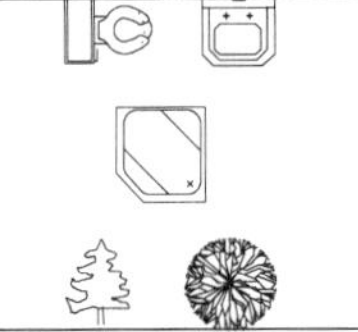

Science

A library of common science visuals for document enhancement or icons. Individual graphics are especially useful for primary and secondary textbook and science teaching materials. Symbols include molecular structures, model atoms, DNA structure graphic and more. Equipment graphics include flasks, beakers, scales, Bunsen Burner, and graduated cylinder. Symbols may be combined in graphics editor to create more complex illustrations and designs.

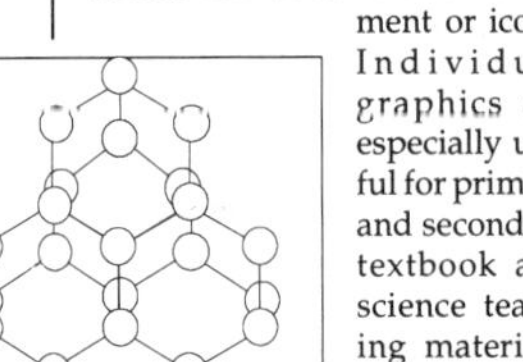

Medicine

A complete library of medical symbols and anatomical graphics which may be used individually or in combination. These libraries are especially useful for general interest medical books, textbooks and teaching materials. Medical equipment graphics include such standard paraphernaila as thermometer, stethoscope, scale, and more. Anatomical projections include labeled full-body illustrations of the muscular, circulatory and nervous systems. Close-up graphics show focused areas of the body with greater detail in labeling.

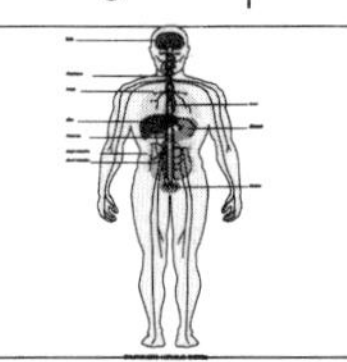

Symbols

A complete collection of graphic symbols which can be used to enhance text or other graphics. Individual symbols may be used in combination to create illustrated flowcharts, diagrams or rebus effects. Standard graphic symbols include standard arrows, 3-D arrows and drop shadow arrows. Icons include mini-graphics of stars, starbursts, telephones, and drop-shadow bullets in round or square forms. Individual sym-

1

Clip-Art Catalog: Ventura frames can be used to create custom layouts integrating pictures, headline text, and other effects. Text is typeset in Palatino. Clip-art from Micrografx Designer.

below, and around it. Place space buffers around, above, and below it. Once you have created the environment, it can be moved, copied and positioned throughout your document with a few strokes of mouse. Frame captions let you automatically enter text at any position around the frame, as well as assign a control name and number to it for automatic document–processing purposes.

Frames can be configured to block space, or entire pages throughout your document, automatically. Repeating frames automatically place repeating illustrations and text throughout the document. Frames let you place a text file on a series of selected pages.

Tools for Frames and Pictures

Frame and picture editing are contained primarily in the Frame mode, and in features on the Edit and Frame menus.

- **Frame mode** contains features to select and edit the base page, which is also the *base frame* in Ventura. Most layout operations are performed in this mode.
- **Cut/Copy/Paste** contains features to move, remove, and place multiple copies of completed frames within a document or between chapter files.
- **Margins & Columns** on the Frame menu is used to set margins and columns inside individual frames.
- **Sizing & Scaling** on the Frame menu is used to size, edit, and crop pictures, as well as set the size and position of individual frames.
- **Repeating Frames** on the Frame menu is used to designate frames as repeating frames which can block space in the layout.
- **Ruling Lines** on the Frame menu can be used to add enhancements to the page design.

Controlling Space and Pictures

Frames are the foundation of the electronic layout system in Ventura. Unlike text, you can't make edits to them outside Ventura. To produce documents efficiently in Ventura, you *must* have a solid working knowledge of frames and how to edit them.

This chapter contains a number of techniques which illustrate the many ways you can design frames to solve document design and production problems. With frames, as with text, your goal should be to reduce repetitive effort to output your documents as fast as possible.

One of the most important time–saving features for Ventura frames is anchoring. This feature lets you link a frame to a specified text position in your document. Then, even if you make comprehensive edits to text, you can instantly snap the frame back into position with a few keystrokes. In the deadline atmosphere of a production department, it is often tempting to take the shortcut and forget frame anchoring, or promise yourself to do it later. Don't fall into that trap. Anchored frames make your documents easier to edit and increase your editing flexibility when it really counts.

Creating Master Frames for Pictures

When creating frames for pictures, you are defining not only the space and the framing for the picture, but defining the actual presentation of the picture itself. It is important to link the entire process of defining the frame into a single step–by–step operation to reduce errors and changes. Unlike paragraph tags, you cannot make simple global edits to frames throughout your document. If you make an error in designing a frame, you must go back to correct that individual frame. If you have many frames that need correction, you must make all of those changes individually.

Building master frames for pictures means designing all details into a single frame which is then copied to all locations in the document which will display a picture.

Recipe: Master Frames for Pictures

Step 1 **Set column snap**

When Column Snap is turned on, frames snap vertically to the nearest baseline of body text. When Column Snap is off, you can draw frames freehand with no constraint. To set column snap, select **OPTIONS•TurnColumn Snap On**

Step 2 **Draw frame**

Enable ***Frame*** mode and select Add New Frame in the Side–Bar. Place the corner of the right–angle frame drawing cursor where the upper left corner of the frame is to appear. Press and hold the left mouse button as you drag the mouse to draw the frame.

Step 3 **Size frame**

Use sizing boxes on the screen or access **FRAME•Sizing & Scaling** and enter dimensions on the Frame Height and Frame Width line.

Step 4 **Set page position**

Access **FRAME•Sizing & Scaling** and set the distance between the top of the page (not the top margin) and the top of the frame on the Upper Left Y line; set the distance between left side of the page (not the left margin) and the left side of the frame on Upper Left X.

Creating Master Frames for Pictures

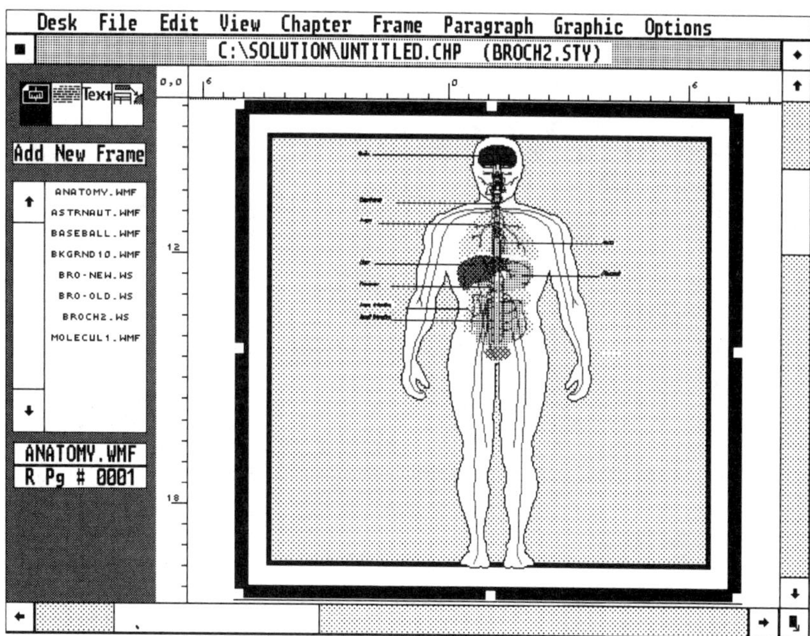

Step 5 **Set ruling lines**

With the frame selected, access any of the ruling lines dialog boxes and define the desired ruling lines above, below, or around. You can also set vertical rules on the left and right edges of the frame, or at any position inside the frame.

Step 6 **Set caption position**

If the frame is to be captioned, assign a caption position to the master frame. Access **FRAME•Anchors & Captions** and use the Caption selector to set the position of the Caption frame.

Step 7 **Set frame background**

To add shading to the frame, select the frame and access **FRAME•Frame Background** and select color and shading.

Step 8 **Set external buffer**

To place an external margin around the frame to prevent text from bumping up against it, select the frame and access **FRAME•Sizing & Scaling**. Enter the desired external margin at the top and bottom of the frame on the Vert. Padding line and enter the value to the left and right on the Horz. Padding line.

Recipe: Placing Enclosed Frames

For complex illustrations, you may draw a page–wide frame which contains several smaller picture frames. Frames drawn inside of other frames do not automatically link to the main frame like Ventura graphics. Enclosed frames allow you to place several pictures along with text in a controlled area.

Step 1 **Draw second frame**

Enable ***Frame*** mode and use Add New Frame to draw a second frame inside the area defined by the main frame.

Step 2 **Reselect file name**

Select the smaller frame. If only the larger frame selects, press Control–Select and select the name of the desired picture or text file in the Assignment List.

Application Notes

- **Blocking frames:** Use frames to block space on the page and place illustrations inside the blocking frame. Turn to page 254
- **Using frames with graphics:** Turn to page 304
- **Uniform picture sizes:** For illustrated applications using a series of uniformly sized and scaled pictures, such as a standard clip–art library, define all values for the picture once, and use frame Cut/Copy/Paste to place frames where desired in the document.

Copying Frames Between Documents

You can copy completed frames to positions in the same chapter, or across chapters. This makes it easy to duplicate the same effect in a number of different chapters without having to repeatedly draw and position all of the elements individually for each chapter.

Recipe: Copy Frames Between Documents

Step 1 **Design frame**

Enable ***Frame*** mode and use Add New Frame in the Side–Bar to draw a frame. Set all attributes, columns, size, position, and enhancements for the frame.

Step 2 **Place frame contents**

Place the desired contents in the frame, whether a text file, a picture file, or a Ventura graphics display.

Step 3 **Select the frame**

Select the frame. Graphics, text, and pictures contained in the frame automatically travel with it and will automatically be loaded into the

Copying Frames Between Documents
Page 249

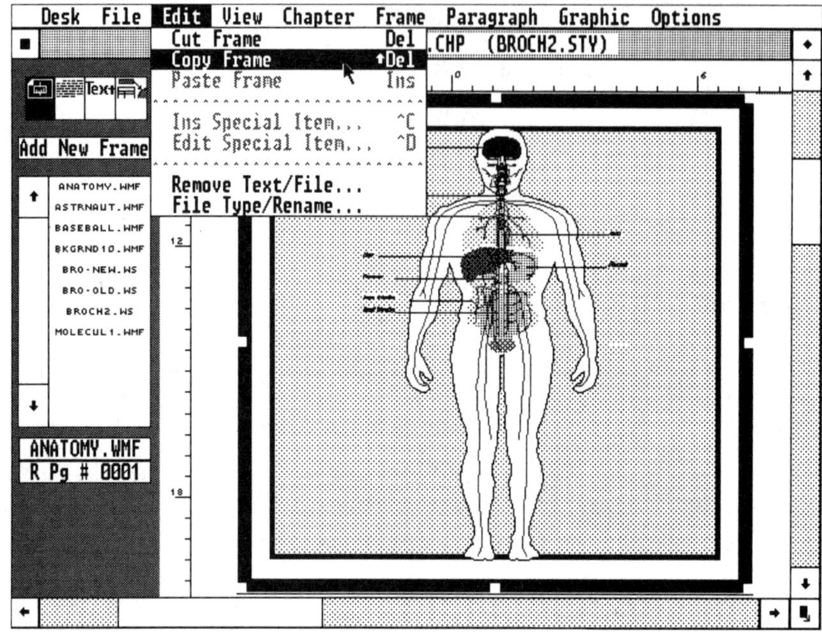

new chapter file. If you are copying a complex illustration made up of a blocking frame with several additional frames inside it, you must press the Shift key and select all frames that make up the illustration before copying it.

Step 4 **Copy the frame**

Select **EDIT•Copy Frame** to load the frame into the clipboard.

Step 5 **Open new chapter**

Access **FILE•Open Chapter** and select the chapter to which to copy the frame. Use PgUp/PgDn keys or access **CHAPTER•Go To Page** to go to the desired page.

Step 6 **Paste frame**

Select **EDIT•Paste Frame** to paste the frame into the new chapter. Select **FILE•Save** to save the frame in the new chapter.

Anchoring Frames to Text

Frame anchoring is a powerful feature to control the position of frames by linking them to a position in text. Frame anchoring is one of the most important production and document editing techniques to master. Used correctly, this feature can save literally hours in document editing and production time.

Unlike text, all frames *must* be edited and positioned in Ventura. And even through there are a number of efficient frame– editing features, such as Cut/Copy/Paste, frames require a great deal of individual editing attention. There is no parallel in the Frame mode for the automatic global changes that take place when you edit a Paragraph tag.

Frame anchoring helps to reduce the amount of individual editing and repositioning by linking a frame to a specific position in the document text. Once anchored, you can automatically force frames to snap back to the page on which their reference text appears. There are a number of uses for frame anchoring:

- Anchoring frames in any document containing a considerable number of illustrations or tables.
- Linking illustrations created through frame–stacking techniques.
- Linking illustrations and text in newsletters and catalogs.

Frame anchoring is a must for any document which contains many illustrations. If you fail to anchor frames, you may have to reposition them throughout the entire document with each editing cycle.

Recipe: Anchoring Frames

Step 1 **Assign frame anchor name**

Enable ***Frame*** mode and select the frame to be anchored. Access **FRAME•Anchors & Captions**. Enter an anchor name for the frame on the Anchor line.

Step 2 **Select text position**

Enable ***Text*** mode. Place the text cursor at the beginning of a string of text to be kept on the same page as the frame. It is a good idea to

Anchoring Frames to Text
Page 251

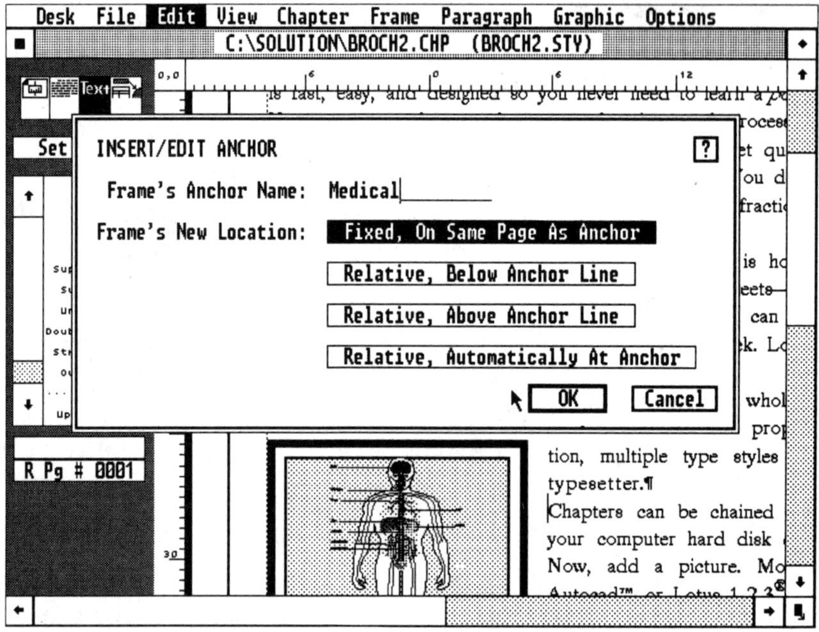

place this anchor in a headline, subheading, or other prominently featured text where the anchor is easy to find.

Step 3 **Place frame anchor**

Access **EDIT•Ins. Special Edit Item** and select Frame Anchor. Enter the anchor name of the frame in the Frame's Anchor Name line. Select the desired anchor option:

▲ **Fixed, On Same Page as Anchor:** The frame will always copy to the same place on the page no matter where the text is.

▲ **Relative, Below Anchor Line:** The frame will always appear below the position of the text.

▲ **Relative, Above Anchor Line:** The frame will always appear above the position of the text.

▲ **Relative, Automatically at Anchor:** The frame will snap to the text baseline at the point where the anchor symbol appears. This is used for special applications.

Step 4 **Re–anchor frame**

When you have performed edits to your chapter and need to re–anchor the frame to the same page as the anchor text, access **CHAPTER•Re–Anchor Frame**. You have two choices:

▲ **This Page:** Will re–anchor only those frames which appear on current page.

▲ **All Pages:** Will re–anchor all pages in the chapter.

☞ CAUTION: For long chapter files, it is sometimes necessary to re–anchor frames several times for all frames to display on the correct pages.

Recipe: Anchoring Frames in the Word Processor

Because frame anchoring is a multi–step process, involving operations in both the Frame and Text modes, it can add significantly to the time involved in creating a document first draft. You can reduce the amount of time necessary to do this by creating and assigning draft frame anchor names to text in the word processor file, recording the names used on a draft hard copy, then going frame to frame and assigning the draft anchor names to the correct frames in Ventura.

The easiest way to do this is to prepare a simple macro or key–insert file which contains the basic anchoring code. That code is <$&ANCHOR NAME>. With additional symbols you can specify the specific anchoring option to use in the code. Placing this code bracket using the macro, simplifies the process even further.

Step 1 **Print document draft**

Print a draft of your document text in either Ventura form or simple word processor text form.

Step 2 **Place anchor text attributes in text**

In your word processor, place code brackets for frame anchor at the position where the frame is to be anchored in the text. Determine a frame anchor name and insert it into the code brackets. At the same time, *write the frame anchor name in the correct position on your printed copy.*

Step 3 **Draw and copy frames**

Access Ventura Publisher and load your text file.

Step 4 **Draw frames and load pictures**

Access **FILE•Load Text/Picture** and load all pictures to be placed in the document. Draw frames in the correct place in the document.

Step 5 **Enter frame anchor names**

Select frames on screen. Using your printed text with the anchor names in place, access **FRAME•Anchors & Captions** and enter the correct frame name which will link the frame to the desired text.

Step 6 **Load pictures into frames**

Place picture files into the desired frames. When not working directly on pictures, select **OPTIONS•Hide All Pictures** to save editing time.

Application Notes

- **Anchoring codes:** A listing of the correct anchoring codes to place in word processor text files can be found in the Appendixes.
- **Pre–formatting text:** Place frame anchor codes directly in word processor text file to save time. Turn to page 477.
- **Long documents** Anchor illustrations to easily identified text elements like headings or subheadings. This makes anchor code easy to find in Ventura or in text processor during editing and production.

Designing with Stacked Frames

Frames are controlled areas in a Ventura document, and they can be stacked, or pasted on top of one another as easily as sheets of paper. Stacking frames on top of one another allows you to create many different layout and design effects.

On the first level, frames serve to block space in a document for illustrations and graphics. Once you create a blocking frame, you can then position several smaller picture or text frames within it. Some of the principal uses for stacked frames are:

- **Blocking document space:** Draw frame to block an open area on page. Text and pictures can be placed in smaller stacked frames.
- **Special layout effects:** Draw overlapping and offset frames to control text flow and place pictures.
- **Special illustration effects:** Double stack pictures and place pictures behind text blocks for special layout effects.
- **Technical considerations:** Place elements in order when printers don't recognize transparent graphics.

When using stacked frames, remember the importance of frame anchoring. If you define a delicate document effect with frames, the only way maintain that effect through normal editing is to anchor every frame in the layout to an identified area of text.

Recipe: Stacking Frames

Step 1 **Draw base frame**

The base frame is usually the largest frame in a stack, used to block space on the page. Enable ***Frame*** mode and use Add New Frame in the Side–Bar to draw the base frame to the desired size. You may enter frame dimensions and position with numeric values by accessing **FRAME•Sizing & Scaling**.

Step 2 **Draw stacked frames**

Use Add New Frame in the Side–Bar to draw a new frame on top of the original frame. Repeat this procedure for each stacked frame.

Step 3 **Place frame contents**

Use Control–Select to select the desired stacked frame and place the desired text file, illustration, or Ventura graphic drawing in the frame.

Editing Stacked Frames

When editing stacked frame layouts, select the frame containing the text picture or graphic you are working on. By clicking on the screen,

Designing with Stacked Frames
Page 254

Ventura tends to select the largest frame in the vicinity, usually your blocking frame. To select stacked frames, use Control–Select.

Step 1 **Select desired frame**

Press the Control key as you point at the desired frame and click the mouse button. Ventura may select the base frame and others in the stack first. Continue clicking until your frame is selected. Use the filename displayed in the Current Selection Box to verify you have selected the right frame.

Step 2 **Make edits to selected frame**

With frame selected, make the desired edits to the frame.

Recipe: Hollow and Opaque Frames

Although Ventura frames do not have hollow and opaque settings as Ventura graphics do, the same effect may be created using the Frame Background feature. Frames are hollow or transparent unless a solid color is set for the Frame Background.

Step 1 **Set solid or hollow frame**

▲ **Hollow frames:** This is the default value of all frames. To change an opaque frame to hollow, enable ***Frame*** mode and select the frame. Access **FRAME•Frame Background** and set Pattern: Hollow. Selected color doesn't matter.

▲ **Transparent frames:** Access **FRAME•Frame Background**. Set desired color and set Pattern to *any setting but* Solid.

☞ CAUTION: Verify that your printer is capable of printing transparent frames. PostScript printers, for instance, cannot.

▲ **Opaque frames:** Access **FRAME•Frame Background** and set Color: White or desired background color and set Pattern: Solid. This suppresses anything appearing beneath the frame, including the display of the column guides and rules in the base page.

Step 2 **Send to Back, Bring to Front**

When using opaque frames, you can create situations in which a stacked frame is hidden behind an opaque frame. Ventura contains no formal Send To Back/Bring To Front feature for frames. You can, however, use frame Cut/Copy/Paste features to cut the partially hidden frame and then paste it on top of the opaque frame.

▲ **Select hidden frame:** Enable ***Frame*** mode. Press the Control key while selecting the hidden frame. Use the file name displayed in the Current Selection Box to verify the correct frame is selected.

▲ **Cut frame:** Select **EDIT•Cut Frame** to cut the frame and place it on the invisible clipboard.

▲ **Bring frame to front:** Select **EDIT•Paste Frame** and the hidden frame will be pasted on top of the opaque frame.

Recipe: Moving Stacked Frames

Once you have created a stacked frame effect, you can easily move or copy it to a different place in your document, or into another chapter using multiple frame select and Cut/Copy/Paste.

Step 1 **Multiple select all frames**

Enable ***Frame*** mode. Press the Shift key as you select all stacked frames which make up the complete layout. If you are having trouble selecting one or more frames in the stack, simultaneously press the Control key as you select frames. When completed, you should see sizing boxes around each of the selected frames on screen.

Step 2 **Place multiple frames in the copy clipboard**

To move multiple frames from one place to another, select **EDIT•Cut Frame**. To copy them, select **EDIT•Copy Frame**. Both options place the multiple frames into the clipboard.

Step 3 **Place multiple frame in destination**

Once the multiple frames are in the copy clipboard, you can move them to a new place inside the chapter or to a new chapter file:

▲ **Inside the chapter:** Go to the page on which the multiple frame is to appear and select **EDIT•Paste Frame**.

▲ **In new chapter:** Select **FILE•Save** to save current chapter. Access **FILE•Open Chapter** and select the name of the chapter to receive the multiple frames. Go to the page where to place the multiple frames and Select **EDIT•Paste Frame**. Select **FILE•Save** to save the frames and the files they contain into the new chapter.

Recipe: Anchoring Stacked Frames

When creating effects using stacked frames, it is extremely important to anchor the frames to a string of text on the page. When the document is edited page position can change as text is added and deleted. If stacked frame effects are not anchored, you may have to individually recreate them, or complete an exhaustive round of frame Cut/Copy/Paste operations to move them back into position.

When assigning anchor names to stacked frames, use names that make it clear which is the base, or blocking frame. For enclosed frames, create an easy–memory method, such as using the eight–digit filename of the text or picture file contained in the frame as its anchor name.

Step 1 **Assign frame names**

Enable ***Frame*** mode and select the frame to be anchored. Access **FRAME•Anchors & Captions**. Enter the anchor name on the Anchor line. Repeat this operation for each frame in the stack. Write down each anchor name as you assign it. Note: it doesn't matter whether anchor names are in all caps, upper and lowercase, or a combination of both. Ventura will read them regardless.

Step 2 **Assign anchor positions**

Enable ***Text*** mode. Place cursor into a string of text which you want to appear on the same page as the multiple frame layout. Access **EDIT•Ins. Special Edit Item** and select Frame Anchor. Enter the anchor name on the Frame's Anchor Name line and select the desired anchor option. When working with stacked frames, it is better to select the Fixed, On Same Page As Anchor option to reduce confusion and possibility of error. Repeat this operation for each frame in the stack.

☞ CAUTION: Depending on the anchoring option selected, position of individual frames in the stacked layout may have to be adjusted.

Application Notes

- **Stacked frames with graphics:** When developing a complex illustrations using stacked frames, do not attach all graphics to the blocking frame. To apply graphic enhancements to a picture in the stacked frame effect, select that picture and draw the graphics. Using this approach, the graphics stay with the picture, even if the stacked frame effect is edited or revised.
- **Shading and design effects:** Experiment with different shading and design effects in your stacked frames. Remember that any solid color setting will make the frame opaque and overprint anything behind it.

Creating Picture Composites

In some applications, you may want to combine one or more pictures into a single illustration or effect. You can convert and combine pictures using an external graphics or drawing program and load the completed picture into Ventura.

This technique is best used with pictures created in Line–Art drawing software, such as Micrografx Designer, Corel Draw or GEM Artline. Bit–mapped image files, which are collections of dots, will appear transparent when placed on top of other pictures. But some vector graphic formats can draw pictures as clusters of two– dimensional shapes, just like Ventura graphics. Files created in this way can appear as opaque when placed inside a Ventura frame, and can overprint anything behind them. Experiment with different picture files to see if they appear opaque or transparent inside frames.

If pictures are opaque, they can be placed into individual pictures into frames and stacked them on top of one another. By sizing and positioning the stacked frames, you can integrate different pieces of art into a single layout. This is very useful when the pictures to combine are of different types, for example, a GEM file (Line–Art) and a PC–Paintbrush file (Image).

Recipe: Picture Composites

Step 1 **Select and load artwork**

Before you begin laying out picture composites, load all the artwork you will need. Access **FILE•Load Text/Picture**. Select Line–Art or Image options and the target file format. If you are loading more than one file in a single format, set # of Files to Several. Repeat this operation for files in each format you are using so that all picture files to be used in the composite appear in the Assignment List.

Step 2 **Draw blocking frame**

Enable ***Frame*** mode and use Add New Frame in the Side–Bar to draw the blocking frame. The frame should be large enough to comfortably contain the complete picture composite.

Creating Picture Composites
Page 260

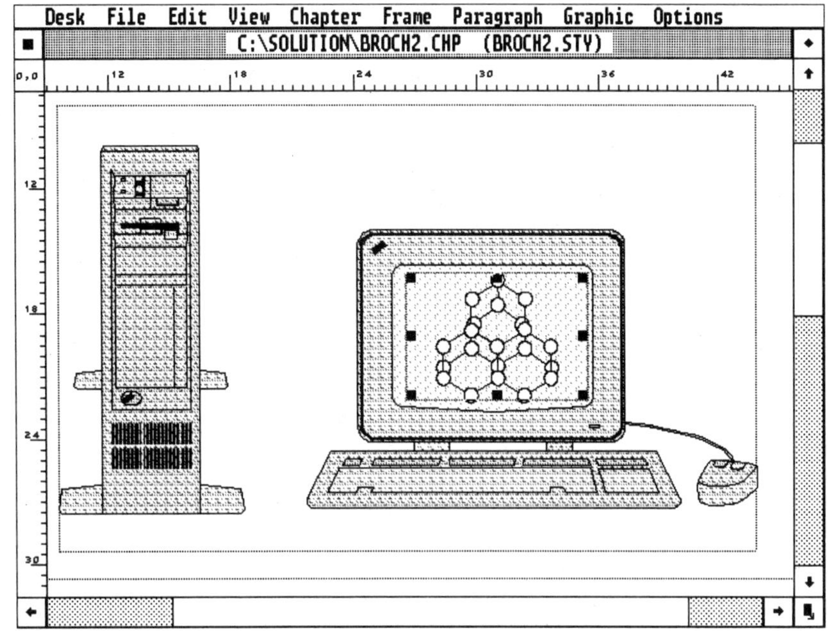

Step 3 **Draw stacked frames and load artwork**

Use Add New Frame in the Side–Bar to draw additional frames to contain the artwork for the picture composite.

Step 4 **Position stacked frame**

Place cursor inside frames, press and hold the mouse button and drag the frames into position to achieve the desired effect. To make fine adjustments to frame size and position, access **FRAME•Sizing & Scaling**. Adjust frame size using Frame Height and Frame Width. Adjust frame position using Upper Left X and Upper Left Y.

Step 5 **Anchor completed illustration**

Enable ***Frame*** mode. Select each frame in the composite, access **FRAME•Anchors & Captions** and assign an anchor name. Enable ***Text*** mode and place anchors in text for each frame.

Application Notes

- **Series effects:** Show the same illustration with different pictures moving into various positions over other pages.

- **Multiples:** Stack multiple copies of the same picture into a pattern or design by copying the picture frame and pasting a number of copies of it.
- **Shading effects:** Add shading patterns to one or more frames in the picture composite to add color or shading to the illustrations.
- **Ripple pages effects:** Using opaque frames with ruling lines, create frames that look like "pages." By creating a stack of offset opaque frames, create a pattern of rippling pages, each showing different text or illustrations.
- **Graphic forms:** Add geometric forms and shading by drawing Ventura graphics into one or more of the frames in the picture composite. Turn to page 304
- **Title elements:** Add titles and text to the picture composite using Box Text graphics in one or more of the frames of the picture composite. Turn to page 310.

Placing Pictures and Backgrounds

Many high–end graphic programs such as Corel Draw and Micrografx Designer offer ready–made background patterns and elements to be used as backgrounds for your pictures and illustrations. The editing capabilities in the third party graphics program provide the means to customize the backgrounds and design them in geometric and free–form shapes.

These custom backgrounds let you devise a texture and look for an entire page or a section of a page. By stacking pictures and text over a background, you can create many exciting and interesting designs and visual enhancements.

This technique is best used with pictures created in Line–Art drawing software, such as Micrografx Designer, Corel Draw or GEM Artline. Bit–mapped image files, which are collections of dots, will appear transparent over the background. But some vector graphic formats can draw pictures as clusters of two–dimensional shapes, just like Ventura graphics. Files created in this way can appear as

Placing Pictures and Backgrounds

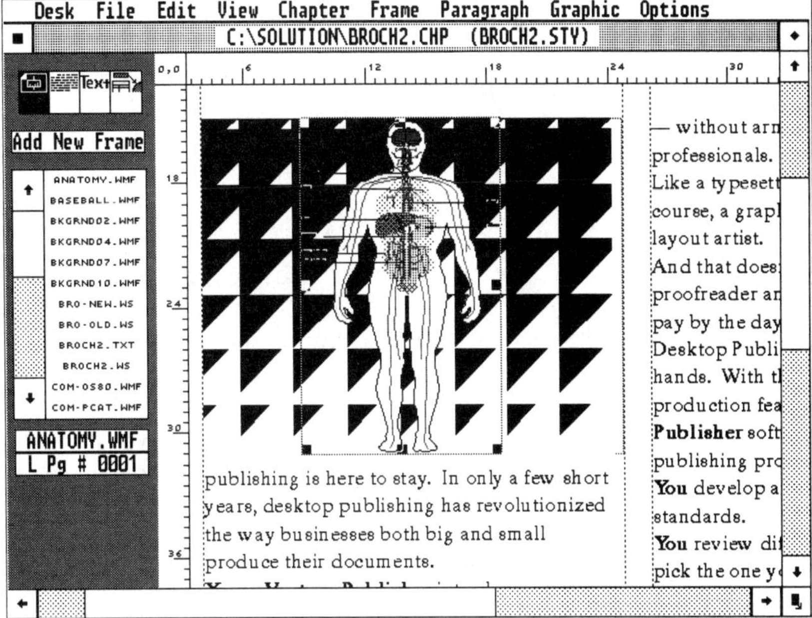

opaque when placed inside a Ventura frame, and can overprint any text or picture background behind them.

Files used to illustrate this concept are drawn from Micrografx Designer clip art and GEM Artline sample files. When using this technique, experiment with your drawing package and clip art files to see if they appear opaque or transparent in a frame.

If files appear transparent, you can use the Graphics Link Plus or other picture conversion software to convert them into a format where you can edit them together with the picture background into a single unified picture element.

Backgrounds available include ornamental patterns, radiating fountain patterns, and a variety of other optical effects. With stacking frames, you can easily incorporate these elements in your documents.

Recipe: Pictures and Background Elements

Step 1 **Place and size background**

Enable ***Frame*** mode and use Add New Frame in the Side–Bar to draw a blocking frame.

Step 2 **Load and stack picture elements**

Access **FILE•Load Text/Picture**, select Line–Art or Image and the target file format to load picture files. With ***Frame*** mode enabled, use Add New Frame to draw frames to hold pictures.

Step 3 **Position pictures over background**

Move frames over the background elements in the position you want.

Step 4 **Anchor completed illustration**

Anchor all frames, including the background frame, to a section of text which must appear on the same page as the illustration.

Application Notes

- **Picture file conversions:** Turn to page 484.
- **Create illustrated text:** Use backgrounds to create illustrated text effects. Turn to page 123.
- **Use with graphics:** Use custom backgrounds in combination with graphic effects. Turn to page 332.
- **Use in page design:** Use custom backgrounds as part of page design using repeating frames. Turn to page 330.

Creating Freeform Framing Effects

Ventura graphics allow you to create simple graphic forms, but they don't have the custom editing effects necessary to create complex geometric or freeform shapes to use as backgrounds for pictures and display text elements.

You can, however, use third–party products such as Corel Draw, Adobe Illustrator, Windows Version or GEM Artline to create a virtually infinite number of freeform picture backgrounds. When you have created the desired background shape, save it in a Ventura Publisher compatible file format. Once in Ventura you load the background form like any picture file and stack the picture to be framed on top of it.

For use as framing elements, it is best to design forms that have a solid white interior with framing lines and/or drop shadow effects around the perimeter.

Recipe: Freeform Framing Effects

Step 1 **Design background shapes**

In third–party program, design irregular, freeform shapes to serve as frames.

Step 2 **Export to Ventura compatible files**

Use the Save As or Export command in the third–party software to save the completed freeform frames into a Ventura compatible Line–Art or Image file format.

Step 3 **Load all files to Ventura**

Load Ventura Publisher and enable ***Frame*** mode. Access **FILE•Load Text/Picture** and select Line–Art or Image, the target file format, and

Creating Freeform Framing Effects

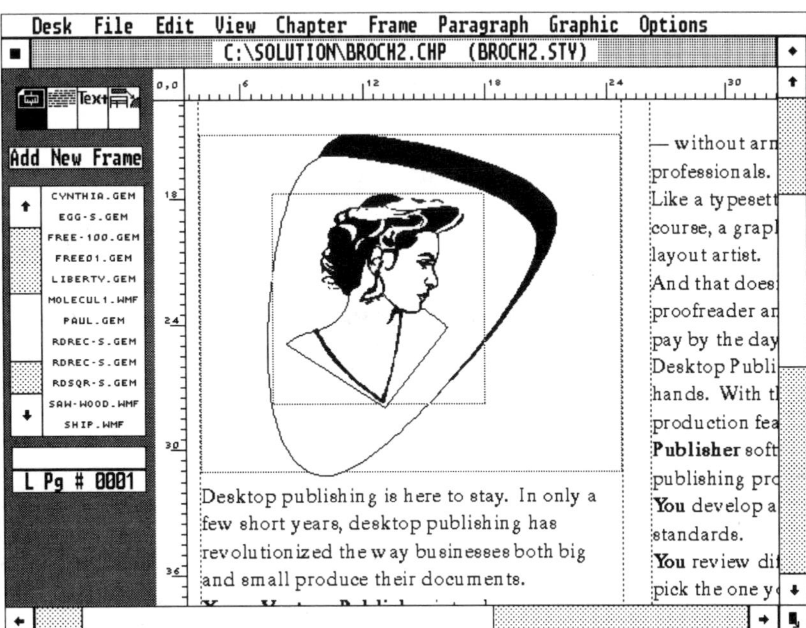

the desired files. Repeat this step with all target file formats until all background and picture files are shown in the Assignment List.

Step 4 **Place background**

From ***Frame*** mode, use Add New Frame to draw a frame to contain the background frame. With the frame selected, select the name of the desired background in the Assignment List.

Step 5 **Stack picture**

Use Add New Frame to draw a stacked frame on top of the background. Select the name of the desired picture file in the Assignment list. Use sizing boxes on screen to edit size and position of frame.

Step 6 **Anchor finished illustration**

Anchor all frames in the layout to a section of text that will appear on the same page as the layout.

Application Notes

- **Design library:** Use irregular shapes and backgrounds for display applications and designs.
- **Creating text runarounds:** Turn to page 284.
- **Picture file conversions:** Turn to page 484.
- **Create illustrated text** Use freeform backgrounds to create illustrated text effects. Turn to page 123.
- **Use with graphics** Use custom backgrounds in combination with graphic effects. Turn to page 332.
- **Use in page design** Use custom backgrounds as part of page design using repeating frames. Turn to page 330.

Using a Library of Standard Backgrounds

When working with pictures in Ventura, you may wish to create a variety of standard geometric and irregular framing effects for your pictures. One great time–saving technique is to create a family of basic framing forms in a third–party software package and load those graphics into a subdirectory on your hard disk where they will always be available.

When you want a custom background or framing effect, choose the background form that is closest to the effect you want to create. By distorting the aspect ratio of the background picture, using the picture scaling features in the **FRAME•Sizing & Scaling** dialog box, you can stretch or flatten the basic form into an infinite number of background shapes. In this way, a simple drop–shadow square graphic can be customized into an infinite number of custom rectangular framing backgrounds by changing the sizing & scaling values.

With a library of these framing effects available on your hard disk, you'll always have easy and fast access to picture framing effects. This is especially convenient for irregular, freeform frames and filled geometric shapes such as triangles and pentagons which cannot easily be created in Ventura graphics.

Recipe: Standard Background Forms

Step 1 **Create background family**

In third–party software package, design set of standard backgrounds and drop shadow graphics to have available as needed.

Step 2 **Load files to styles directory**

Copy picture files to a subdirectory other than \TYPESET on your hard disk. The library of background files will always be available for any document you are creating.

Step 3 **Load background file**

Enable ***Frame*** mode and use Add New Frame in the Side–Bar to draw a frame to contain the background file.

Step 4 **Size the background**

Size the background to the desired size using screen–sizing boxes or by accessing **FRAME•Sizing & Scaling** and entering desired Frame Width and Frame Height.

Using a Library of Standard Backgrounds
Page 266

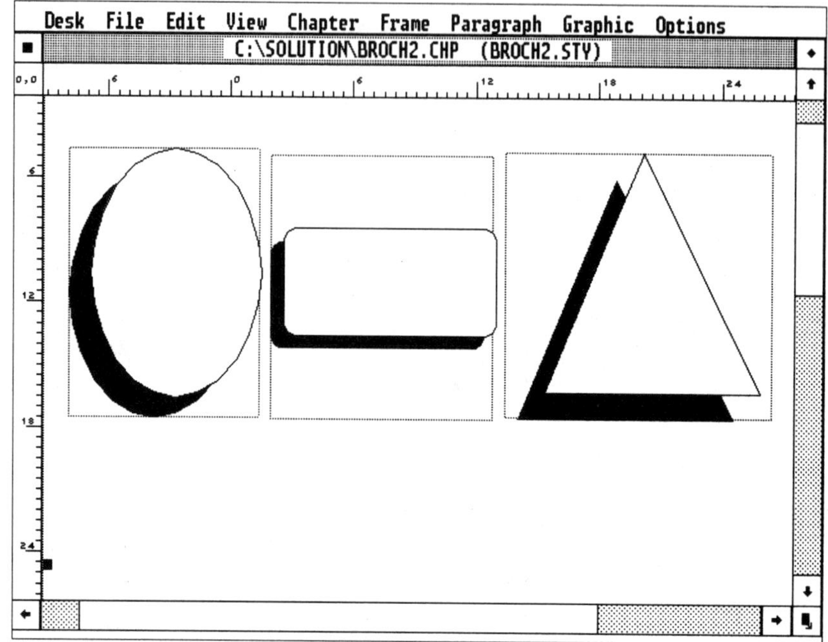

Step 5 **Shape the background**

Produce a variety of different backgrounds from the same file by using horizontal or vertical distortion. Select the frame containing the background, access **FRAME•Sizing & Scaling**. Set Picture Scaling: By Scale Factors.

▲ To flatten the background, decrease Scale Height and/or increase Scale Width.

▲ To narrow the background, decrease Scale Width and/or increase Scale Height.

Step 6 **Draw stacked frame**

From ***Frame*** mode, use Add New Frame to draw a stacked frame.

Step 7 **Place picture**

Access **FILE•Load Text/Picture**, select Line–Art or Image, and select the target file format of the picture to place.

Step 8 **Anchor completed illustration**

Anchor all frames to a position in text.

Application Notes

- **Store in \STYLES subdirectory:** Store production files on the hard disk. Turn to page 471.
- **Picture file conversions:** Turn to page 484.
- **Create illustrated text:** Use backgrounds to create illustrated text effects. Turn to page 123.
- **Use with graphics:** Use custom backgrounds in combination with graphic effects. Turn to page 332.
- **Use in page design:** Use standard backgrounds as part of page design using repeating frames. Turn to page 330.

Designing with Shading Effects

Using stacked frames, you can integrate many different visual effects into a single interesting illustration or layout by adding shading value to frames containing pictures and experimenting with hollow and opaque presentation.

Recipe: Shading Effects

Step 1 **Draw blocking frame**

Enable ***Frame*** mode and use Add New Frame in the Side–Bar to draw the blocking frame.

Step 2 **Select shading and presentation**

A variety of options to place shading in the blocking frame are available:

▲ To shade the entire frame, access **FRAME • Frame Background** and select the desired color and pattern.

▲ To draw a shaded background in a simple geometric shape, Enable ***Graphic*** mode and draw the desired graphic shape. With the graphic selected, access **GRAPHIC•Fill Attributes** and select the desired shading pattern.

▲ Create a freeform background pattern in third–party graphics software and load it into the frame.

Step 3 **Design stacked frames**

Draw additional frames over the blocking frame. Define a special presentation for each. To make frames opaque, access **FRAME• Frame Background** and set Color: White, and Pattern: Solid.

Step 4 **Complete illustration**

Position all stacked frames against the background.

Step 5 **Anchor completed illustration**

Anchor each frame to a position in text.

Application Notes

- **Using stacked frames:** Turn to page 254.
- **Creating picture composites** Use shading effects in multiple picture compositions. Turn to page 260.

Designing with Shading Effects
Page 269

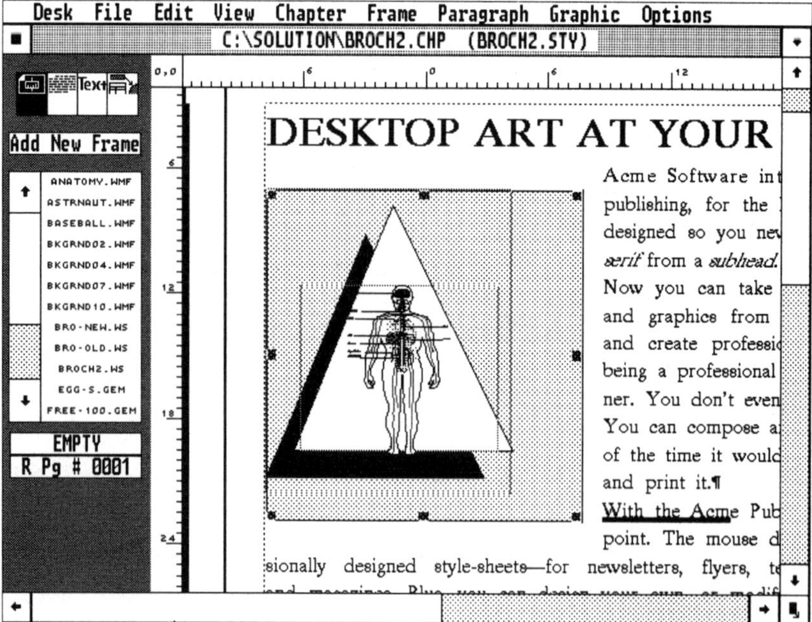

Creating Backgrounds with Frame Rules

Ruling line effects used with frames can also produce backgrounds for pictures. Ruling line attributes can be customized to create a virtually infinite number of background line thicknesses, shading, colors, and dashed effects.

Ventura line graphics don't support dashed lines, but ruling lines do. By assigning custom ruling lines above, below, or around frames, you can create a number of unique and eye–catching backgrounds and enhancements. Use the Ruling Box Around feature to place a pattern of three concentric solid or shaded lines in your frame. Use ruling line above and below features to place ruling framing lines at the top or bottom of your frame.

Backgrounds with Frame Rules

Step 1 **Draw frame**

Enable ***Frame*** mode and use Add New Frame in the Side–Bar to draw the frame.

Step 2 **Assign Ruling Line Above Frame**

Access **FRAME • Ruling Line Above**. A ruling line for a frame must be frame wide. Select desired color, shading pattern and dashed options. Enter line thickness on Height of Rule lines, and spacing between lines on Space Below Rule lines.

Step 3 **Assign Ruling Line Below frame**

Access **FRAME • Ruling Line Below**. A ruling line for a frame must be frame wide. Select desired color, shading pattern and dashed options. Enter line thickness on Height of Rule lines, and spacing between lines on Space Below Rule lines.

Step 4 **Move Ruling Line Below**

Move Ruling Line Below to appear outside of the frame by entering a drop down value on Space Below Rule 3 line and selecting Minus.

Creating Backgrounds with Frame Rules
Page 271

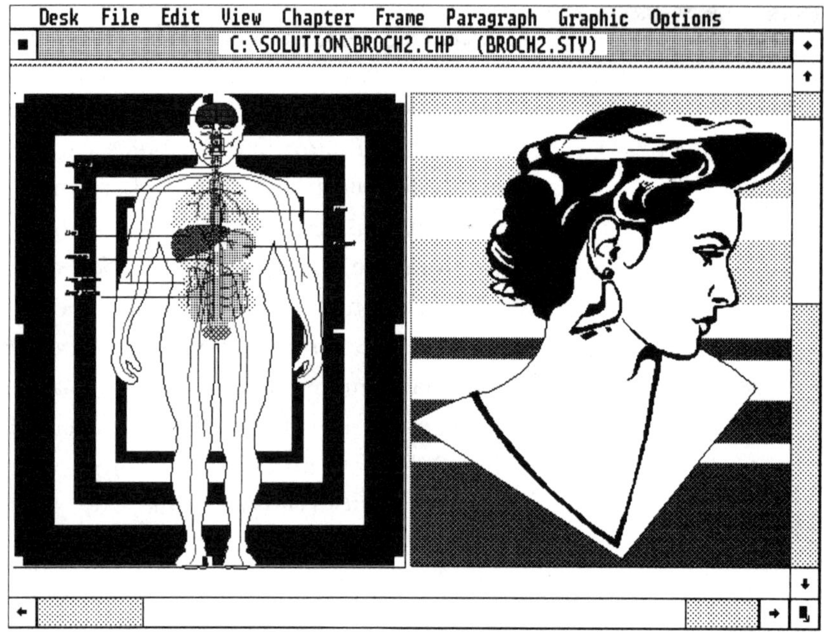

Recipe: Backgrounds with Ruling Box Around

Step 1 **Draw frame**

Enable ***Frame*** mode and use Add New Frame in the Side–Bar to draw the frame.

Step 2 **Assign Ruling Box Around**

Access **FRAME•Ruling Box Around**. A ruling box for a frame must be frame wide. Select desired color, shading pattern, and dashed options. Enter line thickness on Height of Rule lines, and spacing between lines on Space Below Rule lines.

Application Notes

- **Mix and match Above and Below:** By altering the space below and the space above rules, you can drop the Ruling Line Above down to overlay or mix with Ruling Line Below. Try giving each set of lines a different shading or thickness value and experiment with positioning the lines.
- **Title elements:** Use shading and frame rules to create document title elements. Place text in frame and enhance with graphics.

- **Use with Ventura graphics:** Turn to page 310.
- **Link to text with auto–anchor:** Use frame background and ruling line enhancements in frames auto-anchoredto the text baseline. Turn to page 291.

Sizing and Scaling Pictures

Ventura's sizing and scaling features let you manipulate the size, position, and aspect ratio of pictures. When used in concert with stacked graphics, these features provide a variety of editing and picture effects in Ventura Publisher.

To make a picture fit perfectly into a frame, change the Scale Width to match the width of the frame. Ventura will then rescale the picture and tell you what the frame height should be for the picture to fit perfectly into the area. Once you have defined this relationship, you can size and scale the frame on screen and in the dialog box.

Some pictures contain a large area of white space around the actual picture material. You may have to use Sizing & Scaling to zero in on the actual picture area to get around this problem.

To define the size and position of the picture frame to the last fractional point, identify this in the Sizing & Scaling dialog box. *You should make height & width settings to the frame before beginning picture scaling operations.* If you change the frame size after scaling a picture, you will have to rescale.

Recipe: Sizing and Scaling Pictures

Step 1 **Set frame dimensions**

Enable ***Frame*** mode and use Add New Frame in the Side–Bar to draw a frame. Access **FRAME•Sizing & Scaling** and set the exact desired dimensions of the frame.

Step 2 **Place picture**

Access **FILE•Load Text/Picture** and load the picture to be placed in the frame.

Step 3 **Select picture scaling**

Access **FRAME • Sizing & Scaling**. Pictures automatically are scaled to Fit In Frame. If there is a large buffer of white space in the picture file itself, the actual picture area may seem very small inside of the frame. To resize the picture, set Picture Scaling: By Scale Factors.

Step 4 **Set Scale Width**

If you set the scale width to equal the width of the current frame, the picture will scale to fit that measurement. To scale the picture to fit the frame, enter the numeric value from the Frame Width line onto the Scale Width line.

Step 5 **Set scale height**

Once you have scaled the width, the picture resizes to match that width. To perfectly fit the picture into a frame while maintaining its aspect ratio, you must resize the height of the *frame* itself to accommodate the picture. The actual height of the picture will be visible in gray on the Scale Height line. Enter the numeric value from the Scale Height line onto the Frame Height line and the picture will be displayed correctly.

Step 6 **Resizing the picture**

Once the picture is scaled to the right width and height, you can resize the picture using the sizing boxes. The aspect ratio you have defined will be maintained.

Recipe: Scaling to Fit

Using Aspect Ratio: Distorted, you can force a picture to fit into a defined space by violating its aspect ratio. The principle here is the same as with regular scaling. Match the Scale Width of the picture to the actual Frame Width, and match the Scale Height of the picture to the actual Frame Height.

Sizing and Scaling Pictures
Page 273

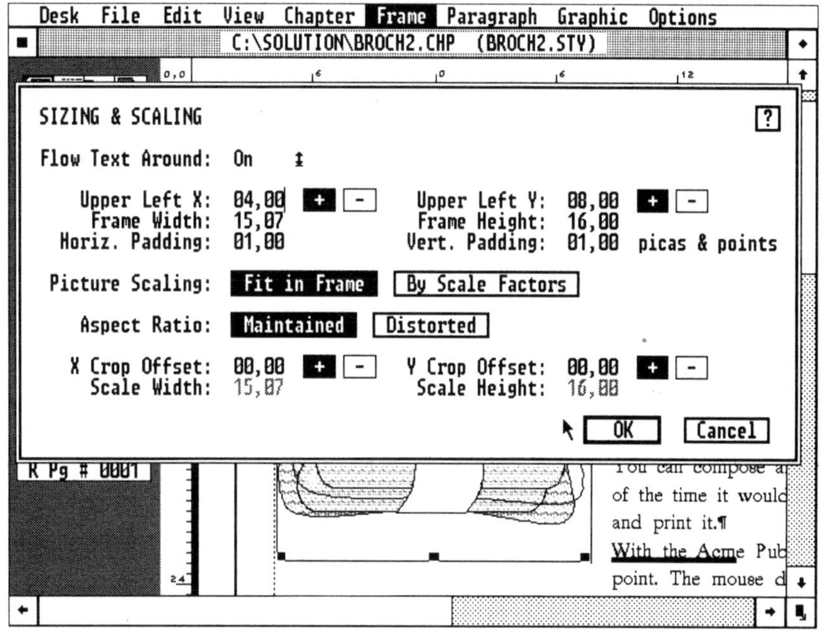

Step 1 **Enable Distorted Scaling**

Enable ***Frame*** mode and select the frame containing the picture. Access **FRAME•Sizing & Scaling**. Set Picture Scaling: By Scale Factors, Distorted.

Step 2 **Set Frame Size**

Enter dimensions on the Frame Width and Frame Height lines.

Step 3 **Match Picture Scale Width**

Enter the numeric value from the Frame Width line on the Scale Width line.

Step 4 **Match Picture Scale Height**

Enter the numeric value from the Frame Height on the Scale Height line. The appearance of the picture will be distorted but it will fit in the defined frame.

Recipe: Onscreen Cropping

In Ventura, you can crop a picture directly from the screen. This allows you to set the position of the picture in the frame, or select a portion of the picture to appear in the frame. Note that during the cropping operation, not all of the picture file may be visible onscreen. When the operation is finished, the complete picture is visible again.

Step 1 **Select picture**

Enable ***Frame*** mode and select picture to be cropped.

Step 2 **Initiate screen crop**

Place the mouse cursor inside the frame. Press and hold the Alt key while pressing and holding the mouse button. The cursor changes to the cropping cursor (an open palm). Drag the mouse to position the picture as desired.

Step 3 **End cropping operation**

Release the Alt key and mouse button when positioning is correct.

Cropping by the Numbers

Step 1 **Select picture**

Enable ***Frame*** mode and select frame with picture to be cropped.

Step 2 **Measure crop offsets**

Use Screen Rulers to measure the distance that the picture is to be moved.

Step 3 **Set picture scaling**

Access **FRAME•Sizing & Scaling** and set Picture Scaling: By Scale Factors.

Step 4 **Set X Crop Offset**

Enter the distance the picture is to move horizontally on the X Crop Offset line. Select Plus to move left by that distance, select Minus to move right by that distance.

Step 5 **Set Y Crop Offset**

Enter the distance the picture is to move vertically on the Y Crop Offset line. Select Plus to move up by that distance, select Minus to move down by that distance.

Application Notes

- **Third–party autoscaling:** Once frame size has been defined, use third–party products like The Graphics Link Plus and to automatically scale a series of pictures to exactly fit those dimensions.

Scaling Pictures for Design Effects

Using Sizing & Scaling, you can stretch and flatten pictures as well as increase them to a specific size. This allows you do make visual edits directly in Ventura without having to return to source software.

The distorted scaling option can be used in a similar way to copyfitting with text. If you have a picture that must fit into a defined space, use slight vertical or horizontal distortion to fit the picture into the frame. In combination with cropping features, you can zero in on any part of a picture and scale it to fit in any area.

Recipe: Scaling Pictures for Design Effects

Step 1 **Select picture**

Enable ***Frame*** mode and select the picture to be scaled.

Step 2 **Size frame**

Access **FRAME•Sizing & Scaling** and enter exact dimensions for Frame Width and Frame Height.

Step 3 **Enter scale values**

Set Picture Scaling: By Scale Factors and select Aspect Ratio: Distorted. Enter the numeric value from the Frame Width line on the Scale Width line. Enter the numeric value from the Frame Height line onto the Scale Height line.

Recipe: Progressive Distortion Effects

To design an effect that shows the same illustration progressively changing size and shape in a series, or over several pages, work directly in Ventura, rather than going through complex editing procedures in the source software.

Step 1 **Draw blocking frame**

Enable ***Frame*** mode and use Add New Frame in the Side–Bar to draw the blocking frame.

Step 2 **Place picture**

Draw stacked frame. Access **FILE•Load Text/Picture** to load the desired picture into the Assignment List. Select the stacked frame and load the picture into the frame.

Step 3 **Copy picture**

With the picture frame selected, select **EDIT•Copy Frame** to place the frame in the invisible clipboard. Go to the new page where the frame is to appear. Select **EDIT•Paste Frame** to place additional copies of the frame. If it is to appear on the same page, the copy will directly overprint the original. Select copy and move into position. Repeat operation as many times as necessary.

Step 4 **Enable distorted picture scaling for each copy**

Select a frame containing the picture and Access **FRAME•Sizing & Scaling**. Set Picture Scaling: By Scale Factors and select Distorted.

▲ To flatten the picture, decrease the Scale Height and/or increase the Scale Width.

▲ To narrow the picture, decrease the Scale Width and/or increase the Scale Height.

Step 5 **Complete illustration**

Set scaling and distortion values for all copies of the picture and position them as desired.

Step 6 **Anchor illustration**

Anchor all illustration to a position in text.

Scaling Pictures for Design Effects
Page 277

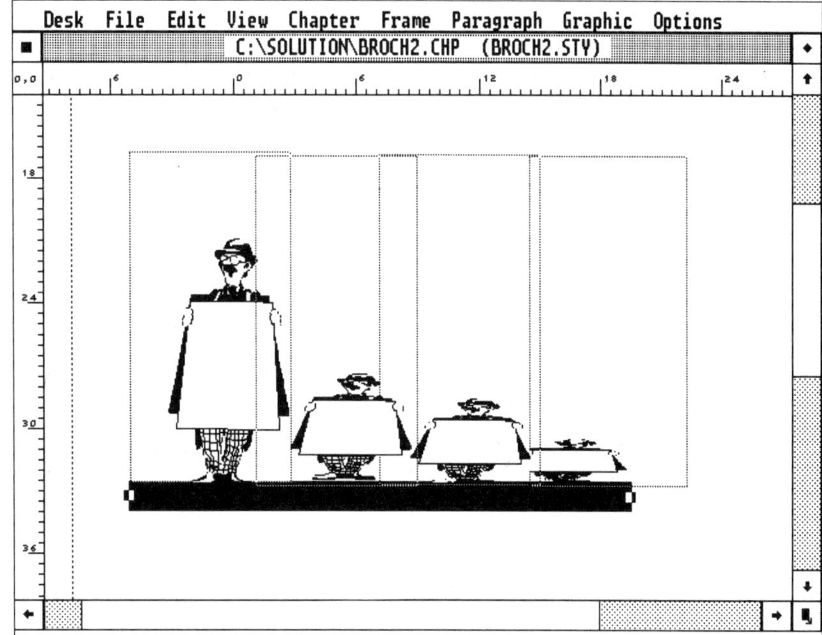

Application Notes

- **Special effects:** Use distortion in combination with frame stacking and graphics. By experimenting with horizontal and vertical distortion separately or together, you can create variations and refinements of standard picture files, icons, and images.

- **Preview picture editing:** Distortion allows you to see what a given picture will look like in the context of your document layout. Before making changes to a picture in a third–party graphics or drawing package, use distorted scaling to see how the revised image might look in your application.

Creating Captions

Ventura makes it easy to link captions to a picture. You simply tell it to place a caption at the top, bottom, left, or right of the picture, and a generated frame is automatically created. You can create many of exciting effects with captions, using the available features in Ventura.

Recipe: Captions

Step 1 **Create frame**

Enable ***Frame*** mode and use Add New Frame in the Side–Bar to draw a frame. Place desired text, picture, or graphics in the frame.

Step 2 **Turn on caption**

With frame selected, access **FRAME•Anchors & Captions**. Select the desired position of the Caption frame using the Caption option.

Step 3 **Enter caption text**

Enable ***Text*** mode. Place cursor on the end of file marker in the caption frame and enter the caption text directly into the caption frame. You have two ways to accomplish this:

- ▲ Type caption text directly into frame.
- ▲ Load prepared text file containing caption text. With the cursor on the end of file marker, access **FILE•Load Text/Picture**, select Text and the target word processor format. Set Location: Text Cursor, and select the desired file.

Recipe: Customizing the Caption Frame

The caption frame is generated to match dimensions with its reference frame. That is, captions on the top or bottom must always be the same width as the main frame. Captions at the left or right must always be the same height. However, Ventura provides a wide choice of options to customize the caption frame.

Step 1 **Size caption frame**

Increase the size of the caption frame by selecting it and using the sizing boxes. For specific sizing requirements, select the caption frame and access **FRAME•Sizing & Scaling** and enter the desired value for the frame width or height.

☞ CAUTION: Ventura does not permit the contact edge of a caption frame to be wider or taller than its parent frame. If you use Sizing & Scaling to increase the contact edge of the caption frame, the parent frame will increase in size to match.

Creating Captions
Page 279

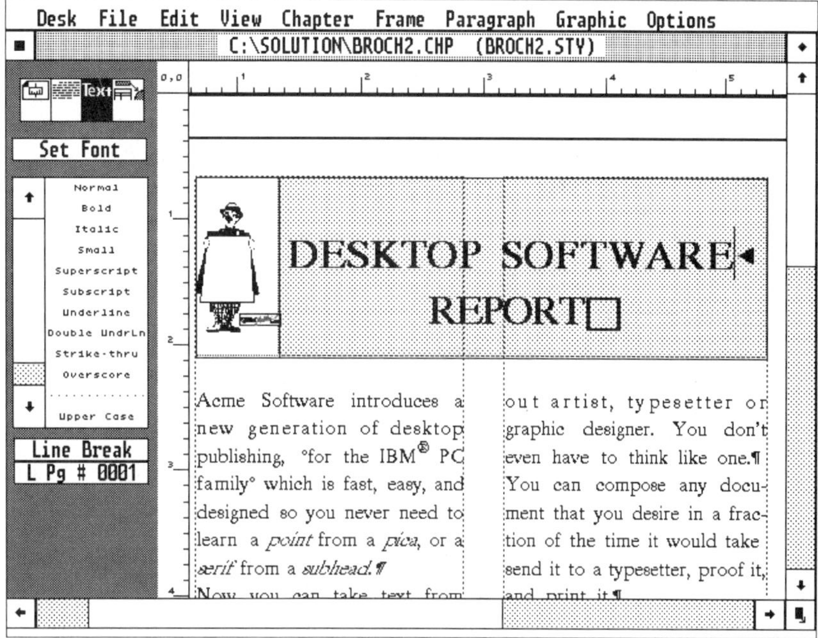

Step 2 **Set caption frame margins**

To set margins inside the caption frame, access **FRAME•Margins & Columns** and set margin and column values. Caption frame Margin & Column values may be different from those in the parent frame.

Step 3 **Set caption frame padding**

If you have set padding values to the parent frame, those values are *not* automatically assigned to the caption frame. To match padding values, select the caption frame and access **FRAME•Sizing & Scaling**. Enter matching horizontal and vertical padding values.

Step 4 **Set caption frame rules**

Ruling lines assigned to the parent frame don't automatically appear on the caption frame. To apply ruling lines to the caption frame, select the caption frame, and access the desired ruling line dialog box on the ***Frame*** menu.

Step 5 **Set caption frame background**

Frame background and shading set for the parent frame do not automatically transfer to the caption. To apply shading values, select the caption frame, access **FRAME•Frame Background**, and set the desired values.

Creating a Caption Label

In applications where you need to number illustrations and/or tables, you must enter the Figure # or Table # code into the caption label line in the **FRAME•Anchors & Captions** dialog box. You can also use the caption label line to enter a short descriptive string of text, such as **Figure [#]: March Sales, Western Region**.

The caption label can be useful in longer publications in several ways. If a standard caption label text format is used, you can make a special caption label sort using the Table of Contents features to create a list of illustrations or tables. In addition, the Professional Extension includes cross–referencing features which can find and insert caption label text at any point in chapter or publication text.

Step 1 **Create caption**

Enable ***Frame*** mode and select frame and access **FRAME• Anchors & Captions**. Position the caption frame using the Caption option.

Step 2 **Set caption label**

Place cursor on Label line and select Figure # or Table # to set the numbering symbol.

Step 3 **Enter caption label text**

Enter any related text to include in the caption label on the caption line; for example: *Figure [#]: Sample 1.*

Step 4 **Enter caption text**

Enable ***Text*** mode. Place cursor on the End of File marker. Enter caption text directly on screen, or load a text file to the text cursor.

☞ CAUTION: You cannot edit caption label text entered in the dialog box from the screen. You must return to the Anchors & Captions dialog box to make any changes to it.

Application Notes

- **Caption label cross–referencing:** Turn to page 410.
- **Create list of illustrations:** Use a special Table of Contents sort to assemble a complete list of tables or illustrations with correct page references. Turn to page 372.
- **Use side captions:** Side captions let you enter and lock a string of text to a picture. You can create many interesting effects by experimenting with side captions and resizing the caption frame.
- **Place photo credits:** In newsletter or magazine layouts, you can place detail information, such as the photo credit, to the side of your frame by creating a special rotated tag using small (6 to 8 point) text to display the caption. To do this, draw a Box Text graphic, enter the photo credit text and apply the rotated tag.
- **Create illustrated sidebars:** By resizing the caption frame, you can create a "caption" that is the length of a short article or sidebar. Using this technique, article are linked into a single sidebar element, which can easily be moved around the document or across chapters.
- **Create illustrated headings:** To create a unified, illustrated heading element, draw a small frame and place an illustration or graphic. Place a right side caption, and expand the caption frame to the width of the page. The caption frame is now large enough to receive large headline text. This unified headline element can now be copied anywhere you want in the document. If you set the headline text values using Set Font instead of a paragraph tag, you can copy the title box across chapters without having to create a new tag.
- **Graphic enhancement:** Link Ventura graphics to the main frame to serve as background or enhancement to the caption text.
- **Frame anchoring:** Turn to page 251.

Creating Text Runarounds

Text runarounds are design effects which wrap text around the irregular shape of an illustration or other graphic element on the page. You can force text to flow around picture forms by drawing a series of blocking frames that control the position of text.

To produce a text runaround effect, place a picture in a frame, remove text flow around from that frame so that text can pour in over the picture. Then, build a system of blocking frames to move text from the picture area.

Recipe: Text Runarounds

Step 1 **Draw picture frame**

Enable ***Frame*** mode and use Add New Frame in the Side–Bar to draw a frame to hold the picture.

Step 2 **Remove text flow around**

Access **FRAME•Sizing & Scaling**. Set Flow Text Around: Off.

Step 3 **Draw blocking frames**

To control the position of text overprinting the picture, use Add New Frame in the Side–Bar to draw new frames on top of the picture, pushing the text away from the picture area. Draw as many frames as necessary to place the text where desired.

Recipe: Single–line Frame Runaround

For a more detailed runaround effect, you may wish to use single line runarounds. This technique is based upon the Options: Line Snap feature. When turned on, it forces frames to vertically snap in increments of the Body Text interline spacing, in short, one–line–high frames.

In this technique, draw the picture frame and remove the text flow around as in the standard runaround. Then cover the entire picture with a grid of one–line–high frames. By adjusting the horizontal dimension of the frames, you can neatly fit each line of text exactly where you want it.

Step 1 **Draw picture frame**

Enable ***Frame*** mode and use Add New Frame in the Side–Bar to draw a frame for the picture. Access **FRAME•Sizing & Scaling** and set Text Flow Around: Off. Access **FILE•Load Text/Picture** to load the picture into the frame.

Step 2 **Draw master one line blocking frame**

To force frames to snap vertically to the nearest baseline, Select **OPTIONS•Turn Line Snap On**. Use Add New Frame to draw a frame over the picture, which is the full width of the picture and only *one line high.*

Step 3 **Copy and position one line blocking frames**

With the one–line–high frame selected, select **EDIT•Copy Frame** to load the frame into the invisible clipboard. Select **EDIT•Paste Frame** to paste additional copies on the screen. Use the mouse to select and move the copies into position over the picture. Repeat this procedure until the entire picture is covered with a grid of one–line–high frames.

Creating Text Runarounds

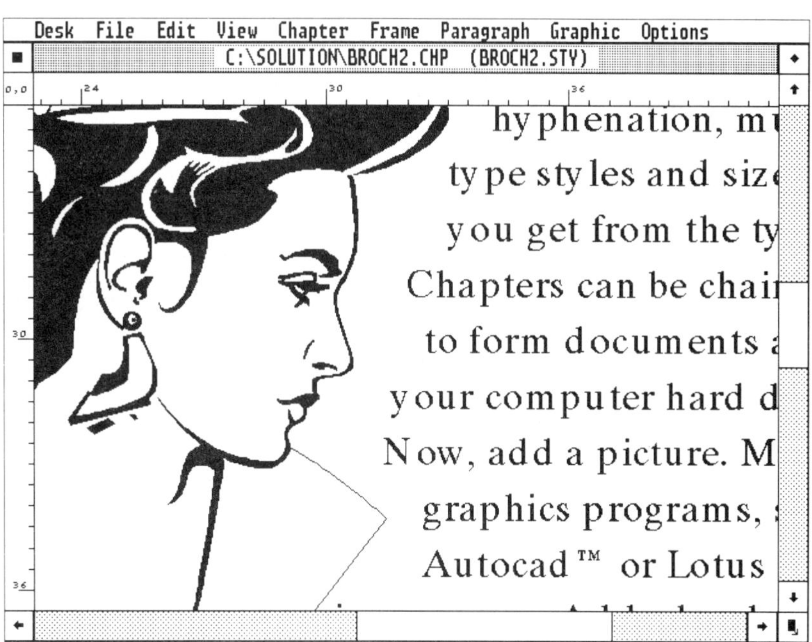

Step 4 **Adjust one line frame width**

To create the detailed runaround effect you wish, use the mouse to adjust the width of each of the one–line–high frames to match the outlines of the picture form. As you reduce the width of the frames, text will flow in and fit neatly next to the picture.

Application Notes

- **Experiment with runaround effects:** Try using frames of different sizes to block text. Using one–line–high frames permits the most detailed and exacting placement of text.
- **Full–page illustrations** For full–page design elements in an advertisement or catalog, place the illustration in a full–page frame and access **FRAME•Sizing & Scaling**. Turn Text Flow Around to Off. Then place individual frames over the illustration to block text.
- **Control text with Margins & Columns** For special page layouts which involve one or more text runarounds, place illustration in frames with Text Flow Around set to Off. Then stack a special frame on top and set special margins and columns to control the text flow on the page. Use blocking frames to keep the text from overprinting the illustration.

Designing Stairstep Runarounds

Using the basic concept of runarounds, you can create runarounds for circular or irregular forms between columns, or for irregular shapes anywhere on the page.

One commonly used effect is the *stairstep runaround* in which the picture is placed in a corner position. Text is made to stairstep neatly down an angled line beside the picture. The best technique for this effect is a variation of single line frame runarounds.

Recipe: Stairstep Runarounds

Step 1 **Draw picture frame**

Enable ***Frame*** mode and use Add New Frame to draw a frame. Access **FRAME•Sizing & Scaling** and set Text Flow Around: Off. Use **FRAME•Load Text/Picture** to load the desired picture.

Step 2 **Draw master one line blocking frame**

To force frames to snap vertically to the nearest baseline, select **OPTIONS•Turn Line Snap On**. Use Add New Frame to draw a frame over the picture, the full width of the picture and only *one line high*.

Step 3 **Copy and position one line blocking frames**

With the one–line–high frame selected, select **EDIT•Copy Frame** to load the frame into the invisible clipboard. Select **EDIT•Paste Frame** to paste additional copies on the screen. Use the mouse to select and move the copies into position over the picture. Repeat this procedure until the entire picture is covered with a grid of one–line–high frames.

Step 4 **Draw graphic guide line**

Enable ***Graphic***. Select line graphic icon and draw a diagonal line to serve as a guide when positioning stairstep runaround frames.

Step 5 **Match blocking frames to guide line**

Enable ***Frame*** mode. Use mouse to edit the width of the one–line–high frames so that they align along the guide line.

Step 6 **Delete guide line**

Enable ***Graphic*** mode. Select the diagonal line and select **EDIT•Cut Graphic** to remove it.

Application Notes

- **Experiment with runaround effects:** Try using frames of different sizes to block text. Using one–line–high frames permits the most detailed and exacting placement of text.
- **Angle runarounds:** Use stairstep runaround concept to create angled or irregular geometric text flow around effects. Draw line

Designing Stairstep Runarounds
Page 286

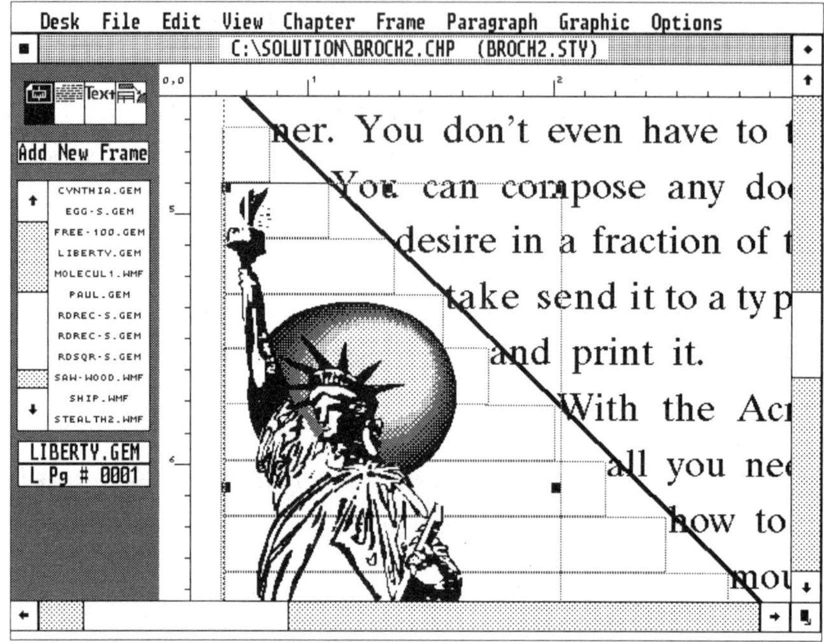

graphics in angle pattern desired and use them as a guide to position one–line–high frames.

- **Circle runarounds:** Use circle graphic to draw curved guidelines around picture element. Use curved form as a guide to position one–line–high frames.

Creating Master Runaround Frames

If you develop many documents requiring runarounds, you can significantly reduce the time necessary to produce them by creating a master runaround frame which then can be copied into your chapters from the \STYLES directory.

A master runaround frame consists of a picture frame with the text flow around turned off, covered by a grid of one–line–high frames. By copying the master frame into the chapter file, all you have to do is load the picture into the picture frame and adjust the width of the blocking frames.

Note that the one–line runaround idea assumes that the one–line–high frames are the same height as the Body Text interline spacing in the document. If you design documents in several standard Body Text sizes, you may want to develop master runaround frames which are ready to load into your chapters.

Recipe: Create Master Runaround Frames

Step 1 **Draw frame**

Enable ***Frame*** mode. Select **FILE•New** to clear the screen. Use Add New Frame in the Side–Bar to draw frame to hold picture. Access **FRAME•Sizing & Scaling** and set Text Flow Around: Off.

Step 2 **Create runaround frame grid**

Draw a one–line–high frame which is as wide as the picture frame. With the one–line–high frame selected, select **EDIT•Copy Frame** to load the frame into the invisible clipboard. Select **EDIT•Paste Frame** to paste additional copies on the screen. Use the mouse to select and move the copies into position over the picture. Repeat this procedure until the entire picture is covered with a grid of one–line–high frames.

Step 3 **Save in chapter file**

Access **FILE•Save As** and enter the name for the template chapter.

Step 4 **Copy to \STYLES directory**

Using Copy All in the Multi–Chapter Operations dialog box, copy the template chapter to your hard disk directory of production files.

Recipe: Copy Master Runaround Frame

Step 1 **Open frame chapter in \STYLES directory**

Access **FILE•Open Chapter** and load the template chapter on screen.

Step 2 **Multiple select all frames**

Enable ***Frame*** mode. Press the Shift as you select all frames on the screen. Simultaneously press the Control key to select the picture frame beneath the grid.

Creating Master Runaround Frames
Page 288

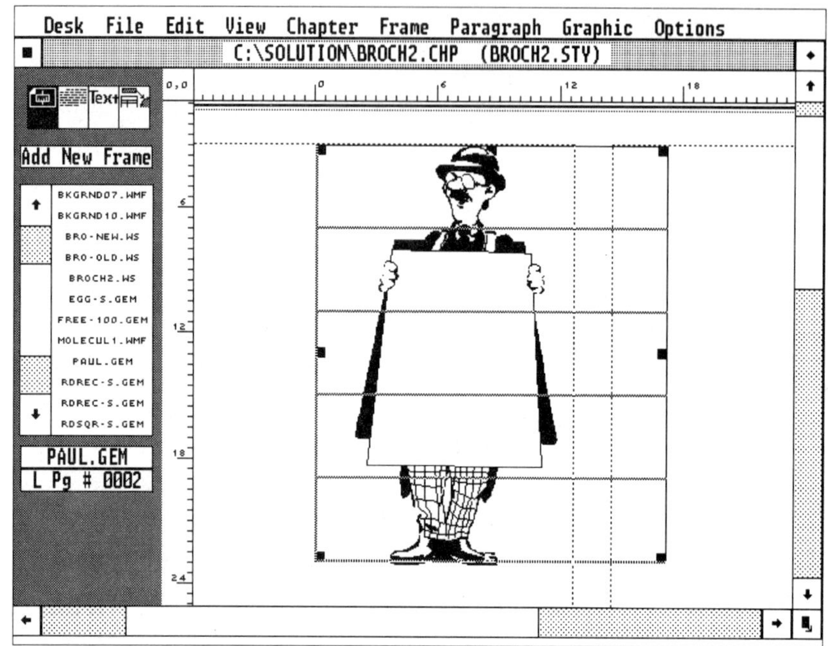

Step 3 **Copy multiple frame**

Select **EDIT•Copy Frame** to load the multiple frame group into the invisible copy clipboard.

Step 4 **Paste into document**

Access **FILE•Open Chapter** and select the chapter where the runaround frame template is to be. Go to the desired page and select **EDIT•Paste Frame** to place the template.

Step 5 **Load picture**

Use Control–Select to select the picture frame under the grid. Load the desired picture into the frame.

Step 6 **Size blocking frame width**

Use the mouse to adjust the width of each of the one–line–high frames in the grid.

Application Notes

- **Production files:** Maintain a backup store of defined runaround frames for use with standard size illustrations. Cut/Copy/Paste features save significant time even with runaround frame grids.
- **Custom frame backgrounds:** Build a standard runaround frame which contains a ready–made freeform and picture background already in place. Bring the completed background into the chapter and place the picture over the background and the runaround effect works immediately. Turn to page 266.
- **\STYLES subdirectory** Store templates in production subdirectory on hard disk for easy access. Turn to page 471.

Designing with Automatic Anchoring

Automatic frame anchoring offers a different twist on Ventura's standard anchoring features in that it locks the frame to the actual position of the anchor in the text. This allows you to draw very small frames which are smaller than the text interline spacing and lock those frames into the text line.

Automatic anchoring lets you place picture files and graphics and **use them just like individual letters**.

An automatically anchored frame enters text as if it were one of the other characters. You must make special allowances to determine the text spacing for documents containing auto–anchored frames. There are two approaches you can use:

- **Automatic Text Expansion:** Using Paragraph Typography: Grow Interline To Fit, set the Body Text interline spacing to automatically expand on lines which contain an auto–anchored frame. This keeps the text from overprinting the frames, but it can result in massive disruption of your text spacing, which makes for a very muddled document effect, especially in multiple column applications.
- **Expand Interline Spacing:** By expanding interline spacing of body text, you can create uniform text spacing which can uniformly

accommodate larger auto–anchored frames. When using this option, turn Grow Interline To Fit Off.

To maintain a uniform flow of text when using auto–anchored frames, make sure that the frame height of all auto–anchored frames is less than the value set for text interline spacing. This lets you turn Grow Interline To Fit off, and avoid the uneven display of text that results when it is turned on.

In display applications, this means you can use scanned fonts or special characters in your text. You can also link graphics directly into text and make them follow when the text is moved. Combined with other features, automatic anchoring becomes a valuable tool that permits you to develop interesting and sophisticated in–text illustration effects.

Recipe: Auto–Anchor Pictures into Text

Step 1 **Check interline spacing**

Enable ***Paragraph*** mode. Select a paragraph of Body Text. Access **PARAGRAPH • Spacing** and write down the interline spacing value. If your frame height is less than this value, it will fit easily into text.

Step 2 **Set Grow Interline To Fit**

With a paragraph of Body Text selected, access **PARAGRAPH • Paragraph Typography**. For text spacing to automatically expand to accommodate character frames, set Grow Interline To Fit: On. Otherwise set it to Off.

Step 3 **Create character frame**

Enable ***Frame*** mode and use Add New Frame in the Side–Bar to draw the character frame in text. *Text may appear disrupted on the screen.* Place desired picture or graphic in the frame.

Step 4 **Assign frame anchor name**

With frame selected, access **FRAME • Anchors & Captions** and enter the desired anchor name on the Anchor line.

Designing with Automatic Anchoring
Page 291

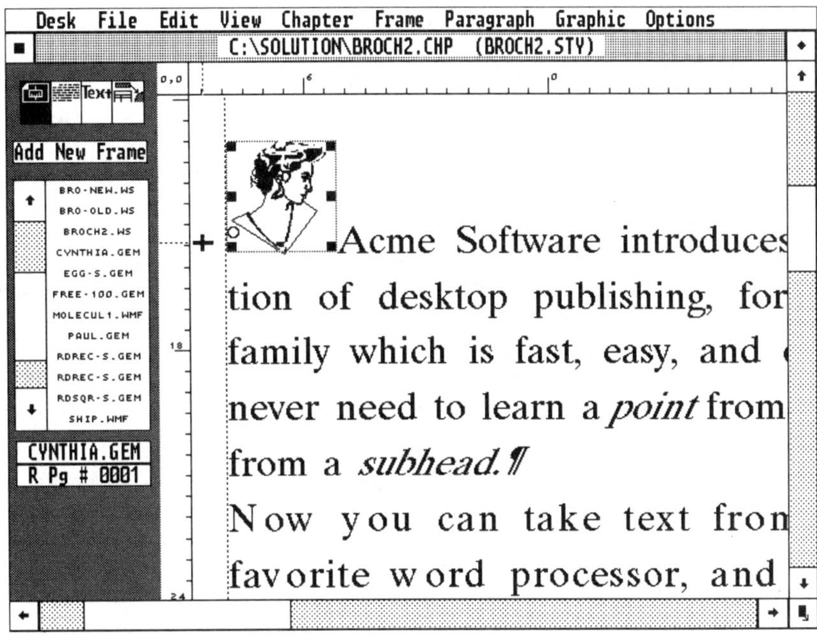

Step 5 **Place frame anchor**

Enable ***Text*** mode. Place cursor at the exact place in text where the frame is to be anchored. Access **EDIT•Ins. Special Edit Item** and select Frame Anchor. Enter the anchor name on the Frame's Anchor Name line and select Relative, Automatically At Anchor.

▲ Note: Automatic anchoring automatically turns off the text flow around so that the frame fits into the text line. The auto–anchor feature forces the frame to snap to the text baseline and nothing can cause the frame to be moved from that position.

Recipe: Master Frame and Copies

Once you have created an automatically anchored frame, you can place copies of it anywhere in a document simply by placing a frame anchor in text and referencing the frame anchor name.

Step 1 **Identify location of copy**

In ***Text*** mode, place text cursor in the exact place in text where copy of the automatically anchored frame is to appear.

Step 2 **Place automatic frame anchor**

Access **EDIT•Ins. Special Edit Item** and select Frame Anchor. Enter the anchor name on the Frame's Anchor Name line and select Relative, Automatically At Anchor.

Recipe: Editing Frame Copies

Even though many copies of a single mini–frame can be placed, only one active frame may be selected at one time. To change the appearance of the mini–frame, or change or edit its contents, select the master frame, make the changes and they will be reflected instantly in every one of the copies.

Sometimes when attempting to select a frame, Ventura may not cooperate. Use the text cursor to add a space before or after any of the frame copies to make the active frame and you can then select and edit it.

Step 1 **Select active frame**

Enable ***Frame*** mode. Select one of the frames on screen. If the frame to edit *does not select*, enable ***Text*** mode, place cursor either before or after the frame and press the spacebar. Return to ***Frame*** mode and select the frame.

Step 2 **Edit master frame**

Make any desired edits to the frame. Note that any and all changes to the frame will be instantly reflected in every single copy of the frame in your document.

Application Notes

- **Graphic heads with tags:** Anchor mini–frames into headline text and draw graphics anywhere you want around the headline text. Create elaborate headline effects anywhere in your document.
- **Working with graphics:** Turn to page 314
- **Placing scanned drop caps:** One of the interesting uses for auto–anchored frames are placing special characters directly into your text. You can purchase a variety of display fonts in special art

books at your art or graphic design supply dealer. Using a scanner, you can turn these display characters into picture files which can be loaded into auto–anchor frames.

- **Creating custom drop caps:** Use this technique to place custom rotated or reverse–text drop caps. Turn to page 114.

Designing with Key Caps, Icons, and Rebus Effects

With automatic anchoring, you can place a number of mini–illustrations directly into text as characters. In applications such as a computer reference manual which features graphic representations of the keys in the text, you can use automatic anchoring to define a series of auto–anchor frames which display pictures of the keys right in the teaching text. Similarly, this feature allows you to create text and graphic sentences for rebus effects in display layouts.

Designing with Key Caps, Icons, and Rebus Effects

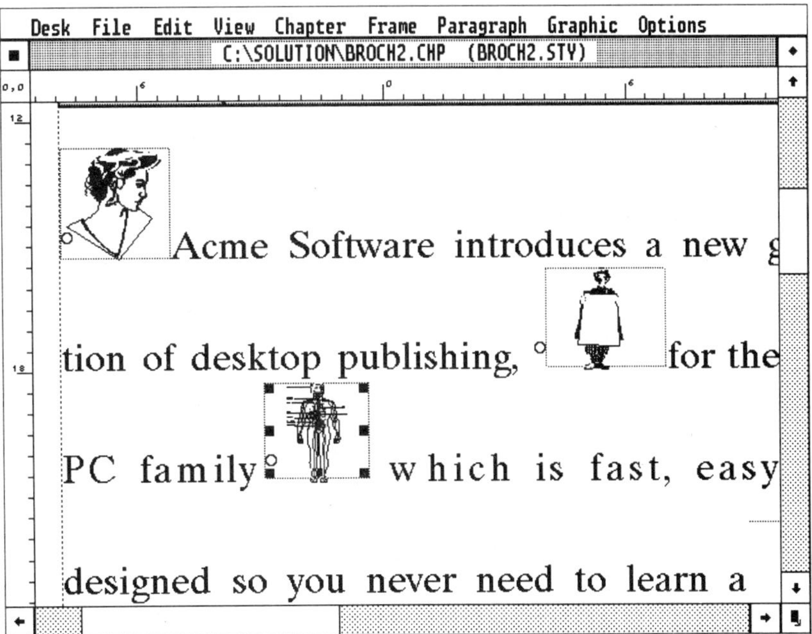

Automatic anchoring lets you place a copy of the original character frame simply by putting another anchor attribute in text. Use this to save a great deal of editing time by using macro or insert files in your word processor to place the automatic anchor detail for each key cap everywhere you wish it to appear in the text.

Recipe: Placing Key Caps

Step 1 **Define master frames**

Enable ***Frame*** mode and use Add New Frame in the Side–Bar to draw a master frame for each key cap.

Step 2 **Place and anchor key caps**

Place picture files for each key cap into one of the character frames. For each frame, access **FRAME•Anchors & Captions** and enter an anchor name descriptive of the key cap. *Write down the exact anchor name for the key cap on a reference sheet.*

Step 3 **Key caps in text**

In word processor, enter the correct anchor text in the desired position in file using the attribute code <$&ANCHOR NAME[–]>. Using the reference list, enter the name of the anchor for the desired key cap inside the brackets.

Application Notes

- **Graphic enhancements to text:** Attach Ventura graphics to the auto–anchor frame. Graphics do not have to be contained inside the frame, and can appear anywhere in relation to text. The anchor frame will always snap to the text baseline, thus forcing the graphics to appear in the same place in relation to the text.
- **Rebus effect:** Insert pictures and icons into text to create integrated text and picture rebus for advertising layouts and special headline presentations.

Mailmerge Printing with Repeating Frames

Many word processors contain features for mailmerge printing. These features type names and addresses on a mailing list into form letter text, automatically creating a whole set of letters. For simple form letter applications requiring higher quality fonts, graphics, and illustrations, use Ventura to mailmerge print.

Mailmerge printing is easy to accomplish using repeating frames. Write the form letter text, place it in a frame, and place the company logo in a separate frame at the top of the page, leaving space between the frames for the name and address. Load a text file containing the names and addresses and salutations into the base page, and make both the logo and letter frames into repeating frames. Automatically, Ventura repeats the form text and logo to as many pages as there are names in the list.

Mailmerge with Repeating Frames

Step 1 **Create text files**

In the word processor, create the text files for the mailing list and the form letter text.

Step 2 **Design style sheet**

In Ventura, select an existing or default style sheet as the base and access **FILE•Save As New Style** to create a new style sheet for the form letter.

Step 3 **Set single sided pages**

Access **CHAPTER•Page Size & Layout**. Set Sides to Single and verify Start On is set to right.

Step 4 **Place letter logo**

In Ventura, Enable ***Frame*** mode and draw a frame at the top of the page to contain the logo. Design logo elements. Access **FRAME• Repeating Frame** and set to repeat on Right pages.

Mailmerge Printing with Repeating Frames
Page 297

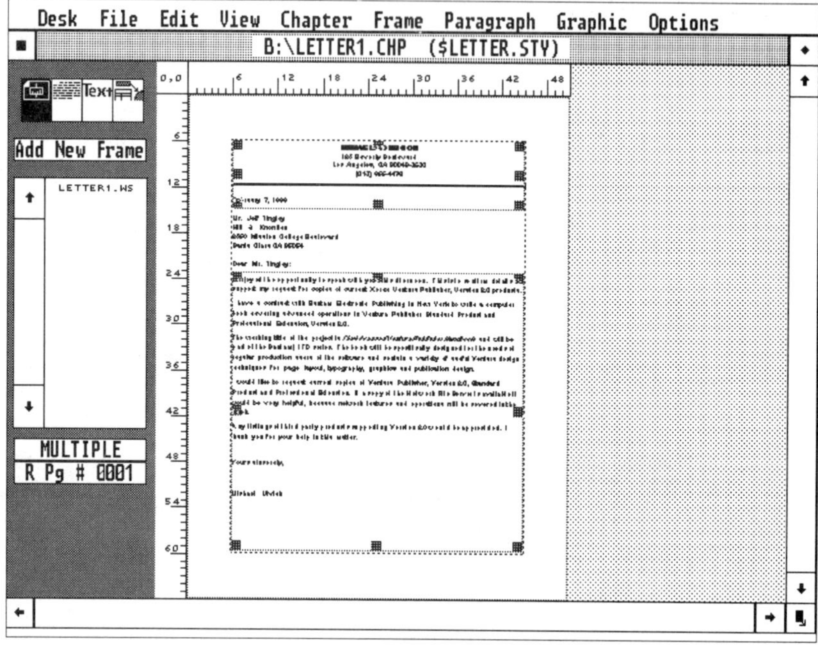

Step 5 **Place letter text**

Access **FILE•Load Text/Picture** and load the text file containing the form letter. Enable ***Frame*** mode and draw a frame to contain the letter text. Leave enough space between the top and bottom frames to display a single mailing list address.

Step 6 **Design form letter text**

Enable ***Paragraph*** mode and use features of the **PARAGRAPH** menu to design the text for the form letter.

Step 7 **Set repeating frame**

Enable ***Frame*** mode, select the letter frame, and access **FRAME• Repeating Frame**. Set frame to repeat on Right pages only.

Step 8 **Load mailing list**

Access **FILE•Load Text/Picture** and load the text file containing the mailing list. Select the base page and load the file. Check the position of addresses between the two frames.

Step 9 **Print form letters**

Access **FILE•To Print** and print completed form letters.

Application Notes

- **Standard form letters:** Create standard form letter chapters which you can print on demand.
- **\STYLES subdirectory:** Store a mailmerge template in the production subdirectory on the hard disk. Turn to page 471.

CHAPTER 7

Graphic Enhancements

Fine Tuning Text and Pictures

The revolution in computer graphics over the last several years has brought an incredible variety of powerful business graphics, drawing and computer artwork packages into the marketplace. Ventura's open architecture is designed to work with the best of these programs. You can devise your own artwork in powerful bit-mapped or vector graphics-based programs and import your files into Ventura. Using external third-party graphics utilities you can convert files from one format to another, and files created in one package can be edited in another.

Then what do you need with Ventura's own on-board graphics package? Ventura Publisher's Graphic mode is, essentially, a simple GEM-based drawing package. And when compared feature for feature with outside graphics programs, it seems very simple. Too simple perhaps. But because the Graphic mode is *inside* Ventura, it has powers that no other graphics package can match. It lets you enhance illustrations and graphics with added visual elements and text. And, it allows you to create specialized text applications, like

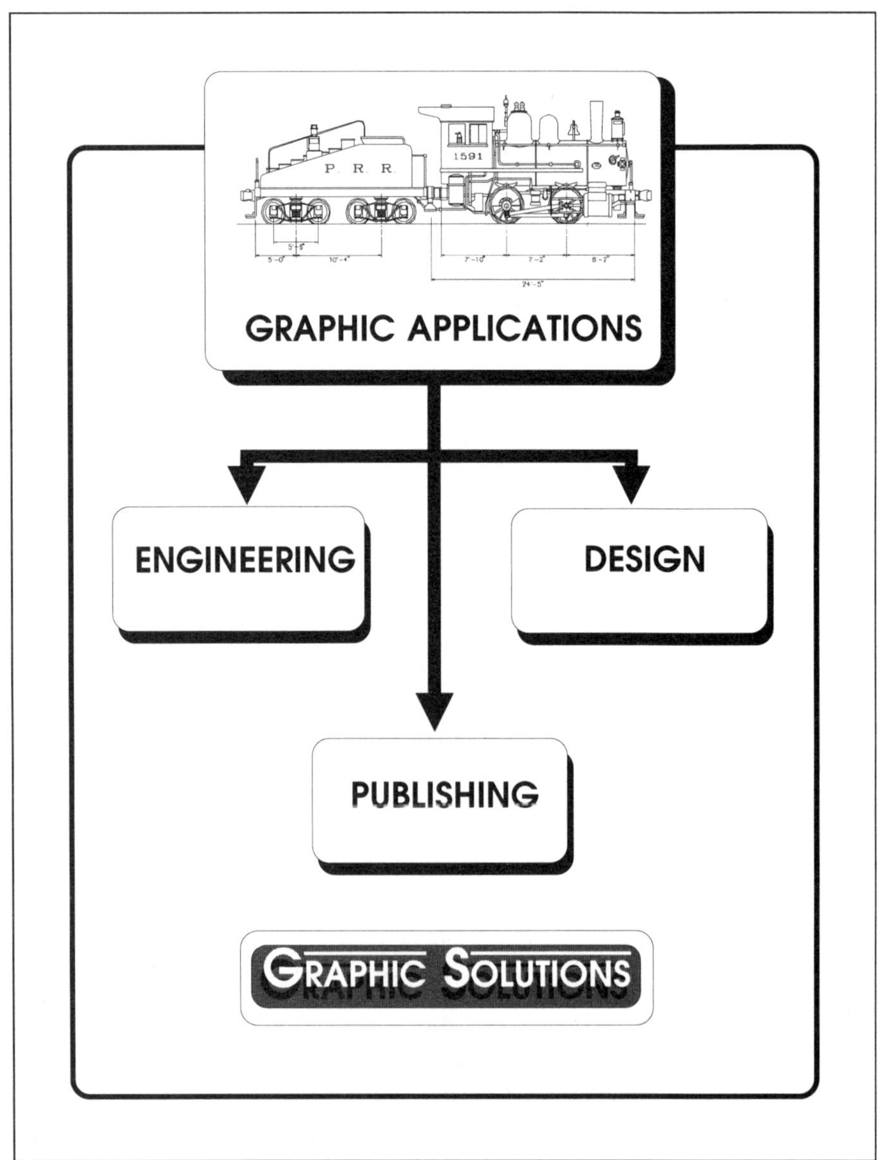

Overhead Transparency Master: Ventura graphics can be used to create a variety of visual effects including geometric forms for flowcharts and diagrams. When graphics are stacked in clusters, they can create more sophisticated designs, including drop shadow forms and text. Text is typeset in ITC Avant Garde. Artwork created in AutoSketch.

tables, organization charts, and diagrams. And it provides extraordinary flexibility for solving design problems.

The Graphic mode includes basic geometric form drawing tools supported by line and fill customizing dialog boxes and a few other positioning features. But when these tools are combined with the power of the other Ventura modes, the number of graphic effects you can easily generate in Ventura is truly surprising.

In addition to visual editing capabilities, the Graphic mode simplifies the design and positioning of special text elements. Place title text in a Box Text graphic and move it anywhere on the page. Place graphic headers and footers. With text in a box text graphic, create special tags and place it anywhere in your document layout.

Graphic Enhancement Tools

Developing graphics involves tools in all four modes of Ventura Publisher and the Graphic menu.

- **Graphic mode** contains graphic drawing icons, editing features, and graphic enhancements.
- **Frame mode** contains features which can be used to move complete graphics in frames, as well as make enhancements to frames containing graphics.
- **Text mode** contains features to enter and edit text placed in Box Text graphics.
- **Paragraph mode** contains features to create custom paragraph tags for text in Box Text graphics.
- **Graphic menu** contains features to place graphics in position as well as set custom values for line and shading in graphic forms.

Shortcuts for Document Production

This chapter contains a group of techniques to show you how to use Ventura graphics in document design, production, and editing. The focus of most of these techniques is the use of graphics as an editing and enhancement tool.

As you work with the Graphic mode, you will discover the startling number of sophisticated design effects you can create. By stacking graphics, you can do everything from drop–shadow text to special text enhancements for headlines.

Designing and Copying Master Graphics

When working with graphics, it is always best to draw master forms and then use the Cut/Copy/Paste features to copy and edit them. This is especially critical when you are creating a complex graphic cluster, like a table grid. Building the grid from a master graphic can save you significant amounts of time in design and production.

Graphics do not have an equivalent to the Sizing & Scaling dialog box for frames. You can't go into a dialog box and set exact dimensions and positioning for graphic forms. The closest you can come to this capability is the graphic grid. By defining a graphic grid, graphics can be forced to snap horizontally and vertically in distinct increments of space which makes their size and shape easier to control.

Once you get used to the idea and concept of master forms and designs, Ventura's Graphics mode becomes an easy–to–use power tool for document design and production.

Even though it is not required by the software, it is *always better to draw graphics with a frame selected.* This attaches the graphic to the frame and lets you easily move the graphic, or a complete graphic cluster within a document or between chapter files. When you are using Ventura graphics for illustration or design effects on a page, attach them to a frame for much greater control over their position in the document.

Recipe: Master Graphics

When drawing a master graphic, have the rulers enabled on screen. Reposition the ruler zero point to the spot where you begin drawing the graphic, so you can measure the graphic on screen using the tracking lines.

Designing and Copying Master Graphics

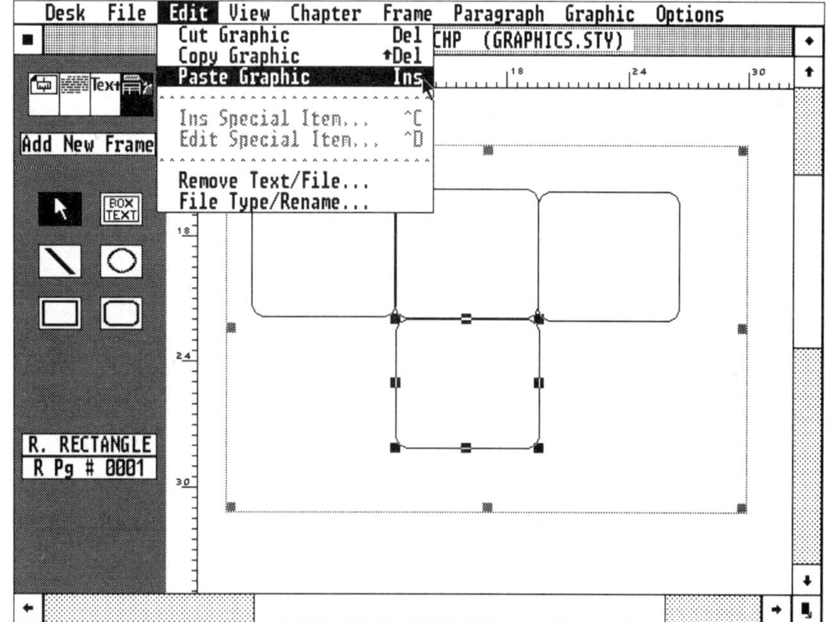

Step 1 **Position page for graphic drawing**

Make sure you have enough room in the Working Area to draw the desired graphic. If you are not confident that you do, go to Reduced or Facing Pages View.

Step 2 **Draw anchor frame for graphic**

Enable ***Graphic*** mode and use Add New Frame in the Side–Bar to draw a frame.

Step 3 **Set ruler zero point**

To draw the master graphic to a specific size, use screen rulers to measure the graphic. Select **OPTIONS•Show Rulers**, and place cursor on the zero box (**0,0**) at the intersection of the horizontal and vertical rulers. Press and hold the mouse button as you drag the four–way arrow cursor to where the upper left corner of the graphic is to appear.

Step 4 **Draw graphic**

Select the desired graphic icon in the Side–Bar. When moving the cursor into the Working Area, the cursor changes to an icon representing the currently selected drawing tool. You have three ways you can draw the master graphic:

▲ **Freeformdrawing:** No constraints or grids enabled. Draw freely on the screen.

▲ **Graphic grid:** Grid settings are enabled. Graphic forms snap to invisible lines in the defined vertical and horizontal grid set in the **GRAPHIC•Grid Settings** dialog box.

▲ **Constrained drawing:** Depress Alt key while drawing to generate a perfect circle, squares, or straight lines that are directly vertical, horizontal, or at 45° angles.

Step 5 **Set line attributes**

Access **GRAPHIC•Line Attributes**. Set the desired thickness of the line around the graphic, the color, and the line ending format. End styles in the left column are applied to the *point at which your line begins*. End styles in the right column are applied to the *point at which your line ends*. You can automatically apply a custom set of line settings to other graphics in two ways:

▲ **Save to:** Saves current settings and automatically applies them to all graphics drawn afterward.

▲ **Load from:** Applies previously saved line attributes to an existing graphic form.

Step 6 **Set fill attributes**

Access **GRAPHIC•Fill Attributes**. Set the color, fill pattern, and transparency of geometric graphics.

☞ CAUTION: Certain printers *do not print* transparent graphics, including PostScript printers. To determine your printer's capabilities, print CAPABILI.CHP, included with the sample files in the \TYPESET subdirectory.

Recipe: Copy Master Graphic

Step 1 **Copy graphic form**

With master graphic selected, select **EDIT•Copy Graphic** to place it in the invisible clipboard.

Step 2 **Paste copies**

Select **EDIT•Paste Graphic**. Ventura directly overprints the copy of the graphic, and does not offset it. The screen looks the same, but the copy is there, directly on top of the original.

Step 3 **Move the copy into position**

Place mouse cursor on the graphic so that it does not touch any of the graphic sizing boxes. Press and hold the mouse button until the four–way arrow cursor appears. Drag the copy of the graphic into position.

Application Notes

- **Designing flowcharts:** Turn to page 318.
- **Creating master graphic clusters:** Turn to page 314.
- **Creating table grids:** Turn to page 321.

Moving and Sizing Graphics

Graphics are moved and resized using the mouse in exactly the same way as with frames. You can move the graphic form or cluster by moving its anchor frame or by moving the graphic itself.

Recipe: Move and Size Graphics

Step 1 **Move graphic form**

From ***Graphic*** mode, select graphic and move it to the desired position. A graphic does not have to be inside its anchor frame. As long as the graphic was drawn when the frame was selected, it is anchored to that frame, even if the graphic form is physically outside of the frame.

Moving and Sizing Graphics
Page 307

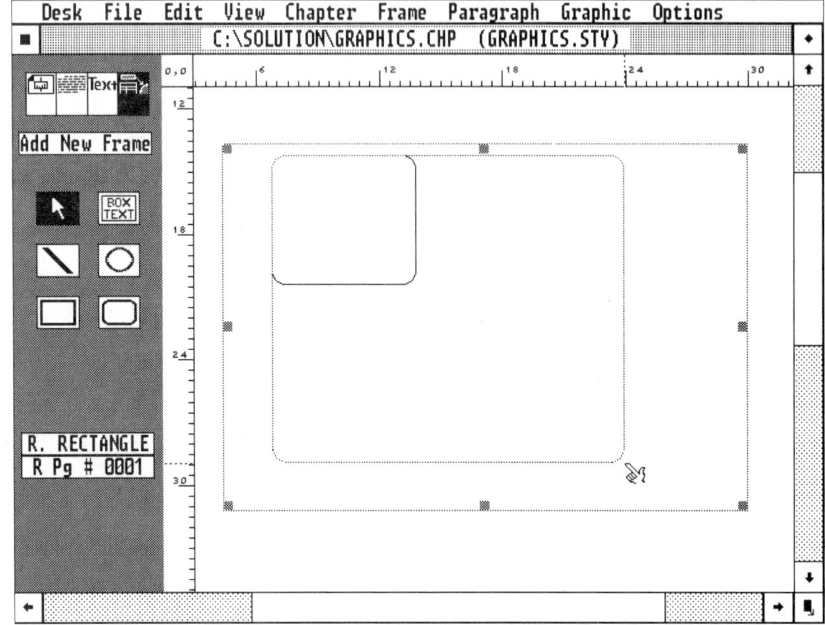

Step 2 **Size graphic**

Place cursor on sizing boxes and adjust size. If you press Alt key during resizing, the graphic will resize only to a perfect shape or line angle. If you resize with the grid turned on, the graphic will snap to positions in the defined grid.

Recipe: Graphic Grid

The graphic grid is invisible and cannot be displayed on the screen. Grid settings are best used when making box charts and similar applications which require a number of different graphic forms drawn to the same size. It is also of use when positioning a number of graphic forms in a larger design, by forcing individual elements of the design to snap to positions on the screen.

If the graphic grid is set in easy–to–compute increments, you can draw graphics to perfect dimensions by counting the snaps as you draw the graphic on screen.

Step 1 **Set grid spacing**

Access **GRAPHIC•Grid Settings**. Enter the desired space between horizontal and vertical grid lines in the spaces provided.

Step 2 **Draw graphic**

To draw a graphic to specification using the grid, count the snaps as you draw (i.e.: 4 snaps when the grid is set to ¼" is an inch), and use the screen rulers as a guide.

Recipe: Perfect Sizing with Frame Overlay

It is not easy to make detailed measurements using the screen rulers or the graphic grid. To draw a graphic to exacting measurements or to fit a specific area in a document use a frame sized in Sizing & Scaling to act as a matrix in drawing your graphic.

Draw rectangle graphics to match the outlines of a perfectly sized frame, or circle/ellipse graphics to touch the frame edges on all sides, for graphics of exact size.

Step 1 **Draw graphic anchor frame**

Enable ***Frame*** or ***Graphic*** mode and use Add New Frame to draw the anchor frame for the graphic.

Step 2 **Draw model frame**

Draw an additional frame to serve as model. When the frame is drawn, access **FRAME•Sizing & Scaling** and set the exact width and height you want for your graphic. To prevent the frame from having any effect on nearby text, set Text Flow Around to Off.

Step 3 **Draw graphic to match overlay**

Enable ***Graphic*** mode and reselect the *anchor frame.* Select the desired graphic icon and draw the graphic to exactly match overlay the model frame. If necessary, check in Enlarged View.

Step 4 **Delete model frame**

Select the model frame and select **EDIT•Cut Graphic**.

Application Notes

- **Design form grids:** By designing a form grid in a frame, you can copy the form anywhere in a document. Make a control copy of the frame in its own chapter file before entering data, and you can enter the prepared grid directly into any chapter.

Designing with Stacked Graphics

As with frames and paragraph tags, you can create various sophisticated effects by stacking graphic forms on top of one another. Some of the effects you can create using stacked graphics are:

- Drop–shadow graphic forms and backgrounds
- Freeform graphic illustration and title elements
- Logos and icons

It is important to note that Ventura graphics can have the attribute of transparency. A transparent graphic can be filled with a gray or colored shading pattern and printed like a screen over other graphics and illustrations. Before designing with this effect, verify that your printer can print transparent graphics. To test your printer's

Designing with Stacked Graphics

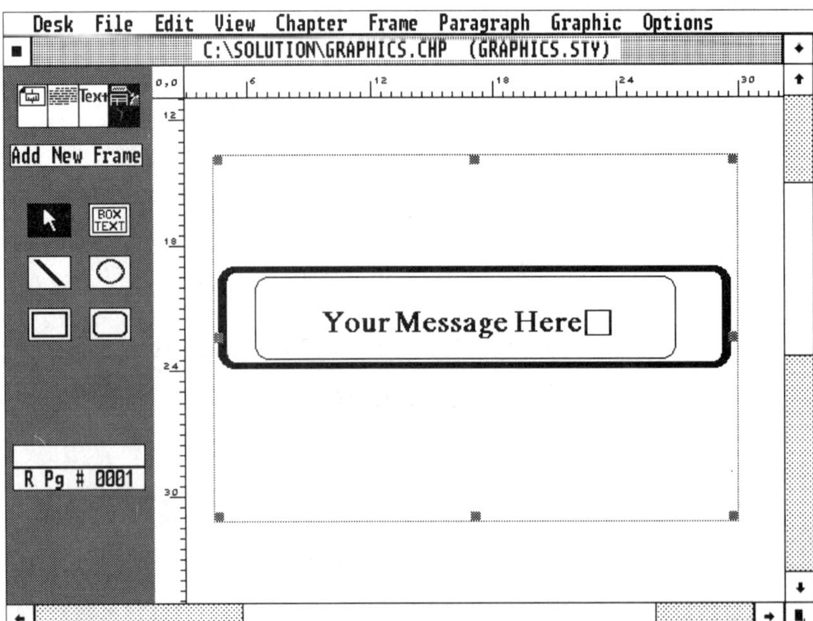

capabilities, you should print out a copy of CAPABILI.CHP, in the \TYPESET subdirectory.

When developing stacked graphics, *always* draw them with a frame selected. This links the complete graphic cluster to the frame and makes it easy to move.

Recipe: Stacked Graphics

Step 1 **Draw frame for graphics**

Enable ***Graphic*** mode and use Add New Frame to draw the frame.

Step 2 **Create base graphic**

Select desired icon in the Side–Bar and draw the first graphic. Set desired attributes using **GRAPHIC•Line Attributes**. Set fill values for geometric graphics in **GRAPHIC•Fill Attributes**.

Step 3 **Draw stack graphics**

Select the desired icon and draw the stacked graphic form. Place the graphic in position over the first graphic.

▲ **Send to Back:** Select **GRAPHIC•Send to Back**.

▲ **Bring to Front:** Select **GRAPHIC•Bring to Front**.

Application Notes

- **Change text colors:** Place identical text tagged with different colors (you can also make the changes in Set Font) and adjust graphics to create drop–shadow effects.
- **Add shaded backgrounds:** Draw shaded graphic forms to act as backgrounds for drop shadow–text and other graphic effects.

Designing Drop Shadow Text

Drop–shadow text is an effect in which text appears three–dimensional by placing a shadow beneath and slightly offset from it. This effect for titles and logos can easily be created using stacked Ventura graphics.

Designing Drop Shadow Text
Page 311

Begin by typing the title element into a box text graphic. Create a paragraph tag and set the typeface, size, style, and color. When the complete Box Text graphic is copied, using graphic Cut/Copy/Paste, a duplicate version of the text is contained in the copy. Create a second tag, based on the first one, and change only the font color. Now there are two strings of identical text in different colors. By slightly moving the top Box Text graphic over the bottom one, a variety of drop shadow effects can be created. This effect can be further enhanced by drawing any shaded geometric form over the two box text graphics and using Send to Back to place it as a background. Drop shadow text offers an infinite variety of design effects for titles and logos.

Recipe: Drop Shadow Text

Step 1 **Draw frame for graphics**

Enable ***Graphic*** mode and use Add New Frame to draw the frame.

Step 2 **Draw first Box Text graphic**

Select Box Text icon and draw graphic large enough to contain text.

Step 3 **Enter text**

Enable ***Text*** mode and place cursor in Box Text graphic. Type desired text into graphic.

Step 4 **Create Drop Black tag**

Enable ***Paragraph*** mode, select the text in the Box Text graphic and use Add New Tag to create Drop Black tag. Access **PARAGRAPH•Font** and set typeface, size, and style. Set color to Black.

Step 5 **Copy graphic**

Enable ***Graphic*** mode and select the Box Text graphic. Select **EDIT•Copy Graphic** and select **EDIT•Paste Graphic** to paste a copy. Select top graphic and slightly drag to the side so both sections of text are visible.

Step 6 **Create Drop White tag**

Enable ***Paragraph*** mode and select the text in the top graphic. Use Add New Tag to create the Drop White tag, based upon Drop Black. Access **PARAGRAPH•Font** and change text color to white.

Step 7 **Position drop shadow text**

Enable ***Graphic*** mode. Select top graphic and move it directly on top of first graphic. Adjust position of Box Text to create drop shadow effects. Experiment with positioning of graphics for different effects.

Step 8 **Place drop shadow background**

Select the circle, rectangle, or rounded rectangle icons and draw a graphic directly on top of the drop shadow graphics. Select **GRAPHIC•Send to Back** and the background appears behind the drop shadow effect.

Application Notes

- **Experiment with typesize:** For drop shadow effects using different fonts and styles, experiment with changing the font size and style in one or more of the Box Text graphics.

- **Use interactive font and tracking:** To experiment on screen, select text in *Text* mode and use interactive font adjustment and interactive tracking to move text in one or more boxes.
- **Multiple stacks:** For more elaborate drop shadow effects, stack multiple graphics with different font colors.
- **Graphic headers and footers:** Use stacked graphic effects in repeating frames at the top or bottom of a page to create graphic header or footer line. Turn to page 328.

Creating Master Graphic Clusters

When developing complex graphic flowcharts, you can reduce the amount of time spent drawing and positioning by breaking the design into a series of small clusters of graphic forms which can be copied and moved into place to form the larger design.

For example, to create an organization chart with a series of drop–shadow boxes, you can develop a master drop–shadow box, then make as many copies as needed to complete the flowchart.

When all elements in a graphic cluster are selected, they can be simultaneously resized, so that the same graphic cluster can be edited into a variety of different sizes.

Recipe: Master Graphic Clusters

Step 1 **Draw frame for graphics**

Enable ***Graphic*** mode and use Add New Frame to draw the frame.

Step 2 **Create graphic cluster**

For each individual graphic, follow this procedure:

▲ **Draw graphic form**. Select the desired icon in the Side–Bar and draw the graphic form.

▲ **Set Line/Fill Attributes**. Access **GRAPHIC • Line Attributes** to set line attributes. For geometric graphics, access **GRAPHIC • Fill Attributes** to set color, shading pattern and transparency.

Creating Master Graphic Clusters

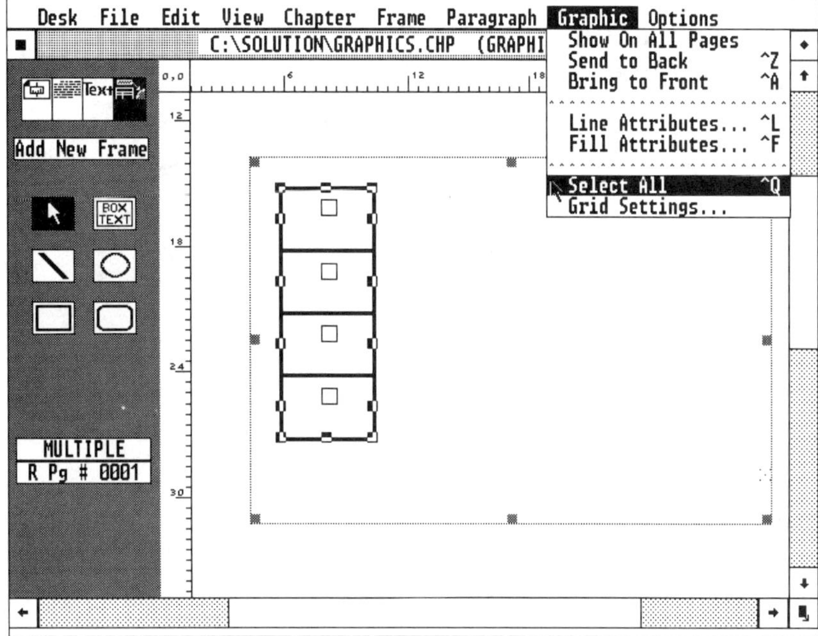

▲ **Size & position graphic**. Use sizing boxes to edit graphic to desired size and move the graphic into position.

Step 3 **Select graphic cluster**

There are two ways to select a cluster of graphics for copying:

▲ Select **GRAPHIC • Select All** to select all graphic forms in the frame. To deselect one or more of the forms, press Shift key and click the mouse pointer on the individual graphics.

▲ **Shift–Select**. Press and hold Shift key as you select the individual graphics you wish to copy.

Step 4 **Copy graphic cluster**

Select **EDIT • Copy Graphic** to place the cluster in the clipboard.

Step 5 **Paste graphic cluster**

Select **EDIT • Paste Graphic** to paste copies of the cluster in the page. Use the mouse to drag the copy off the original

Recipe: Editing Graphic Clusters

A complete cluster of graphics can be sized as a single graphic only *if all elements in the cluster are selected at the same time.*

Step 1 **Resize with sizing boxes**

Select **GRAPHIC•Select All**. Press and hold Shift as you select one of the sizing boxes and drag to resize the grouped graphics.

Application Notes

- **Use graphics with pictures:** Turn to page 262.
- **Create picture backgrounds:** Turn to page 266

Creating Graphic Templates

Once a complex graphic form has been drawn, it is a good idea to preserve the design as a *graphic template* on the \STYLES subdirectory. Keeping graphic templates handy reduces the amount of time and effort required to design and develop new graphic elements for your documents.

Templates allow you to copy a finished graphic form directly into a chapter and edit it to meet your needs. To develop and use templates, *all graphics must be attached to frames.* It is much easier to copy graphics attached to a single frame than to multiple select all elements in a complex graphic form.

Recipe: Graphic Template

Step 1 **Create graphic**

Select **FILE•New** to clear the screen. Access **FILE•Load Diff. Style** to load the desired style sheet. Enable ***Graphic*** mode and use Add New Frame to draw the anchor frame. With the anchor frame selected, draw the complete graphic to be used as a template.

Step 2 **Save the file**

Access **FILE•Save As** and save the template under an easily recognizable chapter file name.

Creating Graphic Templates

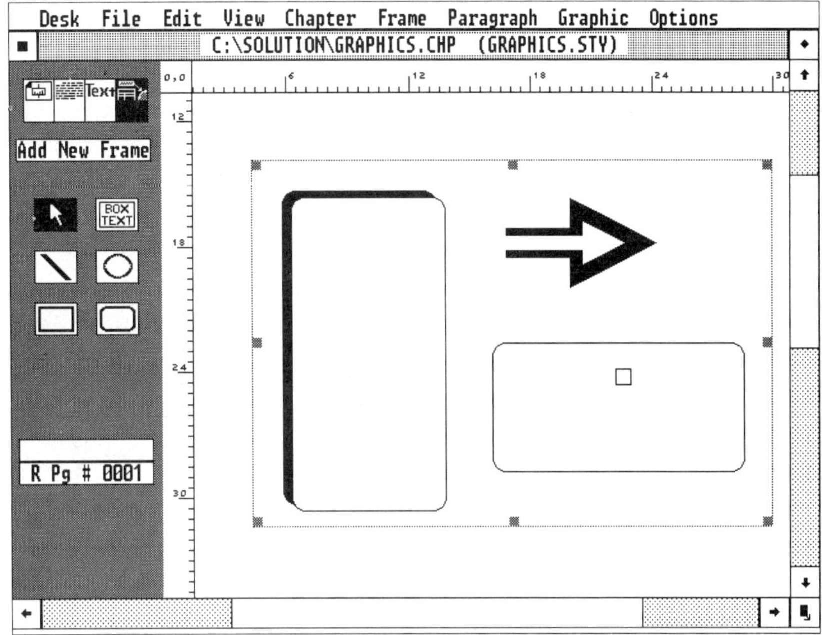

Step 3 **Store on hard disk**

If the template chapter is not on your hard disk, Access **OPTIONS•Multi–Chapter** and select Copy All. Use Copy All to place the template chapter in the subdirectory on your hard disk where you keep Ventura special utilities and files.

Recipe: Placing Graphic Template into Chapter

Step 1 **Select graphic anchor frame**

Access **FILE•Open Chapter** and open the chapter containing the graphic template. Enable ***Frame*** mode and select the anchor frame containing the completed template.

Step 2 **Place frame in clipboard**

Select **EDIT•Copy Frame** to place the frame in the clipboard.

Step 3 **Paste frame in new chapter**

Access **FILE•Open Chapter** and open the chapter where you wish to place the template. Go to the desired page and select **EDIT•Paste Frame**.

Step 4 **Reproduce table template tags**

When you copy the frame from the template chapter, any special tags created for the table grid or flowchart template *will not cross over* to the new document during the copy process. To replicate these tags in the new style sheet, you must recreate them. Create a style sheet report using **PARAGRAPH•Update Tag List** or a third–party product such as Ventura Toolbox to create a reference list of all of the correct tag values.

Application Notes

- **\STYLES subdirectory** Maintain graphic templates in separate chapters and store in production subdirectory on hard disk. Copy frames into current documents to avoid manually drawing individual graphics.
- **Copyfitting:** Fit text elements into defined spaces in the flowchart using interactive font editing and kerning. Turn to page 185.

Designing Flowcharts

The Ventura Graphics mode contains the tools to effectively create flowcharts and diagrams. Master graphics, or master graphic clusters make it even easier. Draw the basic geometric elements that make up the flowchart and make copies of them to maintain uniform appearance. For graphic cluster elements, such as a rounded rectangle and Box Text combination, copy and position the clusters rather than redrawing individual elements.

Recipe: Flowcharts

Step 1 **Draw frame for graphics**

Enable ***Graphic*** mode and use Add New Frame to draw the frame.

Step 2 **Create flowchart box elements**

Each box element is a graphic cluster made up of two parts:

- ▲ **Box Text:** Contains the text that appears in the form.
- ▲ **Framing graphic:** If the flowchart element is not a standard square or rectangle which can be created with Box Text, place rounded rectangle or circular framing graphics behind the box text.

Step 3 **Copy and position design elements**

Draw the principal elements of the flowchart on–screen. To create duplicate forms, select and copy them as graphic clusters rather than drawing new graphics.

Step 4 **Draw connecting arrows**

Select Line icon and draw connecting line between graphid elements in the flowchart. Access **GRAPHIC•Line Attributes** to set the desired arrow and thickness attributes. Select Save To to record settings.

Designing Flowcharts

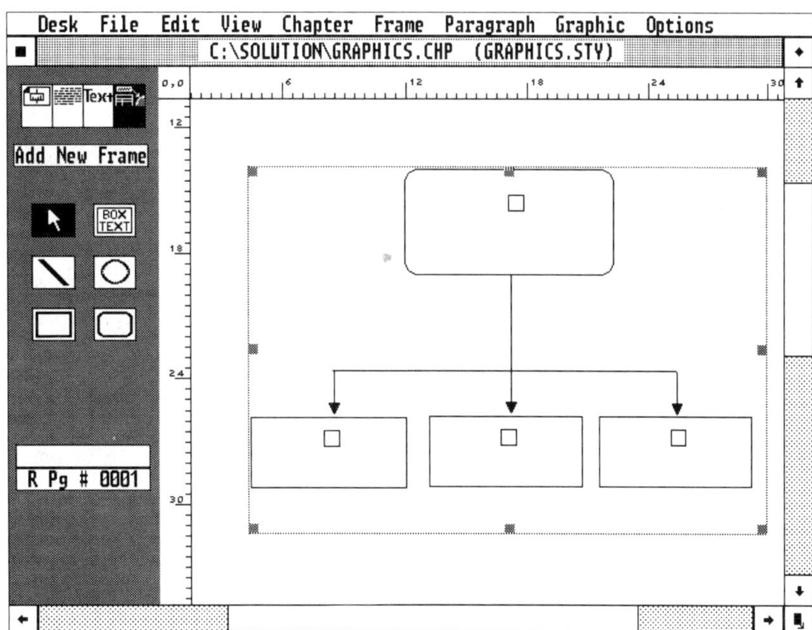

Recipe: Type Flowchart Text

Step 1 **Enter flowchart text**

Enable ***Text*** mode and place the text cursor on the End of File marker in the Box Text graphic. Type text or access **FILE•Load Text/Picture**, select Text and the desired word processor format and set Location: Text Cursor. Select the file containing the prepared text to load into the box text graphic.

Step 2 **Create flowchart tags**

Enable ***Paragraph*** mode. Select text in Box Text graphic. Use Add New Tag to create a custom flowchart text tag. Set desired attributes for the tag using features of the **PARAGRAPH** menu.

Placing Pictures in Flowcharts

For greater visual quality and clarity, you may wish to load picture files, such as clip art icons or other illustrations into a flowchart. Do this by drawing small picture frames within the graphic layout, but remember that frames will not automatically travel with the host frame if it is moved within or across chapters. To preserve your layout, anchor every picture to a string of text in the flowchart itself.

Recipe: Placing Pictures in Flowcharts

Step 1 **Draw picture frame**

Enable ***Graphic*** mode and use Add New Frame to draw frame.

Step 2 **Load picture file**

Access **FILE•Load Text/Picture**, select Line–Art or Image and the target file format. Select all pictures to be placed in the flowchart. Load picture files into frame.

Step 3 **Assign all frame attributes**

Enable ***Frame*** mode, select each picture frame and make all desired edits, set margins, rules, padding, and frame background.

Placing Pictures in Flowcharts

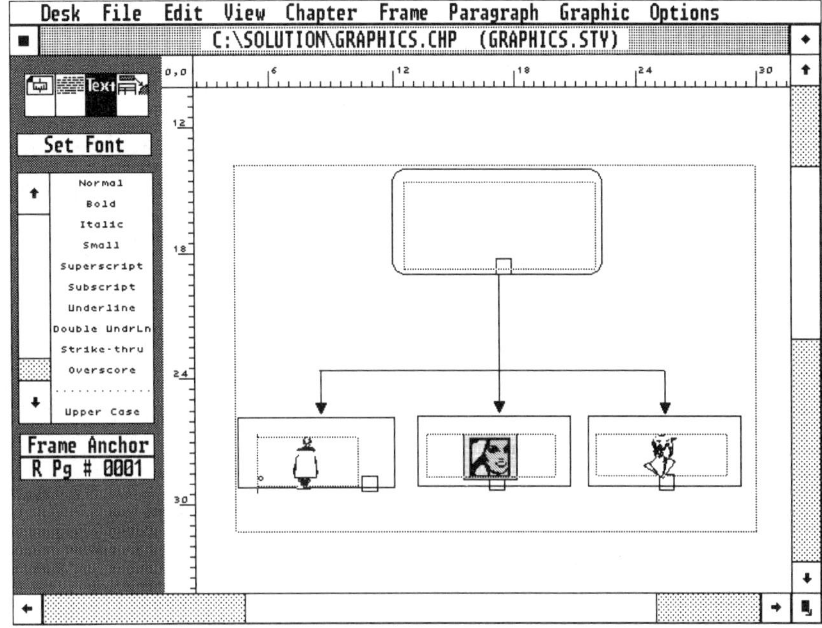

Step 4 **Assign frame anchor name**

Select each frame and access **FRAME•Anchors & Captions**. Enter anchor name for each frame.

Step 5 **Place frame anchor**

Enable ***Text*** mode. Place cursor in one of Box Text graphics in the flowchart. Access **EDIT•Ins. Special Edit Item** and select Frame Anchor. Enter anchor name on Frame's Anchor Line. Select the desired anchoring option.

Application Notes

- **Frame anchoring:** Turn to page 251.
- **Automatic frame anchoring:** Turn to page 291.

Creating Table Grids with Graphics

Ventura's Box Text feature makes it possible to construct table grids for text and data. These features are adequate if you create tables only occasionally. If you regularly produce many tables, you should be using the Professional Extension with its automatic table generation features.

When drawing a table grid you should always enable the graphic grid snap to help accurately draw table cells, and utilize the master graphic concept to its fullest capabilities. Once you have drawn a master table cell, save time by making copies of it. The grid snap helps to snap the cells into position without a lot of delicate and time–consuming positioning. As the grid takes shape, save the file frequently to record your work.

Recipe: Table Grids

Step 1 **Create graphic anchor frame**

Enable ***Graphic*** mode and use Add New Frame in the Side–Bar to draw the blocking frame.

Step 2 **Set graphic grid spacing**

Access **GRAPHIC•Grid Settings**. Enter spacing for Horizontal and Vertical grids on the lines provided.

Step 3 **Draw master table cell**

Select Box Text icon. Draw table cell to the desired height and width.

Step 4 **Set cell attributes**

Access **GRAPHIC•Line Attributes** to set line characteristics for table cell. To place shading in the cell, Access **GRAPHIC•Fill Attributes**.

Step 5 **Create complete table row**

Select the cell and select **EDIT•Copy Graphic**. Select **EDIT•Paste Graphic** to paste copies of the master cell. Use the mouse to move copies into position to form a complete row.

Step 6 **Select table row**

Select **GRAPHIC•Select All** to select all graphics in the row. To deselect individual graphic forms, depress the Shift key as you click the mouse on the specific forms.

Creating Table Grids with Graphics
Page 321

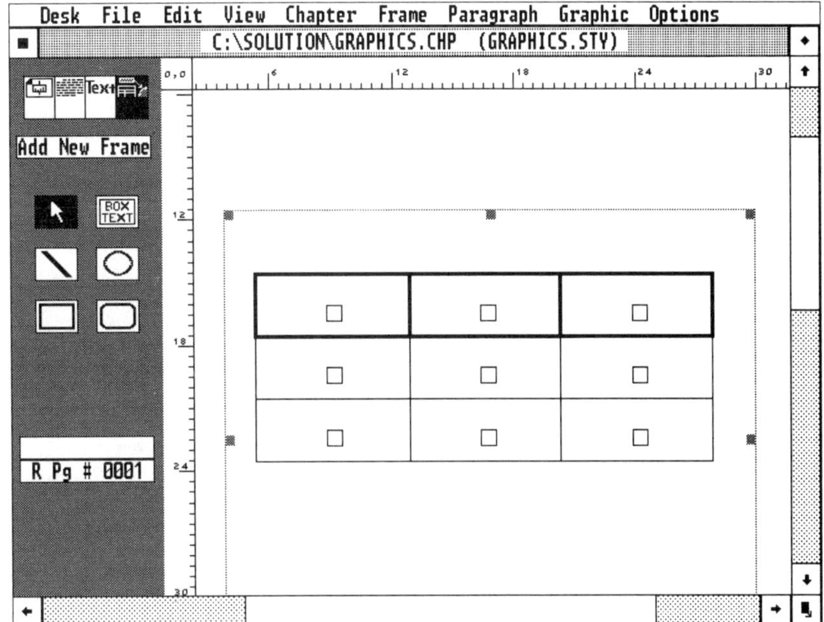

Step 7 **Duplicate table rows**

Select **EDIT•Copy Graphic** to place the complete row of graphics into the clipboard. Select **EDIT•Paste Graphic** to place a copy on the screen. To move the completed row, click and hold the mouse button until all cells are selected then move the row to its new location.

Step 8 **Enter table text**

Enable ***Text*** mode, place cursor on the End of File marker and type the data into the cell.

Step 9 **Set table paragraph tags**

To create special text presentation for the table, enable ***Paragraph*** mode, select table text and use Add New Tag to create a new tag in the Side–Bar. Design table text as desired.

Step 10 **Assign tags to function keys**

To easily apply table tags while entering text, access **PARAGRAPH• Update Tag List**, select Assign Func. Keys and enter table tags in the dialog box. To apply the tag from the function key, enable ***Text*** mode, place cursor on text in table cell and press the appropriate function key.

Step 11 **Apply paragraph tags**

From ***Text*** mode, select text in table cells and apply the desired paragraph tag with the function key.

Application Notes

- **Shade cells for emphasis:** Select an individual cell and define a shading pattern, select Save To to save it. Select other cells and apply the defined shading pattern using the Load From option.
- **Add illustrations:** Add illustrations behind tables or inside of them using auto–anchor frames. Turn to page 453.
- **Drop–shadow table:** Place solid color frame drop shadow frame behind table frame. Access **FRAME•Frame Background** and set color to solid white.
- **Designing tables with horizontal tabs:** Turn to page 103.
- **Professional Extension tables:** Turn to Chapter 11.

Landscape Tables in Portrait Documents

Many business documents include tables as reference material. When a table cannot fit within the width of the portrait page, it must either be redesigned to fit, or turned to print on a horizontal or landscape page.

You cannot place both portrait and landscape pages in the same document in Ventura, but there is a way to trick the software into printing landscape tables in portrait documents. It is a good technique to use if you occasionally design and place tables. But if you regularly develop large–scale table applications for spreadsheet or database files, you should purchase the Ventura Publisher Professional Extension which has a full operating mode devoted to making sophisticated text and data tables.

Landscape Tables in Portrait Documents

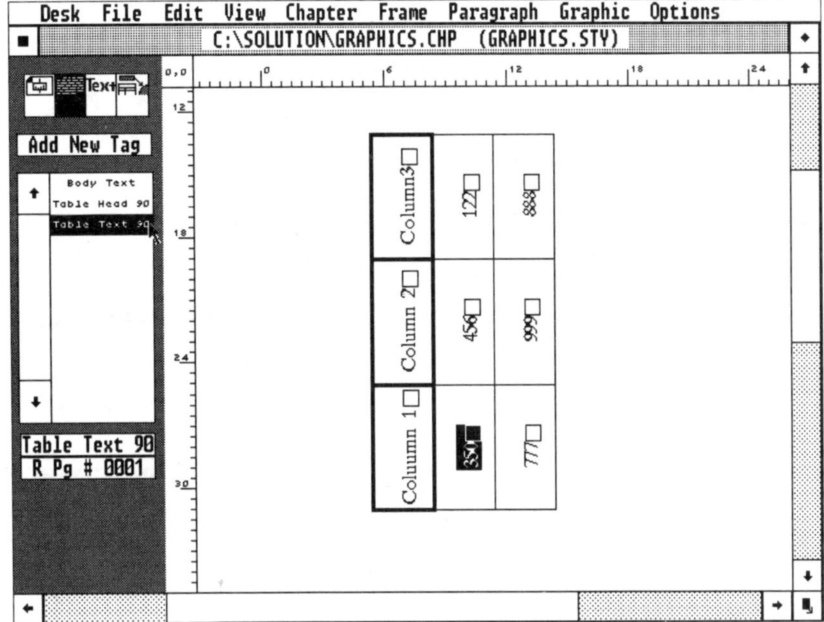

The process of creating landscape tables in portrait documents is a simple one. Draw the table grid using Box Text. Size and place a landscape grid. To display the text, create a special tag that rotates text on its side (settings of 90 or 270) and apply it to the paragraph returns in all the cells of the table grid.

Recipe: Landscape Tables in Portrait Documents

Step 1 **Draw graphic anchor frame**

Enable ***Graphic*** mode and use Add New Frame to draw the frame for the table.

Step 2 **Create landscape grid**

Enable ***Graphic*** mode. Select Box Text icon. Draw table grid on its side, so that the top of the table is actually parallel to the left or right side of the page.

Step 3 **Enter text**

Enable ***Text*** mode and enter text into all cells of the table. Because cells are on their side, all of text may not display until the text is rotated to fit.

Step 4 **Create rotated tag**

Enable ***Paragraph*** mode. Select one of the End of File markers in table cells. Access **PARAGRAPH•Alignment** and set Text Rotation: 270 to move the text a quarter turn to the left. Set Text Rotation: 90 to move the text a quarter turn to the right.

Step 5 **Apply rotated tag to all box text graphics**

From ***Paragraph*** mode, depress the Shift key as you select text in each cell of the table. Apply rotated text tag and text will turn to print in landscape mode.

Application Notes

- **Rotate pictures and icons:** To include icons and illustrations in a landscape table, you will have to rotate the graphics in source software. Ventura does not include a picture rotation feature.
- **Create table headlines:** To create table column and row headlines, simply add Box Text graphics and enter the text. Develop special rotated headline tags, if desired, for special presentation of your graphics.
- **Professional Extension tables:** Turn to Chapter 11.

Creating Graphic Page Frames

Graphics can be placed directly in your base page and repeated on every page of the document. This feature can be used to create graphic framing lines and effects which are impossible to set up with Ruling Box Around. For example, you can surround a page with a rounded rectangle. Or take a rectangular ruling line and place ornamental boxes or patterns at each corner.

Creating Graphic Page Frames

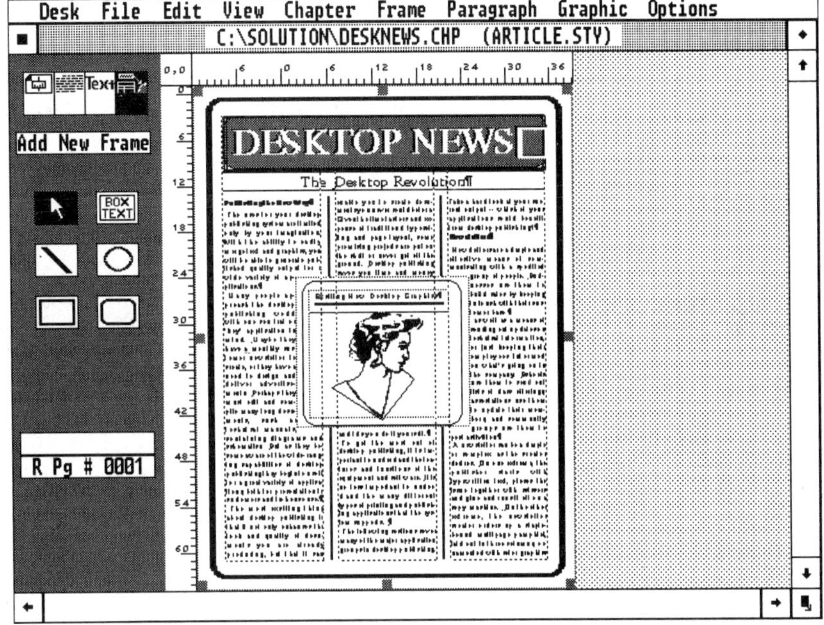

To achieve these kinds of effects draw the graphic forms directly into the base page, *outside* of the column guides, and display that graphic on all pages of the document.

Recipe: Graphic Page Frames

Step 1 **Display full page**

Select **VIEW•Reduced View** to display entire page layout on screen. Note where the page column guides appear.

Step 2 **Draw graphic framing line**

Enable ***Graphic*** mode. From Reduced View, select the desired icon from the Side–Bar. Draw the graphic so that it appears completely outside the margin guides. *If the graphic line appears inside column guides, it may overprint text.*

Step 3 **Show graphic on all pages**

For the page framing line to appear on all pages, select **GRAPHIC• Show On All Pages**.

Step 4 **Set graphic attributes**

Access **GRAPHIC•Line Attributes** to set desired line thickness and color. Access **GRAPHIC•Fill Attributes** and set Pattern: Hollow. To place a shading pattern, specify the color and the shading pattern.

Application Notes

- **Backgrounds:** Place shaded, rounded rectangle in the base page as a background for text.
- **Combined backgrounds:** Stack multiple graphics in the base page as a background for text.

Repeating Graphics

Repeating frames let you control position of page frame graphics on left and right and selected pages in a document. You can accomplish a variety of page design effects and enhancements using Ventura graphics including shaded blocks, grid patterns with a variety of shading textures, and a variety of textured backgrounds for your text or illustrations.

Draw a complete page design element with a small frame selected. The full–page graphic effect is attached to the small frame and that frame becomes a "handle" that allows you to copy, move, and repeat the graphic effect on any or all pages. By using margins and columns to control the position, it can bleed over into the background area, or stay separate from it. These techniques make possible a virtually endless number of design effects.

Recipe: Repeating Graphics

Step 1 **Draw frame**

Enable ***Graphic*** mode and use Add New Frame to draw the frame to use as a handle for your graphics. This frame should be small, about 1 inch square, so it doesn't interfere with the text on the page and is easy to select.

Repeating Graphics

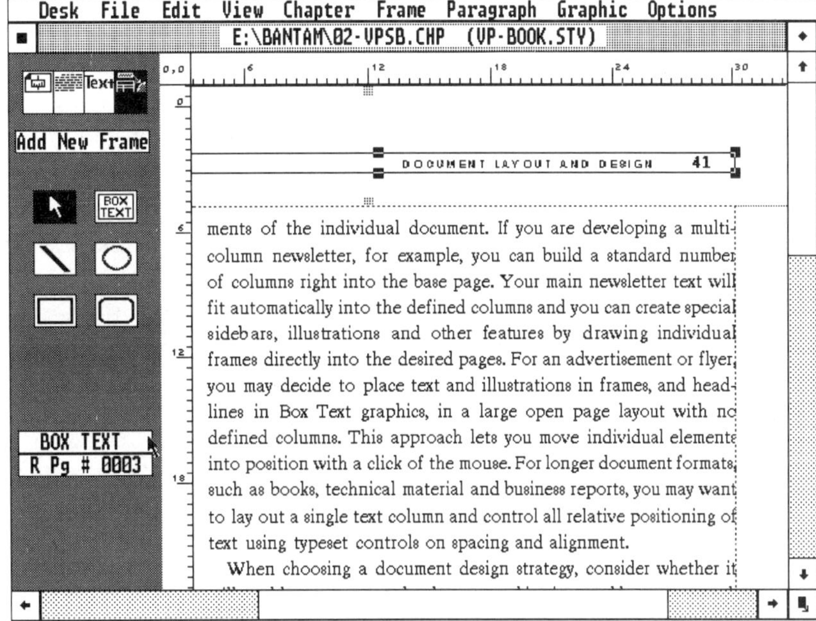

Step 2 **Assign graphic enhancements**

With the frame selected, use the graphic drawing icons to draw the graphic layout to be attached to the frame.

Step 3 **Copy frame to facing page**

If you want a different graphic effect on facing pages, select the frame and select **EDIT•Copy Frame** to load it into the invisible clipboard. Go to the facing page and select **EDIT•Paste Frame** to paste a copy on the page.

Step 4 **Enable repeating frame**

From the ***Graphic*** mode, select the handle frame for the graphic design layout. Access **FRAME•Repeating Frame** and select the pages you wish to display the repeating frame: Left, Right, or Left & Right. For facing pages, set frame on left page to repeat on left pages only, and set the frame on the right page to repeat on right pages only.

Application Notes

- **Master graphics:** Turn to page 304.
- **Stacked graphics** Turn to page 310.

Placing Design Backgrounds with Repeating Frames

You can draw and automatically place up to six complete page graphic design elements using repeating frames. You may decide to create six versions of the same layout and repeat some on left or right pages. This technique can be very useful when developing multi–page display applications, such as ilustrated catalogs.

You can also have a single graphic design element made up of six parts. With repeating frames, you can show all six elements together on a page, or hide certain elements on selected pages.

The principle is to use repeating frames to automatically repeat a graphic design element on each left, right or all pages and use the Hide This Repeating Frame feature to suppress the graphics on pages where you don't want them. Experiment with this technique and you

Placing Design Backgrounds with Repeating Frames

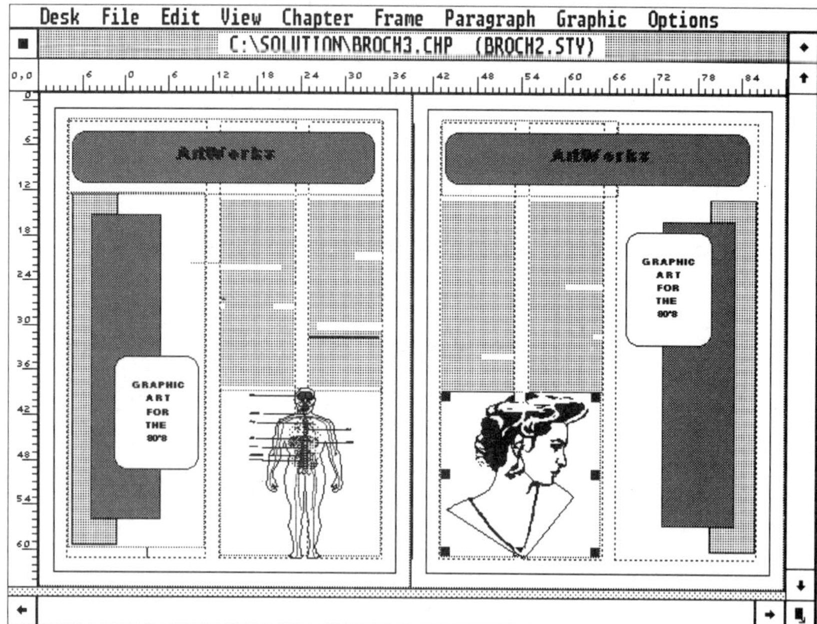

can create many interesting page treatments incorporating graphics, pictures, and repeating frames.

Design Graphics with Repeating Frames

Step 1 **Draw frame**

Enable ***Graphic*** mode and use Add New Frame to draw the frame to use as a handle for your graphics. This frame should be small, about 1 inch square, so it doesn't interfere with the text on the page and is easy to select.

Step 2 **Design graphic layout**

With small handle frame selected, draw the desired graphic background effect.

Step 3 **Copy frame to facing page**

If you want a different graphic effect on facing pages, select the frame and select **EDIT•Copy Frame** to load it into the invisible clipboard. Go to the facing page and select **EDIT•Paste Frame** to paste a copy on the page. Design the desired facing page graphic background.

Step 4 **Enable repeating frame**

From the ***Graphic*** mode, select the handle frame for the graphic design layout. Access **FRAME•Repeating Frame** and select on which pages to display the repeating frame: Left, Right, or Left & Right. For facing pages, set frame on left page to repeat on left pages only, and set the frame on the right page to repeat on right pages only.

Step 5 **Hide repeating frame display**

To suppress the repeating frame on any given page, go to the page, select the handle frame, access **FRAME•Repeating Frame** and select Hide This Repeating Frame.

Application Notes

- **Master graphics:** Turn to page 304.
- **Illustrated text** Use illustrated text effects with graphics in repeating frames. Turn to page 123.
- **Placing pictures and backgrounds** Use pictures and standard backgrounds in repeating frames with graphics. Turn to page 262.

Placing Pictures in Page Designs

By placing pictures in one or more repeating frames, you can add third–party clip art, scanned art, or your own artwork from third party software directly into your graphic page layout. If the text flow around feature for the repeating frame is turned off, your document text will flow over the picture background. Using spacing offsets and margins and column settings, you can develop an integrated page design which incorporates illustrations and graphics as a background to your text.

This opens up a whole new set of possibilities for enhancing display pages in catalogs, brochures, and similar documents. In addition, you can add shaded backgrounds, framing lines, tinting

Placing Pictures into Page Designs

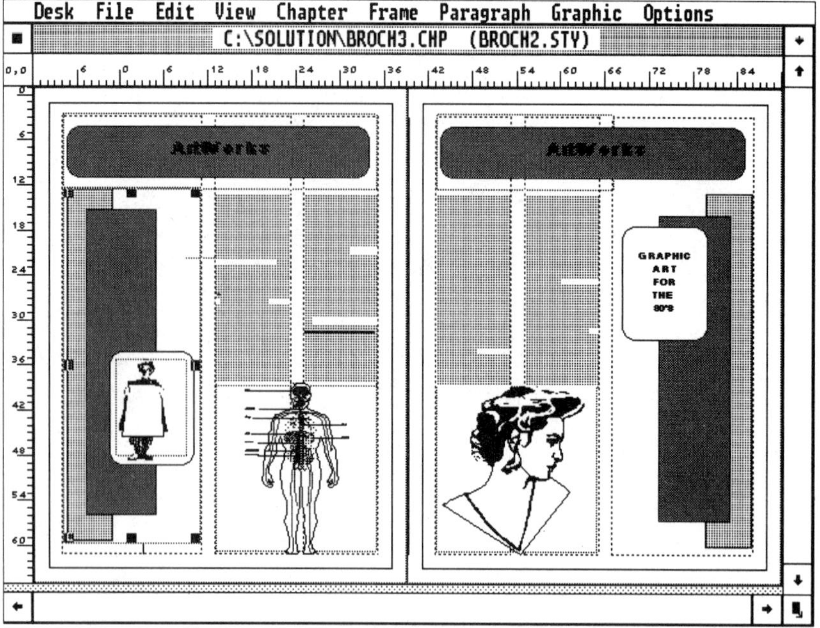

and graphic effects over the picture files. You can use a full featured graphics or drawing program such as Adobe Illustrator, Corel Draw, or GEM Artline to create recurring page design elements.

Remember when creating effects such as these that graphics do not have to be contained in their anchor frame. As long as the frame is selected when the graphics are drawn, it is linked to that frame. If you forget and draw a graphic without an anchor frame, you can select the graphic, cut it from the screen, and paste it into a selected frame.

Recipe: Pictures in Page Designs

Step 1 **Draw frame**

Enable ***Frame*** or ***Graphic*** mode and use Add New Frame in the Side–Bar to draw the frame.

Step 2 **Assign graphic enhancements**

In the ***Graphic*** mode, draw desired graphic design.

Step 3 **Load text or picture**

Enable ***Frame*** mode. Access **FILE•Load Text/Picture** and load picture or text files in the Assignment list. Draw frames and place files where appropriate in the design.

Step 4 **Enable repeating frame**

Select each frame you wish to repeat and access **FRAME•Repeating Frame**. Define the pages on which the picture is to repeat. Use Hide This Repeating Frame to suppress the frame on selected pages.

Application Notes

- **Document signs:** Use repeating graphics to enhance self–study materials with Continue and Stop sign notations and other signpost elements.
- **Page layout and repeating frames:** Turn to page 67.

- **Placing pictures and backgrounds:** Use pictures and standard backgrounds in repeating frames with graphics in page design. Turn to page 262.

C H A P T E R 8

Publication Features

Putting It All Together

You are sitting at your desk staring at a giant stack of 5,000 index cards. Each card contains a separate index entry: a string of text and the page number on which it appears. Your mission, should you choose to accept it, begins with sorting all the index cards into alphabetical order. Then, sort again to check for cross–references between index entries. Finally you must sort through the entire stack and compile the index, complete with the correct page references, without making a single error.

Nightmare visions such as this one don't exist in the Ventura world because Ventura uses the power of your computer system to perform repetitive tasks, which frees up your time and creative energy. Not only does Ventura provide many features for automatic document editing and processing inside of individual documents, it also offers powerful features to automatically process groups of documents.

The publication editing features of Ventura allow you to create sequences of chapter files. Once a sequence has been saved, you can sort and process the material in your chapters in several ways.

Contents

Table of Contents: Ventura's Multi-Chapter editing features allow a variety of automatic sorting operations across a publication list of chapter files. Table of Contents files are automatically generated using specified paragraph tags to find the desired text. Text is typeset in ITC Garamond Light.

The automatic table of contents option searches all your files for the table of contents entries you specify, finds the text, places it in order, writes the complete table of contents into a special text file, which is automatically tagged with special table of contents tags. In a matter of a few minutes, you have a complete table of contents to design and print.

The index option automatically opens every chapter file in your document, searches for all the index entries you have defined, places them in alphabetical order with correct page numbers in place. Then it writes the completed index into an automatically tagged text file which is ready for you to format and print.

Publication renumbering goes through every chapter in the publication, automatically computes the correct beginning and ending page numbers to paginate your sequence of chapters in order. With the Professional Extension, renumbering also finds text markers and writes the correct page numbers to places in the text where you have specified a cross reference.

These powerful features are made possible by Ventura's use of text codes and paragraph tags to mark and define places in documents. During a sort process, Ventura uses these codes to perform sorting tasks that otherwise would take hours and entire print production departments to complete. Ventura also does it much more accurately.

Publication Tools

Publication tools are found primarily in the Chapter menu and the Multi–Operations dialog box of the Options menu.

- **Update Counters** contain controls for pagination within a document or across a complete publication.
- **Multi–Chapter Operations** contains all file management tools and special editing features for complete publication files. This is where chapter files are assembled into publication and special sorting features such as table of contents and index generation are activated.

Tips for Effective Production

This chapter contains techniques covering the feature operations you use when assembling, paginating and finishing a complete publication. In addition to covering standard applications for assembling a publication, these techniques focus on some creative uses for publication features to help save you time and money in your document production process.

To get the most out of publication features, it is important to design documents systematically. Ventura uses systems of tag names to identify and pull text into table of contents sort operations, just like it pulls text into header and footer lines with 1st and Last Match. Keep your style sheets clean and uncluttered. Delete useless or duplicate tags. Use a simple tag naming system that everyone in your production department can understand. And make sure your files have been checked over before initiating any sort operation. By taking a little extra time on the front end, you can sit back and relax while Ventura does hours of publication work in just a few short minutes.

Setting Up Page Numbering Systems

Ventura's automatic pagination and counter system provides complete, automatic control over page, figure, and table numbering. Depending on the document requirements, you can paginate by section or document–wide. Using the table and figure numbering system, you can number illustrations and tabular material throughout the document or complete publication.

The most common place to display pagination is in the document header or footer line. But, if you use Ventura's chapter and page cross references, you can place the chapter and/or page numbers anywhere on the page.

There are two types of document pagination systems you can develop in Ventura:

- **Sectional pagination:** Page numbers are sequenced by chapters. Each page number consists of the chapter number and the page number. For example: Page 3–33.

Setting Up Page Numbering Systems

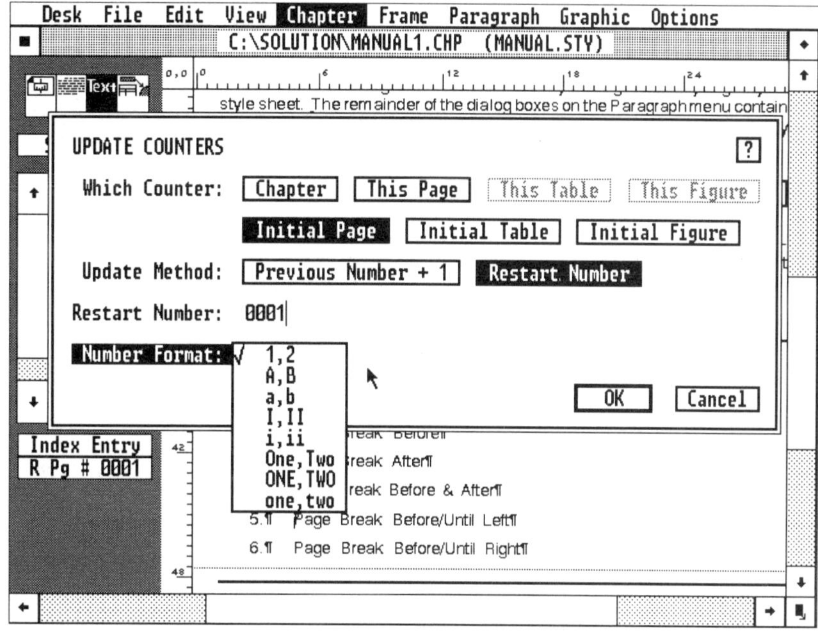

- **Continuous pagination:** Page numbers continue across chapters. For example: Page 125.

Ventura automatically paginates your entire document according to the system you have defined. In addition, you may override pagination commands and set custom pagination values for individual pages, depending on the requirements of the application.

Recipe: Sectional Pagination

Step 1 **Design numbering system**

Decide whether you wish to use sectional or continuous pagination in the document and the format for the page number.

Step 2 **Place chapter and page number in header/footer**

Access **CHAPTER•Headers & Footers**. Turn the desired header or footer on and place the cursor where the page number is to appear on the Left, Center, or Right line. Select the Chapter # at the bottom of the screen. [C#] appears on the line. Enter any desired punctuation. Select the Page # at the bottom of the screen. [P#] appears on the line.

Step 3 **Make counter settings**

Access **CHAPTER•Update Counters**. Select Chapter and Restart Number to enter the correct Chapter Number. Select Initial Page and Restart Number to 1.

Step 4 **Make number format settings**

Select the text presentation of the number for both the chapter and page number.

Recipe: Continuous Pagination

Step 1 **Place page references**

Access **CHAPTER•Headers & Footers**. Place page number where desired on the header or footer line.

Step 2 **Set first chapter initial page to 1**

Access **CHAPTER•Update Counters**. For the first chapter in the continuous pagination sequence, change Initial Page to Restart Number to 1. Select the desired number format.

Step 3 **Set update for all chapters**

For all other chapters after the initial chapter, access **CHAPTER•Update Counters** and set Initial Page to Previous Number +1

☞ CAUTION: If any chapters in the publication contain page number overrides created with the This Page option, they will disrupt the complete continuous pagination sequence.

Step 4 **Save publication**

Access **OPTIONS•Multi–Chapter**. Load all chapters in the publication into the dialog box using Add Chapter. Use mouse to place chapters in the desired order.

Step 5 **Renumber publication**

Select Renumber to begin the pagination sort operation. During this operation, Ventura searches through your publication chapters *twice.* On the second pass, the correct publication page numbers are written to your chapter file.

Step 6 **View publication page number**

You cannot see the publication page number displayed in the Current Page Indicator. To see it, look at the page number displayed in the header or footer line, or open the **CHAPTER•Update Counters** dialog box and select This Page. The publication page number will be displayed.

Recipe: Custom Pagination Override

In some cases, you may want to start numbering pages on a page other than the initial page. For example, in a business report with a cover page and a short table of contents, it makes more sense to begin page numbering with the first page of the actual report text. This is done by using the Update Counters: This Page override.

Step 1 **Restart pagination**

Use keyboard or **CHAPTER•Go To Page** dialog box to display page where you want to reset pagination. Access **CHAPTER•Update Counters** and select This Page. Select Restart Number and enter the page number to restart.

Step 2 **Check update for rest of chapter**

Go to the following page and return to Previous Number +1 so that the numbering continues from that point. If any other This Page overrides are present, they may disrupt page settings.

Step 3 **Edit headers & footers**

Verify that Headers and Footers have been turned off on cover pages and other pages you don't want to number.

Application Notes

- **Developing publications:** Turn to page 351.
- **Renumbering publication:** Turn to page 357.

Designing Book Pagination Systems

Book design applications may require a series of sequential page numbering systems. For example, you may want the front matter in lowercase Roman numerals, then restart the page numbering at 1 with Chapter 1, and finally use a sectional pagination system for the appendices and back matter. This all is easy to accomplish using the features in Update Counters.

When implementing a complex pagination system like this, it is necessary to be careful when making pagination settings for each chapter. To help prevent confusion, it is a good idea to open all chapters of the book *in sequence* and make the correct pagination settings. Once the correct values have been entered throughout the publication, you can relax while Ventura does the work.

Recipe: Book Pagination Systems

Step 1 **Design pagination system**

Identify pagination format for all elements of the publication. Make a list containing all the book chapters *in order* and note the correct pagination format for each. Place a check mark beside all chapters where the pagination format changes, or numbering restarts to a new value.

Step 2 **Place page number references**

For page numbers to print, you must place a page reference in one of two places:

▲ Place a page number reference in header or footer line using the **CHAPTER•Headers & Footers** dialog box.

▲ Place a page cross-reference in a box text graphic on the page. Access **EDIT•Ins. Special Edit Item** and select Cross Ref, P#.

Step 3 **Set initial page for front matter**

Access **FILE•Open Chapter** and open first paginated chapter in front matter sequence. Access **CHAPTER•Update Counters** and set Initial Page to 1. Select number format for front matter.

Designing Book Pagination Systems

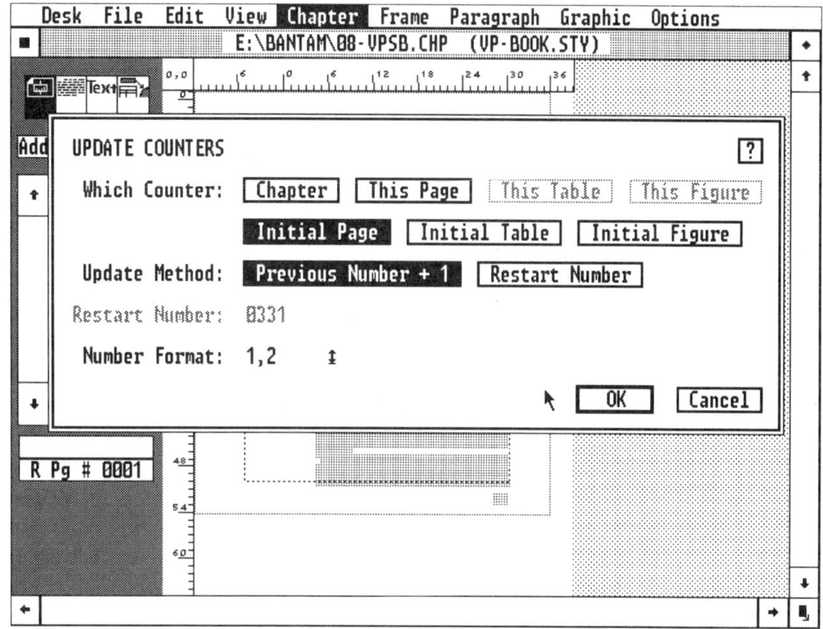

Step 4 **Set update for front matter chapters**

For any succeeding front matter chapters, access **CHAPTER•Update Counters** and set Initial Page to Previous Number +1. Set the same number format for page numbers.

Step 5 **Set initial page for first book chapter**

Access **FILE•Open Chapter** and open first book chapter. Access **CHAPTER•Update Counters** and set Initial Page to Restart Number at 1. Select number format for book chapters.

Step 6 **Set update for book chapters**

For all succeeding book chapters, access **CHAPTER•Update Counters** and set Initial Page to Previous Number +1. Set the same number format for page numbers.

Step 7 **Set initial page for Appendix 1**

Access **FILE•Open Chapter** and open first appendix chapter. Access **CHAPTER•Update Counters** and set Initial Page to Restart Number at 1. Select number format for appendices.

Step 8 **Repeat for additional appendices**

For all succeeding appendix chapters, access **CHAPTER•Update Counters** and set Initial Page to Previous Number +1. Set the same number format for page numbers.

Application Notes

- **Header & Footer tag design:** Set typographic values for header and footer line. Turn to page 237.
- **Set custom typography:** Set custom typography for the page number or other elements in the header and footer lines using text attribute codes. Turn to page 239.

Designing Table and Figure Numbering Systems

In books or technical documents where numbered references to tables and illustrations are necessary, you can set up a chapter–wide or publication–wide numbering system using Update Counters features in concert with Anchors and Captions dialog box.

Table and illustration numbering works in the same way that pagination does. That is, you can set up sectional pagination for tables and figures, or you can number them continuously through an entire publication. Illustrations are numbered separately from tables, giving you the flexibility to create two independently numbered series throughout the publication.

To use these features, tables, and figures *must* be placed inside frames. Each frame which is included in the numbering system *must* have a caption line containing either a figure reference [F#] or a table reference [T#]. Once you have designed your table and figure numbering system, you may override numbering for specific tables and figures anywhere in the publication. The following technique presents the steps used to design document or publication-wide numbering systems for figures or tables.

Designing Table and Figure Numbering Systems

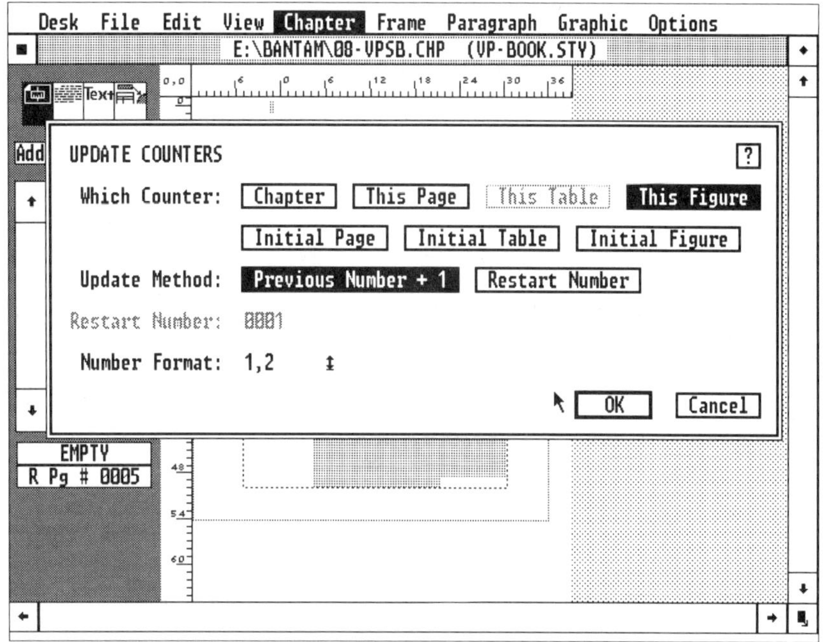

Recipe: Sectional Figure Numbering

Step 1 **Design numbering system**

Choose either sectional or continuous figure numbering for the document and in what format you want the number to appear.

Step 2 **Set chapter and figure references in caption**

Enable ***Frame*** mode and select frame containing the figure or table. Access **FRAME•Anchors & Captions**. Use the Caption feature to select the position of the caption. Use the Chapter # and Figure # features at the bottom of the dialog box to place Chapter and Figure references on the Label entry line.

Step 3 **Make counter settings**

Access **CHAPTER•Update Counters**. Select Chapter and Restart Number to enter the correct Chapter Number. Select Initial Page and Restart Number to 1.

Step 4 **Make number format settings**

Select the text presentation of the number for both the chapter and page number.

Recipe: Continuous Figure Numbering

Step 1 **Set figure references in caption**

Enable ***Frame*** mode and select frame containing the figure or table. Access **FRAME•Anchors & Captions**. Use the Caption feature to select the position of the caption. Place Figure reference only on the Label entry line.

Step 2 **Set first chapter initial figure to 1**

Access **CHAPTER•Update Counters**. For the first chapter in the continuous pagination sequence, change Initial Figure to Restart Number to 1. Select the desired number format.

Step 3 **Set update for all chapters**

For all chapters after the initial chapter, access **CHAPTER•Update Counters** and set Initial Figure to Previous Number +1

☞ CAUTION: If any chapters in the publication contain figure number overrides created with the This Figure option, they will disrupt the complete continuous figure numbering sequence. They must be removed.

Step 4 **Save publication**

Access **OPTIONS•Multi–Chapter**. Load all chapters in the publication into the dialog box using Add Chapter. Use mouse to place chapters in the desired order.

Step 5 **Renumber publication**

Select Renumber to begin the pagination sort operation. During this operation, Ventura searches through your publication chapters *twice*. On the second pass, the correct publication figure numbers are written to your chapter file.

Step 6 **View publication figure number**

You cannot see the publication figure number displayed in the Current Page Indicator. To see it, look in the figure caption frame or select the frame, open the **CHAPTER•Update Counters** dialog box and select This Figure.

Recipe: Custom Figure Number Override

Step 1 **Restart figure numbering**

Use keyboard or **CHAPTER•Go To Page** dialog box to display figure to be numbered. Access **CHAPTER•Update Counters** and select This Figure. Select Restart Number and enter the figure number to restart.

Step 2 **Check update for rest of chapter**

Go to the following figure and return to Previous Number +1 so that the numbering continues from that point. If any other This Figure overrides are present, they may disrupt figure numbering sequence.

Application Notes

- **Sectional figure and table numbering:** Create sectional numbering of tables and figures using Chapter # symbol in the caption label.
- **Editing the caption frame:** Turn to page 279
- **Cross–reference figure or table number:** Turn to page 406.
- **Cross reference caption label text:** Turn to page 410.

Using Matched Left–Right Chapters

Some applications, such as instructor manuals, present different sets of material on facing pages. For example, the instructor text appears on right pages, and its matching text from the participant materials is presented on the facing left pages. Generally, the instructor text is developed in one set of text files and the supporting material in another. The publishing problem is to easily integrate materials from

Using Matched Left-Right Chapters
Page 347

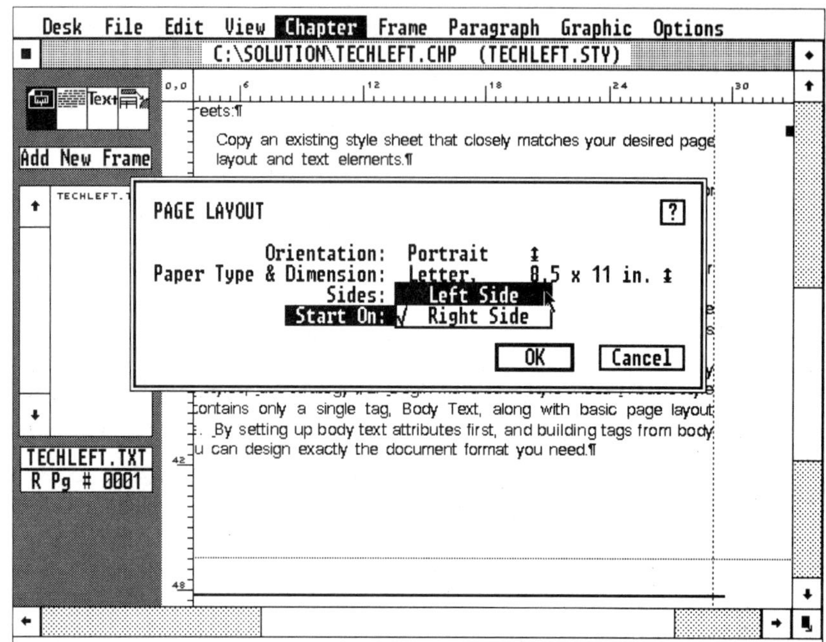

the two sets of text files without an individual laboriously pasting segments of text into frames or some similar approach.

Rather than cutting and pasting page segments into one text file, you can expedite the editing process by creating matched chapters. One chapter contains the text for right pages only and the other contains left pages only. This keeps text files for left and right pages distinct and separate for editing and writing purposes. During final production, the matched chapters allow you to control the correct positioning of text elements and document–wide pagination for the final document. The final document is created by interfiling pages from the two separate chapters.

This technique is implemented through a matched set of parallel style sheets for facing pages of the document. The matched styles differ only in the settings for left/right page margins and basic page settings. This approach helps to save editing and production time throughout the publication process.

Recipe: Left Page Style Sheet

Step 1 **Create left page style sheet**

Access **FILE•Load Diff. Style** to load an existing or basic style sheet, such as DEFAULT.STY in the \TYPESET subdirectory. Access **FILE• Save As New Style** to save it under a new name that includes a notation that it is a left page style.

Step 2 **Set up Page Size & Layout**

Access **CHAPTER•Page Size & Layout**. Set the desired paper type and orientation. Set Sides to Single and Start On to Left. This reduces confusion in production by making the page indicator on the Main Screen show all pages as Left.

Step 3 **Set up page margins**

Access **FRAME•Margins & Columns**. Set up page margins and columns as desired for the left page in the document.

Step 4 **Design document text**

Use features of the Paragraph menu to design the document text.

Step 5 **Set up page break**

Enable ***Text*** mode and pull down a free paragraph return. Enable ***Paragraph*** mode and select the text. Use Add New Tag in the Side–Bar to create a Page Break tag. Access **PARAGRAPH•Breaks** and set Page Break to After.

Recipe: Right Page Style Sheet

Step 1 **Copy left page style sheet**

With the Document Left style sheet currently selected, access **FILE•Save As New Style** and save it under a new name that includes a notation that it is for right pages.

Step 2 **Edit right page layout**

Access **CHAPTER•Page Size & Layout** and change Start On to Right. This causes the page indicator to show only right pages.

Step 3 **Edit Document Right style**

Make all necessary changes to the layout and text elements for the right pages in your document. Try to maintain the same tag names for ease and convenience in editing.

Recipe: Editing with Matched Chapters

Step 1 **Load text into correct style sheet**

Load text for left and right chapters into the correct style sheet and save as chapter files.

Step 2 **Use breaks to control page matches**

Print out copies of both left and right page chapters. To force text items relating to the content to appear on facing pages, place page breaks in text to balance the two chapters.

Step 3 **Interfile final product**

Print and interfile the two chapters for the final product.

Recipe: Matched Chapter Pagination

Pagination for matched chapter files can be set up in two distinct ways. Either let page numbers parallel, so that the content page has the same number as its supporting page, or set continuous pagination for the two chapters which can be interfiled to create seamless sequential pagination.

Step 1 **Parallel pagination**

Match page numbers: Give the content and its facing page matching or similar numbers by paginating straight through both chapters.

Step 2 **Continuous pagination**

To continuously paginate matched chapters, you must trick Ventura to do it by changing both style sheets back to double–sided pages.

▲ **Set double pages:** For both left and right style sheets, access **CHAPTER•Page Size & Layout** and set Sides to Double.

▲ **Block facing page:** To prevent any text from appearing on the double page, block it with a repeating frame. For the Document Right chapter, draw a full page–frame over the left page. Access **FRAME•Repeating Frame** and set frame to repeat on Left pages only. Set a repeating frame to block the right page in the Document Left chapter.

▲ **Set initial page:** For the Document Right chapter, access **CHAPTER•Update Counters** and set the Initial Page to Restart Counting at 1. This gives all right pages odd numbers. For the Document Left Chapter, set Initial Page to Restart at 2, giving all Left pages even numbers.

▲ **Print Left/Right only:** To avoid wasting paper, print only the pages in the chapters with data on them. When printing chapters, access **FILE•To Print**. For the Document Right chapter, set Which Pages to Right. For the Document Left chapter, set Which Pages to Left.

Application Notes

- **Facing page application:** Where different text patterns occur on facing pages, this technique lets you maintain integrated text for material on left and right pages throughout the publishing process without cutting and pasting text in your text file or in Ventura.
- **Long document layout** Turn to page 43.

Creating a Publication

A publication in Ventura is simply a list of chapter files. The publication file allows you to perform sorting and assembling operations including table of contents creating, indexing, and continuous page renumbering. These powerful capabilities are possible because Ventura's publication editing system has the power to automatically open chapter files, search through them and extract information, and write new information into the chapters.

Publication features are all controlled through the **OPTIONS•Multi–Chapter** dialog box. This dialog box contains many of the same features as appear on the File menu, including New, Open,

Creating a Publication
Page 351

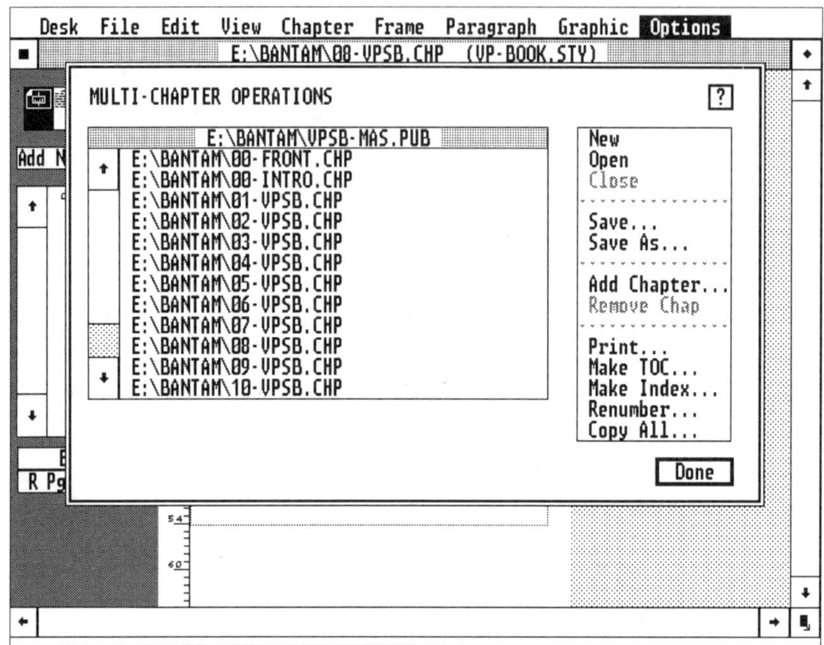

Save, and Save As. In this dialog box, these features are used to open and edit *publication* files.

Always assemble a complete publication in the correct document order. The order in which chapters are listed is the order that pages are assigned, tables of contents assembled, and index entries sorted.

Recipe: Creating a Publication

Step 1 **Access Multi–Chapter Operations**

Access **OPTIONS•Multi–Chapter**. If another publication is listed in the window, select New to clear the screen.

Step 2 **Build publication list**

Select Add Chapter. In the Item Selector, use the Backup Button to specify the drive where the *chapter files* to be listed are stored. Select the name of a chapter to place in the publication. The name of the chapter will appear in the Multi–Chapter Operations list. Repeat this operation for each chapter of your publication. When assembling a long list of files, it is faster to select and load chapter file names by double–clicking on the mouse.

Step 3 **Position files for publication**

To move a file in the publication list, place mouse cursor on the file name. Press and hold the mouse button as you drag the file name to the desired position in the publication list.

Step 4 **Save publication**

To name the publication, select Save As, and assign a publication name. The new publication name appears in the Multi–Chapter Operations title bar. To save subsequent changes to the publication list, select Save. Note that no screen overlay appears during the Save operation.

Application Notes

- **Long document layout** Turn to page 43.
- **Copy publication to floppy disk** Turn to page 355.

Assembling a Print Queue

To print a number of related (or unrelated) files in progression which are not intended to be published together, you can create a publication file simply to provide a print queue. This saves the need to load each chapter file individually and print it.

Before printing the queue, you should check all chapters for print stoppers. If chapters are designed in oversize pages, or contain even a single hidden picture, the print process will stop and display an overlay selector. The print process won't resume until a response is made to the overlay. If you have not removed the stoppers from your chapter, you must be present during the print operation to respond to the overlay message.

Assembling a Print Queue
Page 353

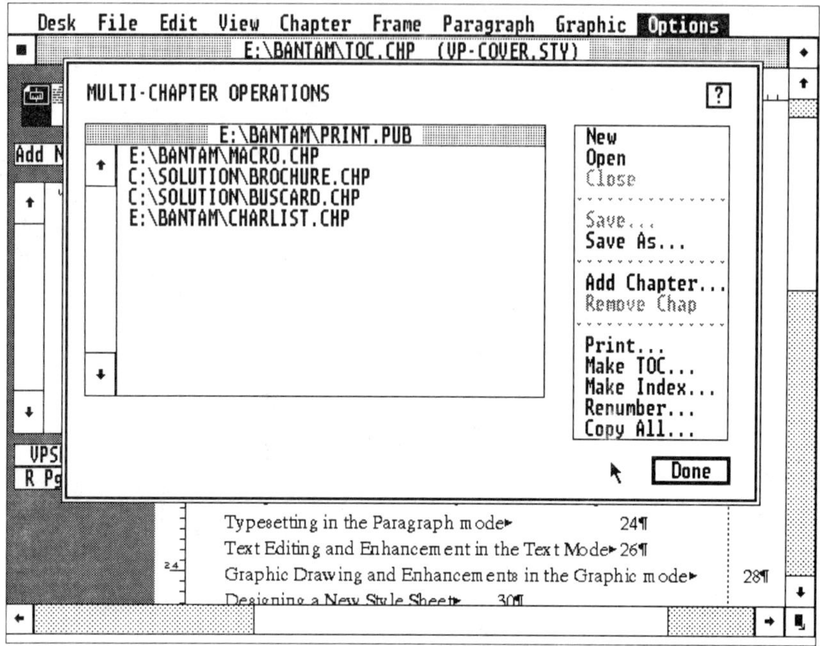

Recipe: Print Queue Publication

Step 1 **Check files**

Before assembling the print queue, check files for elements that may stop the print sequence. If these elements are in your files, you will have to be present to respond to the overlays Ventura places during the print cycle.

▲ Any files using oversize page style sheets (such as Double or Broadsheet) will cause Ventura to stop the print process with an overlay asking if you want to shrink or overlay print them.

▲ Any files with hidden pictures cause Ventura to stop the print cycle to ask if you want to hide or print all pictures.

Step 2 **Assemble files**

Access **OPTIONS•Multi–Chapter**. Use Add Chapter to load all files to be printed and use mouse cursor to place them in print order.

Step 3 **Save as print publication**

Use Save As to save the list of files. Use a standard, reusable name, such as PRINT.PUB. Each time you make a new print list, select the same file name. When Ventura prompts you to rename the file, select the Override option. This helps prevent cluttering your system with a lot of useless files.

Step 4 **Print all pages**

To print, select Print in the **Multi– Chapter** dialog box. Remember to set Which Pages to All. Identify the number of copies if more than one is desired.

Application notes

- **Designing with oversize pages:** Turn to page 54.
- **Downloading fonts:** If any chapter in the print queue contains custom fonts which have not been downloaded to your printer, the rate of printing may slow significantly as Ventura downloads all the custom fonts for *each printed page.* Before beginning the print queue, download all the necessary fonts and tell Ventura they are now resident in the printer. Turn to page 485.

Using Copy All

The Multi–Chapter dialog box is also home to one of the most important features in Ventura Publisher: Copy All. Ventura chapter files contain a list of all the files which make up a document, including the name of the style sheet, all the text files, all the picture files, and any other related files. For each file, the chapter file contains the correct drive and subdirectory where that file is located.

Because of the special way that Ventura saves and stores documents, chapter files and publications cannot be copied from one place to another using standard MS–DOS Copy commands. If files are copied using simple DOS commands, the chapter file won't be able to find any of the related files that make up the document, and it will crash.

The Copy All feature allows you to copy chapter files or complete publications to another segment of the hard drive or to a floppy disk. During the Copy All operation, the correct drive and location detail

Using Copy All
Page 355

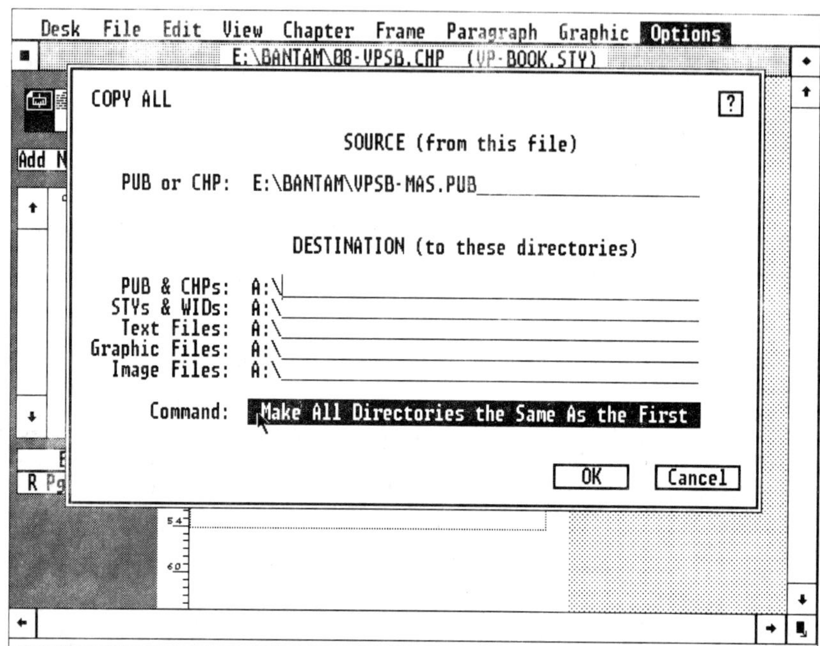

for the document style sheet, text, picture, and related files is written into the new chapter file.

Recipe: Copy All for Publications

Step 1 **Load publication**

Access **OPTIONS•Multi–Chapter**. Select Open and load the desired publication file.

Step 2 **Enter new destination**

Select Copy All. Enter drive and subdirectory destination information for all file types listed. If all files are to be copied to the same destination, enter the destination on the Pubs & Chps line, and select Make All Directories the Same As the First.

Step 3 **Initiate Copy**

Select OK to begin copy operation. During the copy operation, one or more overlays may appear:

▲ **File conflict:** Ventura has found a file with the exact same name at the new destination. The overlay prompts you to keep the old file, overwrite the old file, or cancel the operation.

▲ **Disk space:** If there is not enough room in the new destination, Ventura prompts you to insert a new disk or cancel the operation. If a new disk is inserted, the Copy All operation continues until completed. Write the correct order of the disks created during this process on the label. When copying files off these disks, begin with Disk 1 and continue entering the following disks *in order* as prompted on–screen.

Recipe: Copy All for Chapters

Step 1 **Load chapter file**

Access **OPTIONS•Multi–Chapter**. You can copy a chapter file using Copy All in one of two ways:

▲ **From a publication list:** Click on the name of a chapter in a publication list so the name is highlighted.

▲ **Individually:** Use Add Chapter to load a chapter name into the publication file selector. Click on the chapter name so it is highlighted.

Step 2 **Set up Copy All**

Enter desired destination and initiate Copy All .

Application Notes

- **Check for stoppers:** Periodically check the archive operation to make sure it is continuing. If Ventura cannot find one of the files in one chapter, it will stop the operation and display a query message. You must answer the query for printing to resume.

Renumbering Publications

To paginate a publication across chapters, you must make the correct Update Counters settings to each chapter in the publication and then renumber the publication in the Multi– Chapter Operations dialog box to sort and place the correct page numbers. In this Professional Extension, this process also finds text markers and writes the correct page cross–references to the places you have specified throughout the publication.

When paginating across multiple chapters, there are several important production points to keep in mind.

- Each time you make edits to one or more chapters in the publication, you may change the number of pages in that layout. Adding or losing even one page affects the pagination of *the entire publication.* For pagination to be correct, you must renumber the publication again.
- When the publication pagination changes, publication features such as the table of contents and index must be regenerated to reflect the new page sequence.

After renumbering is complete, you can open any chapter in the publication, and the correct publication page number appears in the **CHAPTER•Update Counters** dialog box or on the screen.

Renumbering Publications
Page 357

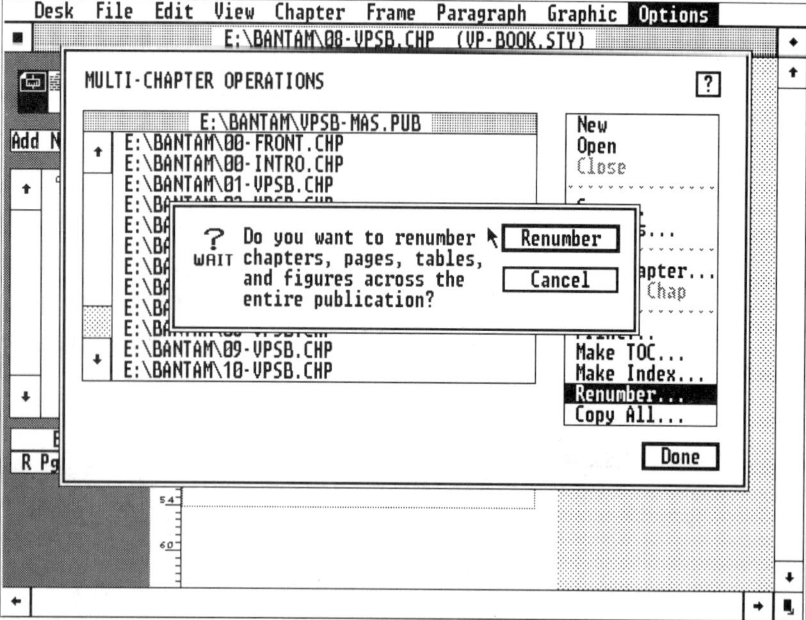

Recipe: Renumbering Publications

Step 1 **Verify pagination system complete**

Before beginning the renumber operation, check each chapter's pagination settings in the **CHAPTER•Update Counters** dialog box.

- ▲ The first chapter beginning with page 1 should be set so that Initial Page has been set to Restart Number at 1.
- ▲ All additional chapters should be set so that Initial Page is set to Previous Number +1.

Step 2 **Place files in correct order**

Access **OPTIONS•Multi–Chapter** and open the publication. Use mouse cursor to position all files in the correct publication order.

Step 3 **Activate renumber option**

Select Renumber in the dialog box and again at the overlay. Ventura will now go through entire publication twice to correctly paginate the list of chapters.

Step 4 **Check numbering**

The sequential page numbers are displayed in the header or footer line, or at the position of the page number cross– reference placed elsewhere on the page. It may also be seen in the **CHAPTER•Update Counters** dialog box for each chapter in the publication.

Application Notes

- **Setting up pagination:** Turn to page 338.
- **Setting up book pagination systems:** Turn to page 342.

Placing Index Entries

Developing an index consists of two key operations. First, you place the index entries and then Ventura sorts them to create the index.

When designing the index, plan out the major details and identify topics and spelling conventions before placing any entries. It is vital to control spelling and place entries using uniformly defined topics.

If you don't, Ventura will generate a collection of misspelled entries with the correct page numbers.

After you have worked with the index process, you can save a significant amount of time by learning to place your index entries directly into text using search and replace features of your word processor.

Recipe: Index Entries

Step 1 **Create index master list**

Make a control list of the key terms in your index. Establish uniform spelling conventions. Words not spelled in the same way, when indexed will be entered under a separate heading.

Step 2 **Identify text to be indexed**

Enable ***Text*** mode and place cursor in front of word to be indexed. Access **EDIT•Ins. Special Edit Item** and select Index Entry.

Step 3 **Design index entry**

A variety of entry formats can be worked into the index:

▲ **Single line:** Places the term with its page number in the index. Select Index entry and enter the term on the Primary Entry line.

▲ **Double line:** Places a list of terms under a common heading. Select Index entry and type the common heading on the Primary Entry line. Type the term on the Secondary Entry line. For each entry in the series, type the same common heading on the Primary Entry line and the terms on the Secondary Entry line.

▲ **Cross reference:** Places a non– numbered cross–reference to other topics and elements in the index. Select See or See Also. Enter the term on the Primary Entry line. Enter the cross–reference name or heading on the Secondary Entry line.

▲ **Sort key:** Place non–alphabet terms into the proper alphabet sequence. For a term like *3–D*, enter *Three–D* on the appropriate sort key line.

Placing Index Entries
Page 359

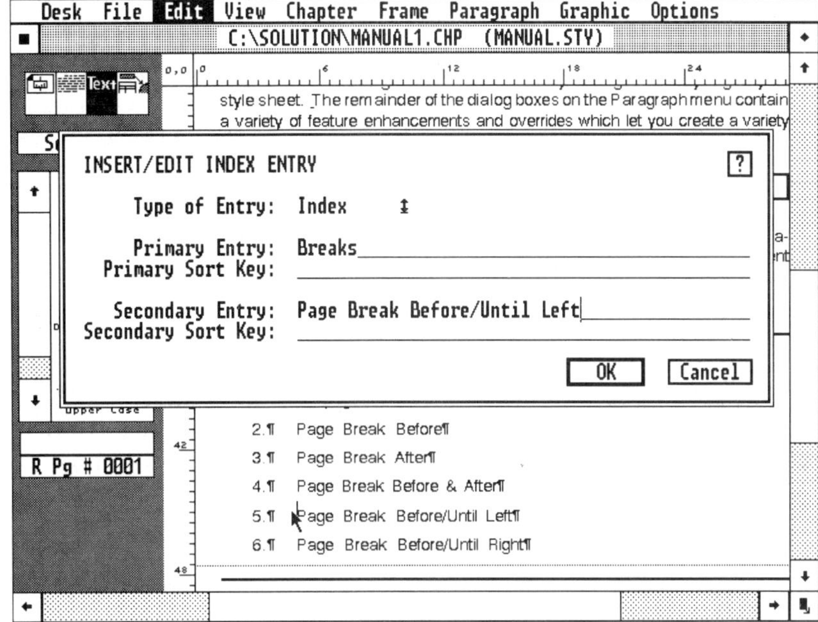

Recipe: Index Entries in the Word Processor

To save time, place index entries directly into a text file using your word processor.

Step 1 **Create macro files**

In a word processor, create macro keys to insert the brackets for index entries directly into text. The macro should read: **<$I>**

Step 2 **Identify text to be indexed**

In the word processor, display the term to be indexed. Place cursor in front of the word and enter the index brackets with the macro.

Step 3 **Place index code brackets**

Enter index text inside brackets using the format: <$IPrimary[Primary Sort];Secondary[Secondary Sort]>:

▲ To place a single–line index entry for the term *Computers* in the word processor, the index entry should read: **<$IComputers>**.

▲ To place a double–line entry for the term *Disk Drive* under the heading *Computers*, the entry should read: **<$IComputers;Disk Drive>.**

▲ To place a double–line entry for the non– alphabetic term *3rd Party Products* under the heading *Computers*, the entry should read: **<$IComputers;3rd Party Products[Third Party Products]>**.

Recipe: Place Index Entries with Search & Replace

Additional time can be saved by using the search and replace features of a word processor to find key words or terms in your manuscript and automatically enter the index entry codes throughout the document.

Set up search and replace to find the term and replace with the that term plus the correctly completed index entry. Indexing this way can save you literally hours of repetitive work.

Step 1 **Identify term**

Identify the term to index. Go into your word processor and run a spelling check on it to verify that all the terms are spelled correctly.

Step 2 **Define search**

Set up the search for the term. For example, Search for: Newsletters.

Step 3 **Define replace**

Set up the replace to insert the term with the correct index brackets. For example: <$INewsletters>Newsletters.

Step 4 **Save frequently**

Save your word processor file after every few index search and replace sweeps to ensure against losing data.

Recipe: Generate Index

When you have placed all index entries in your word processor, assemble the index in Ventura by activating the Index sort.

Step 1 **Save publication**

Access **OPTIONS•Multi–Chapter**. Use Add Chapter to load all chapters into the publication file sorter. Use Save As to save the group of chapters into a publication.

Step 2 **Check location and name of index file**

Select Make Index. The Index File line at the top of the screen defines the location and name of file to which the index will be written. To change the file name or location, enter new name and location directly on the line.

Step 3 **Make Index**

The default values for the index are already defined on the screen. To begin the index generation process, Select OK.

Step 4 **Load Index text file**

When the index generating process is finished, select Done to leave the **Multi–Chapter** dialog box. Access **FILE•Load Text/Picture**, select Text and the Generated file format. Load the generated index text file with the file extension .GEN into the Working Area.

Step 5 **Save Index chapter**

Make sure document style sheet is currently loaded. Select **FILE•Save** to save the generated index into a chapter file.

Step 6 **Place Index in publication**

Access **OPTIONS•Multi–Chapter** and open the publication. Use Add Chapter to load the Index chapter into the publication list. Use mouse to drag the file into the correct position in the publication list. Select Save to complete the operation.

Recipe: Designing the Index

During the index generation process, an index file is automatically tagged with special index tags. Once you have loaded the index file into a chapter, you can define the values for those tags to design the appearance and typographic values of your index.

Step 1 **Show generated tags**

Access **OPTIONS•Set Preferences** and set Generated Tags to Shown.

Step 2 **Define tag attributes**

Enable ***Paragraph*** mode and select index text. Use features of the Paragraph menu to design each index tag.

Application Notes

- **Create term reference list:** Keep a reference list of index terms handy. Invariably, you will come up with new terms to add. Record them all in the master list. Maintain spelling conventions to save editing time after the index is generated.
- **Regenerate after edits:** After each pass in which you place new entries, you must regenerate the entire index for those entries to be included.
- **Automatic updating:** If your index chapter is set up using the generated index tags, each time you regenerate the index, the contents of the index chapter will be automatically updated.
- **Convert index text:** By converting generated index file to your word processor format, you can edit it outside of Ventura. Turn to page 483.

Creating Index Page Ranges

Index entries placed into headlines or other text which is displayed in the header/footer line via 1st/Last Match, can be used to automatically create page range indexes, to show the beginning and ending blocks of a particular block of text.

Recipe: Index Page Ranges

Step 1 **Identify match headings**

Identify document headings to be placed into the header or footer line with 1st or Last Match.

Step 2 **Place index entry**

Place index entries into the text of each of these major headings or subheadings.

Step 3 **Place tag match**

Access **CHAPTER•Headers & Footers**. Place cursor where the heading is to appear. Select 1st or Last Match and enter the tag name of the heading or subheading in the brackets.

Step 4 **Set up index**

When index entries have been placed in all headings, access **OPTIONS•Multi–Chapter** and open the publication. Select Make Index.

Step 5 **Check index ranges**

Verify that the For Each # line in the dialog box is configured to display a page range. A page range is expressed by two page number symbols separated by a dash. When this range is defined, Ventura will enter the beginning page and ending page for the topic, and not list all the pages in between.

Several correct forms of the page range are:

▲ **[C#]-[P#]—[C#]-[P#]:** The default value in the dialog box sets up a page range for a sectionally paginated document.

Creating Index Page Ranges

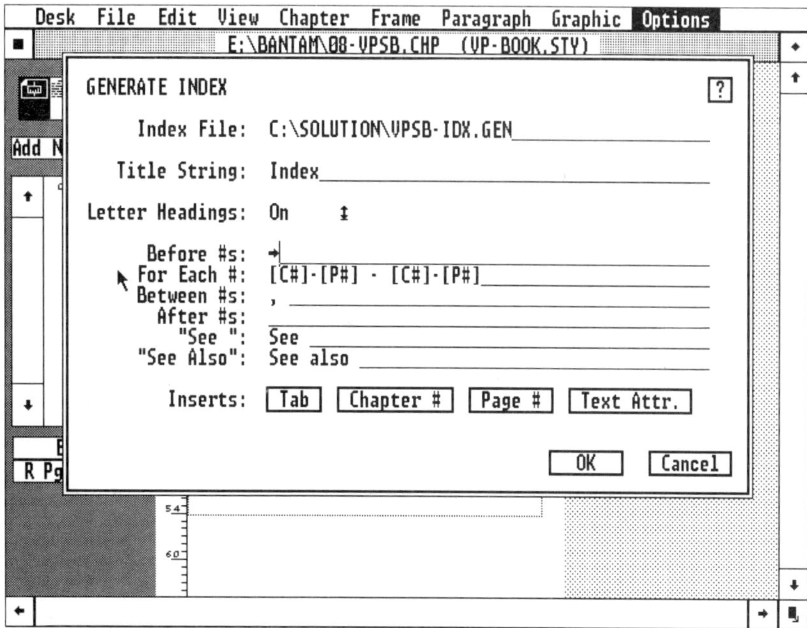

▲ **[P#]—[P#]:** Sets up a page range for a continuously paginated publication.

Step 6 **Make Index**

After you have checked and set up all values in the Generate Index dialog box, select OK to begin index sort operation.

Application Notes

- **Setting up headers and footers:** Turn to page 228
- **Convert index text:** By converting generated index file to your word processor format, you can edit it outside of Ventura. Turn to page 483.

Designing a Table of Contents

A table of contents is one of the Ventura power features that uses paragraph tags as an organizing system. By entering the name of the tags for the text elements shown in a table of contents, Ventura finds all occurrences of the tag, and uses the tag as a handle to pull in the text and put it in publication order. During the operation, the table of contents is written into a separate text file, and automatically tagged with generated tags for each level in the table of contents.

When setting up a table of contents, paragraph tags are used to identify levels in the publication. Make sure that all text which is to be included on the same level in the table of contents is tagged with the *same paragraph tag*. If you have created individual variations of the tag to solve special cases, that text will not be included.

Recipe: Setting Up a Table of Contents

Step 1 **Design table of contents**

Identify the title and heading elements to be included in the table of contents. Write down the paragraph tags for each element in the table of contents, beginning with the title or major heading at the top, and progressing down through subheadings.

Designing a Table of Contents

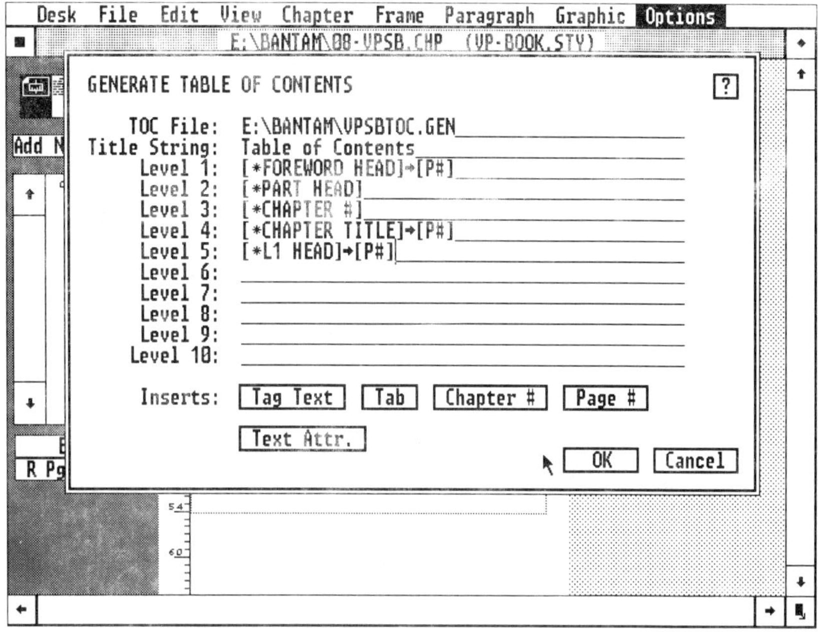

Step 2 **Access table of contents**

Access **OPTIONS•Multi–Chapter** and open the publication. Select Make TOC. The table of contents dialog box appears.

Step 3 **Check location and name of toc file**

On the TOC file line at the top of the screen defines the location and name of file to which the table of contents will be written. To change the file name or location, enter a new name and/or location directly on the line.

Step 4 **Check title string**

If you want to call the file something other than Table of Contents, you may enter that title on the title string line or leave it blank.

Step 5 **Select first tag name**

Place cursor on Level 1. Select Tag Text at the bottom of the screen. Delete the words *tag name* from inside the brackets and enter the name of the first paragraph tag in table of contents.

Step 6 **Apply desired pagination system**

To position the page number in table of contents, place a tab character right after the tag name brackets. Then place the page number format you desire.

▲ If you are paginating sequentially across chapters, place [P#] to place the page.

▲ If you are using chapter by chapter pagination, place [C#]–[P#] to place the chapter and page number in the table of contents.

Step 7 **Complete TOC entry**

Repeat the above process for each additional level in the Table of Contents. When complete, select OK to begin the table of contents sort operation.

Application notes

- **Check tag names:** Always be sure to use the same tag name for all elements in your table of contents. Alternate versions of the same tag in your documents won't be picked up.
- **Stacked tags:** If you are using stacked tags, make sure to use the master tag containing the text of the heading. Turn to page 130.

Editing the TOC

Once the TOC has been generated, it is written to a Generated (ASCII) text file in Ventura with automatically generated tags assigned to each level of text in the file. You can edit those levels and change tags at will.

Recipe: TOC Edit

Step 1 **Load Table of Contents text file**

When the table of contents generation process is finished, select Done to leave the **Multi–Chapter** dialog box. Access **FILE•Load Text/Picture**, select Text and the Generated file format. Load the

Editing the TOC

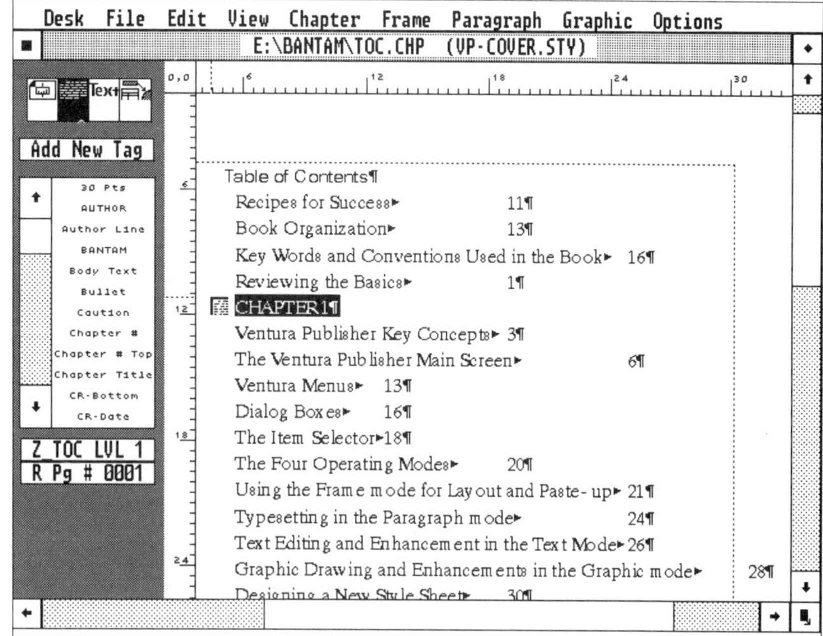

generated Table of Contents text file with the file extension .GEN into the Working Area.

Step 2 **Save Table of Contents chapter**

Make sure that your document style sheet is currently loaded. Select **FILE•Save** to save the generated Table of Contents into a chapter file.

Step 3 **Place Table of Contents in publication**

Access **OPTIONS•Multi–Chapter** and open the publication. Use Add Chapter to load the Table of Contents chapter into the publication list. Use mouse to drag the file into the correct position in the publication list. Select Save to complete the operation.

Recipe: Table of Contents Design

During the Table of Contents generation process, the Table of Contents file is automatically tagged with special Z_TOC tags. Once the Table of Contents file has been loaded into a chapter, define the values for the tags to set typography and position for each level of

TOC text. You may also apply any standard paragraph tag from the Assignment List to the table of contents text.

Step 1 **Show generated tags**

Access **OPTIONS•Set Preferences** and set Generated Tags to Shown.

Step 2 **Define tag attributes**

Enable ***Paragraph*** mode and select Table of Contents text. Use features of the Paragraph menu to design each Table of Contents tag.

Application Notes

- **Set custom typographic values:** Use text attributes to typeset individual sections of Table of Contents text. Process is the same as that used for headers and footers. Turn to page 239.
- **Add text on TOC lines:** You can add text directly on the Table of Contents dialog box entry lines, just like the auto–numbering dialog box. For example, if you want your chapter title text to appear in the Table of Contents line preceded by "Chapter 1," type the text right on the TOC line. Process is the same as that used for auto–numbering. Turn to page 202.

Placing Auto–numbers in the TOC

In some situations, you may want to place the text from more than one tag on a single Table of Contents line. The most visible example of this is for auto–numbering applications. By entering the tag for the auto–number and its reference text on the same line in the Generate Table of Contents dialog box, both will print out on the same line.

Recipe: Auto–numbers in the TOC

Step 1 **Access table of contents**

Access **OPTIONS•Multi–Chapter** and open the publication. Select Make TOC. The Table of Contents dialog box appears.

Step 2 **Place auto–number tag on level 1**

Select Tag Text at the bottom of the screen. Delete the words *tag name* and enter tag name for the heading auto– number. For example, **[*Z_SEC1]**. If you want to place punctuation between the auto–number text and the reference text, enter it between the two bracketed entries.

☞ CAUTION: If the auto–number has a period built in and you add a period here, your TOC file will show 2 periods on the line.

Step 3 **Place reference text tag on level 1**

Select Tag Text at the bottom of the screen. Delete the words *tag name* and enter the name of the desired heading. For example **[*LEVEL 1 HEAD]**.

Step 4 **Identify spacing/punctuation**

Place any desired punctuation before or following the tag entry brackets. Leave spaces on the line by pressing the Spacebar.

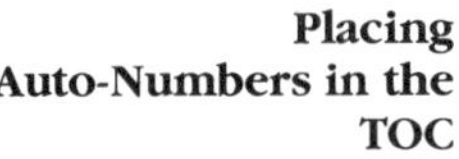

Placing Auto-Numbers in the TOC

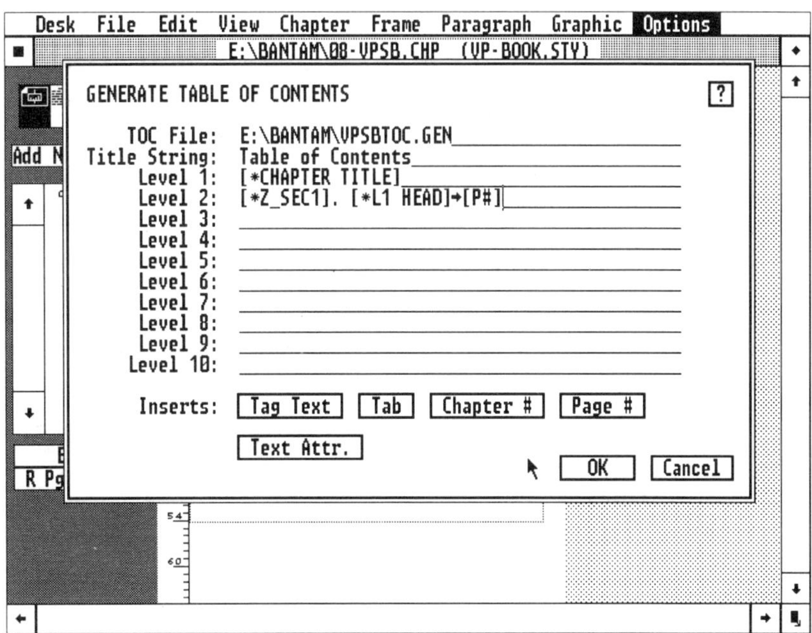

Step 5 **Place page numbers**

Place a tab character after the final bracket on the line and select the desired page display.

Application Notes

- **Place special typography:** Set off the auto– number in bold using the text attributes option.
- **Production auto–numbering:** Create a special checklist of your production auto–numbering system. Turn to page 209.

Creating a List of Illustrations

Documents incorporating a variety of elements including auto–numbered headings, numbered illustrations and tables may require multiple tables of contents. The Table of Contents feature can be used to sort through the publication and assemble specialized tables of contents, such as lists of tables, lists of illustrations and others. For example, running the Table of Contents referencing only the tag for the caption label (Z_LABEL CAP) generates a special table of contents containing the label text for all captioned illustrations in a the publication, with the correct page numbers.

By using the Table of Contents feature as a listing and sorting tool, various document–wide listings of special elements and subheadings are created. For this sorting capability to work, however, it is crucial that all elements being sorted carry the same tag name.

Recipe: List of Illustrations

Step 1 **Set up illustration numbering**

For each illustration in a document, select the frame and access **FRAME•Anchors & Captions**. Enter the caption label on the line provided. This text will be sorted and pulled into the special table of contents file.

Creating a List of Illustrations

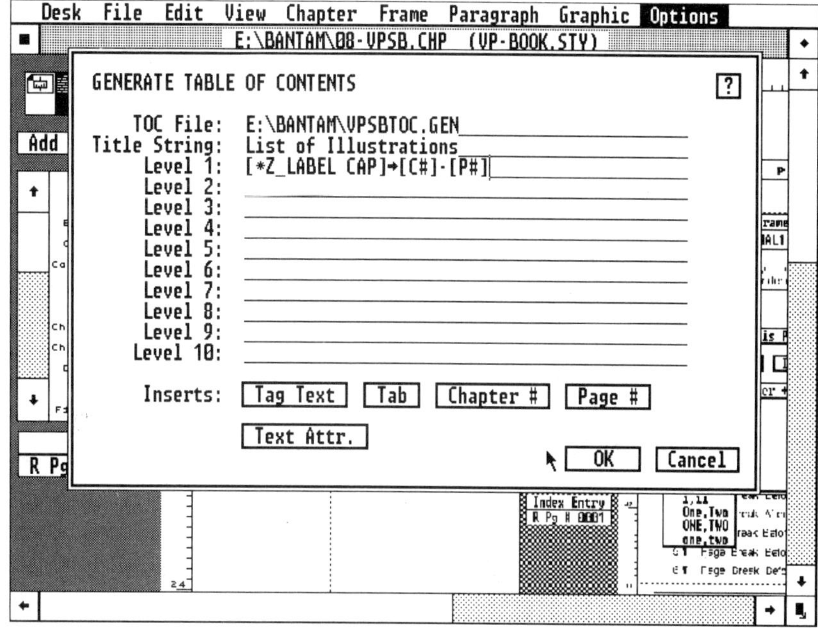

Step 2 **Access Table of Contents**

Access **OPTIONS•Multi–Chapter**. Open the publication file and select Make TOC. The Table of Contents dialog box appears on the screen.

Step 3 **Check name and position of TOC file**

Enter a new name on the TOC File line to prevent the table of contents process from overwriting any existing table of contents file.

Step 4 **Check title string**

Enter a new Title String, for example, "List of Illustrations."

Step 5 **Enter illustration tag: Z_LABEL CAP**

Select Tag Text at the bottom of the screen. Delete the words *tag name* and enter Z_LABEL CAP inside the brackets.

Step 6 **Place chapter and page codes as necessary**

Place a tab character after the final brackets and enter the page symbols as they are to appear.

Application Notes

- **Create Table of Contents for forms and tests:** If you used a special organizing tag for forms and test titles, you can easily use the TOC features to sort them.
- **Using TOC for production reference sorts:** Use Table of Contents to automatically create lists and reports out of your files for use during the editing process. For example, use this feature to develop a listing of all headings and subheadings in your document with page numbers for use during copy editing.

Converting TOC File to Word Processor Format

To make editing easier, convert the Ventura–generated TOC file to your word processor format so you can directly edit and change text elements and reposition them as you wish. The generated text file containing the TOC is a simple ASCII file with completely tagged text. You can convert it to your word processor format using the **EDIT•File Type/Rename** dialog box.

Recipe: Word Processor TOC Text

Step 1 **Select file**

Access **FILE•Open Chapter** and select TOC chapter file. Enable ***Frame*** mode and select the base page. The name of the TOC text file should appear in the Current Selection Box.

Step 2 **Change file name and type**

Access **EDIT•File Type/Rename**. Change the file name appearing on the New Name line to the correct extension for your word processor. For example, for Wordstar, change the file extension to .WS. Select the desired text format.

Step 3 **Save chapter file**

The file conversion is not complete until you save the chapter file. Select **FILE•Save** to create the converted copy.

Converting TOC File to Word Processor Format

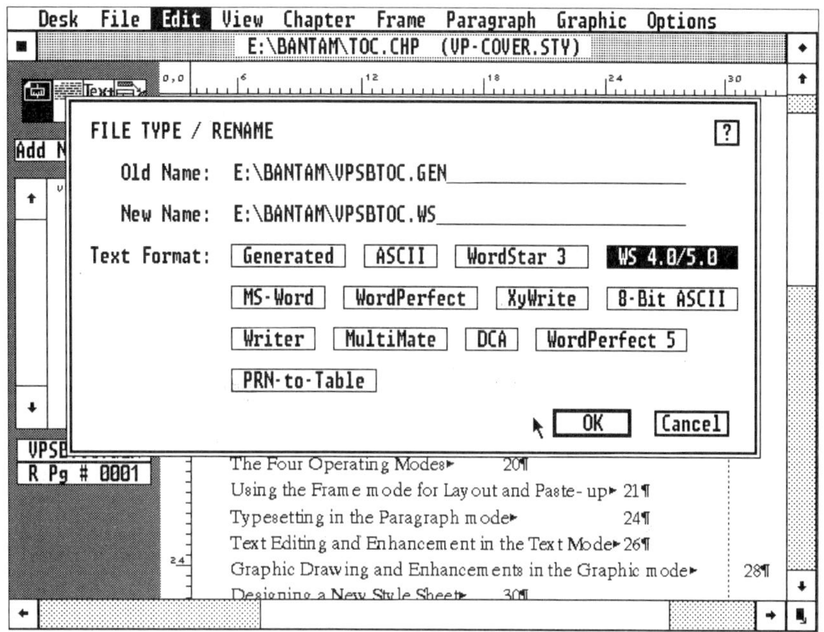

Step 4 **Dispose of duplicate**

When converting text files, Ventura makes a copy of the original text file but *does not destroy it.* To reduce possible confusion, erase the original TOC file with the .GEN extension.

Application Notes

- **Change tag values:** You may tag TOC text with any tags in the current style sheet. You do not have to use, or define values for the generated Z_TOC tags.
- **Save production time:** By editing TOC text directly in word processor, you save production time by making corrections directly into the TOC file. This allows you to make corrections without having to run a new table of contents sort operation in Ventura.

PART II

Working with Professional Extension

CHAPTER 9

Vertical Justification

Professional Typography

For documents to meet the highest standard of professional quality, you must have exacting and comprehensive controls over typography. Ventura's strong commitment to professional typographic standards is evidenced by the system of typographic settings and controls available in the standard Ventura software. The Professional Extension includes an additional set of controls which, when used together, support vertical justification in your documents.

Vertical justification forces text on every page in a document to "justify" to the same point at the bottom, so that all pages have a uniform length. To accomplish this, space must be added in small increments down the page to expand the text without leaving large open spaces or holes.

It is theoretically possible to vertically justify text using the standard software by creating a series of tags set to small increments of space. The problem with this approach is that it requires a great deal of time and effort to put in place, even in a short document.

DESKTOP DYNAMICS

Publishing tools for effective communications

CREATIVE EXPRESSION

The uses for your desktop publishing system are limited only by your imagination. With the ability to easily merge text and graphics, you will be able to generate published quality output for a wide variety of document applications.

Many people approach the desktop publishing world with one central or 'key' application in mind. Maybe they have a monthly customer newsletter to create, or they have a need to design and deliver advertisements. Perhaps they must edit and compile many long documents, such as technical manuals, containing diagrams and schematics. But as they become aware of the wide-ranging capabilities of desktop publishing they begin to use it for a great variety of applications, both for presentation to customers and in-house use.

The most exciting thing about desktop publishing is that it not only enhances the look and quality of documents you are already producing, but that it can enable you to create documents you never could before. Given the time factors and expense of tradi tional typesetting and page layout, some promising projects are put on the shelf or never get off the ground. Desktop publishing saves you time and money and lets you do it yourself.

UNDERSTAND THE SYSTEM

To get the most out of desktop publishing, it is important to understand the features and functions of the equipment and soft ware. It is no less important to understand the many different types of printing and publishing applications that the system supports.

The following sections cover many of the major application groups in desktop publishing. Take a hard look at your current output -- which of your applications could benefit from desktop publishing?

Graphics add Style!

NEWSLETTERS

Newsletters are a simple and effective means of communicating with a specified group of people. Businesses use them to build sales by keeping in touch with their customer base as well as a means of sending out updates on technical informa tion, or just keeping their employees informed on what's going on in the company. Schools use them to send out lists of class offerings, associations use them to update their members, and community groups use them to post activities.

A newsletter can be a simple or complex as the creator desires. On one extreme, the publisher starts with typewritten text, pieces the issue together with scissors and glue and runs it off on a copy machine. On the other extreme, the newsletter creator orders up a staple-bound multipage pamphlet, laid out in three columns, ornamented with color graphics and printed on a 4-color press.

With desktop publishing capability, simple newsletters can get a professional look at a fraction of the time and expense associated with traditional typesetting. Text can be combined with graphics in complex, multi-column formats easily and quickly.

For those individuals who are currently publishing newletters via typesetting and conventional printing technologies, desktop publishing offers the same quality look at a substantially reduced cost. And those individuals who are putting out

1

Newsletter: With vertical justification features, text can automatically be aligned to the same position at the bottom of the page. For layouts with multiple columns, carded vertical justification can align text across columns and facing pages. Text is typeset in ITC Korinna. Artwork was created in Corel Draw.

Professional Extension typography and vertical justification controls let you develop an automatic vertical justification system. By defining a series of limits and spacing values, you can use these Ventura controls to automatically establish vertical justification throughout the document.

A Quick Look at Vertical Justification

Vertical justification in Ventura is a complex process in which the software computes the size of the page, the amount of text on that page, and finally the amount of space which must be added to cause justification. To accomplish this in an automatic, systematic way, you must define vertical justification systems in a different way from most other typographic values.

To begin with, in vertical justification you don't enter set spacing *values*—you define a range of spacing *limits*. Because of the number of variables and computations involved, entering set values would force you to continually change entries for pages of different length and a variety of other reasons. So Ventura lets you control vertical justification spacing changes by setting the highest allowable space it can add above and below frames, between paragraphs, and between lines of text.

When defining settings, keep in mind that they are applied in a set vertical justification sequence. When Ventura goes into a document to add extra space, it follows this step–by–step procedure.

- Add space Above/Below Frames
- Add space Above/Below Paragraphs
- Add space Between Lines of Paragraph

As Ventura processes a document, it can add as little or as much space on the page *up to the defined limit* to accomplish vertical justification.

There are two approaches to vertical justification available in Ventura Publisher. Depending upon specific document requirements, you will probably have occasion to use them both.

Vertical Justification with Feathering

Feathering is the simplest approach to vertical justification. This choice measures the amount of space between the bottom line of text and the defined bottom for vertical justification. It then adds as much space as required between frames, paragraphs and lines to force the text to align to the point of justification.

But because feathering simply stretches text to fit the page or column space, the amount of space added is not consistent. The result is that pages vertically justified with feathering can look unevenly spaced.

In multi–column documents, feathering can also disrupt the uniform text spacing across columns so that text does not line up horizontally. Feathering is, therefore, a "down and dirty" approach to vertical justification when you need a fast, quick solution.

Vertical Justification with Carding

Carding offers a more complex and professional approach for more sophisticated documents. This method adds space for vertical justification in *set increments* of the Body Text interline spacing. Carding allows vertical justification to take place in uniform, controlled increments of space which ensure uniform alignment and presentation on the page.

Using the carding feature, you can set your documents to vertically justify across columns and entire pages. And by applying uniform typographic standards in setting up pages, you can create professional typesetting effects throughout documents.

Vertical Justification Tools

Vertical justification features are contained in the three typography dialog boxes, each of which controls specific parts of the process.

- **Chapter typography** contains the settings which enable vertical justification in your document. Here you set document–wide limits for vertical justification and select the method of vertical justification to be used.

- **Frame typography** contains the override settings for vertical justification within frames. Use this feature to set custom vertical justification limits inside individual frames.

- **Paragraph typography** contains the custom vertical justification settings for each paragraph tag.

Working with Typographic Features

This chapter contains techniques which show you how to get the most out of Professional Extension's typographic design features. Remember that these features only work when the Professional Extension is installed. You can open your chapter file in the standard product, but none of the advanced typography will work there. Keep this in mind when designing and distributing documents in your working environment.

Designing Style Sheets for Carding

To design professional vertical justification effects your style sheets must be typographically precise. Vertical justification with carding adds space to the page in increments equal to the Body Text interline spacing. If the Body Text interline spacing is set to one pica, then carding adds space to the page in increments of *exactly one pica.* To design successfully with carding, you must set up your style sheet so that the interline spacing for each tag is equal to Body Text interline spacing (one pica) or an exact multiple (two picas, three picas, four picas).

When the style sheet has been properly designed as a system of multiples of the Body Text interline spacing, you can produce double–sided, multiple–column documents in which all baselines of text align perfectly across columns and pages.

Recipe: Style Sheet for Carding

Step 1 **Create new style sheet**

Access **FILE•Load Diff. Style** and load a basic style sheet such as DEFAULT.STY from the \TYPESET subdirectory. Access **FILE•Save As New Style** to save the style sheet under a new name.

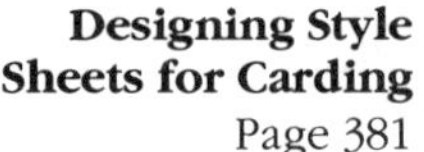
Designing Style Sheets for Carding
Page 381

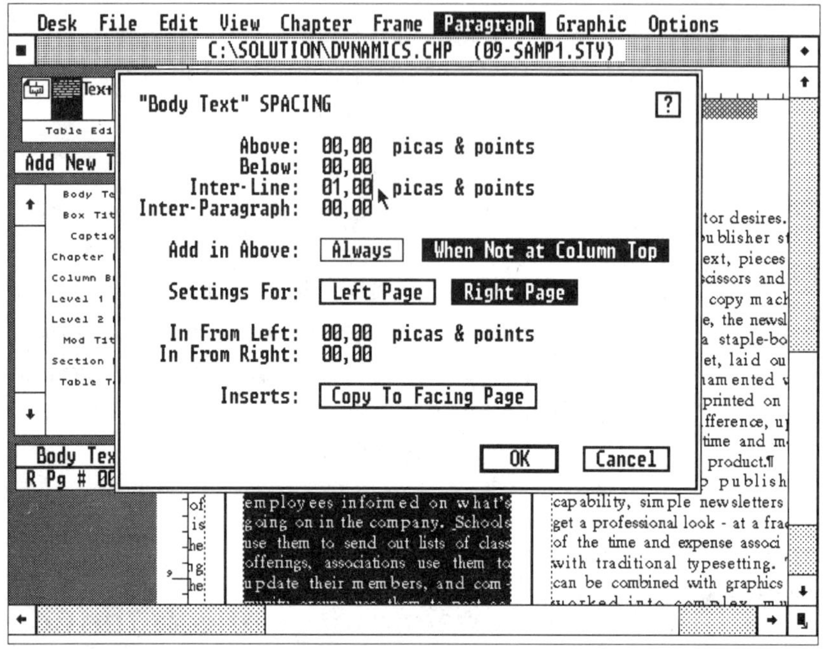

Step 2 **Set body text interline spacing**

Access **FILE•Load Text/Picture**, select Text and the desired word processor format and load a text file into the base page. Enable ***Paragraph*** mode and select a paragraph of body text. Access **PARAGRAPH• Spacing** and set the desired interline spacing.

Step 3 **Position 1st baseline**

Ventura lets you place the 1st text baseline by the height of the selected font or the current interline spacing. When designing with vertical justification, it is important to use the Body Text interline spacing as the uniform spacing value. Access **CHAPTER•Chapter Typography** and set Move Down to 1st Baseline to Inter–line.

Step 4 **Measure column height**

Column height should be an exact multiple of the Body Text interline spacing. Imagine that your page is an electronic version of uniformly ruled paper, with the body text baselines as the rules.

- ▲ From ***Frame*** mode, select the base page and access **FRAME • Sizing & Scaling**. Display the measure in picas & points. The Frame Height figure represents the height of your page in picas & points.
- ▲ Multiply the number of lines desired on the page by the Body Text interline spacing value. For example, 10 point type with 2 point leading has an interline spacing value of 12 points, or 1 pica. 50 lines of text with 1 pica interline spacing represent a column height of 50 picas.

Step 5 **Set top and bottom margins**

To determine the size of the total top and bottom margin, subtract the column height from the height of your page as shown on the Frame Height line. For example, for a 66 pica (11 inches) page, subtract a column height of 50 picas to get 16 picas. Access **FRAME • Margins & Columns** and enter the top and bottom margins for the page so that their total is the total margin height.

Recipe: Designing Text Elements for Vertical Justification

After creating a column which is an exact multiple of your Body Text interline spacing value, you must design text elements as multiples of the interline value. Imagine writing text in longhand on ruled paper. Your smaller letters fit between a single pair of rule lines. Titles and headlines may extend two or three lines high. The rules on the paper provide a uniform placement grid to control the position and the height of the letters you write. When pages of the handwritten text are placed side by side, the text aligns perfectly across pages.

The principle in designing text for vertical justification is exactly the same. When adding text and headline elements to the vertically justified page, their total height must be in *increments of the Body Text interline spacing*. This ensures that all text elements in your style sheet will line up on a uniform pattern of baselines and align perfectly across multiple columns, or across double pages. For each tag you design in the style sheet, go through the following process:

Step 1 **Name the tag**

Enable ***Paragraph*** mode and select the text. Use Add New Tag in the Side–Bar to create the new tag.

Step 2 **Set interline spacing**

Access **PARAGRAPH•Spacing**. Set interline spacing for the tag as a multiple of the Body Text interline spacing value.

Step 3 **Compute total tag height**

When designing your tag, remember that built–in rules and spacing values add to the total tag height. The goal is to have total tag height, including the interline spacing plus additional rules, rule spacing, inter–paragraph and space above/below values, total to a multiple of the Body Text interline spacing. To compute total tag height, begin with the tag interline spacing and add values as shown:

▲ **Space above/below:** Add total value of Above and Below spacing to the total tag height.

▲ **Ruling lines:** Add the total value of ruling lines and ruling line spacing to the total tag height. Note, if the ruling line is dropped to print behind text, as in reverse text effects, you don't need to add the ruling line height.

▲ **Inter–paragraph spacing:** If you are using inter–paragraph spacing in your tag design, add the total value of inter–paragraph spacing to the total tag height.

Application Notes

- **Style sheet reports:** Use style sheet report feature in **PARAGRAPH• Update Tag List** or a third party product like VP Toolbox to check the tag values defined in the style sheet.
- **Print test** During style sheet design process, print documents to check that vertical justification effects are correctly set up. A print test can help you identify problems quickly.

Setting Up Vertical Justification with Carding

Once your style sheet is set up correctly, you can enable a vertical justification system using carding by defining allowable limits for adding space on the page. These tell Ventura how much space it can add between frames, paragraphs and lines of text to justify the page.

Recipe: Vertical Justification with Carding

Step 1 **Enable vertical justification**

Access **CHAPTER•Chapter Typography**. To enable vertical justification in the document, set Vert. Just. Within Frame to Carding.

Step 2 **Set space allowed around frames**

Vert. Just. Around Frame lets you control the position of, and limit the amount of, space which can be added above or below the frames on a page. Depending on the document, you may wish to allow frames to move with the vertical justification or stay locked in place. Remember that the position of your frames depends on the relative position of body text, headings, and other elements.

▲ **Fixed** forces a frame to stay in the same position on the page, even though space may be added above and below it.

▲ **Movable** lets a frame reposition on a page depending on how much space is added above and below it.

▲ **At Top of Frame** defines the maximum amount of space which can be added at the top of frames.

▲ **At Bottom of Frame** defines the maximum amount of space which can be added beneath your frames.

Step 3 **Set space allowed around paragraphs**

You can set the space allowed around paragraphs individually for each tag in a style sheet. Enable ***Paragraph*** mode and select text with the tag to edit. Access **PARAGRAPH•Paragraph Typography**.

▲ By selecting Carding as your vertical justification option, Vert. Just at top of Para. and Vert. Just. at Bottom of Para. have been automatically set to match your Body Text interline spacing.

Setting up Vertical Justification with Carding
Page 385

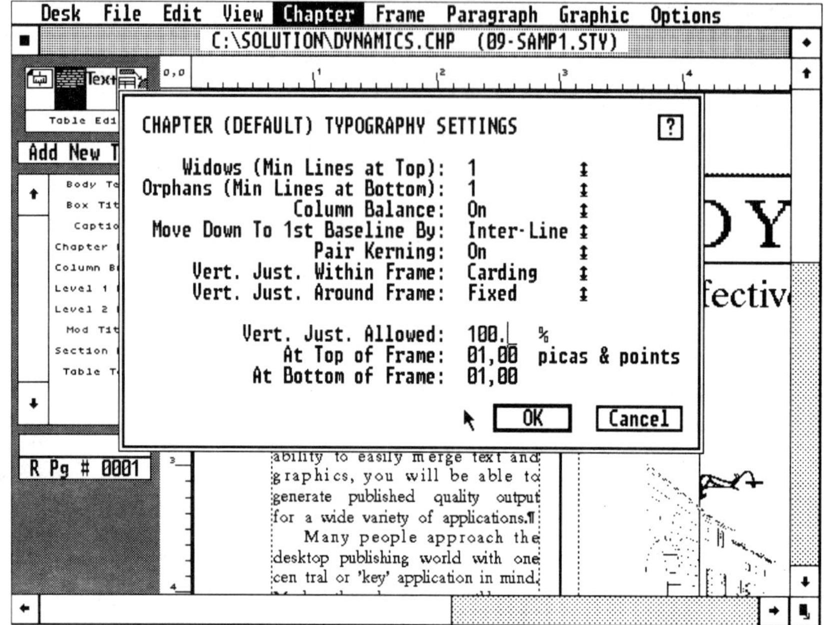

Step 4 **Set space allowed between text lines**

To control the amount of space which can be added between the lines of a paragraph, you may enter the value on the Between Lines of Para line:

▲ For Carding, this value is automatically set to zero. You may change this as long as the new figure is a multiple of the Body Text interline spacing.

Step 5 **Set vertical justification allowed**

If Ventura totals all the limits set for frames, paragraphs, and lines and it isn't enough to move the text to bottom of the page, vertical justification does not take place. This is important, because on short pages (like the last page of a document), you don't want a few lines of text stretched over the full height of the page. Vert. Just Allowed lets you control the amount of vertical justification that takes place.

▲ **Increase the value:** Ventura will attempt to add more space to achieve vertical justification. For example, if Vert. Just. Allowed is set to 200%, Ventura will attempt to double the set limit between frames, paragraphs, and lines to accomplish vertical justification.

▲ **Decrease the value:** Ventura will add less space than the defined limits to accomplish vertical justification. For example, if Vert. Just. Allowed is set to 50%, Ventura will only attempt to add half of the defined limits between frames, paragraphs, and lines. If it cannot add enough space to vertically justify the page, vertical justification is automatically disabled for the page.

Application Notes

- **Suppress for selected tags:** To prevent vertical justification from disrupting spacing values between key tags in the style sheet, disable it for those tags. Access **PARAGRAPH•Paragraph Typography** and zero out Vert Just. At Top of Para and At Bottom of Para. for each tag which is not to have vertical justification space added.
- **Multiple column applications:** Use typographically accurate style sheets to produce all facing page applications.
- **Facing page applications:** Use typographically accurate style sheets to produce vertically justified facing page applications.

Setting up Vertical Justification with Feathering

Vertical justification by feathering is a quick and easy way to force pages to align to a uniform position at the bottom of a page. Feathering is especially useful in simple, one–column applications where exact alignment across pages and columns is not important.

Where carding adds space on a page in measured increments, feathering simply stretches the text to vertically align, adding whatever space is necessary.

Unlike carding, feathering doesn't require a typographically precise style sheet set in uniform multiples of Body Text interline spacing. It simply adds space up to the defined limits to accomplish vertical justification.

Setting Up Vertical Justification With Feathering
Page 387

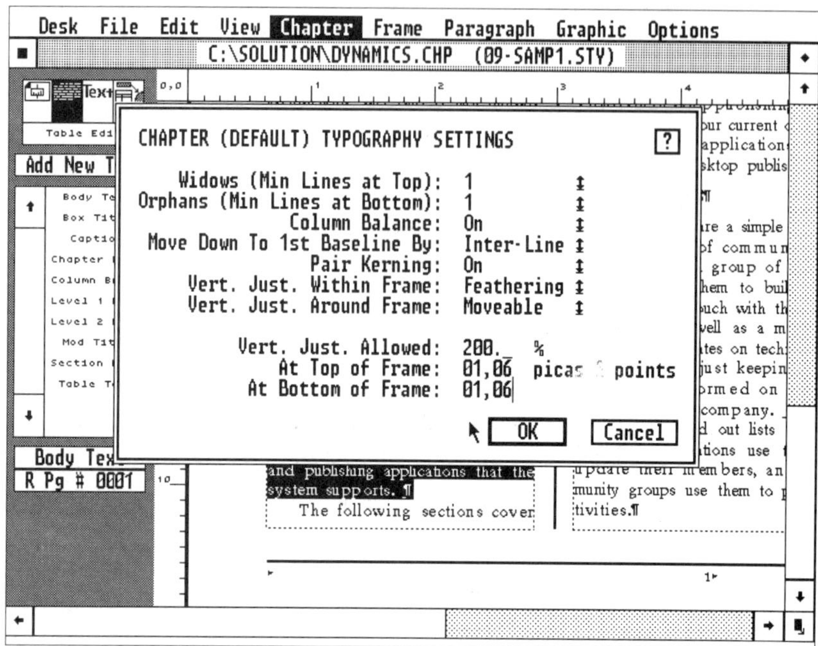

Recipe: Vertical Justification with Feathering

Step 1 **Create new style sheet**

Access **FILE•Load Diff. Style** and load a basic style sheet such as DEFAULT.STY from the \TYPESET subdirectory. Access **FILE•Save As New Style** to save the style sheet under a new name.

Step 2 **Set vertical justification by feathering**

Access **CHAPTER•Chapter Typography**. To enable vertical justification in the document, set Vert. Just. Within Frame to Feathering.

Step 3 **Set limits above and below frames**

Set Vert. Just. Around Frame to Fixed if the frame is to stay in the same position on the page. Set to Movable if you want it to float to a new position on the page as additional space is added.

Step 4 **Set limits above and below paragraphs**

Enable ***Paragraph*** mode and select text which carries a tag you wish to edit. Access **PARAGRAPH•Paragraph Typography** and enter the maximum amount of space above the paragraph on Vert. Just At Top of Para. Enter the maximum amount of space which can be added below the paragraph on At Bottom of Para.

Step 5 **Set limits between paragraphs**

Enter the maximum amount of space which can be added between lines of a paragraph on Between Lines of Paragraph. If you enter too large a value for this option, the appearance of your paragraphs may be significantly distorted throughout the document.

Application Notes

- **One–column applications:** Feathering provides quick and easy vertical justification for most one– column applications.
- **Beware hidden links:** Keep with Next linkages between tags and other defined links can pull text to the next page and leave a big gap on some pages in your documents. If you have this problem, check and revise your tag settings.

Copyfitting with Feathering

Vertical justification with feathering is a quick and easy way to copyfit framed text in your documents. Override settings in the Frame Typography dialog box make it possible to set up custom vertical justification in individual frames, even when you are not using vertical justification in the rest of your document.

When using feathering to fit copy into a defined area, be careful when setting allowable space limits in your tag. The larger the allowable limits set, the more space that Ventura can add to accomplish vertical justification. So, if you set large limits for a widely used tag like Body Text, it could distort the appearance of text outside the frame. To create an open spacing effect using this technique, it is a good idea to create a special tag for the framed text, so you can set the limits exactly as you like.

Designing Style Sheets for Carding
Page 389

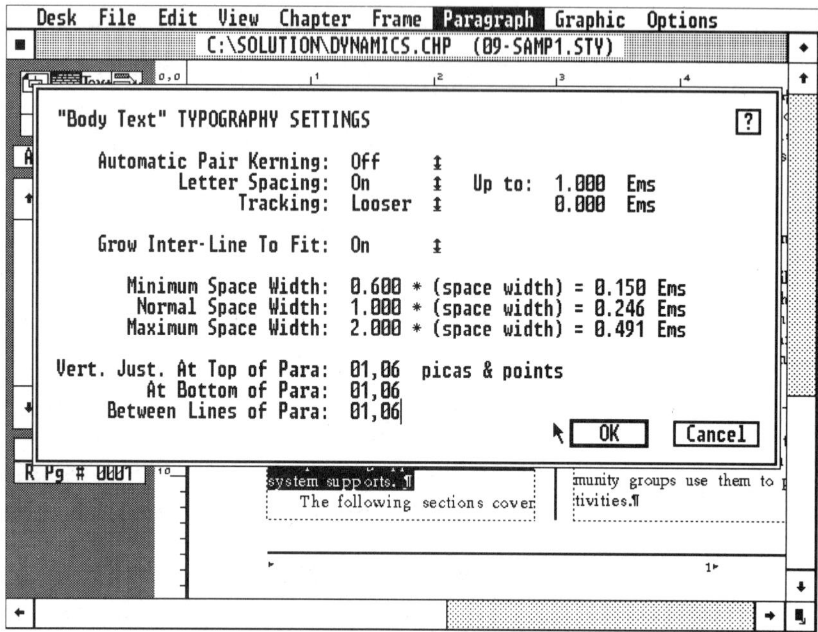

Recipe: Copyfitting with Feathering

Step 1 **Set up vertical justification by feathering**

Enable ***Frame*** mode and select the frame. Access **FRAME•Frame Typography** and set Vert. Just. Within Frame to Feathering.

▲ Note: If Feathering has already been selected in the Chapter Typography dialog box, you don't have to make this setting.

Step 2 **Create special tag**

To create special effects with open spacing, generate a special tag for the framed text. Enable ***Paragraph*** mode, select the framed text, and use Add New Tag in the Side–Bar to enter a new tag name.

Step 3 **Set limits above and below paragraphs**

With the text selected, access **PARAGRAPH•Paragraph Typography** and set the limits Above and Below text.

Step 4 **Set limits between lines**

Enter the allowable limits between lines of text.

Application Notes

- **Text sidebars:** For a quick and efficient way to place sidebar elements in newsletters and other documents, use feathering inside the sidebar frame.
- **Special effects:** If you open the feathering limits between lines of text wide enough, it can automatically spread text to fill an area with broad open spacing. You can use this effect to create special sidebars or designs in display layouts.

CHAPTER 10

Document Information Networks

Placing Instant Information on a Page

Professional Extension expands your publishing power through a system of automatic features designed to free your time by letting the computer perform a complex series of sorts and direct edits to files—all automatically. Features such as auto–numbering, tables of contents and index generation and automatic page numbering across chapters all harness the processing power of your computer to save you time and effort. Add to these the system of automatic cross–references.

Cross–referencing features make it possible to link the reader to key points of information elsewhere in the document right on the current page. Using a system of text markers and cross–references, you can set up networks linking and cross–referencing key points of information throughout the publication. As the publication is edited and repaginated, the correct page numbers for all cross–references are automatically updated without any additional work on your part.

Widgets International

Leaders in Industrial Innovation
123 Sapporro Road
Palos Verdes, CA 90274
(555) 541-1234

November 15, 1987

Mr. J. Smith
Universe of Novelties
123 Main St.
Detroit, MI 98989

Dear Mr. Smith,

It has been called to our attention, Mr. Smith, that you have been having a difficult time with our new widget. Upon reviewing your case, we have found that you have failed to plug your widget into an electrical outlet. As may know, our widget does require power to operate properly.

We take pride in our widgets, Mr. Smith, and we look forward to your continued business. If there are any additional services that you at Universe of Novelties require, please call upon us.

Sincerely,

P. L. Grundy
Customer Service Manager

Form letter: Cross-referencing features can be used to automatically reference page numbers and other information at specific positions in text. For form communications like this one, variable text insertion makes it easy to customize standard boilerplate text. Text is typeset in New Century Schoolbook. Artwork was created in GEM Artline.

This system lets you place references to page and chapter numbers, figure and table numbers, auto–section numbers, caption text and variable insertions. Using this feature, you can literally create an automatic, self–editing cross–referencing system in which page references are automatically changed as the document is edited.

Let's say you want to tell your readers where to find a particular illustration in another chapter of your book. You could find the illustration in the printout and then manually insert the correct page reference in the text. As you rewrite and edit the book, it is likely that these page references may change. Then you must start all over again to find and place the correct page and other references.

With Ventura's cross–referencing system, the cross–reference relationship is defined once. In the case of the illustration, you define the anchor name of the frame containing the illustration and then place a cross–reference notation in text referencing that name. From that point on, regardless if both the text and the picture move to different positions in the document, you can always place the correct page number of the illustration at the cross–reference notation by renumbering the publication. The following sections define the key concepts behind the Ventura cross–referencing system.

Cross–reference

A cross–reference in Ventura is a page number or other element of document information which is inserted at a specific point in the document text. Simple page and chapter cross–references, also available in the standard Ventura package, automatically display the current page number or chapter number anywhere on the page, not just in the Header or Footer line.

With the Professional Extension you can establish cross–references to any page in an entire publication. You can also build cross–references to tables, illustrations, auto–section numbers, captions, and strings of automatically inserted text.

To place a cross–reference in the Professional Extension, the first step is to place a marker in the text to be referenced or assign an anchor name to a picture that is to be referenced. Next, the cross–reference notation is placed into text, noting the marker or anchor of the item to be cross–referenced. During the publication renumbering process, Ventura finds the marker specified, and prints the cross–reference information directly at the correct point in the text.

Markers

A marker is the means to identify the position in text you wish to cross–reference. There are several types of markers you can use in building cross–references:

- **Frame anchor name:** The anchor name you assign to a frame for frame anchoring also serves as the marker name for that frame. By referencing the anchor name of a given frame as a marker you can insert cross–references to that frame's page, chapter, figure number, table number, or caption label directly into text.
- **Text marker:** A text marker is a text equivalent of a frame anchor. It lets you specify a position in text and give it a marker name. By referencing the marker name of a position in text, you can insert a cross–reference to the page number, chapter number, or auto–section number of that text anywhere in a document.
- **Variable name:** A variable name is a special kind of marker used to identify places to insert a string of variable text. You define the string of variable text and give it variable name, then by a variable substitution cross–reference to that name, you can automatically insert the string of text at points throughout documents.

Renumber Publication

Cross–references are generated during the publication renumbering operation. This is a search and process operation similar to the Table of Contents and Index generation process. During the renumbering operation, Ventura goes through a publication in chapter order, renumbering the pages of the chapter as defined, and recording the position of all defined markers and cross–references in text. Then it goes through the chapters again, this time, printing the correct page numbers for markers, frame anchors, and variable names in the cross–reference positions you specified.

Cross–referencing features are powerful time–saving tools, especially for longer applications such as books, technical materials, and reports. Ventura lets you define relationships between elements, and uses the power of the computer to find and place correct references.

Tools for Cross–referencing

Tools for Cross–Referencing are located primarily in the Text and Frame modes, and specifically in the Special Edit Items dialog box on the Edit menu.

- **Special Edit Items** contains all of the cross–reference placement features, including features to place markers, insert cross–references, and enter variable definitions.
- **Anchors & Captions** is where the frame anchor name, which doubles as a frame marker name, is inserted. In addition, the caption label text entered in this dialog box can be cross–referenced and inserted directly into a text.
- **Multi–Chapter Operations** contains the publication renumber feature which sorts all publication files and places correct cross–references into text.

Setting Up the System

This chapter contains a set of techniques which showcase the power of Professional Extension cross–referencing features.

All cross–referencing elements are Special Edit Items written directly to the text file. So, Ventura is designed to save you even more time by letting you place cross–references, markers, and variable definitions directly into the document text file using your word processor. By using macros to enter cross–references and markers into the text as copymarks, hours of editing and placement time can be saved, and when you open the document in Ventura, the cross–referencing system will be ready to go.

This book itself is a testament to the power and scope of automatic document cross–referencing. The cross–references shown after each technique were placed with Professional Extension's cross–referencing system.

Designing a Cross–referencing System

Cross referencing lets you create a system of organization within a document to help the reader access information faster. The reader knows exactly where to turn to find a specific illustration or section of relevant information through the convenience of cross–referencing. In this book, the cross–referencing system was designed as a set of application notes following each technique. Cross–references are placed to instantly link you to techniques positioned elsewhere in the book that relate to the one you are currently reading.

It is vital to plan an approach to the cross–referencing system you will use. That means identifying when, and under what circumstances you will place a cross–reference. Then, you should develop a systematic method of assigning markers so they can be easily edited.

Recipe: Cross–referencing System

Step 1 **Design cross–referencing system**

Make a reference list of the text positions, frames, and other elements to cross–reference. When setting up cross– referencing, always have a hard copy printout to note all marker names and text positions.

Step 2 **Define markers in text**

Enable ***Text*** mode and display the page where you wish to place a marker. Place text cursor at the beginning of the text to be marked. Access **EDIT•Ins. Special Edit Item** and select Marker Name. Enter marker name on the line provided and write it down on the hard copy. Repeat this process for all markers.

Step 3 **Place cross–references**

From ***Text*** mode, display the page where you wish to insert the cross–reference. Place the text cursor at the exact position where the cross–reference is to appear. Access **EDIT•Ins. Special Edit Item** and select Cross Ref. The cross–reference number or text will print exactly where you place the cross–reference item. Be sure to leave a space in front of and after the cross–reference.

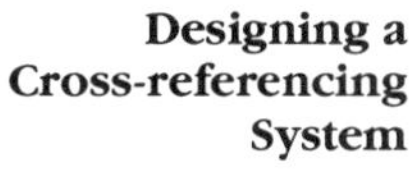

Designing a Cross-referencing System

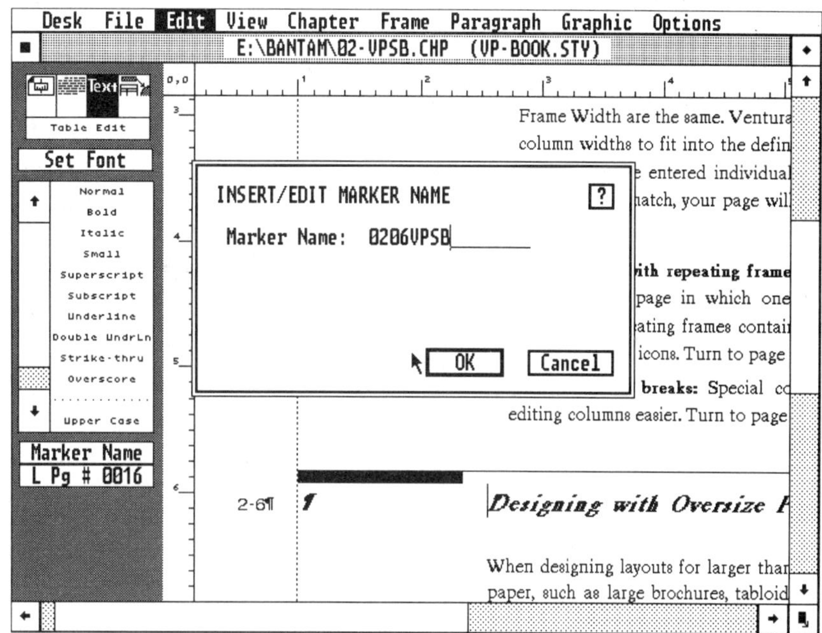

Step 4 **Select the cross–reference**

Enter the marker name you wish to cross–reference on the At The Name line. Select one of several cross–referencing options:

▲ **P#** places the number of the page where the marker appears at the cross–reference position.

▲ **C#** places the number of the chapter in which the marker appears at the cross–reference position.

▲ **S*** places the auto–section number which appears before the marker at the cross–reference position.

Step 5 **Select cross reference number format**

Select the desired number format for cross–references in the text.

Recipe: Cross–referencing Frames

Step 1 **Design cross–referencing system**

Make a reference list of the text positions, frames and other elements to cross–reference. When setting up cross–referencing, always have a hard copy printout to note all marker names and text positions.

Step 2 **Define frame anchors**

Enable ***Frame*** mode and display the frame to be marked. Select the frame and access **FRAME•Anchors & Captions**. Enter the anchor name on the Anchor line and write it down in the appropriate place on the hard copy. Repeat this process for all frames you wish to mark.

Step 3 **Place cross–references**

Enable ***Text*** mode and display the page where you wish to insert the cross–reference. Place the text cursor at the exact position where the cross–reference is to appear. Access **EDIT•Ins. Special Edit Item** and select Cross Ref. The cross–reference number or text will print exactly where you place the cross–reference item. Be sure to leave a space in front of and after the cross–reference.

Step 4 **Select the cross–reference**

Enter the frame anchor name you wish to cross–reference on the At The Name line. You may now select one of several cross–referencing options:

- ▲ **P#** places the page number of the frame at the cross–reference position.
- ▲ **C#** places the chapter number of the frame at the cross–reference position.
- ▲ **F#** places the figure number of the frame at the cross–reference position.
- ▲ **T#** places the table number of the frame at the cross–reference position.
- ▲ **C*** places the caption label text (the text typed into the Label line in the **FRAME•Anchors & Captions** dialog box) at the cross–reference position.

Step 5 **Renumber chapter**

Select **FILE•Save** and access **OPTIONS•Multi–Chapter**. Your file must be saved as a publication before you can access the Renumber option. Either open the publication containing the chapter, or select Save As to save chapter into a publication file. Select Renumber in the selection box to activate the renumbering process and place all cross-references.

Recipe: Multiple Cross–references

You can insert more than one cross–reference at a given position to create multiple cross–reference effects. If you are using chapter–by–chapter pagination, you can insert a cross–reference for the chapter name and a one for the page number. For example, a multiple cross–reference could read: "Turn to page 3–2."

You can also use multiple cross–references to place the page number for an illustration along with the text of its caption label. For example, the following entry is possible: "Please turn to Table 22: Adjusted 1989 Sales on page 156." You must place an individual cross–reference for each element.

Step 1 **Place first cross–reference**

Enable ***Text*** mode and place text cursor where cross–reference is to appear. Access **EDIT•Ins. Special Edit Item** and select Cross Ref. Enter the marker or anchor name in the At The Name line and select the first cross–reference option.

Step 2 **Place punctuation**

The small degree symbol in the text shows where the cross–reference was inserted. Use this character as a reference when placing space or adding punctuation. For two cross–referenced numbers to be hyphenated, place one cross–reference, type the hyphen next to the degree mark in text and place the second cross–reference.

☞ CAUTION: The small degree symbol characters marking cross–references and other Special Edit Items are only visible on–screen if **OPTIONS•Show Tabs & Returns** is enabled.

Step 3 **Place additional cross–references**

Repeat the process for each additional cross–reference.

Step 4 **Renumber chapter**

Select **FILE•Save** and access **OPTIONS•Multi–Chapter**. Your file must be saved as a publication before you can access the Renumber option. Either open the publication containing the chapter, or select Save As to save chapter into a publication file. Select Renumber in the selection box to activate the renumbering process and place all cross references.

Application Notes

- **Use word processor:** Placing markers in text, and cross–references in word processor file saves scrolling and searching in Ventura.
- **Production auto–numbering:** Create numbered marker names for all key headings and subheadings in a long document using production auto–numbering. This makes markers easier to track and cross–reference. Turn to page 209.
- **Print production auto–number list** Use Table of Contents feature to generate a list of text and production auto–numbers. Use this as a reference list when creating numbered marker names. Turn to page 370.

Placing Cross–reference Codes in the Word Processor

You can save a great deal of time by using macros or special insert files to place markers and cross–references directly in your word processor. Like all Special Edit Items in Ventura Publisher, cross–reference codes are written and saved directly into the document text file. To save time, you can type markers, cross–reference notations, and variable text entries directly into the text file without having to page and scroll through your Ventura document.

This technique is especially valuable when working on a long document such as a book, technical manual, or report. For example, the search features of your word processor makes it easy to find specific terms or text strings to cross reference which would take significantly longer to find in Ventura. To save time, create macros to insert the cross–referencing code brackets directly into text.

Recipe: Cross–references Codes in The Word Processor

Step 1 **Set up cross–reference macros**

In a word processor, create macro files to automatically insert the text attributes for cross–references into text:

▲ **<$M[LABEL]>** inserts the marker label into text. Insert the macro at the beginning of text you wish to mark. Type the marker name inside the square brackets. For example: **<$M[MARKER1]>**. Macro text should read: <$M[]>

▲ **<$V[VARIABLE NAME]VARIABLE DEFINITION>** inserts the variable name with its variable text string. Place all variable definitions at the beginning of text file so they are easy to find and edit. Enter the variable name inside the square brackets and the variable definition following the brackets. For example: **<$V[JOHNSON]Johnson Motors, Inc.>** Text for the macro file should read: <$V[]>

Placing Cross-reference Codes in the Word Processor

```
   E:02-VPSB.WS   P3  L53 C1  .00"   Insert Align
═══File═══Edit═══Go to═══Window═══Layout═══Style═══Other══════════EDIT═══
L----!----!----!----!----!----!----!----!----!----!----!--------R
                                                                        <
@L2 HEAD = ^V^BApplication Notes^V^B                                    <
@BULLET = <P10B>Designing Body Text:<P255D> Turn to page
────────────────────────────────────────────────────────────────────────P
<$R[P#,0302VPSB]84>.                                                    <
@BULLET = <P10B>Designing text with spacing:<P255D> Turn to page
<$R[P#,0303VPSB]87>.                                                    <
@BULLET = <P10B>Designing headers and footers:<P255D> Place long
document section names, headlines and other information
automatically in the header or footer line. Turn to page
<$R[P#,0515VPSB]227>.                                                   <
@BULLET = <P10B>Designing auto-numbering systems:<P255D> Use
auto- numbering for section numbering, numbered lists and more.
Turn to page <$R[P#,0502VPSB]192>.                                      <
@BULLET = <P10B>Production page breaks<P255D> Turn to page
<$R[P#,0513VPSB]221>.                                                   <
                                                                        <
@L1 HEAD TOP =                                                          <
@L1 HEAD = <$M0203VPSB>Designing the Display Document Page              <
@FIRSTPAR = Display documents are energetic eye-catching layouts that
seek to immediately involve and interest the reader. They include
such applications as advertisements, catalogs, brochures, flyers and
```

▲ **<$R[TYPE,LABEL, FORMAT]STRING>** inserts the cross–reference into text. Place the text attribute brackets exactly at the position in text where you wish the cross–reference to appear, allowing space, and placing punctuation as desired. Enter the type of cross–reference, a comma, and the marker name or anchor to be cross–referenced. If the number format in which the cross–reference is to be displayed is different than the default numbering system for the chapter, enter the desired number format in the brackets. For example: **<$R[P#,MARKER1,ONE]>** inserts the page number where marker 1 appears at the cross–reference position and the number format is text, all capital letters.

Application Notes

- **Define key macros:** Define standard macros to insert cross–reference and marker name text attribute brackets. This not only saves time, it ensures that brackets are placed accurately.
- **Use search and replace** Using word processor search and replace features, you can place marker text attribute brackets for every occurrence of a single tag. For example, search for **@HEADING1 =** and replace with **@HEADING1 = <$M>**. Once markers have been placed, you simply enter the marker name in the brackets.

Cross–Referencing Page and Chapter Numbers

One of the most common applications for cross–referencing is in book sections or long documents. The correct page number of a text reference can be placed anywhere in a book or other long document.

Recipe: Page and Chapter Cross–References

Step 1 **Design cross–referencing system**

Make a reference list of the text positions, frames and other elements to cross–reference. Make a hard copy printout of the document to note where cross-references are placed.

Step 2 **Define markers in text**

Enable ***Text*** mode and display the page where you wish to place a marker. Place text cursor at the beginning of the text to be marked. Access **EDIT•Ins. Special Edit Item** and select Marker Namc. Enter marker name on the line provided and write it down on the hard copy. Repeat this process for all markers.

Step 3 **Place cross–references**

From ***Text*** mode, display the page where you wish to insert the cross–reference. Place the text cursor at the exact position where the cross–reference is to appear. Access **EDIT•Ins. Special Edit Item** and select Cross Ref. The cross–reference number or text will print exactly where you place the cross–reference item. Be sure to leave a space in front of and after the cross–reference.

Step 4 **Select cross–reference**

Enter page and chapter cross–references in one of two ways:

▲ If you enter nothing in the At The Name line, the number of the current page or chapter will be cross–referenced.

Cross-referencing Page and Chapter Numbers

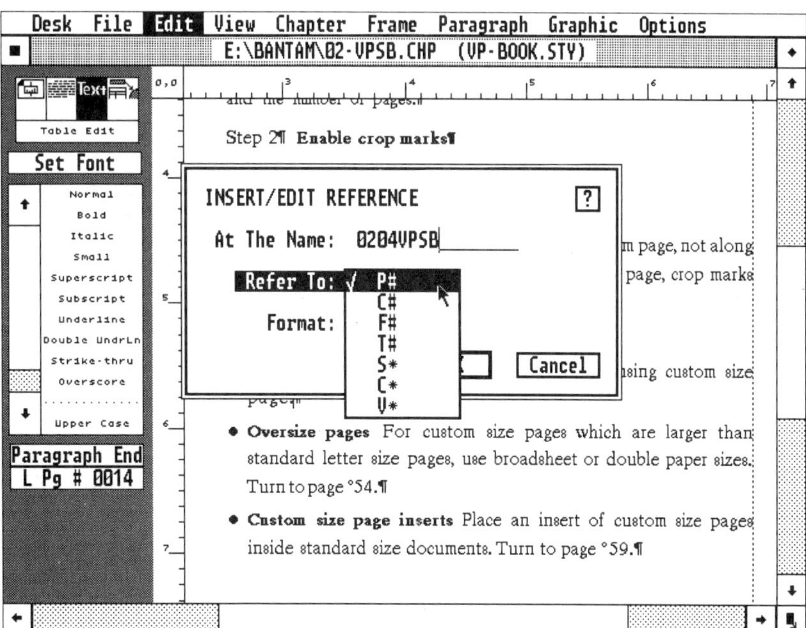

▲ If you enter the marker name to be cross–referenced on the At The Name line, the number of the page the marker appears on will appear at the cross–reference position.

Step 5 **Renumber chapter**

Select **FILE•Save** and access **OPTIONS•Multi–Chapter**. Your file must be saved as a publication before you can access the Renumber option. Either open the publication containing the chapter, or select Save As to save chapter into a publication file. Select Renumber in the selection box to activate the renumbering process.

Application Notes

- **Continued page notes:** In applications where text flows through a series of frames, use page and chapter cross– referencing to automatically generate the correct page number in the expressions: "Continued on page __" and "Continued from page __"
- **Boldface:** Apply boldface text attributes to cross–reference entry in Ventura or in word processor text file.
- **Italics:** Apply italic text attributes to cross– reference entry in Ventura or in word processor text file.
- **Check text position:** After publication is renumbered, the text of page numbers and other cross–reference information is inserted into the document. This can displace the arrangement of documents on the page and the overall position of text in the document. Check pages in Ventura before printing out.

Cross–referencing Tables and Illustrations

You can also cross–reference the correct figure number for an illustration or diagram anywhere in a document. When used in combination with page cross–referencing, you can create a multiple effect, such as: "In Figure 7, page 457, you will see a complete diagram of the process."

Recipe: Table and Illustration Cross–References

Step 1 **Design cross–referencing system**

Make a reference list of the text positions, frames and other elements to cross–reference. When setting up cross–referencing, always have a hard copy printout to note all marker names and text positions.

Step 2 **Define frame anchors**

Enable ***Frame*** mode and display the frame to mark. Select the frame and access **FRAME•Anchors & Captions**. Enter the anchor name on the Anchor line and write it down in the appropriate place on the hard copy. Repeat this process for all frames to be marked.

Step 3 **Define caption label**

To cross–reference figure or table numbers, or caption label text, define them in the **Anchors & Captions** dialog box. The Figure # or Table # reference must be placed somewhere on the Label line.

Step 4 **Place cross–reference position in text**

Enable ***Text*** mode and display the page where the cross–reference is to appear. Place the text cursor at the exact position where you

Cross-referencing Tables and Illustrations

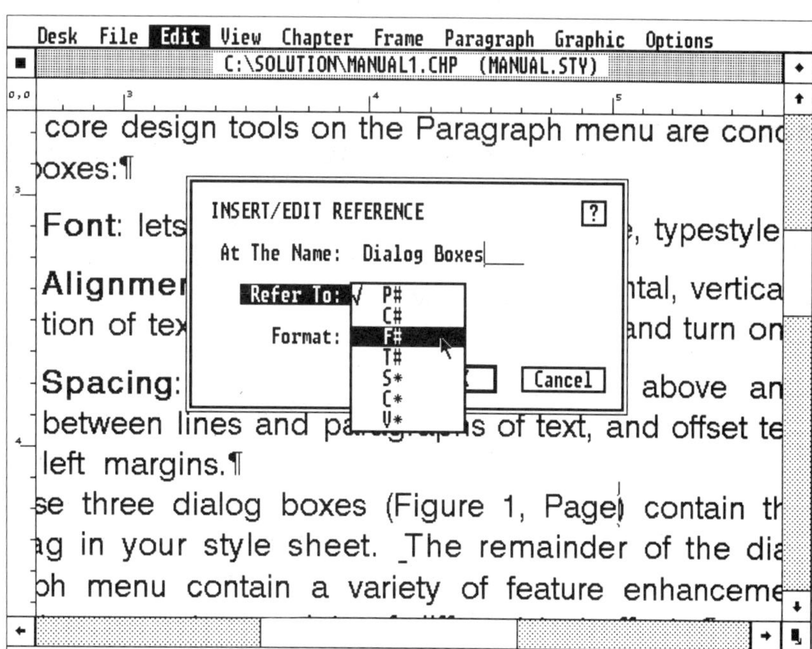

wish the cross–reference to appear. Access **EDIT•Ins. Special Edit Item** and select Cross Ref. The cross–reference number or text will print exactly where you place the cross–reference item. Be sure to leave a space in front of and after the cross–reference.

Step 5 **Select cross–reference**

Enter the desired frame anchor name on the At The Name line.

▲ Select Refer To: F# to cross–reference the number of a figure.

▲ Select Refer To: C# to cross–reference the entire caption label line, including the figure number.

▲ Select Refer To: T# to cross-reference the number of a table.

Application Notes

- **Faster information access:** Cross–references to data tables and illustrations can help the reader access information faster without turning to Index or Table of Contents.
- **Designing tables:** Turn to Chapter 11.
- **Figure and table numbering:** Turn to page 344.
- **Creating the caption label:** Turn to page 279.

Cross–referencing Auto–Numbered Sections

Auto–section numbers can act as surrogates for page numbers if a document is fully auto–numbered. To find a given document heading, all the reader has to do is flip to the auto–section number for the heading.

To cross–reference the auto–section number for a heading, place the marker in the heading text. Because auto–numbers are generated text, you cannot directly edit them, including placing any kind of marker in them. After auto–section number cross–references have been placed into text, Ventura will find the auto–section number immediately preceding the heading marker and print that number at the cross–reference position.

Cross-referencing Auto-numbered Sections

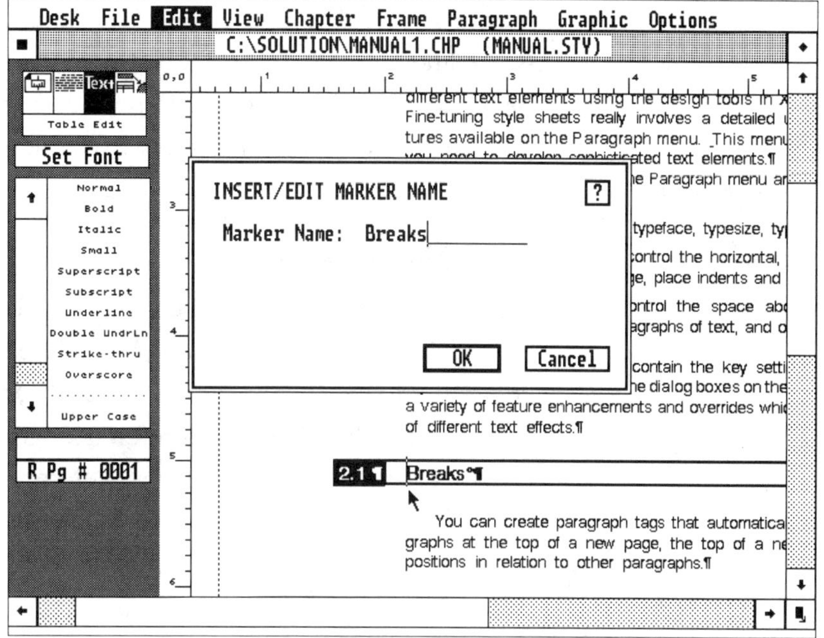

As text is added and deleted from the publication, the auto–number for the heading will automatically change in response to editing changes. Once you have defined the heading marker and the cross–reference position, the correct section number *for that heading* will be placed at the cross–reference positions each time the publication is renumbered.

Recipe: Auto–Number Cross–references

Step 1 **Set up auto–numbering system**

Define the automatic numbering system in document using the **CHAPTER • Auto–Numbering** dialog box.

Step 2 **Place markers in reference text**

Identify auto–numbered headings or other elements to be cross–referenced. Enable ***Text*** mode. Place text cursor at the beginning of the reference text paragraph immediately following the auto–number to make the marker easy to find and edit. Access **EDIT • Ins. Special Edit**

Item and select Marker Name. Enter marker name in the Marker Name line.

☞ CAUTION: The auto–section number itself is text generated by Ventura and cannot be edited from the screen. You cannot place the marker in the auto–section number itself.

Step 3 **Place cross–references**

From ***Text*** mode, display the page where you wish to insert the cross–reference. Place the text cursor at the exact position where the cross–reference is to appear. Access **EDIT•Ins. Special Edit Item** and select Cross Ref. The cross–reference number or text will print exactly where you place the cross–reference item. Be sure to leave a space in front of and after the cross–reference.

Step 4 **Select cross–reference**

Enter the marker name for the section number you wish to cross–reference and select **S***. Cross–references will appear in text after using the Renumber feature in the **OPTIONS•Multi–Chapter** dialog box.

Application Notes

- **Set up auto–numbering systems:** Turn to page 192.
- **Auto–numbers with built–in text:** If auto–number has built–in text, the text will be included in the cross–reference. For more information, turn to page 202.

Cross–referencing the Caption Label

In addition to key document numbers, the cross referencing feature allows you to insert the label string from picture or table captions. This is the text entered in the Anchors & Captions dialog box which may contain figure or table number references. The label string is best used to place titles for your pictures, which can then be used to identify the picture in the text.

Cross-referencing the Caption Label

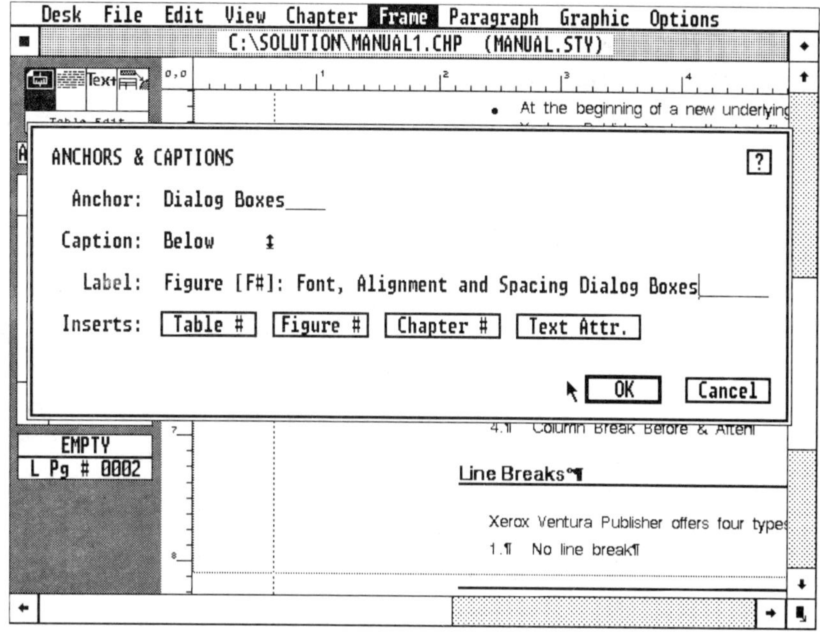

To cross-reference the label string, make sure the frame has an anchor name and that a string of text has been defined on the label line. For this feature, it is not necessary that a table or figure number be used. The anchor name serves as the marker. Now place the caption text cross-ference in text. Remember to write the text leading in and out of the cross-reference to accord with the style used in the caption label. For example, if the caption label reads **Table 6: Western Regional Sales for March**, the surrounding text might read: "Turn to **Table 6: Western Regional Sales for March** for an overview of current patterns of sales in each product category."

When used together with a page number cross–reference, this feature automatically generates references like: "If you turn to **Figure 6: The Ancient Romans** on page **345** you will see how ancient people really lived." Once you have placed markers and defined cross–references, the current caption label text and related page numbers are updated each time you renumber the publication.

Recipe: Cross–referencing the Caption Line

Step 1 **Design cross–referencing system**

List the elements in your document you wish to cross-reference. Print a draft copy of text in Ventura to use as a guide when placing markers.

Step 2 **Define frame anchors**

Enable ***Frame*** mode and display the frame you wish to mark. Select the frame and access **FRAME•Anchors & Captions**. Enter the anchor name on the Anchor line and write it down in the appropriate place on the hard copy. Repeat this process for all frames you wish to mark.

Step 3 **Place cross-references**

Enable ***Text*** mode and display the page where cross–reference is to be inserted. Place the text cursor at the exact position where you wish the cross reference to appear. Access **EDIT•Ins. Special Edit Item** and select Cross Ref. The cross reference number or text will print exactly where you place the cross reference item. Be sure to leave a space in front and after the cross–reference.

Step 4 **Select the caption cross reference**

Enter the frame anchor name you wish to cross-reference on the At The Name line. **C*** places the caption label text (the text which is typed into the Label line in the **FRAME•Anchors & Captions** dialog box at the cross-reference position.

Step 5 **Renumber chapter**

The caption text will not print into your text file until you use the Renumber feature in the **OPTIONS•Multi–Chapter**.

Application Notes

- **Text attributes:** Enhance individual text with text attributes.
- **Caption style standards:** Use the same syntax and structure when writing caption labels in a document. This makes the cross–referenced caption label text makes sense in the surrounding text.

Cross-referencing Variable Definitions

Frequently cycled business documents, such as contracts, pro–forma proposals and form letters consist of standard text containing a number of variable elements, such as date, name, address, and others. Using Professional Extension's automatic cross–referencing system, you can insert variable strings of text into boilerplate documents such as this.

The process is simple. Just define the desired text insertion string and assign a variable name to it. Then insert a variable definition cross–reference in all places in the text where you wish to insert the string, referencing the variable name.

You can define and cross–reference more than one variable string at a time. This lets you create a set of standard boilerplate chapters with all the cross–references defined and in place. To change the variables, all you have to do is go in and change the variable definitions and you have a complete new document.

Recipe: Variable Definition Cross–references

Step 1 **Design variable definition system**

Write down a list of variable names for the strings of variable text in your boilerplate document. Because you will use these names over and over again, they should easily recognized and descriptive such as: DATE, NAME, ADDRESS, CLIENT NAME, etc. Write down the string of variable text to insert opposite each name.

Step 2 **Define variable strings**

Go to the beginning of each chapter to place all of the variable names. Placing them at the beginning makes them easy to find when you want to change the variable definitions. Enable ***Text*** mode and place text cursor at the beginning of the text file. Access **EDIT•Ins. Special Edit Item** and select Variable Def. Enter the variable name on the line provided, and enter the text you wish to insert on the Substitute Text line. Repeat this operation for each variable name and definition on your list.

Cross-referencing Variable Definitions
Page 410

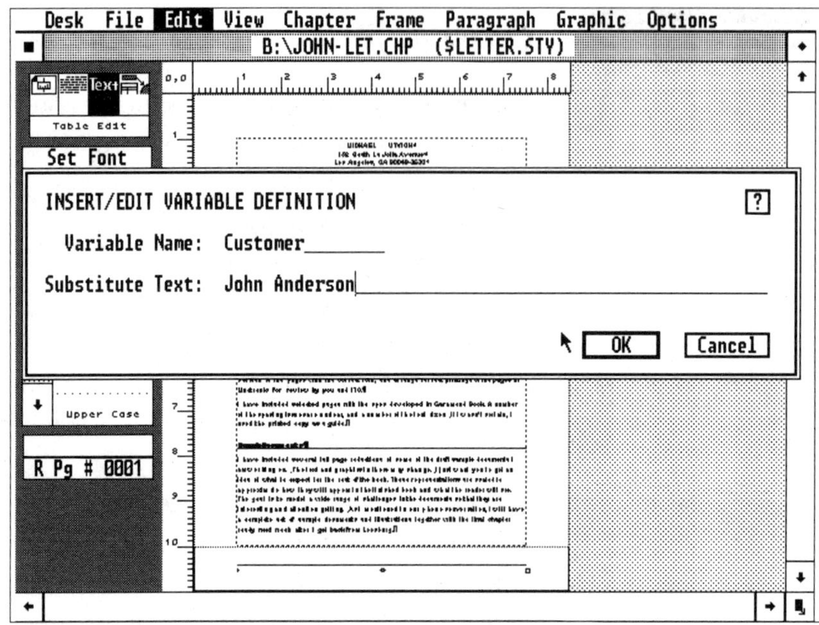

Step 3 **Place cross–references**

Display the position you wish to insert one of the variable text strings. Place the text cursor in the exact place you wish the string to print, remembering to leave space on both sides. Access **EDIT•Ins. Special Edit Item** and select Cross Ref. Enter the Variable Name of the text string you wish to insert on the At The Name line. Select Refer To: V*. Repeat this operation for each position you wish to place variable text in your document.

Step 4 **Renumber chapter**

The variable text strings will not appear in your file until you activate the Renumber feature in the **OPTIONS•Multi–Chapter** dialog box.

Step 5 **Edit chapter**

When using variable definitions, you should always page through and check the position of text in your document following the renumbering operation. By adding a series of text strings into your document, the position of text elements will change.

Application Notes

- **Multiple definitions:** Assign multiple variable definitions to boilerplate text for regularly cycled office documents. Use this technique to create typeset form letters.
- **\STYLES subdirectory:** Keep copies of boilerplate letters and other documents handy in the production subdirectory on the hard disk. Turn to page 471

CHAPTER 11

Working with Tables

Organize Data Instantly

One of the most effective ways to present spreadsheet and database material is in table form. A table grid makes it easier for us to sort, identify, and track information.

The Professional Extension includes the powerful Table Editing mode, which lets you place spreadsheet, database, or word processing files directly into a table grid. Once in the grid, you can typeset and edit the table using the full power of Ventura's four other desktop publishing modes.

The Table Editing mode makes a variety of table applications possible, for applications ranging from technical manuals to simple brochures. Table design and editing tools give you control over the size and relationship of table cells and many tools to configure the overall design of a table.

Ventura Publisher tables are written and stored in document text files using a series of table codes. Even though a table grid may look like a pattern of box text graphic forms, it is not. The grid effect is created through a variation on text ruling line features. All table cell

EXCLUSIVE LISTINGS

ADDRESS	BDR	BATHS	LOT	HEAT	AGE	COST
12 Bartholomew Sq	5	4	0.25	Gas	48	$290,000
46 Prospect Pl	5	2	0.40	Oil	22	$90,000
690 Rice Ave	3	2	0.60	Oil	25	$92,000
903 Ray Rd	2	1	0.30	Oil	45	$42,000
455 Daniels Rd	2	1	0.25	Elec	16	$47,500
12 Garden St	2	1	0.20	Elec	34	$87,500
203 Somerset Ave	4	2	0.60	Gas	12	$95,000
34 Harley Pl	7	5	1.33	Oil	40	$180,000
45 Lynwood Dr	3	2	0.30	Gas	45	$55,000
11 Pomona Rd	3	1	0.40	Oil	30	$80,000
315 Fremont Ave	5	2	0.60	Elec	20	$160,000
19 Auburn St	4	2	0.35	Elec	22	$112,500
122 Stuyvesant Rd	3	2	1.25	Elec	14	$180,000

Real Estate Listings: Ventura tables can automatically accept spreadsheet or database files. Table editing features allow direct editing to individual cells, table rules and text in individual cells. Text is typeset in Times Roman. Data compiled in Lotus 1-2-3. Artwork created in GEM Artline.

separator and framing lines are ruling lines and can be customized through ruling lines features.

Table text files behave in general just like standard text files. They can be loaded into the base page or frames, they can be continued through frames, and they can be copied into existing text files. For convenience in publishing large spreadsheet tables and similar database applications, Ventura accepts ASCII output from Lotus 1–2–3 and a number of other third party spreadsheet and database management software. Properly configured spreadsheet text can auto–load directly into a table grid without any manual data entry or processing. Once in the table grid, you can edit all aspects of the table including the cell size, column widths, thickness, and position of rules as well as the typography directly in Ventura.

Table Editing Tools

Tools for editing tables are concentrated in the Table Editing mode, which is available only in the Professional Extension. Tools to enhance tables are spread through all modes in Ventura Publisher.

- **Table Editing Mode** contains all features to design, edit, and configure tables.
- **Frame mode** features allow tables to be placed in frames and easily moved within a document. Frames can also be used to add illustrations to tables.
- **Text mode** features allow direct input and editing of table text on screen, as well as special font and text enhancements to table text.
- **Paragraph mode** features allow design and editing of custom table ruling lines, as well as special tags for table text.
- **Graphic mode** features can be used to draw graphic enhancements to the table layout.

Creating Tables in Ventura Publisher

This chapter introduces techniques which demonstrate how to develop and edit various text and spreadsheet tables. These techniques focus on the powerful table editing features you can use to design, configure, and customize table layouts.

Keep in mind that tables are a Professional Extension feature and are memory sensitive. Your system must have a minimum of 640K of memory to operate the Professional Extension. At that level of memory, you may only be able to develop small table applications. If you add 1 megabyte or more of expanded memory to your system, you will be able to develop longer and more complex applications in the Table Editing mode.

Designing a Simple Table

On the simplest level, you can use the table editing mode to place a table grid anywhere in document text. Simply place the text or table editing cursor at the end of a paragraph and access the Insert/Edit Table dialog box. In this dialog box, define the required number of (horizontal) **rows** and (vertical) **columns**. When the table grid is generated, each cell will contain a paragraph return symbol. You can enter text directly into the cell using the Text mode.

Recipe: Simple Table in Text

Step 1 **Sketch out desired table**

Draw a sketch of the planned table. Specify the number of columns and estimate the number of rows you will need to enter data.

Step 2 **Place cursor**

You cannot enter a table into text until a cursor has been placed at the location the table is to appear.

- ▲ From the ***Text*** mode, place cursor at the end of a paragraph. Paragraph End, or End of File appears in Current Selection Box.
- ▲ From ***Table Editing*** mode, click the cursor at the beginning of a paragraph. The cursor will appear as a shaded bar over the paragraph, and Before Para appears in the Current Selection Box.

Step 3 **Insert new table**

Once the cursor has been placed, access Insert/Edit Table dialog box from the Text or Table Editing modes:

Designing a Simple Table

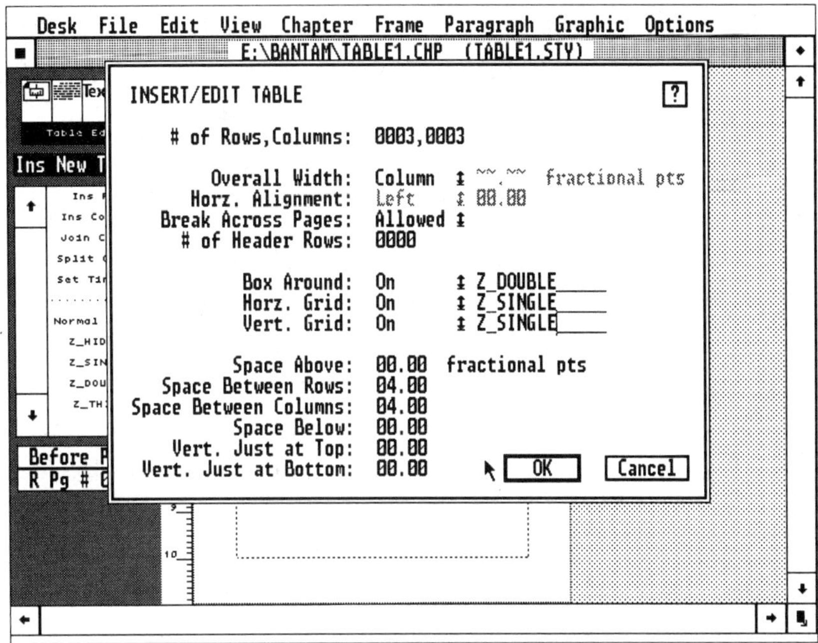

▲ From ***Text*** mode, access **EDIT•Ins. Special Edit Item** and select Table.

▲ From ***Table Editing*** mode, select Ins. New Table in the Side–Bar.

Step 4 **Define row/columns**

In the **Insert/Edit Table** dialog box, enter number of rows, press the Tab key, and enter number of columns.

Step 5 **Define table width**

Unless you specify a custom width, the table will extend to the full width of the frame containing it, or of the column defined in the base page. If you are placing tables in a multi–column style sheet, it is easier to control table width by setting up each table inside a frame.

Step 6 **Set table ruling lines**

Display or hide the table grid by turning the grid lines off or on:

▲ **Box Around** controls the grid line surrounding a table.

▲ **Horz. Grid** controls the horizontal grid lines throughout a table.

▲ **Vert. Grid** controls the vertical grid lines throughout a table.

Control the appearance of the line by using the line tag which appears on the grid line. For example, to add a single line around a table, enter Z_SINGLE on the Box Around line.

Step 7 **Set table spacing**

Automatically control the spacing inside and outside of a table using spacing controls:

▲ **Space Above/Below** controls the space between the table and the surrounding document text.

▲ **Space Between Rows/Columns** controls the space between rows and columns inside the table. Use these controls to increase the size of the table cells and to place space buffers around text entered in the table.

▲ **Vert. Just at Top/Bottom** controls the allowable amount of space which can be added above or below a table during vertical justification.

Recipe: Entering Table Text

Once you have defined the table grid on screen, you can enter text directly into each cell and tag cells using the ***Text*** and ***Paragraph*** modes of Ventura. When text is typed into an individual table cell, the cell will expand the height of its entire row to receive the text.

Step 1 **Enter table text**

Enable ***Text*** mode and place the text cursor on the paragraph return inside the table cell. Enter text in one of two ways:

▲ Type text directly into the cell.

▲ Load prepared text file into the cell. Place text cursor on the paragraph symbol inside the cell. Access **FILE•Load Text/Picture**, select Text and set Location to Text Cursor.

Step 2 **Apply text enhancements**

With the ***Text*** mode enabled, apply any desired enhancements to segments of text in a cell, or to all the text in a cell. You must apply enhancements on a cell–by–cell basis. Ventura doesn't permit selection of text in more than one cell in the ***Text*** mode.

Application Notes

- **Text enhancements:** Enhance text in tables with standard text enhancements and Set Font. Turn to page 169.
- **Custom table text tag:** If there will be more than one table in the chapter, you can to create a custom table text tag for this table alone. Turn to page 439.

Placing Tables in Frames

In Ventura, tables can be inserted directly in a text file or placed in frames. For short table applications, insertion in the text file is acceptable, but as tables grow longer and more complex, it is better to place them in their own frames. Placing a table in its own frame gives you better control over the width of the table and its position on the page. To move the table within the document or between chapters, you simply cut and paste the frame containing the table. By anchoring the table frame, you can link your table to automatically appear next to a specific segment of text in the document.

Recipe: Tables in Frames

Step 1 **Draw the table frame**

Enable ***Frame*** mode and use Add New Frame in the Side–Bar to draw the frame.

Step 2 **Place cursor**

You cannot enter a table into the frame until a cursor has been placed at the location the table is to appear.

▲ From the ***Text*** mode, place a cursor at the end of a paragraph. Paragraph End, or End of File appears in Current Selection Box.

▲ From ***Table Editing*** mode, click the cursor at the beginning of a paragraph. The cursor will appear as a shaded bar over the paragraph, and Before Para appears in the Current Selection Box.

Step 3 **Insert new table**

Once the cursor has been placed, access the Insert/Edit Table dialog box from the Text or Table Editing modes and define the desired attributes of the new table.

▲ From ***Text*** mode, access **EDIT•Ins. Special Edit Item** and select Table.

▲ From ***Table Editing*** mode, select Ins. New Table in the Side–Bar.

Application Notes

- **Save table filename:** To save the table text under its own filename, select the frame and use **EDIT•File Type/Rename** to assign it a name of its own. This takes the table text out of the cap file and increases the security of your table data.
- **Edit table text in the word processor:** To edit table text directly, use the **EDIT•File Type/Rename** dialog box to convert the table file into your favorite word processor format. Turn to page 432.

Placing Tables in Frames
Page 423

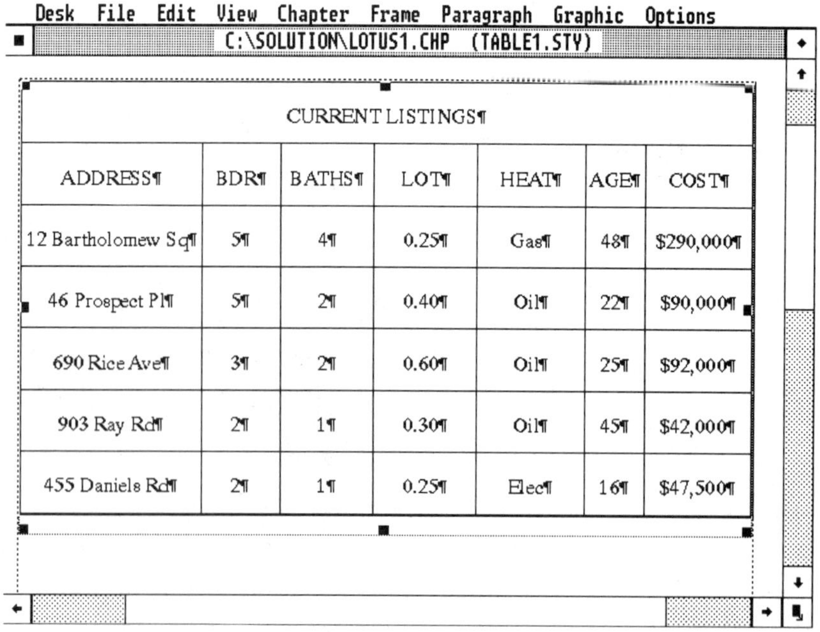

Desk File Edit View Chapter Frame Paragraph Graphic Options

C:\SOLUTION\LOTUS1.CHP (TABLE1.STY)

CURRENT LISTINGS¶						
ADDRESS¶	BDR¶	BATHS¶	LOT¶	HEAT¶	AGE¶	COST¶
12 Bartholomew Sq¶	5¶	4¶	0.25¶	Gas¶	48¶	$290,000¶
46 Prospect Pl¶	5¶	2¶	0.40¶	Oil¶	22¶	$90,000¶
690 Rice Ave¶	3¶	2¶	0.60¶	Oil¶	25¶	$92,000¶
903 Ray Rd¶	2¶	1¶	0.30¶	Oil¶	45¶	$42,000¶
455 Daniels Rd¶	2¶	1¶	0.25¶	Elec¶	16¶	$47,500¶

Selecting and Editing Tables

Once a table has been created, edits to the size and placement of the data in the grid may be required. Ventura provides a full complement of table editing features including:

- Row and column insertion
- Join/Split Cells
- Cut/Copy/Paste
- Cell Tinting
- Interactive column sizing
- Relational column sizing

These features allow you to move data to different positions in the table, combine cells for special presentation effects, highlight cells with color and shading, and adjust the size of elements in a table grid for the best data display.

Recipe: Selecting Table Elements

To make edits to tables, begin by selecting the desired elements in the ***Table Editing*** mode. Unlike ***Frame*** and ***Graphic*** modes, the ***Table Editing*** mode doesn't use black sizing boxes to indicate selection. Instead, a gray line appears showing the position or cell that has been selected.

The location of a cell in the table grid is specified by a set of coordinates. Each coordinate represents a specific point on the table. For example, the coordinate **R31C1** describes a point on the table at the intersection of Row 31 and Column 1. When table elements are selected on–screen, the Current Selection Box displays the beginning and ending points of a selected area. For example, the coordinate pair **R31C1...R39C8** means that the selected area begins at Row 31, Column 1 and extends to Row 39, Column 8.

There are two ways of selecting sections of a table. You may select a position, which is a straight line along the side of one or more cells. You may also drag the mouse to select a complete cell, or a group of cells. In either case, the beginning and end coordinates of the selected area are displayed in the Current Selection Box. Once you

Selecting and Editing Tables
Page 425

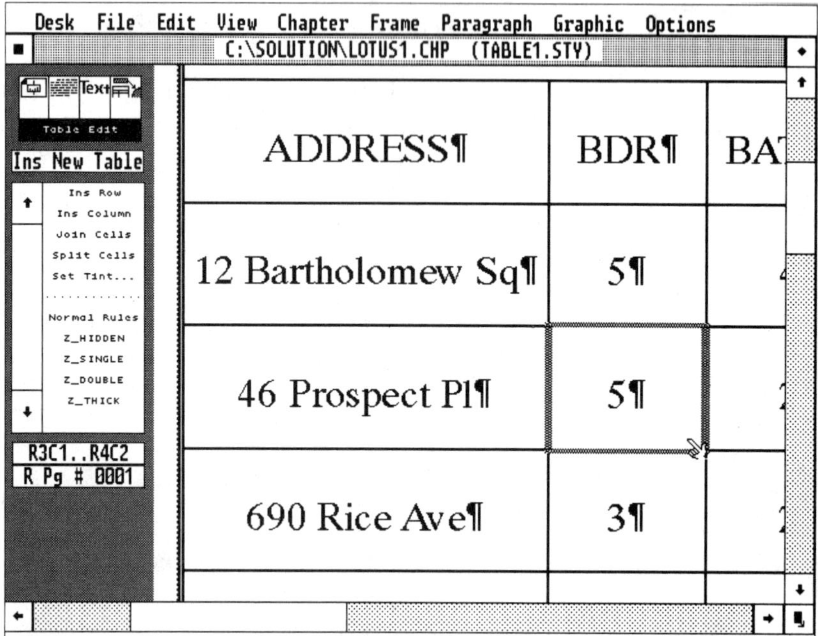

have selected a position in the table you may perform a variety of edits, including changing column width, placing shading, joining cells together, breaking cells apart, and inserting rows or columns.

Option 1 **Select a horizontal position**

Enable ***Table Editing*** mode. Place the mouse on, or close to, the row border to be selected. Click the mouse and a single shaded line will mark your selection. To select the border line of several cells, press and hold the mouse button as you drag the mouse down the row border until all desired segments are selected. With this selection in place, you can insert a row or column, or apply a custom cell ruling line tag to the selected line segment.

Option 2 **Select a vertical position**

Place the mouse on or close to the vertical column border line segment to be selected. Press and hold the mouse button and drag the mouse up, until the vertical cell border is highlighted. To select multiple cells, continue dragging the mouse up until all desired cell borders are selected. With this selection in place, you can insert a row or column, or apply a custom cell ruling line tag to the selected line segment.

Option 3 **Select an area**

From ***Table Editing*** mode, place mouse cursor at the upper left–hand corner of position to select. Press and hold mouse button as you drag the mouse so that the area is encircled by a shaded selection border.

Recipe: Moving and Combining Data

By selecting positions or areas in table, you can add rows of data or insert new columns as needed. You can also move entire blocks of data to new positions within a table.

Option 1 **Insert rows and columns**

Enable ***Table Editing*** mode. Insert a new row or column by selecting the position to insert it:

▲ **Insert a row:** Ventura will insert a row directly above the selected position. Select a position on the first row beneath where the new row is to appear and select Ins Row in the Assignment List. At the overlay, select Insert.

▲ **Insert a column:** Ventura will insert a column in front (to the left of) the selected position. Select a position in the column immediately to the right of where the new column is to appear. Select Ins Column in the Assignment List. At the overlay, select Insert.

Option 2 **Join and Split Cells**

Join and split cells in a table by dragging to select the group of cells to be joined or split. You cannot split cells to a size smaller than that of the column in which the cell appears.

▲ **Join cells:** You can join cells horizontally across rows, vertically down columns, or both. Drag select the group of cells to be joined and select Join Cells in the Assignment List.

▲ **Split cell:** Drag select a cell which has been joined. To split the joined cell into its original cells, select Split Cell.

Option 3 **Cut/Copy/Paste**

Drag select the area to be cut or copied. You can cut or copy a group of rows or columns in a single operation.

- ▲ Select **EDIT•Cut Row/Column** or **EDIT•Copy Row/Column**. The overlay gives you the option to cut or copy selected rows or columns.
- ▲ To paste rows in the table, select a position on the row immediately below where you want to paste the section and select **EDIT•Paste Row/Column**.
- ▲ To paste columns in the table, select the column to the right of the position where the new column is to appear and select **EDIT•Paste Row/Column**.

Recipe: Highlighting Table Cells

In addition to moving data around a table, you can create special highlights to individual cells or groups of selected cells, or remove rules from selected positions and entire cells.

Step 1 **Cell Tinting**

Drag select the individual cell or group of cells to highlight. Select Set Tint in the Assignment List. Select color and pattern.

Step 2 **Table rules**

You can edit table rules by selecting a position on one side of a cell; along a horizontal or vertical rule; or by drag selecting an individual cell or group of cells:

- ▲ **Select a position:** Select a position on a given cell and select the desired ruling line tag in the Assignment List.
- ▲ **Select a group:** Drag select an individual cell or group of cells and select the ruling line tag in the Assignment List.

Recipe: Custom Column Sizing

Once data is in place, you can make adjustments to the relative size of the columns in a table. This means you can balance data in various columns without having to manually rebuild or reconfigure the table.

The simplest way to size columns is to use the screen cursor and drag the column margin to the new position. But, when developing larger, more complex tables, you can edit the column widths using the Table Column Widths dialog box. This dialog box lets you set custom widths in two ways:

- **Fixed Width:** Enter the exact width of the column.
- **Variable Width:** Define the size of each column by proportions. For example, if you want Column 2 to be twice as wide as Column 1, and Column 3 to be three times as wide as Column 1, set the proportional value for Column 1 as 1, for Column 2 as 2 and for Column 3 as 3. Ventura will automatically fit the columns to the width of the margins of the page or frame in the correct proportional relationship.

Step 1 **Sizing columns from the screen**

Enable ***Table Editing*** mode and select a position in the column to edit. Depress and hold the Alt key as you hold down the mouse button. Two vertical column sizing guides appear. Drag the guides to the desired position. Release the Alt key and the mouse.

Step 2 **Relational column sizing**

Select a position on the table to edit. Access **EDIT • Set Column Width**.

▲ **Fixed width:** Select Fixed and enter exact width for each column.

▲ **Variable width:** Identify the smallest column in the table and assign it a Variable Width of 1. Define all other columns in the table as multiples of that value. For example, to set a column to be twice the width of the smallest column, assign a Variable Width of 2.

Application Notes

- **Interactive editing:** Experiment with interactive editing features including Cut/Copy/Paste to edit and move data within tables.
- **Copyfitting:** To make a certain string of data fit into a data cell, use interactive copyfitting. This can prevent an entire table row from expanding in height simply to accommodate extra text in one cell. Turn to page 185.

Creating Spreadsheet Tables

Unless you are creating a short, simple table, entering text directly from the Ventura screen is a long and cumbersome process. Ventura provides another way to load table text: the PRN–to–Table converter.

PRN files are Lotus 1–2–3 files generated using the print–to–filename command. They are essentially ASCII files containing the text of a spreadsheet, database or other text, with all columns separated by a minimum of two spaces. There are no tab characters between columns in PRN files and none are needed. Unlike creating tables with Ventura standard software, you don't need any utility to insert tab characters to cause columns to align.

Once the PRN file of a Lotus spreadsheet (or other software converted to this extension) is ready, load it into Ventura and place it in a frame or the base page. Ventura *automatically creates a table to contain the PRN file*, with all columns of equal width. You can then edit columns and other attributes of the table.

Recipe: Spreadsheet Tables

Step 1 **Create spreadsheet**

Develop spreadsheet in third–party software, such as Lotus 1–2–3.

Step 2 **Output spreadsheet as PRN file**

Lotus allows you to print a spreadsheet to a filename in the ASCII text format. This file is given a .PRN extension (for Print). Use Lotus commands to print spreadsheet to a filename with a PRN extension.

Step 3 **Load PRN file to frame**

When making tables out of spreadsheets, always place the tables in their own frame. If the table is a free–standing table, load the PRN file directly to the base page. The PRN file automatically creates a plain table with columns of equal width.

Step 4 **Edit table settings**

Enable ***Table Editing*** mode and select a position on the table. Access **EDIT•Edit Table Settings** to configure the plain table as you wish.

Creating Spreadsheet Tables

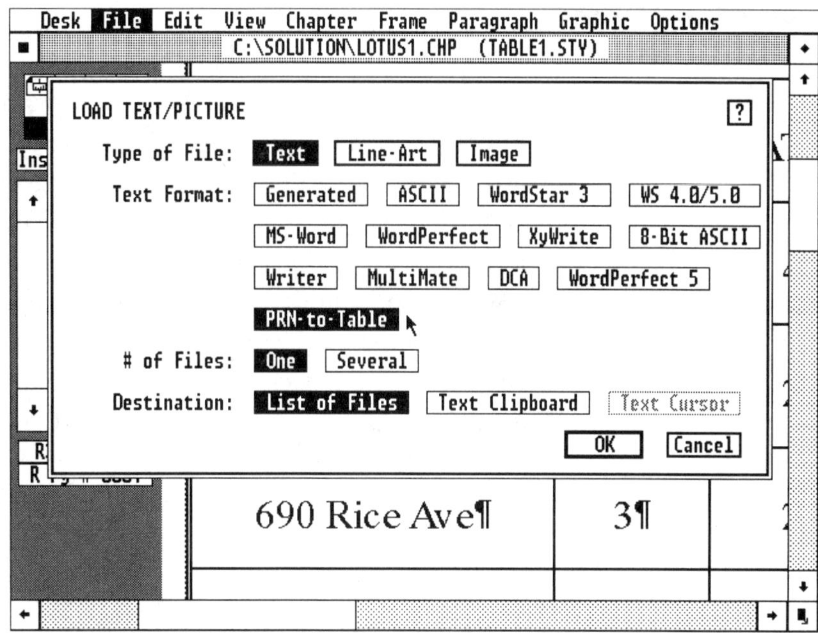

Step 5 **Edit column width**

Because PRN–to–Table creates columns of equal width, some data may be placed in columns which are too tight and others which are too large. Either edit column width directly from the screen using the Alt key, or access the **EDIT•Set Column Width** dialog box.

Application Notes

- **Data integration:** Import data from spreadsheet, database, and text applications into the same document. This saves time when creating reports, proposals, and technical publications.
- **Edit spreadsheet:** To the greatest extent possible edit spreadsheet data in source software, or edit the PRN file in the word processor. This saves production time and a lot of moving and deleting data on screen in Ventura.

Preparing PRN Files For Tables

PRN files can be developed in a word processor or spreadsheet program which can then be loaded directly into a Ventura table. A PRN file is an ASCII text file containing text or data arranged in columns. There must be a *minimum of two spaces* between each pair of columns for the PRN–To–Table converter to read the file correctly.

When producing a PRN file from other spreadsheets or databases, use the Print–to–filename command in that software. Print–to–filename will generally create a clean ASCII file. If Ventura doesn't load the PRN file, open it up in your ASCII word processor (such as WordStar's Nondocument mode) and check to see that there is a uniform two spaces between all columns of data in the file.

Recipe: Making PRN Files in Word Processor

Step 1 **Enter table content**

In an ASCII text processor, such as WordStar's Nondocument mode, enter the text for the table in column form. Maintain a minimum of two spaces between text in columns.

Step 2 **Save table text as PRN file**

Check text to be sure that there is a minimum of two spaces between columns. If data is placed too close, Ventura loads data for all columns into a single cell. Save table text with a PRN file extension.

Step 3 **Load into Ventura**

Load Ventura Publisher. Select frame or base page to receive the PRN file containing the table text. Access **FILE•Load Text/Picture**, select Text and the PRN–To–Table file format. Select the table text file. Ventura automatically formats the text into a table grid.

Application Notes

- **Text attributes:** To assign text attributes to elements of the table text, use word processor codes for boldface and underline before loading the table into Ventura.

Preparing PRN Files for Tables

C:REALTY.PRN P1 L25 C1 .00" Insert Align Column

File Edit Go to Window Layout Style Other EDIT

CURRENT LISTINGS

ADDRESS	BDRMS	BATHS	LOT	HEAT	AGE	COST
12 Bartholomew Sq	5	4	0.25	Gas	48	$290,000
46 Prospect Pl	5	2	0.40	Oil	22	$90,000
690 Rice Ave	3	2	0.60	Oil	25	$92,000
903 Ray Rd	2	1	0.30	Oil	45	$42,000
455 Daniels Rd	2	1	0.25	Elec	16	$47,500
12 Garden St	2	1	0.20	Elec	34	$87,500
203 Somerset Ave	4	2	0.60	Gas	12	$95,000
34 Harley Pl	7	5	1.33	Oil	40	$180,000
45 Lynwood Dr	3	2	0.30	Gas	45	$55,000
11 Pomona Rd	3	1	0.40	Oil	30	$80,000
315 Fremont Ave	5	2	0.60	Elec	20	$160,000
19 Auburn St	4	2	0.35	Elec	22	$112,500
122 Stuyvesant Rd	3	2	1.25	Elec	14	$180,000
87 Newbury St	6	2	0.60	Gas	17	$120,000
1122 Bellevue	6	3	1.00	Gas	9	$140,000
19 Hill Rd	4	2	0.30	Oil	26	$110,000
1 Pond Rd	8	5	2.00	Gas	60	$245,000
384 High St	7	4	1.20	Gas	7	$215,000
2 Beech Ave	4	3	0.40	Gas	11	$175,000

- **Combine spreadsheets:** Combine data from one or more spreadsheet files in word processor and output as a PRN file.

Database Publishing with Tables

Using the ASCII file link, you can print data from your database and enter it into your published documents as a table or column listing. Output the database file in ASCII and load into Ventura using the PRN-To-Filename converter.

Database Publishing with Tables

Step 1 **Create database**

Develop database in third party software, such as dBase III or IV.

Step 2 **Output database as PRN file**

dBase copy command allows you to print database to a filename in the ASCII text format. The correct format in dBase is **COPY TO**

Database Publishing with Tables
433

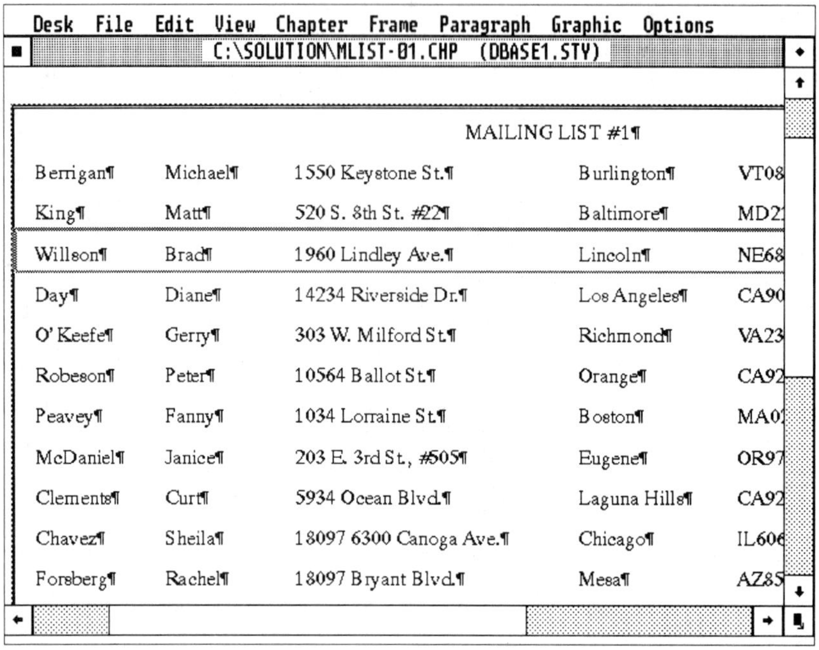

Desk File Edit View Chapter Frame Paragraph Graphic Options

C:\SOLUTION\MLIST-01.CHP (DBASE1.STY)

MAILING LIST #1¶

Berrigan¶	Michael¶	1550 Keystone St.¶	Burlington¶	VT08
King¶	Matt¶	520 S. 8th St. #22¶	Baltimore¶	MD2
Willson¶	Brad¶	1960 Lindley Ave.¶	Lincoln¶	NE68
Day¶	Diane¶	14234 Riverside Dr.¶	Los Angeles¶	CA90
O' Keefe¶	Gerry¶	303 W. Milford St.¶	Richmond¶	VA23
Robeson¶	Peter¶	10564 Ballot St.¶	Orange¶	CA92
Peavey¶	Fanny¶	1034 Lorraine St.¶	Boston¶	MA0
McDaniel¶	Janice¶	203 E. 3rd St., #505¶	Eugene¶	OR97
Clements¶	Curt¶	5934 Ocean Blvd.¶	Laguna Hills¶	CA92
Chavez¶	Sheila¶	18097 6300 Canoga Ave.¶	Chicago¶	IL606
Forsberg¶	Rachel¶	18097 Bryant Blvd.¶	Mesa¶	AZ85

filename SDF. The ASCII TXT extension is automatically added. For other database managers, use comparable print–to–filename procedures to create an ASCII file.

Step 3 **Edit database text in word processor**

Open the database file in an ASCII word processor. Make sure that there are at least *two spaces* between all columns of data on the screen. Rename the edited ASCII file with the extension .PRN.

Step 4 **Load PRN file**

Access **FILE•Load Text/Picture** and load the database PRN file into Ventura via the PRN–To–Filename converter. The PRN file automatically creates a plain table with columns of equal width.

Step 5 **Edit table settings**

Enable ***Table Editing*** mode and select a position on the table. Access **EDIT•Edit Table Settings** to configure the plain table as you wish.

Step 6 **Edit column width**

Because PRN–to–Table creates columns of equal width, some text may be placed in columns which are too tight and others which are too large. Either edit column width directly from the screen using the Alt key, or access the **EDIT•Set Column Width** dialog box.

Application Notes

- **Publish listings:** Do data sorts from your database to publish sales listings, telephone directories, and similar applications.
- **Design table presentation:** To present multiple–column data base information without the table grid, access **EDIT•Edit Table Settings** and turn display for all table rules off.

Designing Multi–page Tables

For long listings or spreadsheets, you can build a table with as many rows as you like. The table will break and print on succeeding pages according to the amount of space available on a page.

Multiple page tables on full pages work best in an expanding frame, that is, insert a new page for the table. This new page can be set up with different values from the main base page. The new base page will add new pages to accommodate the entire table.

Recipe: Multi–page Tables

Step 1 **Add new page**

To place new base page to hold the table, go to the page before the place where the table is to be inserted. Access **CHAPTER•Insert/Remove Page** and select Insert New Page After Current Page.

Step 2 **Load PRN file**

Enable ***Frame*** mode and select the new page. Access **FILE•Load Text/Picture**, select Text and the PRN–To–Table file format. Select the file containing the table. The new page will automatically expand to display the PRN file in its table grid.

Step 3 **Edit table**

Enable ***Table Editing*** mode. Select a position on the table and enter table settings. Edit column width to desired size.

Recipe: Creating Table Headers

To create table header lines that contain labels and other information for each column, define the number of lines you need reserved for a header. For example, if you select three, Ventura will take the top three lines in the table and automatically repeat them at the top of each table on succeeding pages.

Step 1 **Define header rows**

Enable ***Table Editing*** mode. Select a position on the table and access **EDIT•Edit Table Settings**. Enter the number of header rows necessary for the multi–page table.

Step 2 **Enter header row text**

Enter header text directly into the appropriate cells. Page through the table to make sure that header text is displaying correctly.

Designing Multi-Page Tables
Page 435

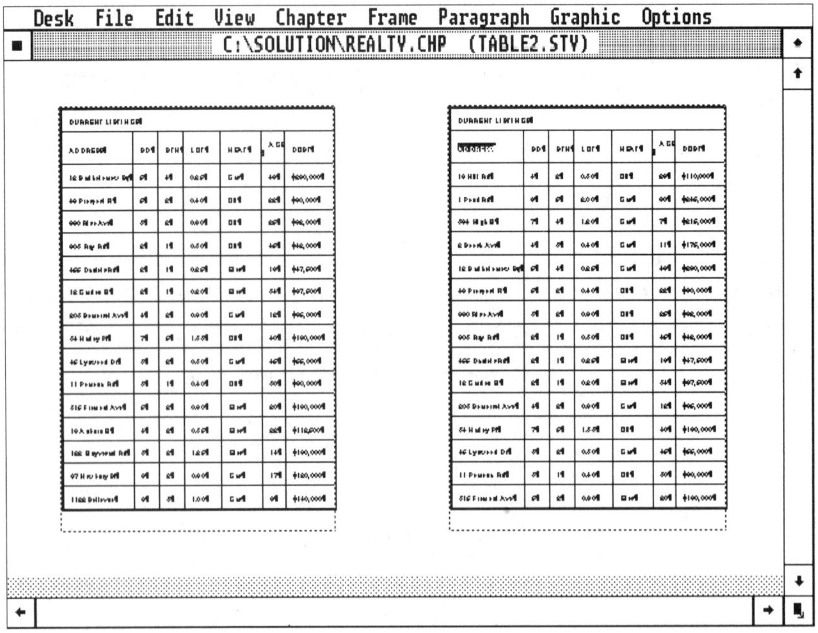

Desk File Edit View Chapter Frame Paragraph Graphic Options
C:\SOLUTION\REALTY.CHP (TABLE2.STY)

Recipe: Special Header Enhancements

Highlight a table header by adding a special text tag to display header text. To place shading in header cells, use Set Tint option in the Assignment List.

Step 1 **Create custom header tag**

Enable ***Paragraph*** mode and select text in a header cell. Use Add New Tag in the Side–Bar to create a new tag for the table header text. Use features of the Paragraph menu to set up the font, alignment, and spacing for the header tag.

Step 2 **Set header tint**

Enable ***Table Editing*** mode. To set off table headers with shading or color, drag select the header cells and use Set Tint in the Assignment List to assign highlighting.

Step 3 **Set header rules**

To set off table headers with special rules select the header cells and apply rules from the Table Editing Assignment List.

Application Notes

- **Multi–page frames:** Turn to page 59.
- **Landscape tables in portrait documents:** Turn to page 324

Flowing Tables Through Frames

In some applications, it is visually effective for a table to flow continuously through a series of half–page frames, or appear on facing pages in half–page frames. Using PRN–To–Table, you can flow table text through a series of frames just like any other text file. The attributes set up for the table will be maintained in all successive frames. Even more spectacular is that any edits made to the finished table will also be automatically reflected in all frames containing the flow–through table.

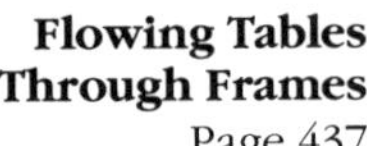
Flowing Tables Through Frames
Page 437

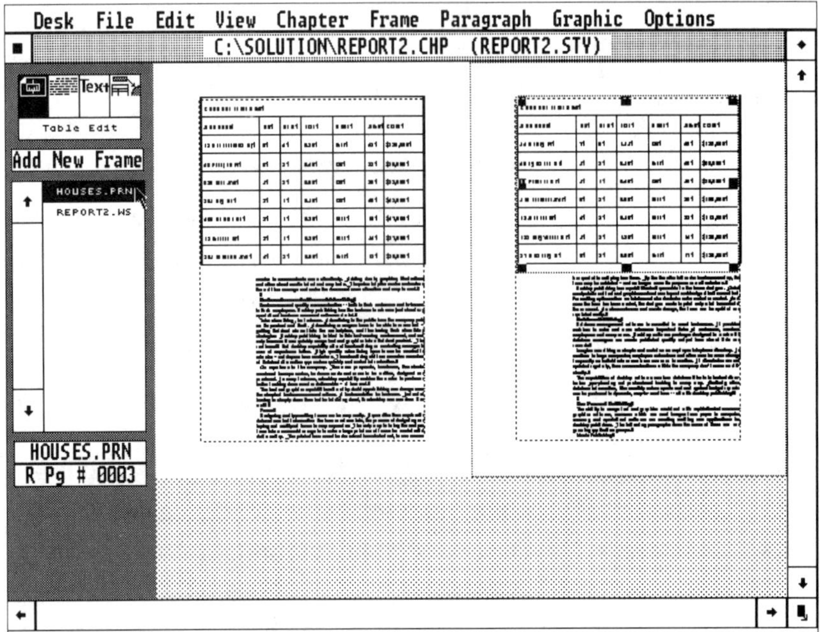

Recipe: Flowing Tables Through Frames

Step 1 **Draw and position frames**

Enable ***Frame*** mode and draw the frames to contain the table file.

Step 2 **Load PRN file**

Access **FILE•Load Text/Picture**, select Text and PRN–To–Table. Select the file containing the desired table.

Step 3 **Load PRN file to initial frame**

From ***Frame*** mode, select the first frame which will contain the table. Select the PRN filename in the Assignment List. The PRN file will appear in its table grid in the frame.

Step 4 **Load PRN file to successive frames**

Select the next frame to continue the table. Select the PRN filename in the Assignment List. The PRN file will appear in its table grid from the point it ended in the previous frame. Repeat this process for all additional frames.

Step 5 **Edit table**

Enable ***Table Editing*** mode. Display one of the frames containing the table. Any edits made to the format in one frame are automatically reflected in all other frames. Use table editing features to set the design and column widths for table data.

Step 6 **Editing table data**

From ***Table Editing*** mode, edit and reposition table data between frames. Insert columns and rows, and Cut/Copy/Paste data between frames containing the same table.

Application Notes

- **Create master frames for text:** Set up table frame attributes before copying through. Turn to page 62.
- **Automatic table positioning:** Use text technique to flow table through a series of frames. Turn to page 64.

Typesetting Tables

To produce higher quality and typographically accurate tables, you can create custom paragraph tags for the header lines and row titles as well as special table text for custom applications.

Table text can be tagged just like other text files. You can select any cell and use it as the basis for a new paragraph tag. To apply a tag to multiple cells, use Shift–Select. You can even set custom tags for the table grid lines to display in the Table Editing Side–Bar, so they can be applied from within Table Editing mode.

New values can be assigned to the Table Text tag, which will instantly affect every cell in the table. This operation can be very helpful when a global typographic change is necessary.

TABLE TEXT is a generic, globally applied tag. It is to tables what the Z_BOXTEXT tag is to box text. If you change the values of Table text, then every other occurrence of Table Text *for every chapter using that style sheet* will change as well. Unless you are dealing with an enormous table it is best to create a new table text tag and apply it to groups of table cells using Shift–Select in the Paragraph or Table Editing modes.

Recipe: Redesigning Table Text

Step 1 **Select table text**

Enable ***Paragraph*** mode and select text in one cell of table. TABLE TEXT or the custom tag specified should appear in the Current Selection Box.

Step 2 **Define new attributes**

Use features of the Paragraph menu to set font, alignment, and other table text attributes.

Recipe: Creating New Table Text Tag

Step 1 **Add new tag**

With Table Text tag selected in ***Paragraph*** mode, use Add New Tag to create new tag name.

Step 2 **Define new attributes**

Use features of the Paragraph menu to set font, alignment, and other attributes for the new table tag.

Step 3 **Apply to table using shift–select**

From ***Paragraph*** mode, depress and hold Shift key as you select cells in the table. Apply the new tag.

Recipe: Custom Table Text Tags

In documents with multiple tables, you may want to assign each table its own version of the TABLE TEXT tag. Then you can assign the typographic values for each table without affecting all the others.

Special versions of Table Text can be created *automatically* using the Rename tag feature of the Update Tag List dialog box. As soon as the first table is defined, use the **PARAGRAPH•Update Tag List** to rename Table Text as Table 1 Text. Immediately, the entire table will

Typesetting Tables
Page 439

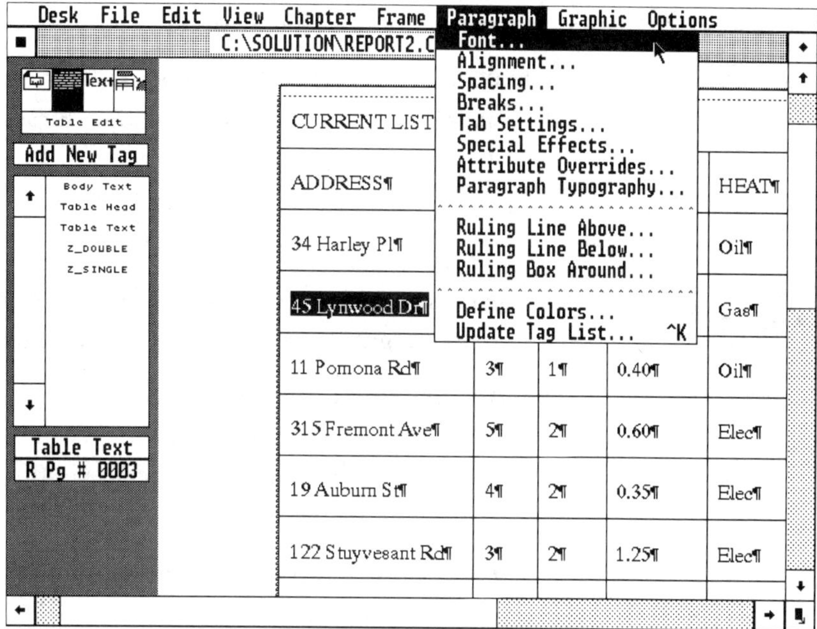

be tagged under the new name. The next table that you create will be given the default tag name, TABLE TEXT. Each table now has its own unique tag and you have typographic control over each table without a lot of time–consuming retagging. Repeat this process for each new table to create a complete system of individual tables with unique tags without manually selecting every cell on the screen.

Step 1 **Create first table**

Enable ***Table Editing*** mode and set up the first table.

Step 2 **Rename Table Text tag**

Select **FILE • Save** to save the chapter. Access **PARAGRAPH • Update Tag List**. Select Rename Tag and enter new tag name as Table 1 Text, or any desired tag name. Save the change to current style sheet. The first table will now carry the new file name.

Step 3 **Create second table**

Enable ***Table Editing*** mode and define the second table.

Step 4 **Rename Table Text tag**

Repeat the process of renaming the TABLE TEXT tag, this time using Table 2 Text, or any desired tag name. Repeat this operation for each table you wish to tag separately.

Application Notes

- **To center text in cell:** Access Paragraph•Alignment and change Horz. Alignment to Center, Vertical Alignment to Middle
- **To rotate text in cell:** Access Paragraph•Alignment and change Text Rotation to desired selection. For settings of 90 and 270, enter the desired height of cell in Maximum Rotated Height line at bottom of dialog box.
- **Landscape tables in portrait documents:** Turn to page 324.

Creating Custom Table Ruling Lines

Custom ruling lines can be defined for a table using the features of the Paragraph menu. Tags for table rules work slightly differently from standard tags. The generic table rules are created using the Ruling Lines features on the Paragraph menu. Using a special feature in the Ruling Lines dialog boxes, the tag is displayed in the Table Editing mode Assignment List. When the table is designed, the ruling line tags can then be enabled to define the Horizontal Grid, the Vertical Grid, and the Box Around the table using the entry lines in the Insert/Edit Table dialog box.

You can create custom table rules either by editing the existing tags (Z_SINGLE, Z_DOUBLE, Z_THICK), or by creating new tags. When custom tags are created, they can be displayed in the Table Editing mode using the Table Rule List setting in the Ruling Lines dialog boxes. Once available in the Table Editing mode, the custom tags can be applied globally to define the entire horizontal grid, vertical grid, or framing box. They can also be applied to selected cell borders directly from the Assignment List.

Creating Custom Table Ruling Lines
Page 442

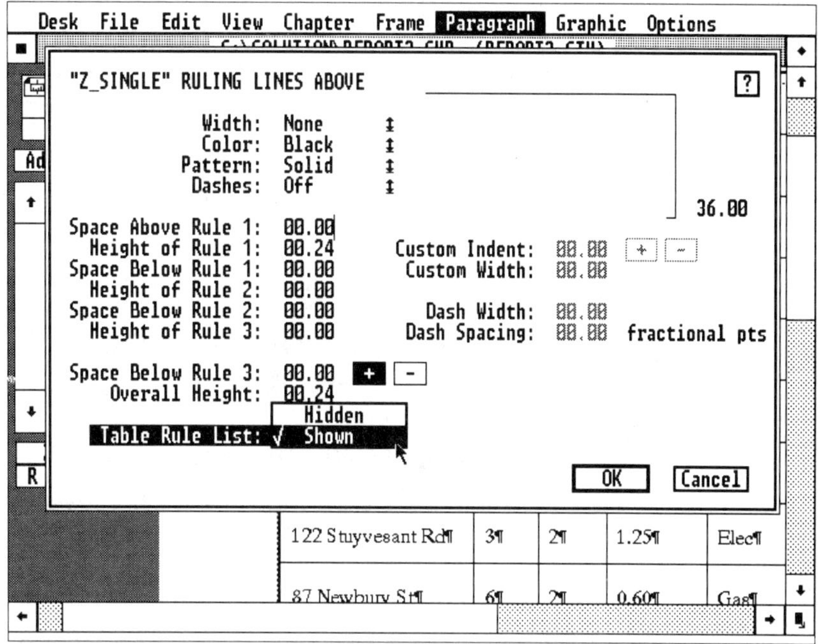

Custom table rules allow you to create special enhancements to certain sections of individual cells, or highlight specific cells anywhere in the table. They add an extraordinary degree of design flexibility to the powerful Table Editing mode.

Recipe: Editing Table Ruling Lines Tags

Step 1 **Show generated tags**

Access **OPTIONS•Set Preferences**. Set Generated Tags to Shown. The generated table rule tags will appear in the Assignment List.

Step 2 **Apply table rule tag**

Enable ***Text*** mode. Pull down a free paragraph return. Enable ***Paragraph*** mode and select the free return. Select the table rule tag in the Assignment List. The rules may not be visible on screen, so check that the correct tag name appears in the Current Selection Box.

Step 3 **Change ruling line attributes**

Access **PARAGRAPH•Ruling Line Above**. Set line thickness, color, pattern and dashes using the features provided.

☞ CAUTION: If you change the attributes of the generated tag, all tables using this style sheet will reflect the change.

Recipe: Making Custom Table Rules

In addition to editing the attributes of existing tags, you can create custom table rule tags and display them in the table rule list.

Step 1 **Apply table rule tag**

Enable ***Text*** mode. Pull down a free paragraph return. Enable ***Paragraph*** mode and select the free return. Select table rule in the Assignment List. The rules may not be visible on screen, so check that the correct tag name appears in the Current Selection Box.

Step 2 **Create new tag**

Use Add New Tag to create a new name. Use any name desired.

Step 3 **Define ruling line attributes**

Access **PARAGRAPH•Ruling Line Above**. Set line thickness, color, pattern, and dashes using the features provided.

Step 4 **Display on table rule list**

To display the new tag in the Table Editing mode Assignment List with the other ruling line tags, set Table Rule List to Shown.

Application Notes

- **Vary Color and shading:** Experiment with different shading patterns to highlight data.
- **Ruling line thickness:** Create emphasis with thick or extra thick ruling lines in solid or shaded patterns.
- **Dashed effects:** Create dashed table rules for special emphasis of selected cells. Turn to page 116.

Creating Sheet Labels with Tables

For business applications, a table can be set up as a matrix for printing sheet labels. Essentially, it is as simple as matching the cell size of the table to the size of the label.

Recipe: Sheet Labels With Tables

Step 1 **Create new style sheet**

Access **FILE•Load Diff. Style** to load a basic style sheet such as DEFAULT.STY from the \TYPESET subdirectory. Access **FILE•Save As New Style** to save it under a new name.

Step 2 **Measure label position**

Measure the sheet of labels and any offset at the top and bottom of the sheet. Access **FRAME•Margins & Columns** and enter these values as the top and bottom margins. Enter left and right margins to prevent the text from printing to the edge of the sheet.

Creating Sheet Labels with Tables

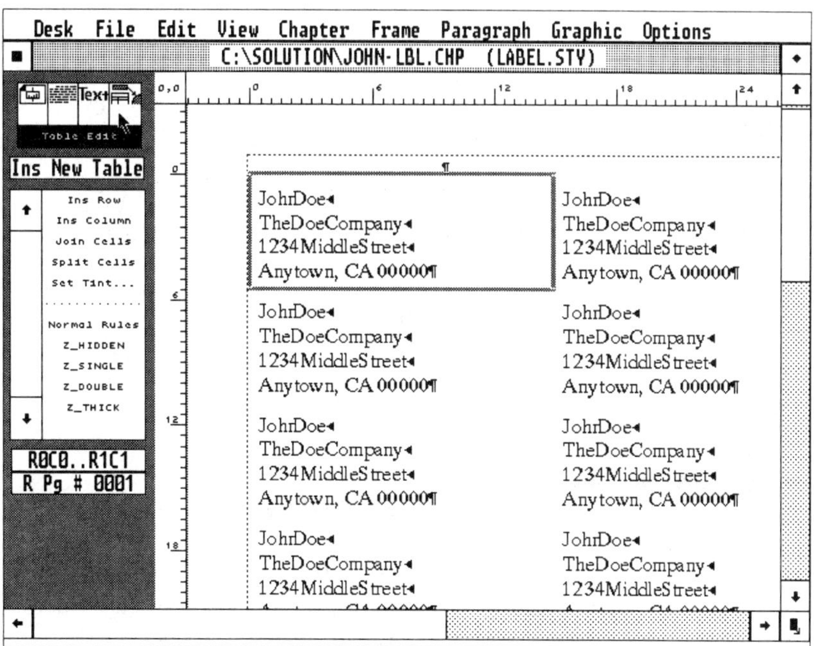

Step 3 **Create table grid**

Enable ***Table Editing*** mode and place a cursor in the base page. Access Ins New Table in the Side–Bar. Enter the number of rows on the label sheet as number of rows, and the number of columns on the label sheet as the number of columns.

Step 4 **Enter label text**

Enter label text in one of two ways:

▲ Type label text in each cell directly from the screen.

▲ Load a PRN file containing the names and addresses to appear on the labels. In this case, you don't need to predefine a table grid.

Step 5 **Set table spacing**

Based on the amount of label text, adjust the size of the cells to conform with the size of the labels. Select a position on the table and access **EDIT•Edit Table Settings**.

▲ Increase Space Between Rows to expand cell height to match label

▲ Adjust Space Between Columns to keep the text from printing right up to the cell (label) edge.

Application Notes

- **Change typesize to fit text:** For label text which contains international or business addresses longer than standard 4–5 lines, create paragraph tag with smaller type size to fit text into label grid.
- **Standard address labels:** Prepare a standard table grid for labels.
- **PRN files with mailing list:** Prepare a PRN file containing a mailing list and load it into a Ventura table. Edit the table to fit the text into a Ventura table. Turn to page 432.

Create a Feature–Function–Benefit Chart

Tables can also be used for text column applications which might ordinarily be done with vertical tabs. Basically, this involves defining a single–or multiple–page table matrix, turning off the table rules and

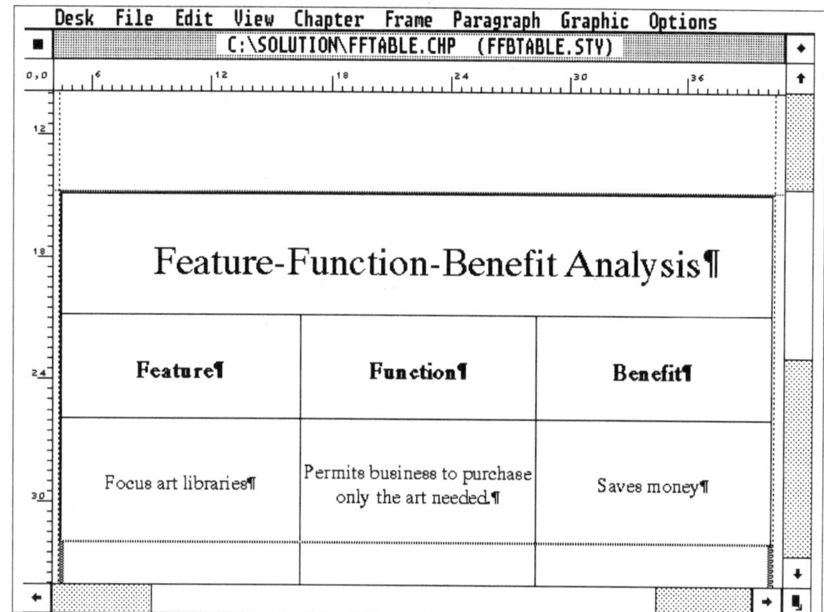

entering the text, either directly in Ventura, or via a PRN file created in your word processor.

This technique is most useful when developing text tables and Feature/Function/Benefit charts. It is not as effective for long, multiple page technical tables and data listings.

Recipe: Feature-Function-Benefit Chart

Step 1 **Create PRN file in word processor**

Type table text in word processor in ASCII mode. Place text in desired column format, taking care to leave a minimum of two spaces between each column.

Step 2 **Load PRN file to Ventura**

Load Ventura Publisher. Access **FILE•Load Text/Picture**, select Text and PRN–To–Table. Load the file containing the text table. The file will appear on the screen in a table grid.

Step 3 **Edit table**

Enable ***Table Editing*** mode. Edit table as desired.

Application Notes

- **Making PRN files:** Turn to page 432.
- **Designing with vertical tabs:** Turn to page 95.

Create Diagrams with Tables

Tables are a ready–made grid, and each line in the grid can be edited separately. This feature lets you design simple diagrams and flowcharts with tables. To do this, simply create a table grid and join clusters of cells to form elements in the diagram or organization chart. By selecting unnecessary lines and hiding individual line rules, you can create a variety of simple flowchart and diagram effects without a whole complex graphic form. Tables do not, however, offer you the variety of visual effects which can be accomplished with graphics. Experiment with table editing features to see how table grids can be used to create interesting diagram and chart effects without drawing complex graphic forms.

Create Diagrams with Tables

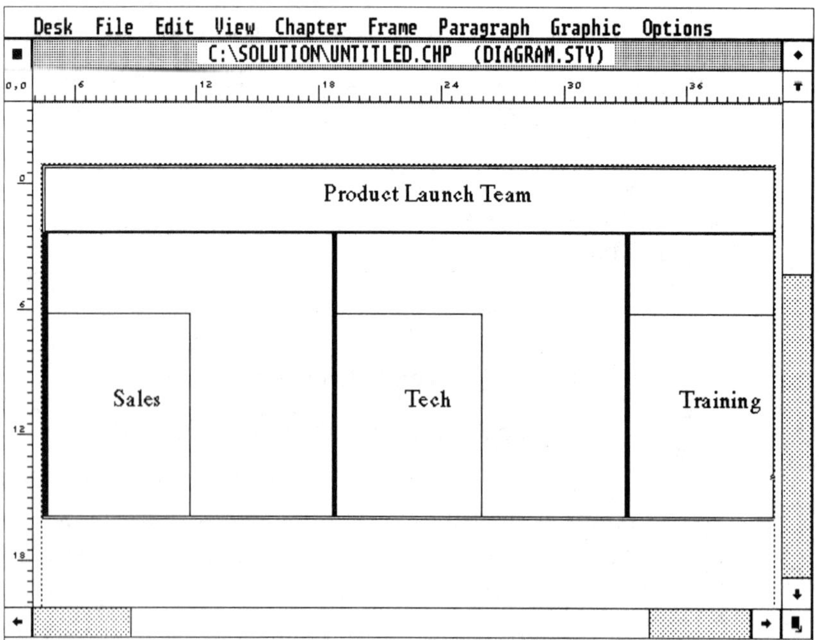

Recipe: Create Diagrams with Tables

Step 1 **Sketch flowchart**

Sketch out the planned flowchart or diagram design you wish to create.

Step 2 **Create table grid**

From ***Text*** or ***Table Editing*** mode, access **Insert Edit/Table**. Set the number of rows and columns to create the table grid.

Step 3 **Join cells to form flowchart blocks**

Drag select groups of cells to form diagram blocks and select Join Cells in the Assignment List.

Step 4 **Hide connection lines**

Select unnecessary vertical and horizontal lines and select Z_HIDDEN in the Assignment List to remove them from the diagram.

Application Notes

- **Custom framing lines:** Unlike Ventura graphics, tables allow you to set a different line thickness for all four sides of a cell. You can create a variety of different design effects by selectively applying custom rules and hiding rules for sides of a cell. Turn to page 425.
- **Designing custom table rules:** Turn to page 442.
- **Overlay picture:** Print diagram over picture for illustrated diagram.
- **Overlay graphic:** Integrate graphic elements into diagram.

Creating Graphic Effects with Tables

A variety of graphic effects can be created by using tables as a graphic grid. By joining clusters of cells, creating custom table rules and setting different hollow/solid tint values you can design graphic enhancements to your pages as well as backgrounds for pictures and graphics.

Recipe: Graphic Effects with Tables

Step 1 **Draw table frame**

Enable ***Frame*** mode and draw a frame to contain the table grid.

Step 2 **Create table grid**

Enable ***Table Editing*** mode and place a cursor inside the frame. Select Ins New Table in the Side–Bar.

Step 3 **Place graphic effects**

Enhance table to create a variety of graphic effects, including:

▲ **Custom ruling lines:** Create ruling lines with dashed and shaded effects in a variety of thicknesses.

▲ **Cell shading:** Set shading and tinting values for individual cells or groups of cells.

▲ **Text in cells:** Place title text or ornamental text in key cells with shading and framing lines.

▲ **Auto–anchor pictures into grid:** Place automatically anchored mini–pictures into grid to create a graphic effect with icons and illustrations.

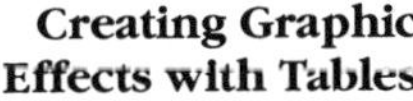

Creating Graphic Effects with Tables

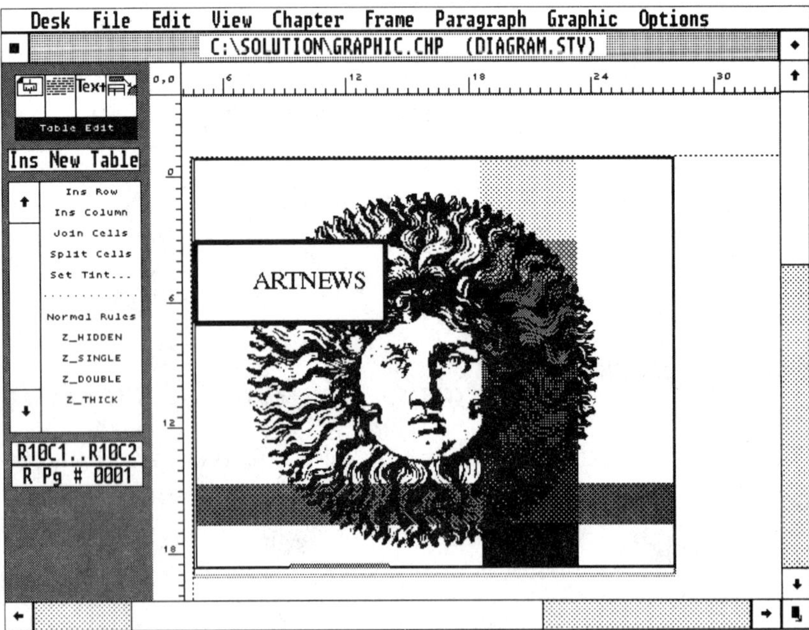

Application Notes

- **Create pattern:** Use join and divide to establish an irregular pattern of graphics.
- **Create color/shading:** Set tint in individual, or clusters of cells.
- **Create shading background pattern:** Remove rules from table and set complete rows or columns to the same tint/shading pattern. In progressive rows, deepen or lighten the pattern.
- **Create framing effects:** Turn rules on and make selective cell edits.
- **Create hollow or opaque cells:** Set tint pattern as solid to create opaque areas of white, black or color. This effect can be used to create a mask effect which blocks portions of the page material beneath the table.
- **Mask effects for pictures:** Stack a frame containing a table grid over a frame containing a picture. Use table grid to mask or enhance portions of the picture.

Designing Form Masters

Most form designs can be reduced to a pattern of one or more tables. By clustering tables together, you can design form masters easily and interactively on the Ventura screen. The top element in a form usually contains areas to receive name, address, telephone, and other key information. The remainder of the form contains organized areas for data, checklists, and controlled areas for special purposes.

For forms which require a variety of custom–size cells, columns and shaded areas, tables can be created in clusters, each with its own row/column structure and attributes. The result is a form master which you can print, revise, and edit on demand.

Recipe: Form Masters

Step 1 **Sketch form**

Sketch out the planned form. Break down the sketch into segments which could be designed as separate tables.

Creating Form Masters

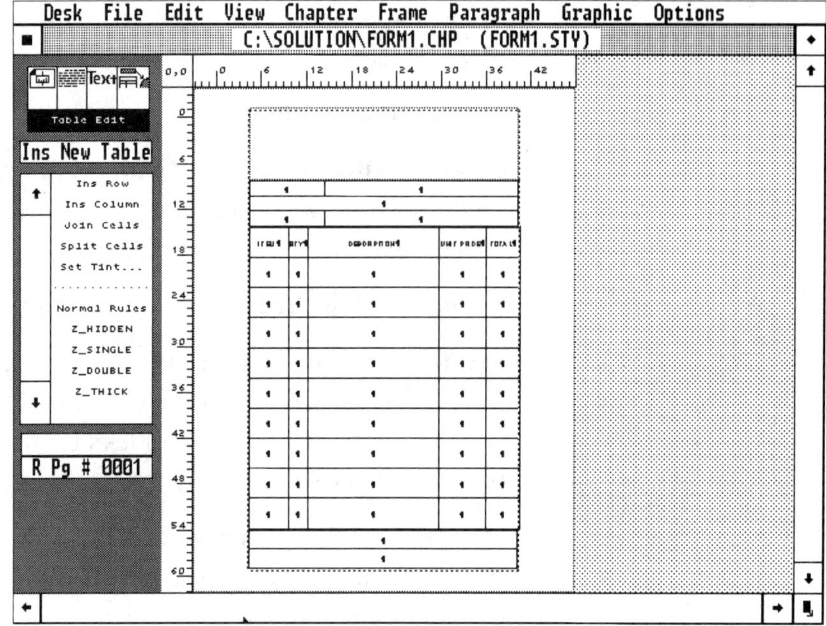

Step 2 **Draw frame**

Enable ***Frame*** mode and draw frame to contain the form master. From ***Text*** or ***Table Editing*** mode, place a cursor in the frame.

Step 3 **Insert first table**

Enable ***Table Editing*** mode, and select Ins New Table in the Side–Bar. Define the number of rows and columns to make up the top table in the form master.

Step 4 **Place second table**

Display the bottom of the first table. From the ***Table Editing*** mode, select the paragraph return or End of File marker beneath the table.

Step 5 **Insert new table**

Select Ins New Table in the Side–Bar to define the second table in the form master. Define the number of rows and columns necessary for the second element in the form.

Application Notes

- **Create labels:** Create a PRN file containing the cell labels for boxes in your form. Load it into Ventura, and design it to specification. Then set its table text to a small size (6 points)
- **Vary rules, shading, and color:** Experiment with line rules, shading and element color to provide emphasis to parts of the tables.

Create Illustrated Tables

Enhance the quality of tables by adding pictures to them as ornamentation or emphasis. Magazine and brochure applications integrating illustrations with tables showing business data are often more eye–catching and involving for the reader.

Tables can be creatively integrated with graphics, background patterns, and third–party illustrations to create a variety of professional and sophisticated effects.

To use tables with visuals, it is a good idea to *always place a table in its own frame.* Tables in frames are more easily moved and edited. In addition, with the table in a frame, you can apply the frame stacking techniques for powerful presentation graphics and illustration materials.

Small tables which are part of an illustration or a graphic layout can be placed directly into a Box Text graphic anchored to the frame containing the picture material. The table can be moved to any point in the overall visual layout, and because it is in a graphic, will automatically move with the frame anywhere within the same chapter or into other documents.

Recipe: Illustrated Tables

Step 1 **Draw illustration frame**

Enable ***Frame*** mode and draw a frame to contain the background illustration.

Step 2 **Define illustration attributes**

Access **FILE • Load Text/Picture** to load the illustration into the frame. Access **FRAME • Sizing & Scaling** to scale the illustration, if necessary.

Create Illustrated Tables
Page 453

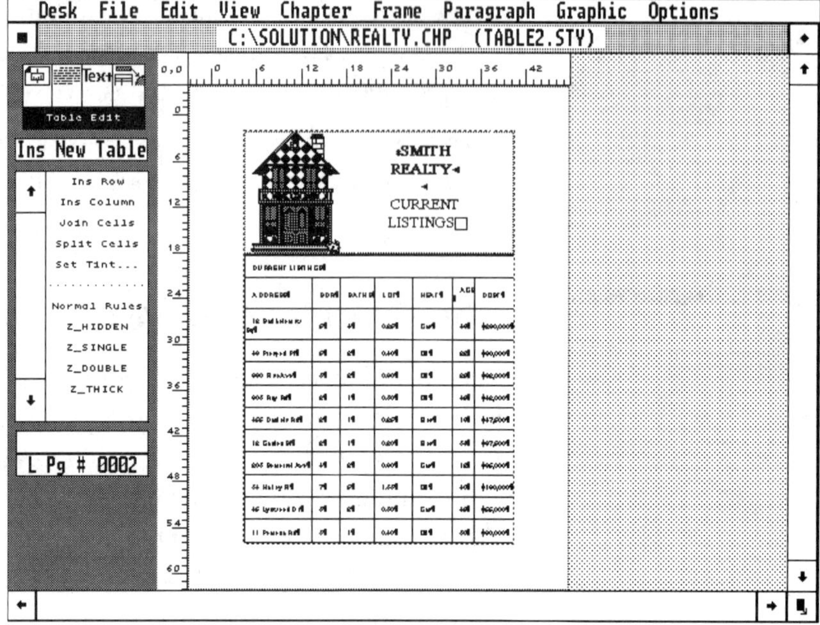

Step 3 **Draw table frame**

Draw a new frame to contain the table next to the frame containing the illustration. Position the frame next to the illustration.

Step 4 **Create and design table**

Enable ***Table Editing*** mode and place the cursor inside the frame. Access **Ins New Table** in the Side–Bar to design the table layout.

Step 5 **Anchor illustration frame to table**

To link the illustration to the table, anchor it to the table text:

▲ Enable ***Frame*** mode, and select the illustration frame. Access **FRAME•Anchors & Captions** and enter an anchor name.

▲ Enable ***Text*** mode and place a cursor in the table text. Access **EDIT•Ins. Special Edit Item** and select Frame Anchor. Enter the Frame's Anchor Name on the line provided, and select the desired anchor option.

Application Notes

- **Pictures and backgrounds:** Use standard pictures and backgrounds with tables. Turn to page 262.
- **Illustrated text:** Use this concept to create illustrated tables. Turn to page 123.

Stacking Tables and Pictures

For more elaborate effects, you can print an entire table on top of a picture or ornamental background. This results in a unified graphic effect with table material featured in black, white, or colored text on top of a picture or graphic.

To integrate data into a picture or graphic layout created in third–party software, turn off the table grid lines, and the data overprint the picture.

Recipe: Stacked Tables and Pictures

Step 1 **Draw illustration frame**

Enable ***Frame*** mode and draw a frame to contain the illustration.

Step 2 **Define illustration attributes**

Access **FILE•Load Text/Picture** to load the illustration into frame. Access **FRAME•Sizing & Scaling** to scale the illustration, if necessary.

Step 3 **Place additional illustrations**

To create a design made up of two or more illustrations as a background for the table, draw frames for all additional pictures.

Step 4 **Stack table frame**

Draw a new frame to contain the table on top of the frame containing the illustration. Position the frame next to the illustration.

Step 5 **Create and design table**

Enable ***Table Editing*** mode and place the cursor inside the frame. Access **Ins New Table** in the Side–Bar to design the table layout.

Stacking Tables and Pictures
Page 455

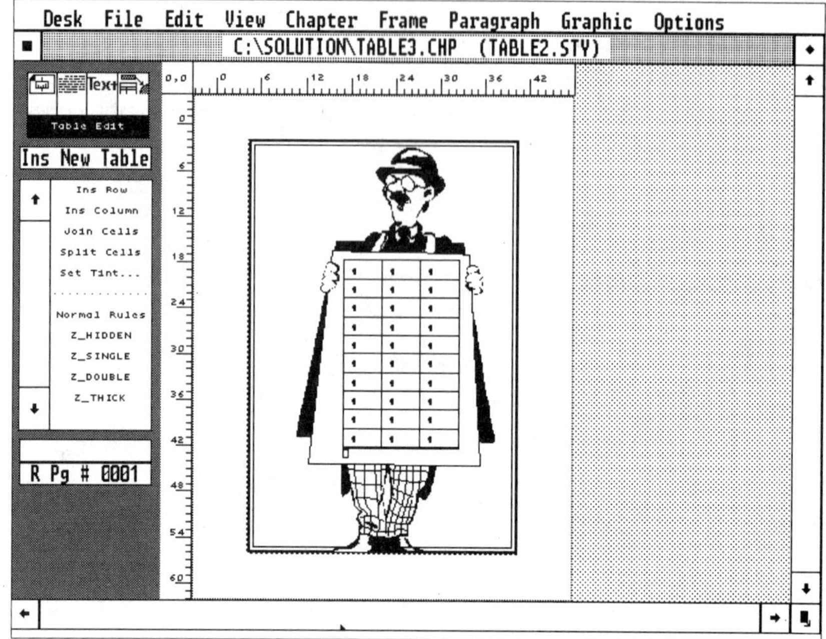

Step 6 **Anchor illustration frame to table**

To link the illustration to the table, anchor it to the table text:

▲ Enable ***Frame*** mode, and select the illustration frame. Access **FRAME•Anchors & Captions** and enter an anchor name.

▲ Enable ***Text*** mode and place a cursor in the table text. Access **EDIT•Ins. Special Edit Item** and select Frame Anchor. Enter the Frame's Anchor Name on the line provided, and select the desired anchor option.

Application Notes

- **Newsletters:** Use this technique to make data more interesting and involving.
- **Pictures and backgrounds:** Use standard pictures and backgrounds with tables. Turn to page 262.

Place Typeset Text in Third–party Graphics

There are a number of third–party business graphics software packages with the capability to create elaborate 3-D graphic effects. The problem is, many of these programs do not have fonts of the same quality as Ventura. This results in business graphics containing poor quality text that sticks out in the middle of your high–quality Ventura typeset document.

You can circumvent this dilemma by using the Table Editing mode to create a data overlay for third–party business graphics. Scale the table cell size to match the layout of the business graph and overlay Ventura typeset data directly over the third–party graphic image.

Depending on the third–party graphic layout, you can use either Ventura tables or graphics to position text and data. This capability can also change the way you create third party business graphics. Simply omit the text in the third–party program. Let the graphic software generate the bar charts and pie graphs and use Ventura to place typeset text.

Recipe: Typeset Text in Third-Party Graphics

Step 1 **Create the third-party graphic**

Design the graphic chart in the third-party software package of your choice. Do not enter text into the chart or graph. Save the file and export in a Ventura–compatible file format.

Step 2 **Draw frame for graphic**

Enable ***Frame*** mode and draw a frame to contain the graphic chart.

Step 3 **Define graphic attributes**

Access **FILE • Load Text/Picture** to load the graphic file into the frame. Access **FRAME • Sizing & Scaling** to scale the illustration, if necessary.

Step 4 **Draw table frame**

Draw a new frame to contain the table next to the illustration. Position the frame over the graphic.

Place Typeset Text in Third Party Graphics
Page 457

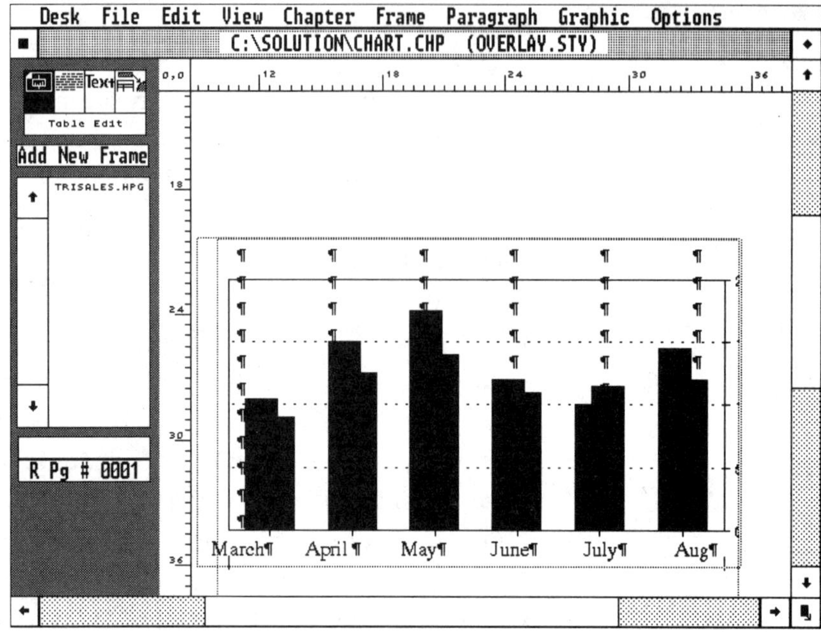

Step 5 **Create and design table**

Enable ***Table Editing*** mode and place the cursor inside the frame. Access **Ins New Table** in the Side–Bar to to set up the table. Turn all table rules Off.

Step 6 **Enter graphic data**

Enter data to display in the graphic chart in the table grid. Use table editing features to join cells to easily position text.

Step 7 **Set typographic value for graphic chart**

Enable ***Paragraph*** mode and select the table text. Use features of the Paragraph menu to design the table text.

Step 8 **Anchor illustration frame to table**

To link the illustration to the table, anchor the file containing the graphic to the table text.

Application Notes

- **Business graphics:** Use with graphics files that don't support Ventura quality printer formats. Eliminate heavily stairstepped or flat text in graphic charts and bar diagrams.
- **Custom table text tag:** Create custom table text tag for the graphic overprint table. Turn to page 439.

Designing Tables with Icons

You can integrate pictures *inside the cells* of tables for graphically enhanced presentations of data and information. The principle is the same as that for automatic anchoring. You simply auto–anchor a frame which has a height less than the current cell into the frame. Once the frame has been defined, you can make additional copies of the auto–anchor frame, thus integrating symbol effects into table.

Recipe: Tables with Icons

Step 1 **Design table**

Sketch out the planned table and identify the icons you want to be placed into the grid.

Step 2 **Draw table frame**

Draw a new frame to contain the table.

Step 3 **Create and design table**

Enable ***Table Editing*** mode and place the cursor inside the frame. Access **Ins New Table** in the Side–Bar to design the table layout.

Step 4 **Draw initial auto–anchor frame**

Enable ***Frame*** mode and draw a small frame inside the table cell.

Step 5 **Place icon or graphic**

Access **FILE•Load Text/Picture** to load picture file into the small frame. Or, enable ***Graphic*** mode and draw the desired graphic form in the small frame.

Designing Tables with Icons
Page 459

Step 6 **Assign anchor name**

Enable ***Frame*** mode and select the small frame. Access **FRAME•Anchors & Captions** and enter an anchor name.

Step 7 **Auto–anchor frame to cell**

Enable ***Text*** mode and place cursor on paragraph return in cell where the icon is to appear. Access **EDIT•Ins. Special Edit Item** and select Frame Anchor. Enter the small frame anchor name, and select Relative, Automatically at Anchor.

Recipe: Place Copies of Icons

Once you have defined the auto–anchor frame for the icon, you can place copies of the icon in more table cells by placing the text anchor on the paragraph return symbol.

Step 1 **Place cursor in other cell**

Enable ***Text*** mode and place cursor on return in another cell.

Step 2 **Access frame anchoring**

Access **EDIT•Ins. Special Edit Item** and select Frame Anchor. Enter the small frame anchor name and select Relative, Automatically at Anchor. Repeat this process to place copies of the icon in additional cells.

Application Notes

- **Using automatic frame anchoring:** Turn to page 291.
- **Placing icons into tables:** Turn to page 295.
- **Add symbols to data:** Mix symbols with data tables for enhanced effects. Symbols can be used to add to title elements in the header line, in which case they print on all pages.

PART III

Production Power

CHAPTER 12

Production Tips and Techniques

Building a Professional Publishing System

The deadline is the bottom line. As you develop your Ventura Publisher software skills and refine your approach to document design, it is with a central goal in mind: to deliver quality documents *on time.* But your skills aren't enough. You need to assemble a publishing system complete with the hardware and software necessary to meet your specific application needs and deadlines.

Ventura Publisher creates a nexus between the hardware and software elements that make up your publishing system. Ventura's open design accepts many different file formats for text and graphics, giving you the greatest possible flexibility for incorporating specific text processing, graphics, and clip–art products to use in developing documents. At the same time, Ventura is compatible with a wide variety of sophisticated hardware options, including dot matrix printers, laser printers, high resolution monitors, and more. Ventura's capabilities let you build a system guaranteed to meet your individual publishing needs.

The current marketplace is brimming with new software and hardware. Technological "revolutions" are released by the hour and are touted as *the* solution to desktop publishing needs. There is no shortage of ways to spend a lot of money on additional equipment and utilities compatible with Ventura Publisher. The array of options and solutions often seems confusing...if not terrifying.

Tips for Efficient Production

This chapter contains information and techniques which will help you set up an efficient print production department using Ventura Publisher. This includes key computer system information about hardware, third–party software and memory.

Production techniques are also included, so that you can reduce repetitive effort and increase effective communication in your production department. Additional information covers key operations in text copymarking, file conversions, file management, and fonts.

Selecting System Hardware: Bigger is Better

As a regular production user of Ventura, your overall goal should be to build a print production system that uses your time as efficiently as possible. A cheap, underpowered computer may cost hundreds of dollars less than a faster model, but when figured with the amount of time lost sitting and waiting for the underpowered system to complete operations, the faster system may well be, dollar for dollar, the better value of the two. The same principle applies to software purchases. Define your present needs, and look about a year into the future. The desktop publishing marketplace is moving so fast that a year from now, there will be new software choices, hardware products, and a whole spate of technological refinements from which to choose.

If you are an independent writer or document designer, your system is probably a PC with a laser printer, perhaps with a picture scanner, all fitting snugly on a desktop in your home office. On the other hand, if you manage a print production workgroup in an intermediate to large company, your publishing system might be multiple PCs and printers and very likely, a network link between systems.

The key elements to consider before selecting the computer hardware for your system are *speed*, *disk storage*, and *memory*. Speed is determined by the microprocessor and other factors in the computer system. Disk storage refers to the amount of hard disk space available in your computer to store files, fonts, pictures, and completed documents. Memory refers to the amount of Random Access Memory (RAM) available in your system, and whether additional expanded memory has been installed.

Processing Power

Ventura Publisher 2.0 and the Professional Extension will technically run on a low–powered system like an IBM XT–class machine or clone. Software operations, however, will take a long time to complete. You will be kept waiting between keystrokes for the processing to complete and the screen to redraw. If you are a regular production user of Ventura, a low–end system will waste your time, and ultimately, your money. On more powerful IBM AT–class machines (286 systems), or even more powerful 386 systems, Ventura will complete publishing operations in the minimum amount of time and effort.

Storage

Ample hard disk storage and floppy disk access in a system is essential for an efficient publishing system. To begin with, Ventura itself takes up between two and six megabytes on your hard disk, depending on how many printer formats and fonts you have installed. Additional space must be allotted for word processing, graphics, spreadsheets, and utilities. As your publishing system grows, you need room to store additional fonts, plus libraries of regularly used icons and graphics.

For more advanced operations, like printing output files to Linotronic or other typesetters, you will need additional room.

Floppy disks make Ventura documents portable, but it is often not possible to copy a heavily illustrated chapter file to a single standard floppy disk. As the quality of PC graphics has improved, the size of PC graphics files has steadily increased. The result is the need for more floppy storage space. A high density floppy disk (a 5 ¼" HD disk stores 1.2 MB, a 3.5" HD disk stores 1.44 MB) in your system is not a necessity, but it's a definite plus.

Conventional and Expanded Memory

The release of Version 2.0 and the Professional Extension has made the amount of memory in your computer one of the most important hardware considerations. Ventura can now use additional memory to enhance processing power and save time in all aspects of the print production process. The Professional Extension will directly access expanded memory in your system, allowing for the design of more complex pages, and the capability to work with much larger text and chapter files without slowing up your system.

Ventura 2.0 and the Professional Extension are the first Ventura Publisher releases to allow access to the additional processing power offered by EMS memory. The PC operating system, MS–DOS, imposes a memory ceiling of 640K bytes of memory. This is sufficient to run a variety of applications, but is limited for large, memory–intensive applications like desktop publishing.

There are two often–confused concepts that you must understand when adding memory to your system. The first is *extended memory.* Extended memory is, literally, an additional board full of memory chips which increase the total memory capability of the hardware system. The problem with using extended memory is getting your software to find and use it. You must have a method of telling your system where the extended memory is and how to access it. Some application software programs simply don't work at all with extended memory.

Expanded memory is a method to configure additional memory so that it can be used with Ventura's Professional Extension and other application software. This method tricks MS–DOS into thinking there is more memory in its basic 640K. Expanded memory manager software creates a bridge between additional memory available in the hardware by moving blocks of memory in and out of MS–DOS standard 640K memory as you work on your application software, enabling you to run many more powerful applications.

Ventura Publisher's Professional Extension directly accesses expanded memory. For best results, use an expanded memory manager which is installed directly into your system configuration. Two popular memory managers that work with the Professional Extension are QEMM–386 and 386 To The Max. Both install your computer's extra memory so that Ventura can access it.

One of the greatest benefits of working with Professional Extension and expanded memory is that you can develop and edit much larger files than with previous releases.

Additional memory increases the amount of text which can fit on a single page in document without triggering a memory overload error message, giving you the capability to develop extremely dense, multi–column applications. It also allows for much longer chapters. A document does not have to be broken into many different chapters, but can consist of two master chapters which are easier to edit and less time–consuming for file management purposes.

Application Software: Integration is the Way

The supporting software in a publishing system forms the base of publishing power. Using third–party software, you can write and edit your document text, develop graphics, draw illustrations, and process data. Ventura was designed for maximum production flexibility. It accepts files from many different word processors, graphics, and drawing programs, as well as databases, spreadsheets, and picture scanners. When designing your publication system with Ventura, use the most powerful software for the job.

Word Processors

Use a Ventura–compatible word processor like WordStar, WordPerfect, or MS Word when writing the document text. Theoretically, you could type an entire document in Ventura's Text mode, but that is not the best way. Ventura's Text mode is designed to perform editing functions, not lengthy text input. It does not contain many of the standard features of the best word processing programs, including macro keys, search and replace features, spell checking, built–in thesaurus reference, and more. Scrolling, typing, and editing are all faster when done on a word processor.

When producing documents in Ventura, use your favorite word processing software package. For multiple–author documents, encourage writers to work in their favorite Ventura–compatible word processors. Once in Ventura, you can load files from different word processor formats into the same document, or convert all of them to a standard format for final production and editing.

Graphics Packages

Ventura's Graphic mode was never intended to replace a full–featured drawing program, but was designed for editing and enhancements. Use more powerful third–party software to develop business graphics, drawing, illustrations, and clip art.

In the past several years a variety of powerful PC–based artwork programs have been released, including Corel Draw, Adobe Illustrator\Windows Version, Micrografx Designer, and GEM Artline. These programs make it easy to develop or make edits to sophisticated artwork, which can then be imported and placed in your Ventura pages.

Given the range of features offered in graphics and drawing software, don't try to make one single package do the jobs of many. Each graphics package performs some functions better than others. Having several different packages available allows you a variety of options when facing a particular graphics task.

The best software is often determined by the specifics of a job and the personnel available to operate it. For special font effects and graphics, an easy–to–use accessible drawing package such as GEM Artline is sufficient. For more complex applications with many fonts, or illustrations, a more powerful drawing package, such as Micrografx Designer, Adobe Illustrator\Windows Version, or Corel Draw is called for. These packages all have many different drawing tools and features which enable you to draw and edit sophisticated illustrations on screen. In addition, a number of these high–end programs have sophisticated font editing and handling capabilities and can be used to create headlines and title elements with special textures, sizing and rotation effects.

As third–party software programs have grown in sophistication, they have also become more uniform in command structure. Software manufacturers have been using the SAA convention for screen displays and pull down menus used in Windows applications and Ventura itself. With menu displays in different programs using the same structure and appearance, and many of the same feature names, learning new software is no longer the daunting task it once was. Especially in the art and graphics area, you can buy a new package and be proficient with it in several days.

Saving Production Time and Money

When designing a production system, it is essential to create standards for regular document applications. Develop a family of tag names to use in *all* style sheets. This reduces the headache of defining and communicating different tag names in every document. Keep the overall system in mind when designing individual documents documents. From a production standpoint, a well–designed style sheet uses a list of tag names easy for *any* user to understand and apply without a complicated reference list.

Organizing Production

To produce documents on deadline, all elements in the production department must be coordinated. Document text from one or more authors must be written and edited. Pictures and graphics have to be created in third–party programs. Spreadsheet and database files require updating and outputting into a format that Ventura can receive. Use the third–party software to develop the elements of a document and then use Ventura as the master integrator—to lay out, typeset, and print the final master.

Personnel Assignments

Perhaps the most important consideration when designing a production department is the one most often overlooked: the people who make the process work. Designing and publishing sophisticated document applications is a complex business, requiring many individual skills. To publish successfully with Ventura, you must identify and develop the individual skills of everyone in your production department.

In a large production department, roles and responsibilities can be assigned based upon individual background and professional strengths. Assign text processing to experienced word processors, and graphics development to artists. Select a core group to train as the final publishing experts, to work in Ventura finalizing page makeup and layout of the document. Because Ventura allows for text and graphics development in third–party products, it is not essential that everyone in the production department be an expert in Ventura operations. When starting up, it is often better to train one or two users to expert level on Ventura to function as "gurus" for the rest of the department.

Failure to implement a strong sense of individual role and relationship in the process can result in disaster, both literally and figuratively. If everyone in a department, regardless of Ventura know–how, is actively working on document design and page layout, each from their own point of view, using their own standards, the result is chaos. Style sheets can be disrupted and ruined and completed documents can be damaged or lost. Style sheets may be created with a system of tag names that only the original designer understands. The net results of disorganization are time lost, money wasted, and missed deadlines.

What is true for groups is equally true for individuals. If you are using Ventura Publisher as your personal publishing system, identify your strengths and weaknesses as they relate to the publishing process. If you need additional training in an area such as graphic design or page layout, spend the money and get that training as soon as possible. Once your skills are developed, you will be able to design documents that look like a whole department designed and published them.

Techniques for Efficient Production

Having the right hardware, software and personnel is the foundation of your production system. To make that system as efficient as possible, your production department should be organized to reduce repetitive effort, and keep all necessary tools, styles and template files close at hand. The following section covers a number of production techniques which can help you create a more efficient production system, including:

- Creating a \STYLES subdirectory
- List of standard tag names
- Pre-formatting text in the Word Processor
- Word Processor tag templates
- Text conversions
- Picture conversions
- Fonts

Each of these techniques is presented to help you better organize and streamline the document production process. By maintaining standard values and communicating these production efficiencies to all members of the production team, you can save time, save money and meet your deadlines.

Creating a Styles Subdirectory

Ventura style sheets and template files should always be kept directly on the hard disk in a special subdirectory, for example, \STYLES. This ensures ready access to standard style sheets, frame templates, graphic templates and often–used illustrations or icons in a central, accessible location.

Avoid using the \TYPESET subdirectory for your custom Ventura style sheets and templates. The \TYPESET subdirectory contains Ventura's teaching and print test files. If Ventura has to be reinstalled, the \TYPESET subdirectory could be deleted and files overwritten. It is better to keep publishing system files in a separate subdirectory.

The \STYLES subdirectory can also be a home to any Ventura file management tools that you use regularly, such as VP Toolbox. Standard production files you should maintain in the \STYLES subdirectory include:

- **\STYLES\STANDARD** Contains standard production style sheets.
- **\STYLES\BASIC** Contains basic style sheets.
- **\STYLES\ICONS** Contains standard graphic icons.
- **\STYLES\CLIPART** Contains frequently used clip art or illustration files.
- **\STYLES\FRAME–TM** Contains Ventura frame templates.
- **\STYLES\WIDTH** Contains backup copies of all current Ventura width tables
- **\STYLES\TOOLS** Contains Ventura file management software such as VP Toolbox.

Maintaining and regularly updating this central production subdirectory puts files you use regularly in Ventura production at your fingertips. All files stored in the \STYLES subdirectory should be backed up and stored on floppy disk in the event files are accidentally erased or revised.

Standard Production Style Sheets

A production style sheet is used to create one or more standard business documents, including business letters, memoranda, letter proposals, reports and other applications. When a style sheet is used in regular print production, it is essential that *no changes be made to that style sheet.* If changes must be made, save the style sheet under a new name using **FILE•Save As New Style**.

If changes are made to a production style sheet, *all documents* which are designed with that style sheet instantly reflect the changes, whether you want them to or not. Making a change to a production style sheet affects not just the current document, but a great many more.

Maintaining the integrity of standard production style sheets is one of the most important ways to ensure smooth document production. To avoid confusion and chaos, there are a number of other style sheet management techniques you can employ.

- **Place local copies:** Avoid designing many documents off the same copy of the style sheet in the hard disk. Instead, use the list of production style sheets in the \STYLES subdirectory as a central archive. When designing a document, load the style sheet from the \STYLES subdirectory, then access the **FILE•Save As New Style**command, click the backup button to display the floppy drive or the hard disk subdirectory where the document is being developed, enter the same style sheet to place a new copy of the style sheet with the rest of the document files. If the central copy is changed or damaged, your document won't be affected.
- **Create style reference list:** Post a list of standard document applications and the correct style sheet to be used for each application. As styles are upgraded, revise the list regularly.

Maintain a complete backup of all production style sheets on floppy disks. To make sure that the production style sheets stored in the \STYLES subdirectory are correct, refresh them regularly from the floppy disk backup copy.

Basic Style Sheets

A basic style sheet is one with a single paragraph tag—Body Text. Ventura comes with a single basic style sheet called DEFAULT.STY which is stored on the TYPESET subdirectory. DEFAULT.STY defines a double–sided letter–size page in portrait orientation, using the Times Roman font. However, most documents you design won't use some or all of these values. And that means you must completely redesign all the basic settings in DEFAULT.STY to develop a custom application.

To save time in design operations, make a set of basic style sheets with the standard page layout characteristics and typefaces you work with regularly. Creating your own set of basic styles saves time when designing new documents from scratch. By defining a unique set of basic design standards in basic style sheets, you can ensure that a group of documents will consistently share the same design basics.

Maintain copies of all basic style sheets on floppy disks. To make sure that the basic style sheets stored in the \STYLES subdirectory are current, regularly refresh them from the floppy disk.

Standard Icons

If you develop applications which use icons for visual enhancement, maintain a library of the most frequently used icons on the \STYLES subdirectory. This can save time searching for the correct floppy disk with the icons, or having to quit Ventura to copy the icons between floppies or into a hard disk subdirectory.

Give all icons simple, easy–to–understand names. If a set of icons is used only for a particular project or department, create a special subdirectory to contain them.

To make it even easier for all production workers to find the icon they need, design a simple icon reference booklet, displaying the icon and its correct filename.

Clip Art

If you use a standard set of illustrations for letter proposals, office memoranda or announcements, store them in a special subdirectory under the \STYLES subdirectory. If illustrations are in a variety of file formats, you should create special subdirectories to contain different groups of them.

To save file space, store only the Ventura–converted version of the file on the hard disk. For Line–Art formats, Ventura converts to .GEM, for Image formats it converts to .IMG.

Frame Templates

For any document which uses standard illustration or frame sizes, save a copy of the frame in a separate chapter and store it on the \STYLES subdirectory. Saving frame templates allows you to open the template chapter, copy the frame, and paste it into the document you are currently working on. This can save you a great deal of extra time and guesswork when trying to exactly reproduce the appearance of an illustration in a document.

Graphic Templates

Complex graphic forms, such as table grids and flowcharts, should be saved in separate template chapters and stored on the \STYLES subdirectory. A bank of ready–made graphic forms can save you a significant amount of time when working to a deadline.

All graphic templates should be drawn when a frame has been selected. You can then copy the frame into its own chapter, and the entire graphic effect (except for any custom tag settings created for it in a style sheet) automatically moves with the frame. To move the complex graphic into a document you are working on, open the graphic template, copy the frame, and paste it into your document.

Custom Width Tables

If you are using a variety of different fonts in production, it is a good idea to develop custom width tables which contain only the key fonts used for specific applications. This helps reduce the large size of some width tables and makes it easier to design documents and archive files.

To make sure that a current copy of all width tables is available, store all your current width tables in the \STYLES subdirectory. In the event a key width table is accidentally deleted or changed, a fresh copy will always be available in the hard disk.

Ventura file management software

Ventura contains the Update Tag List, which supports a variety of file management functions. There are a number of third–party products, such as VP Toolbox, which offer considerably more file management features. Place file management software with the rest of your production resources in the \STYLES subdirectory.

Creating a Family of Standard Tag Names

When working in production, it is best to standardize as much as possible about your system. And that applies especially to paragraph tag names. When assigning copymarking tasks to personnel, uniform tag names used across all style sheets make it easy to identify and place the correct tag in text. For example, many documents use a bullet element. It is much easier if *all* style sheets use the exact same tag name, BULLET, to describe the bullet character. This eliminates confusion and reduces checking and cross–checking at deadline times. This idea should be carried over to headings, columns and column heads, stacked tags, and other elements in a document.

It is a good idea to work up a list showing the standard tag names for document elements used in all style sheets in your production department as a guide to document designers when they are creating style sheets.

Listing: Standard Tag Names

The following is a suggested list of standard tag names. Standard tag names should be easy to remember, and easy to decipher by a user who is not familiar with the style sheet. The more logical your tag names, the easier your style sheets are to work with.

- **LOGO:** Company name on cover page
- **TITLE:** Document title on cover page
- **AUTHOR:** Author name on cover page
- **DATE:** Date on cover page
- **SECTION HEAD:** Document section heading
- **L1 HEAD:** Level 1 heading
- **L2 HEAD:** Level 2 heading
- **L3 HEAD:** Level 3 heading

- **BULLET:** Bullet
- **DASH:** Bullet, Sub 1
- **STAR:** Bullet, Sub 2
- **PPAGE BREAK:** Page break
- **COL BREAK:** Col Break
- **COL 1:** Vertical tabs, left column
- **COL 2:** Vertical tabs, middle column
- **COL 3:** Vertical tabs, right column
- **COL 1 HEAD:** Left column heading
- **COL 2 HEAD:** Middle column heading
- **COL 3 HEAD:** Right column heading
- **BOX 12 NORM:** Box Text, 12 point normal
- **BOX 14 BOLD:** Box Text, 14 point bold

Pre–formatting in Word Processors

One of the most powerful print production capabilities of Ventura Publisher is that text can be pre– formatted in the word processor file. Ventura writes paragraph tags, all text enhancements, and special edit items directly into the word processor file. To save significant production time, you can write all of these features directly into the text file *before* loading the text into Ventura. When a fully tagged text file with all text attributes in place is loaded into its target style sheet, the document appears completely typeset right on the screen.

For regular production users, this capability saves literally hours of time entering enhancements and tagging text. To take the fullest advantage of this capability, set up the word processor with macro or text insert files to insert Ventura codes right into the text. One of the best reasons to maintain a standard list of paragraph tag names is that a standard set of word processor macros can be created to insert these names into your text file. Macros can also be created to insert specific text attributes, for example, <R> for a soft return. To enter special characters and special edit items, create macros to enter the correct text attribute brackets and enter the correct text or codes into the brackets as needed.

Pre–formatting text is the most sensible way to use Ventura for regular print production. Ventura reads some codes directly from your word processor format and it has a number of specific text codes of its own. The following section describes the principal types of codes that can be entered directly into text via a word processor.

Word Processor Text Enhancements

Word processor text enhancements are those text attributes such as boldface and underlining. Each word processor has a different format to enter these text enhancements. For most supported word processors, Ventura reads these enhancements right out of the word processor text file.

To determine which codes Ventura can read directly out of your word processor, check the word processor detail in the Reference Guide. If Ventura does not read the code directly from your word processor, you can create a macro to enter the Ventura equivalent directly into text.

Ventura Publisher Text Attributes

Ventura Publisher defines a number of text attribute codes which you can use. Text attributes are a variety of custom text enhancements and special characters. These codes can be entered directly into your word processor to create text presentation effects, including:

- Enter text enhancements, including boldface, underline, italics, subscript, superscript, and small text.
- Enter non–keyboard characters, such as symbols (registered trademark ®), and foreign language characters (such as é, ä, ç)
- Insert line breaks (soft paragraph returns)
- Change font for selected text
- Change point size for selected text
- Change color for selected text

Each of these codes can be entered directly into the word processor file for a selected string of text. The selected string appears with the correct attributes the moment it is displayed on the Ventura Publisher screen.

When inserting text attribute codes, be aware of their correct format. For attributes that apply to a string of text, two codes must be placed: the code that specifies the effect and the return to normal code. The correct forms in which to place Ventura text attributes are listed below:

- **Special text characters:** Insert the number of the text code in text attribute brackets. For example, the character code for an em–dash: **<197>**.
- **Standard text enhancements:** Insert the text enhancement at the beginning of the selected string and the standard return to normal at the end. For example, to show the word Ventura in medium italic: **<MI>Ventura<D>.**
- **Custom font settings:** Insert the enhancement code for typeface, point size, or color containing the correct numeric code and the specific return to normal code for that enhancement. For example, to show the word Ventura in 36 point type: **<P036>Ventura<P255>**

A list of standard text enhancement and attribute codes appears in Appendix C of this book. Detailed lists of font codes may be found in the Appendix section of the Ventura documentation.

Ventura Publisher Special Edit Items

Ventura Publisher Special Edit Items are special codes inserted to positions in text, including:

- Hollow or filled box character
- Footnote
- Index Entry
- Fraction
- Equation (Professional Extension)
- Frame Anchor

- Cross–references
- Marker Name (Professional Extension)
- Variable Definition (Professional Extension)
- Tables (Professional Extension)

Some of these codes are read by Ventura during publication–wide index sort or renumbering operations, including index entries, marker names, and cross–references. Others mark a specific point on a page for a special feature like frame anchoring, or placing footnotes. Placing these codes individually in Ventura is a time–consuming activity, involving a great deal of page scrolling and repetitive operations.

Instead of entering these items in Ventura, you can simply place them directly into the text file. When a footnote is entered in the text file, Ventura automatically places the text of the footnote on the same page as its reference text. When placing multiple index entries, you can use the powerful search features of your word processor to find all occurrences of a particular word or title string.

A complete list of special edit item text codes appears in Appendix C of this book.

Copymarking with Paragraph Tags

Entering paragraph tags directly into the text file can save you enormous amounts of time and reduce repetitive effort. Once a style sheet has been designed, and the standard tag names identified, make a list of the tags, and assign macro keys to them. When entering paragraph tags into text, here are several key points to keep in mind.

- Tag names must be spelled correctly with the correct spaces between words in the tag name.
- It doesn't matter whether tag names are entered in upper case, lowercase, or a combination.
- It is best to enter tag names IN UPPERCASE to set them off from the rest of the document text.
- Use text entry format **@TAG NAME = Text**.

- Tag names must be placed at left edge of word processor page, preceded by a line break. If tag names get mixed up in the text, the text of the tag name appears on the screen.
- Any tag names which are not in the target style sheet will be shown in the Paragraph mode Assignment List IN UPPERCASE and display the attributes of Body Text.

Copymarking text files with paragraph tags can save you significant amounts of time, whether you are working alone or in a workgroup. In larger production environments, this capability can not only increase efficiency, but can improve the quality of the document development process from the very beginning. By training all document authors and experienced word processors in the production department to write all text files with the tags included from the beginning allows you to publish all drafts for review in Ventura typeset form. Not only does this make the drafts easier to read, but it helps you evolve and refine the ultimate style of the final document as the document is being written.

For long documents involving multiple authors, distribute a complete macro code sheet for the ultimate style or provide a diskette with the macro files already made up. For word processors such as WordPerfect, a complete set of MAC files can be created and given to the authors to use in placing paragraph tags directly into their text as they write it. For those who are not used to working with Ventura, make up a sheet explaining the utility of the copymarks and how easy they are to place in text. The tagged files from the different authors can be integrated into a single Ventura document that has been completely typeset at the text processing level.

Removing Double Paragraph Returns

It is often easier to read text files when paragraphs are set off with a double return. When Ventura Publisher encounters a double return it inserts an extra blank line on the page. To make Ventura Publisher strip out double returns when it receives a text file, insert special paragraph tag **@PARAFILTR ON** = on first line of text file. When text file carrying this tag is saved into a chapter file, Ventura ignores double returns and does not insert an additional line.

Quote and Em–dash Conversions

For greater production efficiency, Ventura Publisher can read standard keyboard symbols for quotes and em–dashes and convert them to the typographically correct character.

- **Quote conversion:** Finds inch marks entered in word processor and changes them into typographically correct open and close quotation marks. Quote conversion automatically ignores any inch marks which appear after a numeral, so that inch marks in standard usage are left untouched.
- **Em dash conversion** changes double dashes (- -) into typographically correct em dashes (—).

To set up quote and em–dash conversion, use the following procedure:

Step 1 **Access set preferences**

Access **OPTIONS•Set Preferences.**

Step 2 **Turn on quote conversion**

Select **Auto Adjustments: Styles** to automatically adjust spacing for tags when font size is increased or decreased.

Step 3 **Turn on em–dash conversion**

Select **Auto Adjustments: "and—** to turn on quote and em dash conversion utility.

Step 4 **Turn on both**

Select **Auto Adjustments: Both** when you wish both utilities to be enabled.

Creating Word Processor Tag Templates

For frequently cycled documents, you can save a significant amount of time by preparing word processor template files with the correct tag values and standard text already in place. For a standard business letter, you can place your name and address with the appropriate tag at the top of file, followed by the date, the name of the addressee, the salutation, and so forth.

The tag names in the template act as a guide when writing the letter, and you are assured of getting the correct tag values and minimizing the amount of time spent in Ventura. To further reduce possible confusion, give your word processor tag template file the exact same name as the style sheet it references. If you have more than one template for the same style sheet, then number the templates: LETTER1.WS, LETTER2.WS, and so on. A simple letter template might look like this:

@LOGO = JOHN DOE<R>123 Center Street<R>Los Angeles, CA 9000<R>(213) 666–6666
@DATE =
@ADDRESS =
@SALUTATION = Dear :
@SINCERELY = Yours sincerely,
@SIGNATURE = John Doe

When using the template, simply copy it into your letter file, enter the text and load the letter file into Ventura, select the correct style sheet, save the chapter, and your letter is finished and ready to print without any additional tagging or editing.

Text Conversions

In situations when you receive text files from different authors in a number of different formats, you may wish to convert them to the same format for ease of editing in your favorite word processor.

Ventura Publisher provides a bridge between supported word processor formats so that you can translate a file from *WordPerfect* format to *WordStar* and back again. When converting text in this manner, Ventura does *not* preserve text formatting in the word processor file, including tab indents, centered lines, or extra spaces.

Recipe: Convert Text Files

Step 1 **Select text file**

Enable ***Frame*** mode. Select base page or individual frame containing text file.

Step 2 **Rename file**

Access **EDIT•File Type/Rename**. Place cursor on the New Name line and change the file extension for the target word processor format. Select Text Format for the target word processor format.

Step 3 **Save chapter file**

Access **FILE•Save As** create the converted copy.

Note that the transfer process does not erase the original file, it merely makes a copy of the file in the newly selected format. If you don't want the file in the original format, you should delete it from the disk.

Picture Conversions

Ventura Publisher recognizes two different types of art files. *Line–Art* files are vector graphics which are stored as a pattern of coordinates. *Image* files are pictures stored in bit–map form.

When Ventura opens any format of Line–Art file except GEM, it immediately makes a copy of the file in GEM format. Similarly, for every Image file not in IMG format, Ventura makes a copy of the file in IMG format.

You can use these automatic conversions to save disk space. By deleting the original Line Art file (i.e.: AutoCAD format) or the original Image file (i.e. Paintbrush format), and loading the Ventura

GEM/IMG copy, you reduce the amount of disk space required to store your documents significantly.

Picture files can be converted outside of Ventura using a powerful graphics conversion package like The Graphics Link Plus. This makes it possible to convert files to a Ventura–supported format, such as .IMG, before loading the files in Ventura itself. External graphics conversion software offers the additional benefit

Loading and Managing Fonts

The fonts that are available to you are determined by your printer. Ventura contains standard fonts and custom width tables for supported printer formats listed in the installation screen. In addition to standard printer fonts, there are a variety of third–party font options available from vendors including Adobe Systems and Bitstream.

As you develop more sophisticated designs and applications, it is likely that you will wish to use fonts which are not available in the standard typefaces provided. Ventura accepts a variety of third–party font products. For installation and creation of Ventura compatible fonts, your best source of information is the font documentation and the documentation for your printer. To bring third–party fonts into Ventura, you must understand several key concepts about how fonts are presented on the screen, and how they are printed on the page.

Screen and Printer Fonts

Each typeface which is available in Ventura is made up of two separate font sets. What you see on the screen are *screen fonts* and what you get from the printer is created by *printer fonts.* The correct relationship between the two font sets is set by the font metrics recorded in the *width table.* These terms and concepts are commonly used in desktop publishing products, and to make intelligent purchases of font products you must understand a number of key points about each of them.

- **Screen fonts** display text on the screen. Often screen fonts are generic font shapes which approximate the design of a specific font. Some custom font packages, such as Bitstream Fontware, have the capability to generate high–resolution screen fonts which are accurate representations of specific typefaces. The quality of what you see on the screen is determined not only by the quality of the screen fonts, but by the resolution of the screen itself. A VGA (Virtual Graphics Array) gives you a high–resolution presentation of the page which lower screen display standards including EGA and CGA cannot.

- **Printer fonts** are contained in the printer, or stored on the hard disk of the computer. There are two principal types of printer fonts:
  - — **Outline fonts** such as PostScript use a single character outline which is expanded to the specific point size requested. The advantage of outline fonts is that the outline can be continuously expanded in one point, or ½ point increments.
  - — **Bit–mapped fonts** such as HP Laserjet format create individual characters as bit–mapped images. Every character in every style and point size must have a separate bit– mapped image. Bit–mapped fonts require more hard disk and printer storage space than outline fonts, and generally offer only a specific set of typesizes and styles, rather than continuous one point increments.
- **Character Width Table** contains the specific dimensions of each character in the printer font set. It uses these *font metrics* to set the correct size of the screen fonts in the Ventura Working Area. The selection and type of fonts which are available in the **PARAGRAPH•Font** dialog box is determined by the currently selected width table. When designing documents, you should *always* use the width table for the printer that will be used to print the final version of the document.

When shopping for third–party font products, do not buy any product that does not have specific Ventura Publisher installation support. You cannot use any third–party font product in Ventura without a custom width table that allows the fonts to be printed in your specific printer format. Without specific Ventura Publisher installation support, a third–party font product is worthless to you.

Recipe: Installing Custom Fonts

Before you install third–party fonts into Ventura Publisher, you must install the fonts in Ventura–compatible form and create a Ventura width table for your printer format. The specific installation procedures vary, depending which font products you have purchased. As you install fonts, it is important to keep in mind the three key concepts: screen fonts, printer fonts, and width tables.

Bitstream Fontware is a leading third–party font product which allows you to create bit–mapped fonts for HP Laserjet and other printer formats. It also allows you to generate PostScript outline fonts for PostScript–compatible printing devices. Fontware does this by means of a central installation program which allows you to specify printer format, screen resolution for screen fonts, and other key data. The installer then creates Ventura–compatible versions of typefaces loaded into the installer. During the process, printer fonts, screen fonts, and a width table are created.

To use the new fonts in Ventura, you must either load the custom font width table and use it by itself, or merge it into the width table containing your standard printer fonts. By merging width tables, you have access to all of your available fonts in a single width table.

Step 1 **Install custom fonts**

Follow the installation procedures provided by the font vendor to create Ventura compatible printer and screen fonts and a Ventura width table.

Step 2 **Load standard width table**

Access **OPTIONS•Set Printer Info**. Verify that the correct printer device is selected and that the width table containing standard fonts for that printer format is currently loaded. If it is not, use the Load Different Width Table selection to load the standard width table.

Step 3 **Save as new width table**

Access **OPTIONS•Add/Remove Fonts**. Before merging width tables, save the standard width table under a new name. Select Save as New Width Table and enter the desired name.

Step 4 **Merge width width tables**

Select Merge Width Tables. Use the Backup Button if necessary to display the drive and subdirectory where the custom width table is located. Select the custom width table and select OK to begin the merge process.

Step 5 **Scroll through typeface selector**

Scroll through the typeface selector in the **OPTIONS•Add/Remove Fonts** dialog box to make sure that all fonts in the custom width table have been merged into the standard width. The fonts are now available for design in the **PARAGRAPH•Font** dialog box.

Recipe: Printing with Custom Fonts

Once custom fonts have been installed in Ventura, you can design on the screen and print documents with them. To print with custom fonts, you must understand the key distinction of whether printer fonts are stored in the computer and must be *downloaded* to the printer or are *resident* in the printer. Resident fonts are stored in the printer's memory and are available upon demand. Many laser printers come with a standard set of resident fonts.

Download fonts are custom or add–on fonts which are stored in the computer memory. These fonts can be used only if they are downloaded into the printer's memory. Ventura automatically downloads custom fonts, but it downloads the entire font *for each page in the document.* This results in print times of five minutes per page and higher on a PostScript printer. Most font vendors include a *font downloading utility* program with their fonts. This is a simple package you can use to download custom fonts into the printer memory before accessing Ventura Publisher. Once inside Ventura, access **OPTIONS•Add/Remove Fonts**and change the specified font location to Resident. Now Ventura knows that the custom fonts are available in the printer, and doesn't download the entire font set for each page. The result is fast, efficient printing with custom fonts.

Step 1 **Download fonts to printer**

Before accessing Ventura Publisher, use the font downloading software provided by the font vendor, download the fonts into the printer memory.

Step 2 **Access Ventura Publisher**

Load Ventura Publisher and open a chapter to be printed using the new fonts. Access **OPTIONS•Set Printer Info** to verify that the width table which contains the custom fonts is loaded.

Step 3 **Set fonts to resident**

Access **OPTIONS•Add/Remove Fonts**. Select the custom typeface to be printed. Check the font location toggle at the bottom of the Style column. If it reads *Download*, click the mouse on it once to display *Resident*. Select *each style* for the typeface (i.e.: Normal, N-Italic, Bold, B-Italic) and set the location toggle to *Resident*.

Step 4 **Begin print operation**

Now that Ventura has been told the custom fonts are Resident in the printer, it will print pages in the same time it takes for standard fonts. Access **FILE•To Print**, set all desired print parameters and begin printing.

☞ CAUTION: Unless your printer has a special hard-disk for permanent storage of custom fonts, the custom fonts are erased from the printer memory when the system is turned off. However, the Resident location designation remains in the width table. If you don't download custom fonts to the printer after each time the system is turned off, Ventura will print the page in a generic font, usually Courier, because it cannot find your custom fonts in the printer memory.

Custom Editing Width Tables

In addition to the font metrics, Ventura Publisher width tables contain the identified kern pairs and specifications for the typeface. As you produce more sophisticated applications, you may have need to make edits to kern pairs identified for the typeface and the exact kerning values specified for the kern pairs. Appendix K of the Ventura Publisher documentation covers the detailed process of editing the kern pairs and making custom change to the width table files.

LetrTuck, a third–party utility program from Edco Services, makes it easier to edit and set custom values for kern pairs in the Width Table. This allows you to make custom changes to text presentation for documents that require special attention to typographic detail. LetRTuck allows you to increase kerning for identified kern pairs and add additional kern pairs to the width table.

Custom Headline Fonts

For display document headlines and other design challenges which require elaborate, stylized graphic text, some high–end drawing packages let you develop and edit headline fonts directly on screen. Corel Draw contains a formidable set of special text editing and formatting tools which let you develop a virtually infinite variety of different illustrated fonts for graphic headlines and other applications. GEM Artline is an accessible, easy–to–use product that lets you stretch, twist and reshape font characters just like graphics. Developing headline graphics in third–party drawing software places a whole new approach to headline design at your fingertips.

Designing Your Own Fonts

In addition to purchasing third–party fonts, you have the additional option of purchasing a program that lets you enhance or design your own fonts. Publisher's Typefoundry is a leading type design product which allows you to develop a variety of custom typefaces for bitmapped printer formats (i.e.: HP LaserJet) or outline printer formats (i.e.: PostScript).

Tools provided in the font editor allow you to reshape individual characters and implement design values across the entire character set. If you are actively involved in developing display applications which require custom fonts, or you are interested in creating your own version of symbol font families like Zapf Dingbats, make sure that whatever package you purchase offers complete support for Ventura Publisher, including the capability to develop width tables for all custom fonts you create.

Appendixes

How This Book Was Created

Recipes in Action

The challenge of this book was to create an interactive design and print production tool for Ventura Publisher which would allow you to directly access information and step-by-step techniques. Rather than narrative text, information is broken out into self-contained recipes. Each recipe is made up of four parts. The technique illustration shows how the finished result will appear on the Ventura screen, or a key dialog box used in entering the technique. The chapter lead presents an overview of the technique and uses for it. Each step in the recipe contains a step overview followed by detailed instructions. Each technique ends with a list of application notes describing ways in which you can experiment with the presented operation and cross-references to related techniques.

The elegant book design by Nancy Sugihara displays all of these elements in an open, accessible and visually pleasing way. Using a coordinated set of headings with offset text, the design makes it easy to identify the different elements in the technique as you flip through the pages. To help you find specific elements faster, illustration captions, recipe heads and application note heads are placed in the open area to the left of the main text block. As the book was being written, a Ventura style sheet was created to match the design specs.

This book was made possible by a number of unique features and capabilities of Ventura Publisher 2.0 with the Professional Extension. During development and production, a number of interesting design and production challenges arose that may be similar to production problems you have encountered. This section provides an overview of some of those challenges and how they were solved using recipes in this book. For your convenience, cross-references are shown to all techniques discussed.

Text Processing

Text was developed using WordStar, versions 5.0 and 5.5. For maximum efficiency, a number of WordStar features and function key assignments were customized using the WSCHANGE utility. Principal paragraph tags from the book style sheet were assigned to Wordstar Shorthand macro keys. In addition, the WordStar file import command (^KR) was assigned to one of the main function keys. At a single stroke, the import command could import additional prepared text files containing keystroke instructions (for example: Access **PARAGRAPH•Font**). To eliminate spelling problems and discrepancies for names of Ventura menus, dialog boxes and other features, a system of special import files were created for all Ventura feature names and instructions.

Text for the book was pre-formatted in the word processor (see page 477). Correct paragraph tags for the book style sheet were entered into the text as the book was written. Text enhancements, including boldface, italics and custom font changes were placed using macro and special function keys.

Most major text editing throughout the project was done in the word processor, including entering copyedit and proof changes, spell checks, and codes for markers and cross-references.

Page Design Elements

The book was typeset in ITC Garamond Light, a custom font provided by Adobe Systems in PostScript format. The page design presented a number of design challenges which were resolved using techniques presented in the book. The main heading for each technique is composed of a page-wide hairline rule matched with a short, thick left-aligned rule. This was accomplished using stacked tags to create a paired ruling line effect (see page 153). The heading used to display Recipes and Application Notes uses a hanging indent created using vertical tab effects (see page 95).

Following each heading, the first paragraph of body text has no paragraph indent. This was created using a special @FIRSTPAR tag in which the paragraph indent was suppressed.

Body Text in the book is set in 11 point ITC Garamond Light with 4 points of leading. To keep strings of text in boldface from overpowering the line, all occurrences of boldface in Body Text throughout the book are set one point smaller, in 10 point. To accomplish this, each string of boldface text was given a combined point size and text attribute code string. The initial boldface command set the point size and Ventura's boldface command: **<P10B>**. The ending command returned both the point size and the text presentation to normal: **<P255D>**. Seen from the word processor, a typical keystroke command with Ventura codes in place looked like this: Access **<P10B>PARAGRAPH<195>Font<P255D>**.

Header Line and Page Numbers

Header lines containing the name of the book and current chapter and the current book chapter are contained in a hairline rule box which is the width of the page and exactly one pica high. This effect was not created using standard headers and footers, but with repeating graphics (see page 328). A special frame was drawn at the top of right and left hand pages containing a one-pica high Box Text graphic. The graphic was correctly sized and placed in the frame using tiny frames as templates to measure and position the graphics (see page 180). The page numbers were placed into the Box Text graphics using simple page number cross-references (see page 93).

Auto-numbered Steps

Steps in all recipes were numbered using automatically restarting lists (see page 204) which were set to restart to 1 following main headings and recipe headings. The word *Step* was entered as built-in text in the auto-number (see page 202). As text was edited, and steps were added or deleted in the word processor, the steps were correctly re-numbered each time that a chapter was opened in Ventura.

Production Auto-numbering

When copyediting had been completed and all techniques had been placed in their final order, the book entered final production. At that time, a production auto-numbering system was set up to number all main technique headings in the book (see page 209). The numbering system was sectional, and consisted of the chapter number and a sequence number. For example, the technique in Chapter 2 called "Creating Custom-size Pages" is the fourth main heading in that chapter, and the production auto-number for it was **2-4**. To create a reference list of the production auto-numbers, a special table of contents sort was run (see page 370) and a list was printed from the generated file.

Cross-referencing System

Once the production auto-numbering system had been created, it was used to create sequentially numbered marker names for each of the main headings used to implement the cross referencing system. For example, the marker name for "Creating Custom-size Pages" described above is **0204VPSB**. By using sequential numbers linked to a heading, it saves a great deal of time placing and checking cross-reference codes (see page 402).

After markers had been placed, then page reference codes were entered in the application notes section. To ensure that the code values were typed correctly, word processor search and replace features were used to find all page reference positions and insert the correct code and brackets. Search was set to find the expression: **Turn to page #**. It was then replaced with the expression: **Turn to page <$R[P#,VPSB]>**. Note that the search and replace expression included part of the marker name. The only step necessary to identify the correct marker to reference was to type in the number of the correct marker, using the the numbered reference list.

Once frames for all figures had been placed into text, the Ventura .CAP file for each book chapter contained a blank Z_CAPTION tag line for each caption frame. Rather than page through the document in Ventura and enter the correct codes into the caption frames, the cross-references were typed directly into the .CAP file in WordStar's Nondocument mode (see page 404).

Illustrations

All screen shots used as illustrations were created with HotShot Graphics. A series of special sample documents were placed into the C:\SOLUTIONS subdirectory to be used in illustrations. In addition, actual book chapter files, located in the hard disk E drive were used to illustrate some techniques. Using HotShot's built-in file conversion system, all screen shots were converted to .IMG format for use in Ventura.

Sample Documents

Full-page sample layouts were designed using a variety of custom fonts and third party graphics software products. Once the layouts were complete, they were printed to Encapsulated PostScript files using the Print to Filename setting in the **OPTIONS•Set Printer Info** dialog box.

APPENDIX A

Third Party Products

Introduction

One of Ventura's greatest strengths as a desktop publishing product is that it accepts the output of third-party graphics, word processing, spreadsheet and data management software. The following is a list of software and utilities used in the creation of this book.

Drawing Software and Clip-Art

Adobe Illustrator, Windows Version

Adobe Systems Inc.
P.O. Box 7900
Mountain View, CA 94039
(415) 962-2000

AutoCAD
Autosketch

Autodesk, Inc.
2320 Marinship Way
Sausalito, CA 94965
(415) 332-2344

Corel Draw

Corel
1600 Carling Avenue
Ottawa, Ontario K1Z 8R7
(613) 728-8200

GEM Artline

Digital Research Inc.
70 Garden Court, P.O. Box DRI
Monterey, CA 93942
(408) 443-4200

The Graphics
Link Plus

Harvard Systems
1661 Lincoln Boulevard, Suite 101
Santa Monica CA 90404
(213) 392-8441

HotShot Graphics

Symsoft, Inc.
P.O. Box 4477
Mountain View, CA 94040
(415) 941-1552

MicroGrafx
Designer

Micrografx
1303 Arapahoe
Richardson, TX 75081
(800)272-3729

Publisher's Picture Pak

Marketing Graphics Inc.
4401 Dominion Boulevard, Suite 210
Glen Allen, Virginia 23060-3379
(804) 747-6991

Data Processing Software

Lotus 1-2-3

Lotus Development Corporation
55 Cambridge
Boston MA 02142
(617) 577-8500

dBase IV

Ashton-Tate
20101 Hamilton Avenue
Torrance, CA 90502
(213) 329-8000

Fonts and Typeset Utilities

Bitstream Fontware

Bitstream, Inc.
215 First Street
Cambridge, MA 02142
(800) 522-3668

Adobe Type Library

Adobe Systems Inc.
P.O. Box 7900
Mountain View, CA 94039
(415) 962-2000

Publisher's Type Foundry

Z-Soft Corporation
450 Franklin Road, Suite 100
Marietta, GA 30067
(404) 428-0008

LetRTuck

EDCO Services, Inc.
12410 North Dale Mabry Highway
Tampa, FL 33618
800-541-2255
813-962-7800

Ventura Utilities

VP Toolbox 3.0

SNA, Inc.
P.O. Box 3662
Princeton, N.J. 08543
(609) 683-1237

VP Tabs

The Laser Edge
360 17th Street, Suite 203
Oakland, CA 94612
(415) 835-1581

User Support

Ventura Publisher User Group (VPUG)

Ventura Publisher User's Group (VPUG)
7502 Aaron Place
San Jose, CA 95139
408-227-5030

Ventura Keyboard Shortcuts

Commands

Addition Button (Add New Frame, Add New Tag, or Set Font)	^2
Assign Function Keys	^K
Bring To Front (Graphics)	^A
Cancel Dialog Box	^X
Clear Selection line in dialog box	^Escape
Copy	Shift + Delete
Copyright©	^ + Shift + C
Cut	Delete
Delete to the right of cursor	Delete
Delete to the left of cursor	Backspace
Discretionary hyphen	^hyphen
Double quote, close	^ + Shift +]

Double quote, open	^ + Shift + [
Edit Special Item	^D
Em dash —	^]
Em space	^ + Shift + M
En dash –	^[
En space	^ + Shift + N
Enlarged View	^E
Figure space	^ + Shift + F
Fill Attributes (Graphics)	^F
Frame Mode	^U
Go to Page	^G
Go to first page	Home
Go to last page	End
Go to next page	PgDn
Go to previous page	PgUp
Graphic Mode	^P
Insert Special Item	^C
Line Attributes (Graphics)	^L
Line Break	^Enter
Non-Breaking Space	^Spacebar
Normal View	^N
Paragraph Mode	^I
Paste	Insert
Recall last dialog box	^X
Reduced View	^R
Registered trademark®	^ + Shift + R
Renumber Chapter	^B
Save	^S
Select All (Graphics)	^Q
Send to Back (Graphics)	^Z
Show/Hide Tabs & Returns	^T
Show/Hide Side-Bar	^W
Text Mode	^O
Thin space	^ + Shift + T
Trademark™	^ + Shift + 2
Update Tag List	^K

Ventura Text and Font Attribute Codes

Font Attributes

Standard text enhancements

Medium weight type	<M>
Bold weight type	<B>
Italics	<I>
Double Underline	<=>
Underline	<U>
Overscore	<0>
Strike-through	<X>
Small	<S>
Superscript	<^>
Subscript	<v>
Return to Normal	<D>

Color codes

White	<C0>
Black	<C1>
Red	<C2>
Green	<C3>
Blue	<C4>
Cyan	<C5>
Yellow	<C6>
Magenta	<C7>
Reset color to normal	<C255>

Custom font codes

Change typeface	<Fnnn>
Return typeface to normal	<F255>
Change point size	<Pnnn>
Return point size to normal	<P255>
Change base line jump	<Jnnn>
Return base line jump to normal	<J255>
Begin kerning	<Knnn>
Return kerning to normal	<K0>
Kern/Tracking	<B%nnn>
Return	<B%0>

Text Attribute Codes

Box (Hollow)	<$B0>
Box (Filled)	<$B1>
Cross-reference current chapter number	<$R[C#]>
Cross-reference current page number	<$R[P#]>
Discretionary hyphen	<->
Em space	<_>
En space	<~>

Figure space	<+>
Footnote	<$Ftext>
Fraction	<$Enumerator/denominator>
Fraction	<$Enumerator over denominator>
Hidden text	<$!text>
Index	<$IPrimary[Primary sort key];Secondary[Secondary sort key]>
Line break	<R>
Non-Breaking Space	<N>
Frame anchor below	<$&anchor name[v]>
Frame anchor fixed on page	<$&anchor name>
Frame anchor above	<$&anchor name[^]>
Frame anchor automatically at anchor	<$&anchor name[-]>
Thin space	<I>
Deleting double paragraph returns	@PARAFILTER ON =

APPENDIX D

Ventura Character Table

Special Text Characters

This character table shows the correct character codes for the standard VP International character set, Symbol and Zapf Dingbats. It is used to identify codes for special text characters.

Decimal	Standard	Symbol	Dingbat
32			
33	!	!	✁
34	"	∀	✂
35	#	#	✃
36	$	∃	✄
37	%	%	☎
38	&	&	✆
39	’	∋	✇
40	(	(	✈
41	)	)	✉
42	*	∗	☛
43	+	+	☞
44	,	,	✌
45	-	−	✍
46	.	.	✎
47	/	/	✏
48	0	0	✐
49	1	1	✑
50	2	2	✒
51	3	3	✓
52	4	4	✔
53	5	5	✕
54	6	6	✖
55	7	7	✗
56	8	8	✘
57	9	9	✙
58	:	:	✚
59	;	;	✛
60	<	<	✜
61	=	=	✝
62	>	>	✞
63	?	?	✟
64	@	≅	✠
65	A	Α	✡
66	B	Β	✢
67	C	Χ	✣
68	D	Δ	✤
69	E	Ε	✥
70	F	Φ	✦
71	G	Γ	✧
72	H	Η	★
73	I	Ι	✩
74	J	ϑ	✪
75	K	Κ	✫
76	L	Λ	✬
77	M	Μ	✭
78	N	Ν	✮
79	O	Ο	✯
80	P	Π	✰
81	Q	Θ	✱
82	R	Ρ	✲
83	S	Σ	✳
84	T	Τ	✴
85	U	Υ	✵
86	V	ς	✶
87	W	Ω	✷
88	X	Ξ	✸
89	Y	Ψ	✹
90	Z	Ζ	✺
91	[	[	✻
92	\	∴	✼
93	]	]	✽
94	^	⊥	✾
95	_	_	✿

Decimal	Standard	Symbol	Dingbat
96	‘	‾	❀
97	a	α	❁
98	b	β	❂
99	c	χ	❃
100	d	δ	❄
101	e	ε	❅
102	f	ϕ	❆
103	g	γ	❇
104	h	η	❈
105	i	ι	❉
106	j	φ	❊
107	k	κ	❋
108	l	λ	●
109	m	μ	❍
110	n	ν	■
111	o	ο	❏
112	p	π	❐
113	q	θ	❑
114	r	ρ	❒
115	s	σ	▲
116	t	τ	▼
117	u	υ	◆
118	v	ϖ	❖
119	w	ω	◗
120	x	ξ	❘
121	y	ψ	❙
122	z	ζ	❚
123	{	{	❛
124	|	|	❜
125	}	}	❝
126	~	~	❞
127			

Decimal	Standard	Symbol	Dingbat
128	Ç		
129	ü	ϒ	❡
130	é	′	❢
131	â	≤	❣
132	ä	⁄	❤
133	à	∞	❥
134	å	ƒ	❦
135	ç	♣	❧
136	ê	♦	♣
137	ë	♥	♦
138	è	♠	♥
139	ï	↔	♠
140	î	←	①
141	ì	↑	②
142	Ä	→	③
143	Å	↓	④
144	É	°	⑤
145	æ	±	⑥
146	Æ	″	⑦
147	ô	≥	⑧
148	ö	×	⑨
149	ò	∝	⑩
150	û	∂	❶
151	ù	•	❷
152	ÿ	÷	❸
153	Ö	≠	❹
154	Ü	≡	❺
155	¢	≈	❻
156	£	…	❼
157	¥	|	❽
158	¤	—	❾
159	ƒ	↵	❿

Decimal	Standard	Symbol	Dingbat
160	á	ℵ	①
161	í	ℑ	②
162	ó	ℜ	③
163	ú	℘	④
164	ñ	⊗	⑤
165	Ñ	⊕	⑥
166	ª	∅	⑦
167	º	∩	⑧
168	¿	∪	⑨
169	“	⊃	⑩
170	”	⊇	❶
171	‹	⊄	❷
172	›	⊂	❸
173	¡	⊆	❹
174	∈	∈	❺
175	»	∉	❻
176	ã	∠	❼
177	õ	∇	❽
178	Ø	®	❾
179	ø	©	❿
180	œ	™	➔
181	Œ	∏	→
182	À	√	↔
183	Ã	·	↕
184	Õ	¬	➘
185	§	∧	➙
186	‡	∨	➚
187	†	⇔	➛
188	¶	⇐	➜
189	©	⇑	➝
190	®	⇒	➞
191	™	⇓	➟

Decimal	Standard	Symbol	Dingbat
192	„	◊	➠
193	…	〈	➡
194	‰	®	➢
195	•	©	➣
196	–	™	➤
197	—	∑	➥
198	°	⎛	➦
199	Á	⎜	➧
200	Â	⎝	➨
201	È	⎡	➩
202	Ê	⎢	➪
203	Ë	⎣	➫
204	Ì	⎧	➬
205	Í	⎨	➭
206	Î	⎩	➮
207	Ï	⎪	➯
208	Ò		
209	Ó	〉	➱
210	Ô	∫	➲
211	Š	⌠	➳
212	š	⎮	➴
213	Ù	⌡	➵
214	Ú	⎞	➶
215	Û	⎟	➷
216	Ÿ	⎠	➸
217	ß	⎤	➹

Index

B

C

G

H

I

J

K

L

P

Q

R

S

T

U

V

W